FRANK R. SCOTT was for many years a professor of constitutional law at McGill University and is a well-known Canadian poet. He is the author of *Overture* and *Eye of the Needle*, and co-author of *New Provinces, Social Planning for Canada*, and *Evolving Canadian Federalism*.

Frank Scott's career is unique among Canadians of this century. As a constitutional lawyer, civil libertarian, teacher, and poet, he has helped to shape Canada's national awareness and culture.

Comprising some thirty articles and occasional pieces from four decades, *Essays on the Constitution* reflects the achievements of a legal scholar whose interests and concerns have always been in the vanguard of Canadian political thought and closely attuned to practical matters of national policy. Dr Scott became renowned early in his career as a defender of the civil liberties of persecuted groups, including the Jehovah's Witnesses in Quebec, the Communists in Toronto, and the interned Japanese of British Columbia. An adamant critic of the constitutional decisions of the Judicial Committee of the Privy Council, which he felt seriously damaged Canadian federalism, he has also explored the constitutional implications of Canada's evolution within the Commonwealth and the changing forces of federal-provincial relations. In recent years his central theme has been the problems of language policy and biculturalism.

The essays in this volume provide a remarkably coherent appraisal of constitutional, political, and legal developments in recent Canadian history. Their appeal lies not only in their insights into the form and functioning of Canadian politics, but also in their unity and scope as the work of a man who has been one of the most influential of twentieth-century Canadian political thinkers.

FRANK R. SCOTT, C.C., Q.C., F.R.S.C.
formerly Macdonald Professor and Dean of
the Faculty of Law, McGill University

# Essays on the Constitution

## Aspects of Canadian law and politics

UNIVERSITY OF TORONTO PRESS
TORONTO AND BUFFALO

© University of Toronto Press 1977
Toronto and Buffalo
Printed in Canada

**Canadian Cataloguing in Publication Data**

Scott, Frank R., 1899-
    Essays on the Constitution

    Bibliography: p.
    Includes indexes.
    ISBN 0-8020-2238-3 bd. ISBN 0-8020-6297-0 pa.

    1. Canada. Constitution — Addresses, essays, lectures.
    2. Canada — Constitutional law — Addresses, essays,
    lectures.  3. Canada — Constitutional history —
    Addresses, essays, lectures.  I. Title.

    KE4199.5.S36      342'.71'02      C77-001406-2

This book has been published during the
sesquicentennial year of the University of Toronto

Law is enforced by the State because it is law;
it is not law merely because the State enforces it.

Sir Frederick Pollock


Order the beauty even of beauty is ...

Thomas Traherne

# Preface

These essays and papers are selected from among those I published during the more than forty years (1928-1971) of my teaching law at McGill University, Montreal. They are arranged for the most part in chronological order so as to reflect the progressive changes, both in external and domestic affairs, to which the Canadian constitution had to adapt in that period. When it is remembered that the British North America Act, Canada's basic constitutional document, was drawn up in 1867, in the heyday of *laisser-faire*, it is remarkable that the adjustments were made with so few formal amendments to the written text. Imperial, international, and inter-provincial relations, being founded more on convention than on written law, were flexible enough to admit of frequent modification by administrative agreement as Canada shed her colonial inheritance and became an independent nation-state. It was in the distribution of legislative powers between the central and provincial governments that the rigidities and uncertainties, largely the result of judicial interpretation, became soon apparent, and which led the federal government to rely increasingly upon the approval of federal-provincial conferences before attempting to legislate on many matters of obvious national importance. As has frequently been remarked, in its political operation Canada has now one of the most decentralized federal constitutions in the world.

Because I have included in this volume not only essays of strict legal analysis but others which show my political preferences, I felt it might be useful to the reader to explain briefly how I came to accept the particular social and economic philosophy which is evident in the pages to follow. I was born in 1899 in Quebec City, in the rectory of St Matthew's Anglican Church. My father, Archdeacon Frederick George Scott, a poet and chaplain with the Canadian forces in the First World War, used to tell me how as a boy in Montreal he remembered the guns on top of Mount Royal saluting the first Dominion Day, 1 July 1867. When I was eight years old, I watched the great pageant on the Plains of Abra-

ham celebrating the tercentenary of the founding of Quebec by Samuel de
Champlain in 1608. I grew up understanding the import of the nostalgic motto
of Quebec – *Je me souviens.* Every St Jean Baptiste parade on 24 June por-
trayed scenes from the *ancien régime.* French Canada and its history were all
about me. I only left the province once for a short visit to Ottawa before I went
to Oxford in 1920 to read history and to spend vacations travelling in England
and on the continent.

I came back to Montreal in 1923 and became a law student at McGill the following year. I was immediately caught up in the new wave of nationalism in English Canada stimulated by a pride in the military achievements of the Canadian
Army in the First World War, by the country's newly acquired place in world society, and by a growing strength in the developing economy. My friends and con-
temporaries believed our country had a bright future, given its traditions, its man-
power, and its resources. We did not question the form of federalism that was
adopted at Confederation, based on a parliamentary system of government on the
British model for Ottawa and the provinces, a central government endowed with
adequate power to look after the general interests of the whole country, and, instead of a melting-pot, a recognition and constitutional guarantee of religious and
linguistic rights hopefully intended to preserve the cultural dualism in the federation. At the same time we were determined to rid the constitution of all vestiges
of colonialism and to clothe Canada with the full powers of a nation-state, beyond
what her separate membership in the League of Nations in 1920 had already given
her. This spirit of national independence helped to reduce the racial tensions
which had been exacerbated by the conscription issue in the world war. The Balfour Declaration of 1926 and the Statute of Westminster of 1931 were hailed
everywhere as great forward steps, marking the change from Empire to Commonwealth. An editorial in *Le Devoir*, then the leading exponent of Quebec's nationalism, even suggested that 11 December, the day the Statute of Westminster was
signed, should be made a national holiday.

I started to teach constitutional law in 1928 and, as Stephen Leacock might
have put in, the next year the whole North American economy collapsed. One
could not live through the Great Depression and remain politically unaffected.
The human misery cried out for relief, the failed institutions for reform. When all
the provinces were virtually bankrupt, the primary responsibility for reducing unemployment and providing welfare on an adequate scale was clearly federal. Few
dared to question the need for a strong federal authority in those days. Nor could
old ideas about free competition and freedom of trade continue unchallenged.
While remaining a full-time teacher and never seeking public office, I became active in the League for Social Reconstruction, Canada's version of the English Fab-
ian Society, and in the Cooperative Commonwealth Federation (the CCF), Can-

ada's democratic socialist party, the predecessor of the present New Democratic Party. This involvement sharpened my insight into the nature of law and particularly of constitutional law. I saw that every legal change involves a choice of values, a selection of objectives, and in this sense I was greatly attracted to the concept of law as social engineering being then advanced by the great American jurist, Roscoe Pound. Changing a constitution confronts a society with the most important choices, for in the constitution will be found the philosophical principles and rules which largely determine the relations of the individual and of cultural groups to one another and to the state. If human rights and harmonious relations between cultures are forms of the beautiful, then the state is a work of art that is never finished. Law thus takes its place, in its theory and practice, among man's highest and most creative activities.

The depression of the 1930s showed Canadians that in a great crisis provincial governments were incapable of effective remedial action, while the federal government, which alone provided a rallying point for serious reform, was thwarted by the fundamental law of the constitution as seen through distant eyes. It has long been my opinion that the weakening of Canadian federalism, so evident today, began with the interpretations of the constitution by the Judicial Committee of the Privy Council in England acting as Canada's court of last resort. Its crucial holdings in such cases as the *Companies Reference* case (1914), the *Board of Commerce* decision (1922), the *Snider* case (1925), and the three decisions in 1937 on Mr Bennett's 'New Deal' legislation (namely, the References on the *I.L.O. Conventions,* the *Natural Products Marketing Act*, and the *Employment and Social Insurance Act*) by denying federal jurisdiction in areas of great national importance, seemed to me to break the back of our constitutional structure. This was defending provincial autonomy and locking us in 'water-tight compartments' with a vengeance. Yet every day was bringing us and still brings us more links of dependence one upon another.

From this impasse we were freed suddenly, but not permanently, by the outbreak of war in 1939. At once the 'emergency doctrine' in the constitution became effective, and the federal government for the duration was able to pursue a unified policy virtually without serious legal impediments. The unemployed were absorbed into war industries and the armed forces, production was doubled without any foreign investment, inflation was kept under control, and even the prairie drought disappeared. A strong central government, given a clear objective, seemed almost capable of working miracles. Canada's war effort, it was generally agreed, compared favourably with that of any of the Allied powers. Instead of provincial governments disappearing, they also increased in activities and income, and the cultural life of the country, whether French or English, was greatly stimulated and given new opportunities of expression in such recent federal agencies as the

Canadian Broadcasting Corporation and the National Film Board. Indeed, during the dictatorial régime of Premier Duplessis in Quebec many francophone dramatists, novelists, and poets found a haven of freedom in these federal agencies which they would never have enjoyed in provincial employment.

The economic strength gained during the war continued into the post-war period. Canada became an important trading power with the second highest standard of living in the world. But the economic disparities within the country were not removed, though greatly alleviated by the acceptance of the principle of equalization grants from the richer to the poorer provinces. The policy of 'orderly decontrol' inaugurated by Mackenzie King after the war, resulting in the withdrawal of the federal parliament from the jurisdictions it had occupied in order to carry on the war, gave back great authority to provincial governments now richer and more able to become active on their own behalf. In particular, this period saw a continuous expansion of the claims of the government of Quebec as a centre of French-Canadian culture in North America, and therefore as the representative, not of a province, but of a nation. So the 'two nation' theory of Canada was born, and its consequences have been steadily developed to the point where, as I write these lines, the new government in Quebec of the Parti québécois (elected in November 1976 when this book was already in proof) is embarked upon a program of independence for the physical territory now included in the whole province, though Quebec contains a native population of Indians and Eskimos who are wards of the federal government, an English-speaking minority of over a million people (close to 20 per cent of the total), and the separation would leave almost as many French-speaking Canadians scattered among the other provinces. This challenge is so recent, and its outcome so uncertain, that I may be excused any attempt to analyse it in the preface to a volume of essays on a Canada that did not contemplate its own destruction. What I feel about it will be evident in the essays themselves. I do not believe that a Balkanized Canada, least of all a small independent French state in the middle of it, could withstand the ever increasing strength of American commercial and financial corporations – the new form of Manifest Destiny.

Apart from a few elisions and minor changes, I have reprinted these essays and papers as they originally appeared. I have not attempted, because the task would have been impracticable, to bring them up to date. I am conscious that they contain many repetitions, and some opinions I would not put forward today in the form in which I expressed them thirty or forty years ago. Increasing strength in Canada's provinces was inevitable given their size and, in most of them, their resources. That government should be as close as possible to the people being governed is a wise precept; so also in the modern world is the inescapable fact of interdependence of peoples, one upon the other, and the need to create governments large enough to deal effectively with the problems they are called upon to solve. There was nothing ignoble in the original concept of Canadian federalism.

My special thanks are due to my former colleague on the McGill Law Faculty, Professor Gerald E. LeDain (as he then was) now of the Federal Court of Appeal, for his invaluable assistance in the selection and arrangement of the material; to Dean Ronald Macdonald of Dalhousie Law Faculty who also read the manuscript and gave me his warm encouragement and support; to Professor J.R. Mallory of the Department of Political Science, McGill, for helpful advice; to Mr Arnold Banfill of the McGill Law Library who did careful proof-reading and prepared the index of cases and the bibliography; and to Ms Pat Lagace who composed the index of topics. I should like also to acknowledge debt to McGill University; there were several occasions when its administrators were, I know, 'eyeing me dubiously as I pursued my course', but its Faculty of Law in Montreal, Canada's third largest English-speaking city, as well as the second largest French-speaking city in the world, where the civil and the common law intermingle and where Canadian financial and industrial corporations first developed on a large scale, gave me an intellectual and sociological vantage point from which to study those aspects of constitutional law which most commanded my attention – the supremacy of public government over private corporate power, the enlargement and protection of human rights, and the free development of Canada's two principal cultures alongside the other ethnic groups, now a quarter of the Canadian population, who also wish to preserve their languages and traditions.

F.R. Scott
15 March 1977

# Contents

# ESSAYS ON THE CONSTITUTION

# Political Nationalism and Confederation

*A paper read at the Annual Meeting of the Canadian Political Science Association, 1942. The economic aspects of Confederation were dealt with at the same meeting by Professor D.G. Creighton. Canada was then at war, the Depression was over, the War Measures Act had concentrated all powers necessary for wartime planning in Ottawa's hands, the Royal Commission on Dominion-Provincial Relations (Rowell-Sirois Report) had recommended important constitutional changes, and there was a renewed interest in the origins, nature, and purposes of the British North America Act of 1867.*
From the *Canadian Journal of Economics and Political Science*, 8, 1942, 386-415

To Canadians living in the 1860s, as to Canadians of the 1940s, the world seemed a very dangerous place. In many respects the threats to Canadian survival must have appeared even greater then than now. The American Civil War brought large-scale fighting closer than the present campaigns in Europe or Asia. The Fenian raids, apparently backed by wide American support, looked more ominous than U-boats in the St Lawrence. The most disastrous international alignment that could ever befall Canadians – a war between the United States and Great Britain – appeared once again imminent. Internally there were equivalent dangers. The constitution of 1841 had broken down in the province of Canada, rendering stable government impossible. Political deadlock had been reached. Though French Canadians were able to enjoy the gratifying spectacle of British Canadians caught in the very constitutional trap – equal representation regardless of population – which had been designed to assure British supremacy, the situation could not continue. The economic outlook was no brighter. Imperial preferences had disappeared with the free trade movement, and though a successful readjustment had been made by the Reciprocity Treaty of 1854 this too was about to end. Notice of the cancellation of the Treaty was given by the United States in March, 1865. Thrust out into the economic world first by England, Canadians were rejected a second time by their other mainstay. And when they looked westward for new frontiers, they saw an advancing wave of American settlement, backed by western railways,[1] threatening to engulf the unsettled prairies.

Such a situation was indeed a challenge. One false step, and all might have been lost. Without some new political concept large enough to embrace all the factors and stimulating enough to command the allegiance of widely differing communities and races, Canada might have disappeared from the map. That concept was found in Confederation. Canadians – and for convenience I use the term in its current sense to include all the peoples of the British North American provinces – found the solution of their difficulties in the idea of nationalism. The force which was then at work unifying Germany under the first Reich, and Italy under the House of Savoy, operated to bring together under one political system the scattered peoples north of the American border. 'Let us build a great nation in this great country' – that was the rallying cry that pulled victory out of seeming defeat. The deadlock of the 1860s was resolved by an expansion of outlook and a widening of the political horizon, so that the forces which on the old plane were in conflict, on the new plane could work in collaboration.

Like most political events in which the chief actors profess high aims, Confederation had its more materialistic aspects. To certain financial and railway interests the union of the provinces was primarily a means of saving shaky investments. The near bankruptcy of the Grand Trunk Railway was one of the causes of Confederation – perhaps the most potent cause in changing the British government's lukewarmness of 1858, when Cartier, Ross, and Galt met with such discouragement in London, to its enthusiasm of 1864–7, when British pressure on the Maritimes to accept the Union was carried to a point that evoked charges of tyranny. A fact to which Canadian historians have drawn far too little attention was the union in 1863 through the International Financial Society, Limited, of the two largest corporations with a stake in Canada, the Grand Trunk Railway and the Hudson's Bay Company.[2] A unification of their directorates preceded political union in Canada by just four years. E.W. Watkin was the John A. Macdonald of the banking houses. Yet even when all allowances necessary for a Marxian interpretation of Confederation are duly made, the political fact of union remains. A new country was created, with purposes, plans, and aspirations to which the constitution bears witness. The temporary profit of a few capitalists is of small con-

1 The Northern Pacific was chartered in 1864.
2 The fullest account of this transaction will be found in R.G. Trotter, *Canadian Federation: Its History and Achievements* (London, 1924), chap. XIII ff.; and in the same author's 'British Finance and Confederation' (Canadian Historical Association Annual Report, 1927, p. 89). See also G.P. deT. Glazebrook, *A History of Transportation in Canada* (Toronto, New Haven, 1938), pp. 193–4, 230.

sequence beside the long-range principles on which the political structure was intended to rest. What were those principles?

## NATIONAL UNION

Though it is obvious, the fact must be emphasized that the first purpose of Confederation was union. The British North America Act was entitled 'An Act for the Union of Canada, Nova Scotia, and New Brunswick, and the Government thereof ... '; and throughout the Act it is the word 'Union,' not 'Confederation' that is used. A number of small and weak provinces were to be brought together into a single state out of which would grow 'a new nationality.' Toward this new nation and its central government the allegiance of all the citizens was expected to turn. Canadian nationalism here follows the pattern of many similar movements. The pettiness of politics and of public life in the individual provinces, the inefficiency of their local economies, the scant opportunity they offered to men of ability and ambition, were constant themes in the addresses on Confederation. By 1867 men had come to dislike provincialism. By contrast with this meagre life of the past, bright hopes were painted for the future. And while these hopes were somewhat overcoloured they do show the currents of thought and the desired goal of Canadian development. They show the purposes of Confederation, without which the law of the constitution is lifeless.

'I hope to see the day ... when there will be no other term to our patriotism, but the common name of Canadian, without the prefix of either French or British.' So wrote Thomas D'Arcy McGee,[3] and this vision of a new nationality in North America was shared by all the leaders of the Confederation movement. It is a belief constantly referred to by the public men of the times. Nor was it a sudden growth in the troubled sixties, but the product of a long-maturing Canadian consciousness. Colonel Morse's early thoughts about a 'great country' in North America were purely visionary. Later references to the idea show the growth of more solid plans. Lord Durham, himself a believer in federal union, expressed his gratification at finding 'the leading minds of the various colonies strongly and generally inclined to the scheme that would elevate their countries into something like a national existence.'[4] With the winning of responsible government, the coming of free trade, the new threats from the south and the growth of little Englandism, the sense of national opportunity in the northern provinces grew rapidly. Might not union, wrote Sir Edmund Head in 1851, result in 'rais-

3 Letter to his constituents, 1859. Quoted by A. Brady in *Thomas d'Arcy McGee* (Toronto, 1925), p. 53.
4 Sir Charles P. Lucas (ed.), *Lord Durham's Report on the Affairs of British North America* (3 vols., Oxford, 1912), vol. II, p. 305.

ing up on this side of the Atlantic a balance to the United States – a power so united as never to be absorbed piecemeal and so important in itself as to take an independent position if at any time hereafter the remaining ties with Great Britain might be severed?'[5]

Elgin saw materials in Canada 'for the future of Nations'; A.T. Galt dreamed of 'a nation worthy of England from her North American possessions.'[6] The 'great object and the great question' discussed at the Charlottetown Conference, said Cartier, was whether 'there could not be any means devised by which the great national fragments comprised in each of the British American Provinces could be brought together and made into a great nation.'[7] 'Shall we be content to maintain a mere provincial existence,' he asked during the Confederation debates,[8] 'when by combining together we could become a great nation?' Instead of being 'half a dozen inconsiderable colonies,' said George Brown, 'we would rise at once to the position of a great and powerful state.'[9] 'To you and your colleagues,' wrote Lord Monck to Macdonald, 'is really due the honour of having founded a "new nationality."'[10] A new nationality meant something that had not existed before: something obviously different from the old status of a mere British subject. The phrase 'new nationality' appeared in the Speech from the Throne in the Canadian Parliament of 1865. Macdonald saw Canada as 'standing on the very threshold of nations and when admitted we shall occupy no unimportant position among the nations of the world.' 'It needed no prophet,' said Colonel Gray of Prince Edward Island, 'to foretell that the day was coming when they would take their places among the first nations of the world.'[11] Later he referred to 'the dream of my life,' in which he hoped 'to be one day a citizen of a great nation extending from the Great West to the Atlantic seaboard.'[12] Some more realistic advocates of na-

---

5 Memorandum of 1851. Cited by Chester Martin, 'Sir Edmund Head's First Project of Federation' (Canadian Historical Association Annual Report, 1928, p. 25).
6 Chester Martin, *Empire and Commonwealth: Studies in Governance and Self-government in Canada* (Oxford, 1929), p. 351.
7 The Hon. E. Whelan, *The Union of the British Provinces: Written Immediately after the Conferences Held in Charlottetown and Quebec in 1864, on Confederation, and the Accompanying Banquets Held in Halifax, St. John, Montreal, Ottawa, and Toronto* (reprinted, Gardenvale, Toronto, 1927), p. 24.
8 *Ibid.*, p. 59.
9 John Hamilton Gray, *Confederation: or, the Political and Parliamentary History of Canada, from the Conference at Quebec, in October, 1864, to the Admission of British Columbia, in July, 1871* (Toronto, 1872), p. 37.
10 Sir Joseph Pope (ed.), *The Memoirs of the Right Honourable Sir John Alexander Macdonald, First Prime Minister of the Dominion of Canada* (2 vols., Ottawa, 1894), vol. I, p. 303.
11 Whelan, *Union of the British Provinces*, p. 145.
12 A.G. Doughty (ed.), 'Notes on the Quebec Conference, 1864' (*Canadian Historical Review*, vol. I, March, 1920, p. 28).

tionhood spoke of the need for Canada possessing a separate flag and currency of her own.[13]

These utterances – which could be multiplied many times[14] – were not all rhetoric. A sense of potential strength and future growth was in the spirit of the times, even though economic need and political deadlock were more immediate spurs to constitutional change. The very use of the word 'parliament' for the federal legislative body, and of the lesser term 'legislature' for the provincial assemblies, shows that 'the framers of the [Quebec] resolutions were thinking not in terms of a new province but of a new nation, with names as well as institutions copied from the mother of parliaments.'[15] Confederation was Canada's coming of age, the start of a national career.[16] Provincialism was to be left behind.

The boundaries of the new nation were to be the three oceans to the east, north, and west. Union was intended to bring together everything north of the United States boundary, from Newfoundland to Vancouver Island – Alaska being alone excluded. 'One great nationality,' said D'Arcy McGee, 'bound, like the shield of Achilles, by the blue rim of the ocean.' Atlantic, Arctic, Pacific – here were natural frontiers of the finest sort. Only the southern boundary appeared artificial, and here the railways would be added to the St Lawrence to provide an east-west line of communication. Within this huge domain there would be room for nationhood.

The problem of bringing together the remainder of British North America, after Canada, Nova Scotia, and New Brunswick had united, occupied the first years of the Dominion government. The Hudson's Bay Company territories were transferred and the province of Manitoba created in 1870. British Columbia joined in 1871, and Prince Edward Island in 1873. By this date the national structure as conceived by the Fathers was virtually complete. Newfoundland, however, refused to join, and her abstention led in 1927 to the loss of a considerable portion of Labrador owing to the odd definition of its 'coast' by the Privy Council; just as the Alaskan boundary award of 1903 cut off part of the Pacific coast claimed by Canada. In 1880 an Imperial Order in Council[17] annexed all British possessions in North America, except Newfoundland, to Canada.

---

13 E.g., Joseph Howe and Sir Edmund Head.

14 See J.S. Ewart, *The Kingdom Papers* (Ottawa, 1911–14), vol. II, pp. 369 ff.

15 W.M. Whitelaw, *The Maritimes and Canada before Confederation* (Toronto, 1934), p. 260.

16 Even consular powers for Canada were suggested at the London Conference, though no decision was taken. See Sir Joseph Pope (ed.), *Confederation: Being a Series of Hitherto Unpublished Documents Bearing on the British North America Act* [hereafter referred to as Pope, *Confederation Documents*] (Toronto, 1895), p. 112.

17 July 31, 1880.

A NEW STATUS

Confederation was brought about without any formal disturbance of the relations between Canada and the British Crown. Though Sir Edmund Head in 1851 had seen that union would eventually enable Canada to stand alone should the imperial tie be severed, and though the independence of Canada and the other colonies was frequently prophesied and discussed by public men in the fifties and sixties, nevertheless the Fathers were agreed that they wished to remain associated with the British Empire. Indeed, Confederation was looked upon as the best means of preventing annexation to the United States. The 'perpetuation of the connexion with the Mother Country' was one of the purposes mentioned in the Quebec and London Resolutions. But there were various types of 'connexion' to choose from; and 'connexion' can exist between equals. Both the Maritimes and the Canadas had already passed through the stage of Crown dependencies and had become largely self-governing colonies. Was the new nation to be just another such colony, like Nova Scotia or New Brunswick? Macdonald, Cartier, Tupper, Langevin, and other leading statesmen thought not. Confederation, they hoped, would change the self-governing colonies into a united nation with a status like that of a partner or ally of Britain. It was intended to carry colonial development beyond the point of mere responsible government, and to end the era of subordination. Without ending the imperial connection, the dominating position of Great Britain was to be ousted by the federal government, from which the provinces would depend as they formerly depended from England.

The colonies that united in 1867 were all 'provinces' of the Crown of Great Britain. Each was equal in status to the others, and all were inferior to Britain. The term 'province' was part of the official name of Canada under the constitution of 1841. At Confederation a new government, above that of these provinces, was created. If it too were a 'province,' it would seem to be not at all superior to its parts. It had to be something more free and independent than a province or colony. So we find the Fathers concerned with changing the name and raising the inferior status of the country. The speeches made during the tour of the delegates to the Charlottetown and Quebec Conferences, both in the Maritimes and in the Canadas, abound in references to the new rank. A 'new order' was indeed in the hearts and minds of the Fathers of Confederation. Canadians are often given to thinking in grandiose terms, perhaps as much to cover past failures as to reflect future opportunities, and every constitution has been launched on rhetoric. Yet the prophecies and visions of the period come astonishingly close to later developments in the field of imperial relations. There are few ideas in the Imperial Conference report of 1926 that are not present in Canada in the 1860s. The Hon. T. Heath Haviland, one of the few early supporters of Confederation in Prince

Edward Island, may have been a little fanciful when he said: 'The practicability of a Confederation of the Provinces and territories of British North America, to their utmost extent and limits, into a great national power, is, with respect to geographical difficulties, fast ceasing to be regarded as a mere visionary idea. The empire of which it would form the foundation, would in extent, be inferior only to those of Russia, China and Brazil, and, in commanding position, its advantages would be equal to those of all the three combined.'[18] But such language was typical of the times, and men thinking in such terms were obviously not contemplating a colonial subordination. Mr Haviland saw that a new Canadian empire would have to be much freer in its external relations, and sought, not too unsuccessfully, to solve the riddle of continued imperial relations under such circumstances.

It was not to be presumed, however, that the Federal Government, although, in some sense, it would be independent could, without some very material modification of the relation of the Provinces to the Mother Country, be permitted the power of making war, and of concluding treaties of peace and commerce, on its own account, as the government of an entirely independent country. The power of regulating the intercourse and relations of the Confederated Provinces would, on the contrary, be confined to such adjustment of trade and commercial intercourse and relations with foreign states, as could not be prejudicial, in any very material or aggressive degree, to the interests of Great Britain, and as would not involve her actual divesture of all authority over them.[19]

Here some 'relations with foreign states' are contemplated, and even the power of making war and peace is being tentatively approached.

Nowhere is the spirit of national independence more evident than in the speech of Cartwright, and the touch of political bitterness, so characteristic of the man, does not obscure the passionate love of country.

My own years are not very many, Mr Speaker, but yet even I can remember when Canada was but a petty province, an obscure dependency, scarce able to make its voice heard on the other side of the Atlantic without a rebellion; forgotten or ignored, as if, as the French Minister said when he signed the treaty for its surrender, 'it mattered not what became of a few barren acres of snow!' And yet, sir, in less than thirty years I have lived to see Canada expand into a state equal in numbers, in resources and power of self-government to many an independent European kingdom – lacking only the will to step at once from the position of a de-

18 Prince Edward Island Assembly, *Debates*, 1867, p. 152 (speech of May 8, 1866).
19 *Ibid.*, p. 153.

pendency to that of an ally – a favoured ally of the great country to which we belong, and to take that rank among the commonwealth of nations which is granted to those people, and to those only, who have proved that they possess the power as well as the wish to defend their liberties. This, sir, is what I think Canada can do; and if, as I believe, this project of Confederation would contribute most powerfully to enable us to do so, there are few sacrifices which I would refuse to make for such an object – much more, forgive my honourable friends yonder for having in time past spoken somewhat over harshly and hastily of each other. Let them only persevere, let them only go on and complete the task which I will say they have so nobly begun, and they will have made good their claim – I do not say to the forgiveness – but to the regard, the affection, the esteem of very many who shall hereafter bear the name of Canadian.[20]

Tupper saw the desire for a new status as the chief reason for the success of the union movement. 'I can discover,' he told the Nova Scotian Assembly, 'no other cause why there has been so great a co-operation among all classes of intelligent people of our country in respect to the union of these colonies than the desire that possessing these advantages we should at the same time advance to a more national position and render our institutions more secure.'[21] 'A more national position' meant something above a mere colony. He too was clearly thinking of a change in the control of Canada's external and imperial relations, for he goes on to remind his listeners of the way their international interests have been disregarded in the past.

We have evidence of the most tangible and positive character, both in Nova Scotia and New Brunswick, how insignificant is our position in the estimation of the parent state. What was the complaint when the Reciprocity treaty was submitted to the house, that came from both sides? That the Imperial Parliament, in negotiating the treaty, had not thought it necessary to ask the opinion of Nova Scotia statesmen, though the great fisheries that surround this country were to be surrendered ... where was New Brunswick when a large slice was cut off from her territory – when the whole of British North America was disfigured by the Ashburton Treaty? The opinion of a single statesman in New Brunswick was not asked.[22]

20 Canada, Province of (1841–66), *Parliamentary Debates on the Subject of Confederation of the British North American Provinces* [hereafter referred to as *Confederation Debates*] (Quebec, 1865), p. 825.
21 Nova Scotia Assembly, *Debates*, April 10, 1865, pp. 210-11.
22 *Ibid.*

During the Confederation debates Langevin, the Solicitor-General, quoted from an article which pointed out how unfavourable was the position of a Canadian by comparison with that of an American citizen: the latter was free to rise to the presidency, ranking with 'the proudest monarchs of Europe,' but 'the British American could not reasonably aspire even to become the governor of his native province; and if he were to go to England, all the influence which he could command would probably not procure him a presentation to his sovereign.' 'Does not that show,' added Mr Langevin, 'that the position of a Canadian, or of any other inhabitant of the colonies, in England is a position of inferiority? We desire to remove that inferiority by adopting the plan of Confederation now submitted to the House.'[23]

By the Resolutions adopted at Quebec and London, the 'rank and name' of the Confederation were to be determined by the Queen.[24] Macdonald said during the debate on the Resolutions that he did not know 'whether we are to be a vice-royalty, or whether we are still to retain our rank and name as a province,' but he had no doubt that the rank the Queen 'will confer on us will be a rank worthy of our position, of our resources and of our future.'[25] In his great speech he too foresaw the new Commonwealth relationship that was emerging: 'Gradually a different colonial system is being developed – and it will become, year by year, less a case of dependence on our part, and of overruling protection on the part of the Mother Country, and more a case of a healthy and cordial alliance. Instead of looking upon us as a merely dependent colony, England will have in us a friendly nation – a subordinate but still a powerful people – to stand by her in North America in peace or in war.' His use of the word 'alliance' is significant, and many others used the term at this time. Allies can be equals, but colonies, provinces, and dominions are mere British possessions. Even Cardwell, the Colonial Secretary, said of the proposed new Canada, that to Great Britain 'the *alliance* of so great a State will be of infinite advantage.'[26]

Mr Dunkin, the most perspicacious opponent of Confederation, warned where this nationalism might lead. He pointed out that the Quebec scheme would tend to independence, 'for disguise it how you may, the idea that underlies this plan is this, and nothing else – that we are to create here a something – kingdom, viceroyalty or principality – something that will soon stand in the same position towards the British Crown that Scotland & Ireland stood in before they were legislatively united with England; a something having no other tie to the Empire than

---

23 *Confederation Debates*, p. 370.
24 Quebec, no. 71; London, no. 68. See also Pope, *Confederation Documents*, p. 74.
25 *Ibid.*, p. 43.
26 Cited in New Brunswick Assembly, *Debates*, 1865, p. 149 (italics mine).

the one tie of fealty to the British Crown ... '[27] History has proven him correct in his analysis of the new relationship, though he would have been surprised had he known how long a time was going to elapse before even the Canadians understood what had been accomplished. Similarly Mr Gilbert attacked the scheme in the New Brunswick legislature: 'Did they intend to establish a Viceroy here with all the pomp & circumstance of Royalty?' With good North American distrust of monarchical pomp he wanted no officer of New Brunswick, 'kissing the boney hand of a viceroy.'[28] Mr McLelan in Nova Scotia warned that hitherto England had been the 'embodiment of our nationality,' but 'this confederation comes in and proposes a new order of things.'[29] Mr Bourinot in Nova Scotia feared that 'the formation of such a nation would lead to independence of England.'[30]

In London, we know that Macdonald pressed hard for the name 'Kingdom of Canada' for the new country. It was an idea that had been in his mind for some time. At Halifax in 1865, speaking of the Charlottetown Conference, he had said, 'We all approached the subject feeling its importance, feeling that in our hands were the destinies of a nation; and great would be our sin and shame if any different motive had intervened to prevent us carrying out the noble object of founding a great British monarchy in connection with the British Empire, and under the British Queen.'[31]

Cartier spoke in similar vein. 'We know very well that, as soon as confederation is obtained, the Confederacy will have to be erected into a Vice-Royalty, and we may expect that a member of the Royal Family will be sent here as the head.'[32] The term 'Kingdom of Canada' actually appears in two of the draft bills drawn up by the delegates to the London Conference;[33] it was now not just a whim of Macdonald's, but the considered wish of the entire Canadian delegation. The first draft bill, produced by the British Law Officers of the Crown, had been liberally sprinkled with the word 'colony'; the 'colonies' were to be 'united into one colony'; this term the Canadian delegates struck out entirely.[34] Certain British officials treated the Union 'much as if the BNA Act were a private bill uniting

27 *Confederation Debates*, p. 527.
28 New Brunswick Assembly, *Debates*, 1865, p. 126.
29 Nova Scotia Assembly, *Debates*, 1865, p. 260.
30 *Ibid.*, p. 268.
31 Gray, *Confederation*, p. 45.
32 Whelan, *Union of the British Provinces*, pp. 26-7.
33 The third and fourth drafts. See Pope, *Confederation Documents*, pp. 158, 177.
34 The story of this first struggle for equal status is best told, as one might expect, in
   J.S. Ewart, 'Imperial Projects and the Republic of Canada' (Ewart, *The Kingdom Papers*,
   vol. II, pp. 374–85). See also Lionel Groulx, *La Confédération canadienne, Ses
   Origines: Conférences prononcées à l'Université Laval* (Montreal, 1917–18), p. 225.
   Most Canadian historians treat the incident as though it had little significance.

two or three English parishes,'[35] and Lord Derby objected to the Canadian proposal, on the ostensible ground it might hurt American susceptibilities. So the word 'Dominion' was substituted for 'Kingdom.'[36] Thus the desire of Canadians to achieve a title unequivocally descriptive of a partnership was thwarted. Old concepts of empire barred the way to a recognition of Canadian nationality, and hindered its development at its very birth. As Macdonald later wrote, 'A great opportunity was lost' of having Canada declared to be 'an auxiliary Kingdom.'[37]

The 'name' given to the union was Canada; its 'rank' was that of a 'Dominion.' What is a 'Dominion?' No one knew. Canadians wished it to indicate a new and more equal status under the Crown. But the ambiguity in the term 'Dominion,' implying both 'rule over' and the 'territory ruled' left the real status quite in the air. Virginia was a 'Dominion' before the American Revolution. The law of the constitution knew only of colonies after 1867. 'Half-a-dozen colonies federated are but a federated colony after all,' said the sceptical Dunkin.[38] When in 1880 Canada wished to give her newly-appointed representative in London a diplomatic status, again the British objected on the ground that it implied too great a separation between the countries. The Conference of 1887 was a 'colonial' conference. In 1889 the British Interpretation Act took care to include the Dominions within the term 'colony,' thus restoring the definition of the first draft of the BNA Act which the Canadians had rejected. Not till the turn of the century did the term 'Dominion' come to imply a relationship approximating what Canadians had hoped to achieve in 1867, and not till the Balfour declaration of 1926 and the Statute of Westminster of 1931 was the equality of status first aimed at in 1867 officially declared. The word 'colony' ceased to be applied to Canada, by constitutional law, only in 1931. The result of those later changes was to make even the term 'Dominion' obsolete, for a Dominion had become by implication something not equal to Great Britain; the word for too long had been associated with the middling status of colonies whose foreign policy was not

35 Macdonald's phrase (Pope, *Memoirs of Sir John Alexander Macdonald*, vol. I, p. 313).
36 *Ibid*. It is odd that the Fathers, who knew the Americans better than Lord Derby did, never anticipated this objection. The only suggestion I have found in the Confederation debates to the possible dislike in the United States of a Canadian monarchy was in Perrault's speech (at pp. 621–2), and he was an opponent of the whole scheme. It has been suggested that it was the British who were offended at the implication of equality. See O.D. Skelton, *The Life and Times of Sir Alexander Tilloch Galt* (Toronto, 1920), p. 410.
37 Cited in Ewart, *Kingdom Papers*, vol. II, pp. 384–5.
38 *Confederation Debates*, p. 525. Taché also expected the continuance of colonialism (*ibid*., p. 228). Dunkin, who preferred an imperial federation, was inconsistent in his attack, since at one moment he was arguing that Confederation would leave Canada a colony and at the next that it would make her independent.

their own and who were not separate persons in international law. At the time of the Royal visit of 1939, Canadians were beginning to ascribe again to themselves, as a constitutional novelty, the term 'Kingdom of Canada' which British influence compelled them to remove from the draft of their own constitution seventy-three years before. Three generations of Canadians were compelled to live in a state of mental confusion about their status, because the delegates to London did not have quite enough courage and determination to insist that the British 'connexion' should be established on their own terms. And because the term 'Dominion' is still used the confusion continues.

The concept of a new status in 1867 was not incompatible with the existence of the technical legal doctrine of imperial parliamentary sovereignty – any more than the concept of democracy in England is incompatible with the legal doctrine of the royal veto. The BNA Act was primarily the work of Canadians; it was the first time they had ever prepared a constitution for themselves. Constitutional practice had become settled by 1867 that legislation by the imperial parliament for the self-governing colonies in North America, on any matter of constitutional importance, would only occur at their request. Hence the legal power of the imperial parliament to legislate for Canada after 1867 remained merely as a useful underlying principle giving legal force and rigidity to the constitution, and available as a method of constitutional amendment whenever Canada should invoke its application. The existence of this element of 'subordination' does not detract from the reality of the desire for equality. A bold suggestion was once made that the BNA Act, by giving the Dominion parliament 'exclusive' legislative powers in certain subjects, operated as a renunciation by the imperial parliament of its power to legislate in these fields for Canada, but the law courts held firmly to the old view that no such abdication of sovereignty occurred.[39] It was to get rid of this legal anomaly of sovereignty being vested in one only of several 'equal partners' in the British Commonwealth that the Statute of Westminster was passed in 1931.

MINORITY RIGHTS

The new nation to be created was to be composed of many races. This was abundantly clear to all, and in consequence Canadian nationalism began with the theory of duality if not plurality of cultures. The aboriginal population was Indian and Eskimo, of whom many remained. French explorers had been here from the sixteenth century; British traders – in Hudson Bay – from the seventeenth. The British themselves were composed of the four principal races that inhabit the

---

39 *Reg.* v. *Taylor*, 36 U.C.Q.B. at p. 220; *Smiles* v. *Belford*, 1 O.A.R. 436. See W.H.P. Clement, *The Law of the Canadian Constitution* (ed. 1, Toronto, 1892), pp. 57ff.

British Isles. German Mennonites were in Ontario in the early nineteenth century, and United States settlers of all kinds were filtering into the country. The Canadian nation could be a political concept, but not an ethnic one. National unity meant a union of diverse groups in a common political structure for common ends, not an assimilation or an amalgamation. 'We were of different races,' said Cartier, 'not for the purpose of warring against each other, but in order to compete and emulate for the general welfare.'

Confederation came after the major battles of the French Canadian for survival had been won. The British element had made two principal attempts to assimilate him. The first was immediately after the conquest, when it was hoped that the change of laws and institutions would gradually win the 'new subjects' to the new British ways. The Quebec Act reversed this policy. The second attempt was after the 1837 rebellion, when the Act of Union was devised so as to exclude the French language from the law and to secure an English majority in parliament regardless of population. This ended with the victory of the French and English Reformers in 1848 under Lafontaine-Baldwin, the re-introduction of the French language for official uses, and the acceptance of responsible government by Lord Elgin. Those great events, which mark the real birth of the new nationalism that brought union through Confederation, spelled the end of the policy of assimilation. Any hopes there might have been for a 'British' Canada with one language and one law, went up with the smoke of the parliament buildings in Montreal; that conflagration, set by British extremists, was their own funeral pyre. Since then the dualism of the Canadian nation has been a basis of constitutional law and of political theory and practice, however much there may have been conflict over the application of the principle.

The BNA Act must be seen in this context. The framers of the statute did not have to battle over the principle of minority rights, but only over its formulation and extent. The idea of entrenching certain protections in the fundamental law, to formulate a minority bill of rights, was clearly accepted. The story of the various safeguarding clauses has been frequently told; from the point of view of the theory of Canadian nationalism what is important is the recognition of cultural and religious freedom implicit in the arrangement. The element of race as such receives little direct recognition: the Indians are the only race mentioned in the Act (Section 91-24). The protections went to the French and English languages (Section 133), to the Catholic and Protestant religions (Sections 92-12 and 93), and to proportional representation for provinces and sections (Sections 22, 51-2). The inclusion of 'Property and Civil Rights in the Province' as a provincial power, and the exclusion of Quebec from the uniformity provisions of Section 94, preserved the Quebec Civil Code from basic changes except in so far as the provincial legislature might wish to alter it. Some special indirect safeguards for the British minority in Quebec were included (Section 22, the last paragraph, and Section 80).

Out of these different provisions emerges a constitution that fixes certain minimum guarantees for the different groups, leaving further expansion of minority rights to the good sense and fairness of later generations. Since the use of the French language was extended to Manitoba in 1870 and to the whole of the Northwest Territories in 1877, it is evident that the original Fathers of Confederation did not look upon the minority guarantees in the 1867 constitution as being a maximum, but rather as a minimum on which to build. Macdonald had said that 'the use of the French language should form one of the principles upon which the Confederation should be established.'[40] Changes in the position of minorities could be made, but only in the direction of greater rights than those established in 1867.[40a] Hence Section 93 provides that even in provinces where no special privileges exist for separate schools, once they are granted they cannot be taken away again without giving rise to remedial legislation by the federal parliament.

This last provision suggests another important aspect of minority rights at Confederation. To whom is their protection confided? Much that has been said about Canadian federalism in recent years suggests that the powers of the provinces were the protection for minorities. On this interpretation every extension of provincial powers becomes an increase of minority rights. There is little in the BNA Act to justify this view. There the basic protection for minorities rests in the writing of the safeguarding clauses into the fundamental law of the constitution, which cannot be changed without resort to the imperial parliament. Hence the law courts can declare *ultra vires* any law, whether provincial or federal, which conflicts with these provisions. Hence the Supreme Court of Canada, for example, unanimously declared the Manitoba School Act of 1890 invalid. It was the Privy Council which overruled the Court, expanded provincial powers in Manitoba, and hence legalized what the Court had held to be an invasion of minority rights.[41]

The minorities are protected in the constitution primarily against the provinces. Appeals by minorities against provincial legislation lie with the Dominion government under Section 93, and the Dominion veto power can always be invoked. Macdonald said that 'we shall be able to protect the minority by having a strong central government.'[42] Inside the Dominion parliament it is the weight of French

---

40 *Confederation Debates*, p. 944.
40a [Recently Quebec has attempted to challenge this principle: see The Official Language Act, 1974, commonly known as Bill 22.]
41 For an expansion of this idea see my article 'The Privy Council and Minority Rights' (*Queen's Quarterly*, vol. XXXVII, Oct., 1930, pp. 668 ff.); Canada, House of Commons, 1935, *Proceedings, Evidence and Report of Special Committee on the British North America Act* (Ottawa, King's Printer, 1935), pp. 82–3.
42 Pope, *Confederation Documents*, p. 55.

Canadian representation in the Senate and Commons which must count,[43] a weight that constantly increases with the increase of the French population. Provincial powers and minority rights are quite different concepts in the constitution, and the great centralization of the power over national affairs planned for by the Act of 1867 did not appear a menace to minorities. There would not have been a two-to-one majority in favour of Confederation among the French-Canadian representatives unless this had been clear; and the dire predictions of Mr Perrault[44] have not been fulfilled. Attacks on minorities since 1867 have nearly all been provincial, not federal. The exclusive provincial jurisdiction over local matters of property and civil rights, over the provincial constitution and municipal affairs, was an adequate guarantee that 'each of the colonies should preserve its peculiar privileges and institutions, and that there should be no higher power to interfere with them.'[45] The result of associating minority rights with the provincial instead of with the federal power, is to suggest that they are geographically limited exceptions instead of general principles of national unity.

A STRONG NATIONAL GOVERNMENT

No intention of the Fathers of Confederation was more clear than that the new nation was to have a strong central government. The role of the new state in world affairs was to be great, therefore its powers must be great. The supreme object of union was to create a single parliament 'charged with matters of common interest to the whole country.'[46] It was to have 'all the powers which are incident to sovereignty' to use Macdonald's phrase – powers which a mere province, not being sovereign, could not possess. The dangers of disunity were only too evident, both within and without. Narrow provincialism and 'the petty strife of small communities' had disgusted both parties and people. Inside British North America were separate colonial tariffs, different currencies, mean provincial jealousies retarding commerce and industry, scattered military forces, huge unoccupied areas waiting to be organized, and political stalemate. Outside were two dominant facts; a United States rent by the doctrine of 'States' rights,' yet emerging to a new unity under the leadership of the North; and Great Britain no longer interested in economic or military protection for her colonies. These were the three 'warnings' that D'Arcy McGee saw as the chief motives impelling toward union: 'one warning from within and two from without';[47] and their combined

---

43 See J.W. Dafoe, 'Revising the Constitution' (*Queen's Quarterly*, vol. XXXVII, Jan., 1930, pp. 6–7).
44 *Confederation Debates*, p. 623.
45 Hon. Edward Palmer as quoted in Gray, *Confederation*, p. 118. Macdonald spoke in the same sense (Pope, *Confederation Documents*, p. 55).
46 Quebec and London Resolutions, no. 2.
47 *Confederation Debates*, p. 131.

effect was to make the constitution lean to the side of centralization as against local independence. In contrast to the American colonies, which approached union from the position of sovereign and independent states, and gave up their full powers with reluctance, the Canadian provinces came to union as colonies under the sovereignty of a single all-powerful imperial legislature, and departed from that model only because of necessity and in a limited degree.

As the relations between the Dominion and provincial governments came in later years to be matters of great dispute in Canada, it is important to keep alive the views on this subject of the men who drew up the constitution. The clearest expression of opinion, as might be expected, came from Sir John Macdonald. He was himself desirous of a legislative instead of a federal union, but subordinated his views to those of the other delegates when it became obvious that some form of federalism would alone command acceptance. Speaking during the Quebec Conference he said:

The various States of the adjoining Republic had always acted as separate sovereignties. The New England States, New York State and the Southern States had no sympathies in common. They were thirteen individual sovereignties, quite distinct the one from the other. The primary error at the formation of their constitution was that each state reserved to itself all sovereign rights, save the small portion delegated. We must reverse this process by strengthening the General Government and conferring on the Provincial bodies only such powers as may be required for local purposes. All sectional prejudices and interests can be legislated for by local legislatures. Thus we shall have a strong and lasting government under which we can work out constitutional liberty as opposed to democracy, and be able to protect the minority by having a powerful central government. Great caution, however, is necessary. The people of every section must feel that they are protected, and by no overstraining of central authority should such guarantees be overridden. [48]

Further debate on the question arose when the powers to be ascribed to the local legislatures were being discussed. Chandler of New Brunswick objected that 'The Local Legislatures should not have their powers specified, but should have all the powers not reserved to the Federal Government, and only the powers to be given to the Federal Government should be specified.' Tupper replied that at the Charlottetown Conference 'it was fully specified there that all the powers not given to the Local should be reserved to the Federal Government. This was stated as being a prominent feature of the Canadian scheme; and it was said then that it

48 Pope, *Confederation Documents*, pp. 54–5.

was desirable to have a plan contrary to that adopted by the United States.' Macdonald was most emphatic: he said,

I think the whole affair would fail, and the system be a failure if we adopted Mr Chandler's views. It would be adopting the worst features of the United States. We should concentrate the power in the Federal Government, and not adopt the decentralization of the United States. Mr Chandler would give sovereign power to the Local Legislatures, just where the United States failed ... No general feeling of patriotism exists in the United States. In occasions of difficulty each man sticks to his individual state. Mr Stephens, the present Vice-President, was a strong Union man, yet, when the time came, he went with his state. Similarly we should stick to our Province and not be British Americans. It would be introducing a source of radical weakness.[49]

Mr Chandler's opposition was overcome by these arguments, for when on the same evening, Coles of Prince Edward Island moved that 'the Local Legislatures shall have power to make all laws not given by this Conference to the General Legislature expressly,' the Conference records show that 'the same was unanimously resolved in the negative.'[50] This decision to strengthen the federal legislature by giving it general as well as specified powers was not departed from at any later date in the proceedings at Quebec or London.

During the debates on the Quebec Resolutions, in the parliament of the province of Canada, many other references were made to the same idea. The simple formula was this: To the general government, all matters of common interest to the whole country; to the local governments, all matters of local interest in their respective areas. Macdonald stated the position in these terms:

Ever since the union was formed the difficulty of what is called 'State Rights' has existed, and this had much to do in bringing on the present unhappy war in the United States. They commenced, in fact, at the wrong end. They declared by their Constitution that each state was a sovereignty in itself, and that all the powers incident to a sovereignty belonged to each state, except those powers which, by the Constitution were conferred upon the General Government and Congress. Here we have adopted a different system. We have strengthened the General Government. We have given the General Legislature all the great subjects of legislation. We have conferred on them, not only specifically and in detail, all the powers which are incident to sovereignty, but we have expressly declared that all sub-

49 *Ibid.*, p. 86.
50 *Ibid.*, p. 27.

jects of general interest not distinctly and exclusively conferred upon the local governments and local legislatures, shall be conferred upon the General Government and Legislature. – We have thus avoided that great source of weakness which has been the cause of the disruption of the United States.[51]

Later he came back to the point when discussing the Dominion residuary clause:

This is precisely the provision which is wanting in the Constitution of the United States. It is here that we find the weakness of the American system – the point where the American Constitution breaks down. [Hear, hear.] It is in itself a wise and necessary provision. We thereby strengthen the Central Parliament, and make the Confederation one people and one government, instead of five peoples and five governments, with merely a point of authority connecting us to a limited and insufficient extent.[52]

Cartier, the leader of the French-Canadian group supporting Confederation, explained the situation in briefer but similar terms. He said: 'Questions of commerce, of international communication and all matters of general interest, would be discussed and determined in the General Legislature ... Under the Federation system, granting to the control of the General Government those large questions of general interest in which the differences of race or religion had no place, it could not be pretended that the rights of either race or religion could be invaded at all.'[53] Taché, who was chairman of the Quebec Conference, pointed out how, in a Federal Union, 'all questions of a general character would be reserved for the General Government and those of a local character to the local governments, who would have the power to manage their domestic affairs as they deemed best,'[54] Brown, leader of the Upper Canada Reform party, followed in the same vein: 'For all dealings with the Imperial Government and foreign countries we have clothed the General Government with the most ample powers. And finally, all matters of trade and commerce, banking and currency, and all questions common to the whole people, we have vested fully and unrestrictedly in the General Government.'[55]

Galt, who was chiefly interested in the financial aspects of union, argued that under the proposed division of powers the costs of governing the country would not be increased. It was his view that 'we may well doubt whether the aggregate charge will be greater for the General Government, caring for the general interests

51 *Confederation Debates*, p. 33.
52 *Ibid.*, p. 41.
53 *Ibid.*, pp. 55, 60.
54 *Ibid.*, p. 9.
55 *Ibid.*, p. 108.

of the whole, and for the local governments, attending merely to the local business of each sections ... we shall have the legislation of the General Government restricted to those great questions which may properly occupy the attention of the first men of the country; we shall not have our time frittered away in considering the merits of petty local bills.'[56] D'Arcy McGee pointed out that 'In the application of this principle [of federalism] to former constitutions, there certainly always was one fatal defect, the weakness of the central authority.'[57] Langevin, another French-Canadian delegate to the Quebec Conference, said, 'The Central or Federal Parliament will have the control of all measures of a general character, as provided by the Quebec Conference; but all matters of local interest, all that relates to the affairs and rights of the different sections of the Confederacy, will be reserved for the control of the local parliaments.'[58] He pointed out that the central legislature would not injure French Canadians, since it 'will only be charged with the settlement of the great general questions which will interest alike the whole Confederacy & not one locality only.'[59] Cartwright said: 'even where there may be some conflict of jurisdiction on minor matters, every reasonable precaution seems to have been taken against leaving behind us any reversionary legacies of sovereign state rights to stir up strife and discord among our children.'[60]

It was not only in the Canadian legislature that this interpretation was given. Dr Tupper, in the Nova Scotia Assembly, in a speech which deserves to rank beside that of Macdonald for its clarity and vision, used these words:

If a Legislative Union were devised for British North America the people occupying the different sections would not have the guarantee that they have under the scheme devised, that matters of a local character would occupy the attention of the local legislatures, whilst those of a general nature would be entrusted to the General Legislature. Therefore the scheme that was devised gave the centralization & consolidation and unity that it was absolutely indispensable should be given. On the other hand, instead of having copied the defects of the federal constitution – instead of having the inherent weakness that must always attend a system where the local legislatures only impart certain powers to the government of the country – quite a different course was pursued, and it was decided to define the questions that should be reserved for the local legislatures, and those great subjects that should be entrusted to the general parliament ... all the

56 *Ibid.*, p. 70.
57 *Ibid.*, p. 144.
58 *Ibid.*, pp. 367–8.
59 *Ibid.*, p. 368.
60 *Ibid.*, p. 823.

questions of leading general importance should be entrusted to the general government.[61]

Several opponents of Confederation based their opposition precisely on the ground that there was too much centralization. Olivier protested that 'The powers of the Federal Government will be in reality unlimited. The fact of the enumeration of these thirty-seven heads does not in the least restrain the power of the Federal Government from legislating on everything. The exceptions are few.'[62] Joly feared that 'The local parliaments, in the event of that system being adopted, having no part in the government, will soon become perfectly useless, and they will soon be dispensed with, just as in a machine we do away with useless and expensive wheelwork. Nothing will then be left to us but the legislative union.'[63] Mr Perrault wanted to postpone Confederation until French-Canadian influence would be strong enough to demand greater rights: 'We shall not then have our present political rights, which were so dearly obtained by the struggles of a century, replaced by local governments, which will be nothing more than municipal councils, vested with small and absurd powers, unworthy of a free people, which allow us at most the control of our roads, our schools and our lands; but we shall then obtain local governments based on the sovereignty of states, as is the case under the Constitution of the United States.'[64] And Dorion declared: 'The Confederation I advocated was a real Confederation, giving the largest powers to the local governments, and merely a delegated authority to the General Government – in that respect differing in toto from the one now proposed, which gives all the powers to the Central and reserves for the local governments the smallest possible amount of freedom of action.'[65]

The Hon. Mr Coles, one of the delegates to Quebec, speaking of the provincial legislatures under the Quebec scheme, protested that 'The City Council would be a King to such a Legislature. In this House scarcely anything would be left us to do, but to legislate about dog taxes and the running at large of swine.'[66] 'This House would be dwindled down to a level with the small municipal bodies throughout Canada for the management of local affairs,' said Mr Howat.[67] Answering this criticism, the Hon. Mr Haviland contended there would be no 'degradation' of

61 Nova Scotia Assembly, *Debates*, 1865, pp. 207–8.
62 *Confederation Debates*, p. 176.
63 *Ibid.*, pp. 360–1.
64 *Ibid.*, p. 623.
65 *Ibid.*, p. 250.
66 Prince Edward Island Assembly, *Debates*, 1865, p. 68.
67 *Ibid.*, 1866, p. 109.

provincial legislation, which would retain entire control and management of its own local and internal affairs; yet he had to add –

It was true, indeed, that the General Government would, of necessity, exercise supervision of the individual States: but the power of the Federal Government to interfere with the exclusively internal affairs of the Confederated Provinces, would be of the most limited and inconsiderable character ... Under Confederation [he continued] each of the Provinces would retain its own Legislature and Government, for the management of its own local affairs, limited in power only to such an extent as would prevent its operating in favour of its own prosperity at the expense of any of the others.[68]

This was a basic and extensive limitation of local powers. Other opposition speeches in the Maritimes voiced the same idea. The Hon. Mr Hatheway in New Brunswick said, 'If this Confederation scheme had been carried, it would have brought our Legislature down to a mere municipality.'[69] Mr Needham asked: 'What would we have been had Confederation taken place under this scheme? Would we have been a Province? Certainly not. O, it is said we can have a local legislature; so we could, and its powers would be confined to making laws to prevent cows from running on the commons, providing that sheep shall wear bells, and to issue tavern licenses.'[70] Mr Annand, in Nova Scotia, wanted to be informed 'whether this body [the local legislature] is to be only a little more important than a Court of Sessions or a City Council.'[71] 'We will represent a dependency of Canada, with power about as great as the Grand Jury and Sessions of a county,' said Mr LeVesconte.[72] Mr Duncan of Prince Edward Island used the phrase 'little better than a town council.'[73] 'Very insignificant bodies,' said Mr Bourinot.[74]

Finally, if further emphasis is needed, it will be found in the statements of the British sponsors of the British North America bill. Lord Carnarvon, when introducing the bill to the House of Lords, said:

The real object we have in view is to give the central government those high functions and almost sovereign powers by which general principles and uniformity of legislation may be secured in those questions that are of common import to all

---

68 *Ibid.*, at end of 1867, pp. 151–2.
69 New Brunswick Assembly, *Debates*, 1865, p. 116.
70 *Ibid.*, p. 111.
71 Nova Scotia Assembly, *Debates*, 1865, p. 235.
72 *Ibid.*, p. 247.
73 Prince Edward Island Assembly, *Debates*, 1865, p. 65.
74 Nova Scotia Assembly, *Debates*, 1865, p. 266.

the Provinces; and at the same time to retain for each province so ample a measure of municipal liberty and self-government as will allow and indeed compel them to exercise these local powers which they can exercise with great advantage to the community ... In closing my observations upon the distribution of powers, I ought to point out that just as the authority of the Central Parliament will prevail whenever it may come into conflict with the Local Legislatures, so the residue of legislation, if any, unprovided for in the specific classification which I have explained, will belong to the central body. It will be seen, under the 91st clause, that the classification is not intended 'to restrict the generality' of the powers previously given to the central parliament, and that those powers extend to all laws made 'for the peace, order, and good government' of the Confederation, terms which, according to all precedents, will, I understand, carry with them an ample measure of legislative authority.[75]

Mr Adderley, who introduced the bill to the Commons, said, 'The Governor-General will have a veto on all legislation; and the Central Legislation will be invested with a general power of providing for the good government and peace of the country; but without derogating from the general power, certain specified powers are enumerated for the Central Legislature. It will be seen that by these provisions arrangements are made as far as possible for ensuring the unity and strength of the Central Government.'[76] Mr Cardwell pointed out that the Act allowed the local legislatures 'only to deal with those questions which are supposed to be of local concern.'[77] In his first comment on the Quebec Resolutions, he remarked that His Majesty's Government 'are glad to observe that although large powers of Legislation are intended to be vested in Local bodies, yet the principal of central control has been steadily kept in view. The importance of this principle cannot be overrated.'[78]

There was therefore no doubt in the minds of those who put through the Confederation scheme that they were creating a strong federal government fully entrusted with power to legislate on certain specified matters of general concern to the united provinces, and with a residue of authority over all other general matters which would enable it to meet future national needs as they might arise. The specified federal powers were merely examples of the kind of power existing in the general residue. Nowhere is there to be found the slightest hint of the idea that the Dominion residuary powers were only for emergency use; the whole interpretation given by the Fathers negatives any such odd notion. Nowhere is

75 *Hansard, Parliamentary Debates*, 3rd Series, vol. 185, Cols. 563–6.
76 *Ibid.*, Col. 1168.
77 *Ibid.*, Col. 1179.
78 Cardwell to Monck, Dec. 3, 1864 (see *Journals of the Legislative Assembly of Nova Scotia*, 1865, Appendix 3).

there any suggestion that the aim at Confederation was to 'preserve the autonomy of the province,' as suggested in later Privy Council decisions; the aim was precisely to get rid of this autonomy, except in matters of purely local concern. Consistent with this desire for unity are those provisions of the constitution giving the federal government power to veto all provincial laws, to appoint provincial lieutenant-governors, to nominate the judges for provincial superior courts, and to take over local works by a simple declaration that they are for the 'general advantage of Canada.' This preference for a strong central government, however, did not make Canada a legislative union. Within the sphere of their *local* interests the provinces were left free from the legislative interference of the Dominion; there was plenty of room for what Lord Carnarvon called 'local action and wholesome self-government,' and what Langevin told the French Canadians were 'those interests which are most dear to us as a people.' In so far as matters of property and civil rights did not touch general subjects of common interest to the whole country, they were exclusively within provincial jurisdiction. The result of the 1867 agreement was to make Canada a particularly united type of federation. Divisions that occurred later were due to other causes than defects in the structure of the constitution.

The political theory of Canadian federalism thus contrasts sharply with that of the United States. The principal difference is well stated by J.H. Gray, himself one of the Fathers, in his volume *Confederation*.[79] The passage deserves repetition:

At the time of the framing of their constitution, the United States were a congeries of independent States, which had been united for a temporary purpose, but which recognized no paramount or sovereign authority. The fountain of concession therefore flowed upward from the several states to the united government. The Provinces, on the contrary, were not independent States; they still recognized a paramount and sovereign authority, without whose consent and legislative sanction the Union could not be framed. True, without their assent their rights would not be taken from them; but as they could not part with them to other Provinces without the Sovereign assent, the source from which those rights would pass to the other Provinces when surrendered to the Imperial Government for the purposes of confederation, would be through the supreme authority. Thus the fountain of concession would flow downward, and the rights not conceded to the separate Provinces would vest in the Federal Government, to which they were to be transferred by the paramount or sovereign authority.

Thus the Dominion parliament is the creation and the heir, not of the provinces, but of the sovereign imperial parliament, to which alone it is beholden for

79 P. 56.

its supremacy. The London *Times* correctly stated that the British American colonies, not being sovereign states but integral parts of the Empire, 'cannot delegate their sovereign authority to a central government, because they do not possess the sovereign authority to delegate.'[80] In so far as there was a 'compact' at Confederation, it was an agreement on all sides that the 'supreme authority,' the parliament of Westminster, would transfer its sovereignty to the new federal government for all national purposes in Canada, leaving to the former provinces a field of independent local activity, but shorn of a great part of the freedom they had possessed under the earlier constitutions. This theory or compact, the Fathers hoped, would cut the ground from under any doctrine of 'States' rights' in Canada. The Fathers made the supremacy of the Canadian parliament depend, not on provincial consent, but on imperial grant.[81] The provinces did not create the Dominion; 'it derives its political existence,' as Lord Carnarvon said, 'from an external authority.'[82] Only because we have neglected this theory, and because the Judicial Committee of the Privy Council had another theory it preferred to impose for imperialist purposes, has the law and custom of the Canadian constitution deviated so grievously from the agreement of 1867.

## THE MAINTENANCE OF PARLIAMENTARY GOVERNMENT

The early Canadian provinces had achieved the parliamentary system of government after long efforts. The key position in the system – the responsibility of the Crown to the ministers of the day, and the ministry to the majority party in the legislature – had been won less than twenty years before the Quebec Conference. The memory of that victorious struggle was still fresh. The model of the British constitution – as well as that of the American – was constantly in the minds of the Fathers, when preparing the BNA Act. Consequently, although a federal system of government was adopted in preference to a complete legislative union, the parliamentary method of controlling the executive was preserved. Federalism came in by way of exception to the established, operating machinery of parliamentary government. The presidential system of the United States found no sup-

---

80 Cited by Morris, *Confederation Debates*, p. 440. *The Times* suggested Canada's motto should be, not *E Pluribus Unum* but *In Uno Plura*.

81 This use of imperial sovereignty to eliminate provincial sovereignty appears as early as 1851 in Sir Edmund Head's memorandum (Martin, 'Sir Edmund Head's First Project of Federation,' p. 18). It is found too in the letter of Cartier, Galt, and Ross to Lytton, Oct. 25, 1858 (W.P.M. Kennedy, *Statutes, Treaties and Documents of the Canadian Constitution, 1713–1929*, ed. 2, Oxford, 1930, at pp. 537–8). See also quotations from Macdonald, *supra*: and Morris, *Confederation Debates*, p. 440.

82 Speech on BNA Act, cited in Sir A. Hardinge, *The Life of Henry Howard Molyneux Herbert, Fourth Earl of Carnarvon* (3 vols., London, 1925), vol. I, p. 326.

porters, even among those – and there were several – who were loud in their praises of the American constitution.[83] 'A great evil in the United States,' said Macdonald, 'is that the President is a despot for four years ... Every President is the leader of a party, and obliged to protect the rights of a majority. Under the British Constitution, with the people having always the power in their own hands and with the responsibility of a Ministry to Parliament, we are free from such despotism.'[84]

The later growth of Cabinet authority in Canada was to belie this sharp distinction. The Canadians, however, made their choice on the basis of their experience and their observation, and their constitution in this respect remained more British than American. Parliament, in the British tradition of 1867, was composed of the Crown and the representatives of the people in two houses. The business of parliament was conducted by a government, or group of ministers of the Crown made up of leaders of the dominant party in the lower House, acting under a prime minister. These advised the Crown upon the exercise of all its legal powers and assumed responsibility for all its public actions. The Crown was fully controlled by the law and the custom of the constitution; the King's title descended, not by divine right, but in accordance with the Succession Act of 1701 which the British parliament could alter any time it chose. In Canada the Crown had always been represented by an agent, who held office at pleasure. With the idea of parliamentary government went the basic ideas of election and franchise, of freedom of public discussion, of government by consent of the governed, in short, of a political democracy.

Some of the Fathers of Confederation spoke against what they called 'universal democracy,' which in their minds seemed to be a peculiarly American failing, synonymous with lawlessness, insecurity of tenure for public officers, corruption and disrespect for authority. Against this they set their faces, and to the monarchical tradition of their own constitution they attributed their own assumed superiority. This is what Macdonald had in mind when he spoke of working out 'constitutional liberty as opposed to democracy.'[85] But the Fathers did not have any doubts as to the meaning of liberty of speech and of the person, of equality before the law and of self-government. These democratic ideas had already been achieved by Canadians themselves, and made part of their constitutional tradition.

The BNA Act contains no express enumeration of civil rights and liberties, no bill of rights – other than the minority rights – comparable to the first ten amendments of the United States constitution. It does contain, however, a par-

---

83 Macdonald and D'Arcy McGee both praised the United States constitution very highly while criticizing it in detail.
84 Pope, *Confederation Documents*, p. 57.
85 *Ibid.*, p. 55.

liamentary system of government as an integral part of the Act, and thus imports into the constitution the essential concepts of democracy implicit in that system. So long as the word 'parliament' remains in the text of the constitution, there is a bill of rights.[86] This is the significance of the statements in the Quebec and London Resolutions that the delegates 'desire to follow the model of the British constitution, so far as our circumstances will permit,'[87] and that the executive authority 'shall be administered according to the well understood principles of the British constitution.' The idea reappears in the preamble to the BNA Act which declares that the provinces desire to unite 'with a constitution similar in principle to that of the United Kingdom.' Thus Confederation was a compact on self-government and free institutions. No elaboration was necessary among men who themselves had seen Canada achieve many of these rights.

## COMPLETING THE EDIFICE

The BNA Act was only one step in the process of building the new nation. It provided the constitutional framework; the content had to be added. The first problem was the extension of the territorial limits both east and west. This was accomplished, as already indicated, by 1873, with the transfer of the Hudson's Bay Company territories and the admission of British Columbia and Prince Edward Island. At last the dream was realized of one country stretching from sea to sea. To achieve this object Canadians in effect had had to buy back portions of their own country from the absentee owners of Hudson's Bay claims and Prince Edward Island proprietorships.

## RAILWAYS

To complete the political unification two new railways were required, one from Canada east to the Maritimes and the other from Canada west to the Pacific. The first was provided for in the BNA Act itself. Section 145 contains the provision, unusual in any constitution, that 'it shall be the Duty of the Government & Parliament of Canada to provide for the Commencement within Six Months after the Union, of a Railway connecting the River St. Lawrence with the City of Halifax.' The western railway was not referred to in the Act, but formed part of the constitutional agreement between Canada and British Columbia at the time of the latter's entry into the Union.[88] The Intercolonial Railway through to Halifax was

86 This idea first finds judicial acceptance in the *Reference re Alberta Statutes*, 1938 S.C.R. 100, *per* Duff C.J., at p. 134 and Cannon J., at p. 143.
87 No. 3.
88 See schedule to Order-in-Council of May 16, 1871, admitting British Columbia to the union.

completed in 1876, the Canadian Pacific to Vancouver in 1885; the former under public ownership, the latter under private ownership. Of Canada's first transcontinental railways it can be truly said that they are part of the constitution of the country, and the element of private ownership and operation in the Canadian Pacific Railway, themselves due largely to political accident,[89] appear anomalous in this context of public law.

NATIONALIZING DEFENCE

The question of national defence raised important constitutional issues for Canadians before Confederation. Prior to the granting of responsible government British regiments stationed in Canada provided the chief defence for the colony, and the expense of maintaining them was borne by the British treasury. Canadians raised a militia, in varying numbers, in critical times. Since all Canada's external relations were controlled from London the arrangement was just and normal. The two invasions of Canada after 1763 were primarily due to British-American quarrels in which Canada was merely the battleground. After the attainment of responsible government in Canada, however, and the discovery that trade with independent nations could be even more profitable than trade with colonies, the attitude in England began to change. The 'Little Englanders' used the cost of defending colonies as a proof that imperialism was a bad policy. 'An army maintained in a country which does not permit us even to govern it! What an anomaly!' wrote Disraeli to Derby.[90] To which a Canadian would have replied, 'An army paid for by a country which has no separate power over peace and war! What an anomaly!' Nevertheless the attitude of mind in England was made very clear. If Canadians were to govern themselves they must defend themselves. This the Canadian government accepted in principle, and in 1855 was passed the first important Canadian Militia Act;[91] though not without opposition that would scarcely have been overcome but for the 'patriotic enthusiasm' aroused by the Crimean War.[92] This Act was temporary, and when, in response to British pressure in face of the crisis caused by the American Civil War, Macdonald introduced a new bill in 1862 to the Canadian parliament, it was defeated. Canadian judgment was sound on the need for calmness and moderation to placate American

---

89 The Pacific Railway was begun by the Dominion government, and the portions thus built were handed over to the C.P.R. later.
90 Sept. 30, 1866. Cited by C.P. Stacey, *Canada and the British Army, 1846–1871: A Study in the Practice of Responsible Government* (London, 1936), p. 193.
91 18 Vict. c. 77.
92 Stacey, *Canada and the British Army*, p. 94.

feeling.[93] The rejection caused much resentment in England, however, and hastened the British determination to withdraw their troops from North America.

In 1865 a conference occurred in London between certain Canadian ministers and the British authorities, at which the Canadians proposed a general plan for joint defence in North America. By this Canada would assume far greater burdens but Great Britain would still contribute a large share of the expense. This full plan the British refused. The belief had grown in England, reinforced by reports of officers garrisoned in North America during the American Civil War, that Canada was indefensible as against the United States, and that expenditures designed to prevent invasion were next to worthless.[94] The British, in effect, were leaving Canadians to look after themselves as best they could on land, while maintaining naval power in the Atlantic. However the 'mutual' obligations of the two countries for joint defence in wartime were recognized.[95] The desire to help the colonies to protect themselves was one of the reasons why the British government used its influence so strongly in the Maritime Provinces in favour of Confederation. In 1871 the last of the British regiments were withdrawn from Canada save for a small force at Halifax, and the barracks and fortifications were handed over to the Canadians.[96] Thus at Confederation Canada took over the entire local defence of the country, while continuing a military alliance with Great Britain in which mutual obligations were recognized in time of war. Not till after the Dundonald incident of 1904, however, was the Militia Act amended so as to enable a Canadian officer to command the Canadian army.[97]

The last British troops (450) to be sent to assist Canadians in Canada were used for the Red River rebellion in 1870 (caused in part by the too hasty withdrawal of British troops from Fort Garry). These reinforcements did not come for mere love of empire. The first condition exacted for their use was that £300,000 should be paid to the Hudson's Bay Company in satisfaction of their claim for territorial rights ceded to Canada, about which controversy was raging.[98]

## THE NATIONAL COURT OF APPEAL

The creation of a general court of appeal for the federated provinces was one of the federal powers set forth in the Quebec and London Resolutions.[99] It was part

93 The Canadian attitude is set out in a Minute of Council of October 28, 1862, in *Canada, Sessional Papers*, 1863, no. 15.
94 Sir Richard John Cartwright, *Reminiscences* (Toronto, 1912), p. 55.
95 Despatch of Cardwell, June 17, 1865, cited in Stacey, *Canada and the British Army*, p. 187.
96 The agreement as to future military arrangements is in Stacey, *Canada and the British Army*, p. 226.
97 See 4 Edw. VII, c. 23, s. 30.
98 Stacey, *Canada and the British Army*, p. 238.
99 Nos. 29–34 and 28–33.

of the grand design to unify the judiciary by making them Dominion appointees and to harmonize the laws in the common-law provinces through the procedure of Section 94 of the BNA Act. Eventually it was hoped there would be only one bar in the common-law provinces.[100] The Quebec civil law was naturally excepted from the plan, and the judges in the Quebec courts were to be drawn exclusively from the Bar of that province.[101] A legal and judicial union accepting minority rights was to parallel political union.

To carry out this idea two important moves were made in 1869. Macdonald introduced his first bill to establish the Supreme Court of Canada, and also saw to the appointment of the Honourable J.H. Gray as Commissioner for the unification of laws under Section 94. The Supreme Court bill of 1869 and another of 1870 were dropped owing to fears of the French-Canadian members that the civil law might be jeopardized, and the Conservative defeat in 1873 prevented the carrying of the measure; but the Liberals under Mackenzie were able to secure the passage of a similar bill in 1875. The national court came into being eight years after Confederation and it is significant that both Conservatives and Liberals were agreed upon its creation. Of the move to unify the laws of the common-law provinces, nothing more is heard after the brief report presented by Gray in 1871.[102]

From the point of view of the national ideas at Confederation, the formation of the Supreme Court, and the debates and discussions to which it gave rise, are most important. They show that Canadians generally had come to accept the concept of judicial independence from England at this early date. While the prerogative right of appeal was saved by the statute creating the court, the appeal as of right was taken away, and it was expected that the use of the prerogative right would die out or be very rarely exercised.[103] Blake himself, it appears, favoured abolition of the appeal, and his influence was largely instrumental in preventing the disallowance of the Supreme Court Act in London, where the provision restricting the appeal met with strong disfavour.[104] Fournier, the Minister of Justice

100 See Macdonald in Pope, *Confederation Documents*, p. 82.
101 BNA Act, sec. 98; contrast sec. 97, showing the local selection of common-law judges was meant to be temporary.
102 *Canada, Sessional Papers*, 1871, no. 16. See my article 'Section 94 of the BNA Act' (*Canadian Bar Review*, vol. XX, June, July, 1942, 525–44).
103 See Lord Cairns's memorandum to Blake, cited in L.A. Cannon, 'Some Data Relating to the Appeal to the Privy Council' (*Canadian Bar Review*, vol. III, Oct. 1925, at p. 464). Also R.B. Haldane, 'Lord Watson' (*Juridical Review*, vol. XI, 1899, p. 280).
104 For a full account of this see F.H. Underhill, 'Edward Blake, The Supreme Court Act, and the Appeal to the Privy Council, 1875–6' (*Canadian Historical Review*, vol. XIX, Sept., 1938, pp. 245–63).

who introduced the successful bill, expressed what appeared to be the point of view of most French-Canadian members when he said, 'There were very strong reasons in favour of the right of appeal to the Privy Council, but the reasons against it were still stronger.'[105] It is doubtful whether the appeal would have continued had it not been for imperial influences. But Canadian national feeling was not quite strong enough to overcome the obstacles and to take the final hurdle, and as a result the nation-building of the Fathers has been grievously damaged, in the opinion of most authorities, through the reading into the BNA Act of a concept of federalism radically different from that of 1867.[106]

The framers of the Supreme Court Act, as well they might be, were more concerned to protect the Quebec civil law than to protect the appeal to the foot of the throne. Section 4 of the Act established the rule which has been followed ever since, that at least two members of the court were to be from the province of Quebec. This is squarely in line with the general agreement about minority rights, and makes the Court more expert in matters of civil law than the Judicial Committee is ever likely to be.

THE OFFICE OF HIGH COMMISSIONER

Though the incident of the appointment of the first Canadian High Commissioner occurred thirteen years after Confederation, and hence is somewhat outside the scope of this paper, it deserves to be recorded here since it brings so well to the fore the national feeling of those days.

Canada began to assume a new status in the international community immediately after Confederation, as so many Canadians had expected she would. Macdonald inaugurated a new era when he went as one of the three British representatives who negotiated the Treaty of Washington in 1871. That trying experience did not endear him to the subordinate role which he then occupied.[107] In 1878 the question of new commercial treaties for Canada with France and Spain was under consideration, and this time Macdonald was determined that Canada's representative should not play second fiddle. He wished Galt to work out the details of the arrangements, and the British representatives to be confined to the formal negotiations.[108] Other matters, particularly the Pacific Railway, were also pressing. So Macdonald, Tilley, and Tupper prepared a memorandum in which they set out

105 *Ibid.*, p. 247.
106 The overwhelming weight of Canadian authority outside the courts now acknowledges that the Privy Council has interpreted the BNA Act in a manner contrary to the intentions of the Fathers. [See chap. 20, *infra*, note 44.]
107 Macdonald's exasperation at the sacrifice of Canadian interests in the negotiations appears in his correspondence to his colleagues: see Pope, *Memoirs*, chaps. XX–XXI.
108 W.P.M. Kennedy, *The Constitution of Canada: An Introduction to Its Development and Law* (Toronto, 1922), at p. 344.

the need for a permanent Canadian representative in London, who could at the same time represent the Canadian government vis-à-vis the United Kingdom, and also could be specially accredited as Canadian representative to foreign courts.

It was the Canadian desire that the representative should have a 'quasi-diplomatic position at the Court of St James,' with the title of Resident Minister, or some other name 'of equal import.'[109] Canada, they pointed out, 'has ceased to occupy the position of an ordinary possession of the Crown. She exists in the form of a powerful Central Government having already no less than seven subordinate local executive and legislative systems, soon to be largely augmented by the development of the vast regions lying between Lake Superior and the Rocky Mountains. Her Central Government is becoming even more responsible than the Imperial Government for the maintenance of international relations towards the United States, a subject which will yearly require greater prudence and care.'[110]

It was fitting, they felt, that the representative of so important a country should have a status comparable to his duties. The dignity of the office required 'a more expressive title than that of Agent-General,' which was the pre-Confederation term. But once again the attempt of Canadians to raise their country in the eyes of the world was frustrated in London. Sir Michael Hicks Beach wrote to the Marquis of Lorne politely welcoming the suggestion of a permanent representative, but adding: 'Looking, however, to the position of Canada as an integral portion of the Empire, the relations of such a person with Her Majesty's Government would not be correctly defined as being of a diplomatic character, and, while her Majesty's Government would readily accord him a status in every way worthy of his important functions, his position would necessarily be more analagous to that of an officer in the home service, than to that of a Minister at a foreign court.'[111] So another colourless title, 'High Commissioner of Canada in London,' was invented.

## THE GOVERNOR-GENERAL'S INSTRUCTIONS

In 1878 occurred the well-known revision of the Governor-General's instructions so as to eliminate the eight classes of bills which up to that time he had been expected to reserve for imperial sanction.[112] This was another of Blake's contributions to the cause of Canadian nationalism. It cleared the prerogative documents of the chief remaining marks of colonialism and in effect made the Governor-General what he was defined as being in the 1926 Imperial Conference Report – the representative of the Crown alone and not of the imperial government. Had

109 Kennedy, *Documents of the Canadian Constitution*, at p. 676.
110 *Ibid.*
111 *Ibid.*
112 For the list of reserved bills see *ibid.*, at p. 672.

the Canadian idea of a Kingdom of Canada been accepted in 1867, the control of the Colonial Office would have been eliminated at the start.

CONCLUSION

This perspective view shows that the political nationalism in Canada at the time of Confederation was a vigorous and creative movement. It arose out of the peculiar conditions of the British North American provinces, and could only have been built by Canadians for Canadians. It had great vision, but never moved too far from reality. Its principal aim was to achieve those democratic ends which all true nationalism strives for – the elevation of a whole people to new status in the community of nations. Canada was to be 'redeemed from provincialism'; her public men were to move into a larger world where great duties and great opportunities would evoke the great responses.

Because this nationalism emerged from within an established empire which was itself the product of another nationalism – an English nationalism – the problem which the new North American nation had immediately to face was the discovery of a new relationship between itself and this older nationalism, now glorified with the title of British Empire. If Canadian nationalism were to achieve its ends, both political and psychological, every vestige of rule by Englishmen over Canada had to cease. Associating with other nations on terms of equality and in a spirit of cooperation does no harm to any national aspirations; it is indeed a necessary condition of their fulfilment, since the world is bigger than its national units, and the human race more important than any single race. That Canada should continue to associate with her sister nations in the British group on these terms, and that the symbol of the Crown should remain as the distinctive mark of this British 'connexion,' was the solution which the Fathers of Confederation had in mind. But history records how the realization of this concept was frustrated and delayed by the innumerable resistances of imperialism, operating through traditional channels, both in and out of Canada, using at times the blind alleys of imperial federation and retaining always the trump card of judicial appeal. British peoples are apt to pride themselves on their capacity for gradual growth and stable evolution. But there are times when gradualness becomes a mere failure to seize opportunities, and when stability in the face of new needs is simple die-hard Toryism. It is indeed a tribute to the moderation, the patience, and the willingness to compromise of Canadian statesmen, if to nothing else, that they were content to wait more than half a century before the political theories first enunciated at the time of Confederation found their final formulation in the Declaration of 1926 and the Statute of Westminster. What the Canadian people have had to pay for this delay in terms of national unity it would be difficult to estimate.

# II

# The Development of Canadian Federalism

*An early statement of the thesis that judicial interpretation of the British North America Act, 1867, had given Canada a constitution markedly different from the original, and one in which federal powers were dangerously impaired. The evidence lay in the helplessness of the federal government in face of the nationwide problems of unemployment, economic stagnation and human misery caused by the Depression. Later decisions of the Privy Council in England (see 'The Privy Council and Mr Bennett's "New Deal" Legislation' below) strongly confirmed this view, which was first succinctly stated by my former teacher, Professor H.A. Smith, in his article 'The Residue of Power in Canada,' in 27* The Canadian Bar Review, *432.*

From *Papers and Proceedings*, Canadian Political Science Association, 1931, 231-47

The Canadian constitution at the time of its creation presented to the world of political science a novel combination of constitutional principles. England's great contribution had been parliamentary and responsible government; the United States had shown that federalism was the system best adapted to a disunited people scattered over wide areas. Canada was the first nation to weld these conceptions into a new whole, and in so doing she produced a constitution which, it was agreed, embodied the virtues of both its prototypes. But virtues, particularly borrowed virtues, are more easily adopted than retained ... What has become of our federalism? It is a legal morass in which ten governments are always floundering; a boon to lawyers and obstructionist politicians, but the bane of the poor public whose pathetic plea is simply for cheap and efficient government. But this brings me to the subject of this paper.

Since my aim is to trace the development of Canadian federalism, it is necessary that I should attempt to reconstruct the original agreement of 1867 in regard to the manner in which legislative powers were to be distributed between the Dominion and the provinces. This is not really as difficult a matter as it sounds; it is not nearly so difficult as attempting to state the present distribution of powers. The sources for such a reconstruction are the obvious ones: the proceedings and resolutions of the Quebec and London Conferences, the explanatory statements of the public men of the time, the words of the BNA Act and early judicial pronouncements upon them by Canadian judges. From this evidence one may gather the ideas which were the basis of our federalism. The extraordinary thing about these ideas is that everyone at that time seemed to understand what they were. Both the opponents and the supporters of Confederation agreed upon what sort of federal arrangement was being made; they differed only about the outcome and the value of the arrangement.

Turning then to the sources indicated, we find the following conception emerges, clear and definite. The basis for the distribution of legislative powers was to be this – all matters of national importance were to go to the national parliament, all matters of merely local importance in each province were to remain subject to exclusive provincial control. This is declared explicitly by the second of the Quebec Resolutions, which reads as follows:

2. In the Federation of the British North American Provinces the system of government best adapted under existing circumstances to protect the diversified interests of the several Provinces, and secure efficiency, harmony, and permanency in the working of the Union, – would be a General Government charged with matters of common interest to the whole country, and Local Governments for each of the Canadas and for the Provinces of Nova Scotia, New Brunswick and Prince Edward Island, charged with the control of local matters in their respective sections, provision being made for the admission into the Union on equitable terms of Newfoundland, the North West Territory, British Columbia, and Vancouver.

Nothing could be plainer than those words, and they are emphasized by many of the Fathers of Confederation who spoke upon the subject. Macdonald said: 'In the proposed constitution all matters of general interest are to be dealt with by the general legislature; while the local legislatures will deal with matters of local interest, which do not affect the Confederation as a whole, but which are of the greatest importance to their particular sections.'[1]

Sir George Cartier stated that 'under the Federation system granting to the control of the General Government these large questions of general interest in

1 *Debates of the Parliament of the Province of Canada on Confederation* (Quebec: Hunter-Rose, 1865), p. 30.

which the differences of race or religions had no place, it could not be pretended that the rights of either race or religion could be invaded at all.'[2]

Mr Galt argued that under the new system there would be no increase in the expense of government over the old: 'We may well doubt whether the aggregate charge will be greater for the General Government, caring for the general interests of the whole, and for the local governments, attending merely to the local business of each section ... than that which is required for our Government under the present system.'[3]

D'Arcy McGee said that 'Local affairs are left to be dealt with by local bodies and cannot be interfered with by those who have no local interest in them, while matters of a general character are left exclusively to a general government.'[4]

The Hon. L.A. Olivier opposed the scheme because he did not wish to see the local governments crushed under a great central power, and because, as he expressed it: 'The powers of the Federal Government will be in reality unlimited. The fact of the enumeration of these thirty-seven heads does not in the least restrain the power of the Federal Government from legislating on everything. The exceptions are few.'[5]

Finally I may quote the expressions used by Lord Carnarvon when introducing the measure to the Imperial Parliament;

The real object we have in view is to give to the central government those high functions and almost sovereign powers by which general principles and uniformity of legislation may be secured in those questions that are of common import to all the Provinces; and at the same time, to retain for each Province so ample a measure of municipal liberty and self-government as will allow and indeed compel them to exercise these local powers which they can exercise with great advantage to the community.

If it were necessary, other evidence could be adduced to establish my first proposition, namely that the basis of Canadian federalism is the distinction between general and local matters. The very words 'general legislatures' and 'local legislatures,' which are used throughout the Quebec Resolutions, the debates and judicial pronouncements of the time, bear out the same idea. With this in mind, let us examine more closely the actual distribution of legislative powers. We shall begin with the Quebec Resolutions again. But first let me remind you of an incident that occurred in the evening of Monday, 24 October 1864, during one of

2 *Ibid.*, p. 60.
3 *Ibid.*, p. 70.
4 *Ibid.*, p. 145.
5 *Ibid.*, p. 176

the sessions of the Conference. The Hon. Mr Mowat had introduced a motion respecting the powers of the local legislatures. By way of amendment the Hon. Mr Coles of Prince Edward Island moved: 'That the Local Legislatures shall have power to make all laws not given by this Conference to the General Legislature expressly.'

On question put 'the same was unanimously resolved in the negative.'[6] Every group represented at the Conference, therefore, was agreed that the general legislature was not to be bound to a specific list of enumerated powers, but was to have, over and above such enumerated powers, a residue of legislative capacity. This point will be reverted to later.

The list of powers distributed by the Quebec Resolutions to the general and to the local legislatures is found in numbers 29 and 43 respectively. As might be expected, in view of the idea expressed in the second Resolution quoted above, these sections explicitly preserve the distinction between matters of general and matters of local interest. The 29th Resolution opens with these words: 'The general parliament shall have power to make laws for the peace, welfare and good government of the Federated Provinces (saving the sovereignty of England), and especially laws respecting the following subjects.' The list of enumerated subjects follows, the last of which reads: 'And generally all matters of a general character, not specially and exclusively reserved for the local governments and legislatures.' Similarly the 43rd Resolution declares that 'The local legislatures shall have power to make laws respecting the following subjects.' And the last of these is: 'Generally all matters of a private and local nature, not assigned to the general parliament.'

It is to be noticed that the treatment of both general and local legislatures is the same; each has its enumerated powers, each has its residuary powers. The Dominion residuary power is over all matters of a general nature, not specially and exclusively reserved to the local legislatures. This, it is true, seems to imply that some general matters were reserved to the legislatures, just as the provincial residuary power seems to imply that some purely local matters were given to the general government. But such was not the case; no Dominion powers are of purely local interest, and no provincial powers are matters of general interest. The limitations on both residuary powers when read in their context, can only mean that the Dominion was not to be allowed to invoke its residuary clause for the purpose of interfering with provincial autonomy on purely local matters, any more than the province was to be allowed to invoke its residuary clause to support legislation upon some matter of national concern under the pretence that it was of merely local interest. Thus the effect of these clauses will be that beyond the subjects attributed to each, the central legislature will have jurisdiction over

6 Sir Joseph Pope, *Confederation Documents* (Toronto: Carswell Co., 1895), p. 27.

all general matters, whatever they are, and the local legislatures over all local matters, whatever they are.[7] The specifically enumerated powers in each case are examples merely of the sort of power contained in the residues. And it is important to note that the local provincial power over property and civil rights has the all important qualification 'except such portions thereof as are assigned to the general parliament.' The portions so assigned, and therefore outside provincial control, are obviously such matters of property and civil rights as are contained in the matters of general interest given the Dominion either specifically or by residuary grant. Just because a proposed law touches upon property and civil rights is no proof of itself that it was meant to be a provincial matter; the further proof is needed that it touches such rights only in their local aspect. Property and civil rights as part of a matter of national concern were intended to belong to the Dominion. This is further secured by the provision that where there are concurrent powers, Dominion legislation shall prevail over provincial.

When the Quebec agreement was redrafted at London in 1866, and finally put into statutory form for parliament, no changes save of detail were made in the distribution of legislative powers. Sections 29 and 43 of the Resolutions were slightly rearranged, and some words were altered or omitted in an effort to avoid redundancy and gain precision. The education compromise was placed in a separate category as section 93 of the BNA Act; it therefore forms an exception to the general rule. But the original basis of distribution of powers remains. By section 91 of the Act the Dominion Parliament was given authority to make laws for the peace, order and good government of Canada, in relation to all matters not exclusively assigned to the legislatures of the provinces. The matters 'exclusively assigned to the legislatures of the provinces' are, of course, the local matters, whether enumerated or residuary. This is plainly in accord with the 2nd and 29th Resolutions quoted above; the Dominion is to look after general matters, but it is not to deal with local affairs which belong exclusively to the provinces.

The section proceeds to say that 'for greater certainty, but not so as to restrict the generality of the foregoing terms of this section.' In other words, in order to illustrate the general rule without in any way restricting it, certain enumerated powers are to belong to the Dominion. Twenty-nine special subjects are then listed, and the section concludes by saying that any matter covered by the classes of subjects in section 91 is not to be considered as being included in the local matters assigned to the provinces. This last observation scarcely appears necessary, for if a matter if of general interest it obviously cannot be local; it is of importance, however, as showing that when the national interest demands legislation by the Dominion the exclusive powers of the provinces must give way to the

---

7 See quotation from the *London Times*, cited by Dunkin in *Debates on Confederation*, p. 506.

extent necessary to permit the Dominion to act. It was never intended that the provinces should be able to obstruct general legislation for the good-government of Canada on the ground that such legislation might happen to deal incidentally with a subject over which they have exclusive control when the national interest is not involved. And this rule would appear to apply to all matters of general national concern, whether enumerated in section 91 or not, since the list of specific subjects is merely given for greater certainty and not so as to restrict the general principle of Dominion supremacy in matters affecting the whole Dominion.

If we turn to section 92 of the Act we find that the powers there given to the provinces agree equally well with the ideas of the Resolutions. Sixteen specific subjects are assigned exclusively to the local legislatures, the last of which is the residuary clause already quoted giving power over 'generally all matters of a merely local or private nature in the Province.' The Quebec agreement has thus been followed closely in the statute embodying it; all general matters have been granted to the general parliament, all local matters to the local parliaments. The enumeration of specific subjects for both Dominion and provinces merely illustrates the rule.

There are certain other features of our constitution which illustrate the predominance of general over local matters, and show that the Fathers of Confederation were not wedded to any narrow conception of federalism. The Dominion was given power to disallow provincial laws within one year of their passing. This was intended to be used, and has been used, so as to enable the Dominion to prevent one province from imperilling the well-being of the whole country by ill-advised legislation. It has become good politics to say that this power should only be exercised upon provincial laws which are *ultra vires*, but this limitation cannot be supported in law. Then there is the power given the Dominion parliament to secure control of provincial works and undertakings by declaring them to be for the general advantage of Canada. Note the phrase 'general advantage'; it is in keeping with the basic principle that I have been stressing. The Dominion was also empowered to give effect to the obligations of Canada, or any province thereof, arising out of treaties between the Empire and foreign countries, so that *vis-à-vis* the rest of the world Canada was intended to be a unit.

Such was, in brief, the federalism with which we began in 1867. It has, of course, political and administrative aspects, such as the divisions in the Senate, the arrangement of the judiciary, and other matters, with which there is no time to deal in this paper. Enough has been said to show that Macdonald was justified in using the following words in regard to Confederation – words which none dared contradict:

Ever since the [American] Union was formed the difficulty of what is called 'State Rights' has existed, and this has had much to do in bringing on the present unhappy war in the United States. They commenced, in fact, at the wrong end. They declared by their constitution that each state was a sovereignty in itself, and that all the powers incident to a sovereignty belonged to each state, except those powers which, by the Constitution, were conferred upon the general government and Congress. Here we have adopted a different system. We have strengthened the general government. We have given the general legislature all the great subjects of legislation. We have conferred on them, not only specifically and in detail all the powers which are incident to sovereignty, but we have expressly declared that all subjects of general interest not distinctly and exclusively conferred upon the local governments and local legislatures, shall be conferred upon the general government and legislature. We have thus avoided that great source of weakness which has been the cause of the disruption of the United States.[8]

How has our federalism developed since Confederation? What is the present situation in regard to the distribution of legislative powers? These are questions of vital and immediate importance. It is difficult to be accurate and brief at the same time in answer to them, for the interpretation of sections 91 and 92 of the BNA Act has been the battlefield of judges and lawyers for over sixty years, and this warfare, like most warfare, seems to have done more to confuse than to clarify the issue. But the effort to discover what has happened in the courts, and to state in ordinary language the developments of these years, must be made, because the ordinary citizen is just as vitally concerned in this matter as the lawyer. The principal results of this period of interpretation are therefore summarized here.

In the first place, the courts have drawn a totally unjustifiable distinction between the general power of the Parliament of Canada to legislate for the peace, order and good government of the whole country, and its special powers over the twenty-nine topics enumerated in section 91. These enumerated subjects were given, in the words of the act itself, 'for greater certainty, and in no way so as to restrict' the general power. They were simply illustrations of a general principle, inserted so as to avoid any doubt as to the national control of certain essentially national matters. Yet today they have become in effect the sole sources of Dominion power. The examples have swallowed up the rule, and it has now become next to impossible to justify any Dominion legislation unless it can be brought under one of the twenty-nine specific headings. The Fathers of Confederation gave us a living and elastic principle fit for every emergency; the courts have made of it a dead and rigid list. Apparently it would have been better for the Dominion had no specific subjects been assigned to it at all, for then there would have been no escape from the necessity of applying the test of general interest to every Do-

8 *Debates on Confederation*, p. 33.

minion act, and so this basic rule of interpretation would have been preserved. As it is, the Dominion Parliament is permitted to interfere incidentally with provincial powers when legislating upon one of its special powers, like Bills of Exchange or Bankruptcy, but cannot so interfere when exercising the general power itself.

As a result of this interpretation the residuary power of the Dominion over matters of national importance, so explicitly preserved by the opening words of section 91, and so emphasised by the Fathers at the time of Confederation, has been cut down to the vanishing point. It still exists, but can only be employed, we are told by Lord Haldane, in the Lemieux Act case, during occasions of war and national emergency. If in times of tranquility a Dominion act of paramount interest to all the provinces and required for the good government of Canada, but concerning a matter not specified amongst the Dominion subjects, should be found to touch upon any provincial power, it will be declared *ultra vires* and of no effect. One of the provincial powers is property and civil rights, and it being impossible to conceive of any piece of general legislation which is not covered to some degree by this all-embracing formula, the present rule is that the Dominion general power is merely an emergency police power. The distinction between the general and local aspects of property and civil rights seems to have been forgotten. What, to the authors of Confederation, would have been justified by national interest and good government, is now justified only by the existence of a national crisis. The Dominion government is thus permitted in a severe emergency to pass laws which it could not enact in ordinary times in order to prevent the emergency arising! On one occasion the Privy Council, inspired by a rare genius, went so far as to allow the Dominion to legislate for the general advantage of Canada, on an unspecified matter – namely temperance – but this was in 1882. Since then they have changed their minds, and today they hold that the fact that a law is of general interest throughout the whole Dominion and cannot be passed by the provinces alone is not sufficient to justify the Dominion Parliament in legislating. The national Parliament is apparently concerned with peace and order, but not with good government! This extraordinary doctrine, the credit for whose discovery may be entirely attributed to the late Lord Haldane, practically forces upon Canada the American type of constitution with its state residuary power, which we carefully and particularly avoided in 1867; and Canadians who desire to improve the quality of Canadian life by sane and progressive legislation, must now work through nine channels in many cases where the Fathers of Confederation would have permitted them to work through one. The Dominion today is restricted to the control of such national interests as happened to occur to the minds of the framers of the constitution in days when Canada was but a fraction of her present size, and when her economic, agricultural and social development was in its infancy. This is a flat contradiction of the agreement of 1867.

The treatment of the Trade and Commerce clause of section 91 of the BNA

Act is quite in line with the above developments. In 1867 the 'Regulation of Trade and Commerce' was specifically assigned to the Dominion Parliament. It was intended that the general government, which alone could perform the task adequately, should assist and control the economic life of the nation for the benefit of the whole people, and it is noteworthy that the words do not restrict the Dominion government, as the Federal Government of the United States is restricted, to inter-state commerce. With the rapid growth of Canadian industrial life this clause should have proved the most valuable of the Dominion powers, and the one most beneficial to the public. It can scarcely be to the interest of our large commercial enterprises to have to deal with nine different bodies of law throughout the country – although some more cynical than myself have suggested that big business prefers to handle nine small legislatures rather than one big one. But the clause has been practically written out of the constitution, in so far as the internal economic life of the country is concerned. In early cases before Canadian courts it was frequently relied on to support Dominion enactments, but the Privy Council have since instructed us that Trade and Commerce generally belong to the topic of property and civil rights, and thus must be left to the provinces. Trade treaties with foreign governments, and the granting of charters to Dominion companies are about the sole activities which the clause now authorizes. Anything like a wise regulation of Canadian trade and commerce by the Dominion government has now become an impossibility. It is interesting to note, however, that the most recent Privy Council judgment upon the question, the Combines Investigation Act case, seems to indicate that the Trade and Commerce clause may actually mean what it says. Our own Supreme Court in the still more recent Lawson judgment has even dared to rely upon this clause in declaring the Produce Marketing Act of British Columbia *ultra vires*.

In recent years another variation has been played upon the preceding themes. It used to be thought, and possibly still is believed by persons whose knowledge of the BNA Act is historical rather than legal, that every legislative power not belonging to the provinces must belong to the Dominion. This would seem to be a not unreasonable conclusion from the fact that in 1867 the distribution of powers was complete, both the Dominion and the provinces having their residuary clause. The courts, however, taking a lead from the Privy Council in the 'through traffic' case of 1912, have discovered a class of subjects which do not belong in their totality either to the Dominion or to the provinces. Legislation affecting these subjects must be enacted by both Dominion and provinces before it can possess validity. The Dominion does its part, the province or provinces do theirs, and thus only can the object be achieved. We knew of Dominion powers; of provincial powers; even of concurrent powers, but this is neither Dominion nor provincial, nor concurrent. It is positively Athanasian. In theory it involves the existence of a third depositary of sovereignty in the Canadian constitution – a mysterious body composed of the Dominion plus nine provincial legislatures. Here is a good subject for research by some eager political scientist. The difficulties in the way of government become absurdly great when ten parliaments must be brought into action before a desired law can be passed. And in view of the extent to which provincial powers have grown since Confederation this type of legislation seems likely to increase.

The extent to which the Dominion power has been reduced by the courts in favour of the provinces is best seen by considering some of the subjects now of national importance which the Dominion Parliament is unable to deal with fully. The control of grain is one. In 1925 the Supreme Court felt obliged to rule that certain sections of the Canada Grain Act were *ultra vires*, and yet as Chief Justice Anglin pointed out, the grain trade of Canada is a matter of national concern and of such dimensions as to affect the body politic of the Dominion.[8a] Part of the difficulty created by that decision was overcome later by declarations by the Dominion Parliament that certain grain elevators were 'works for the general advantage of Canada'; but this is an indirect method of getting control, and the aims of the Fathers would seem to have been considerably frustrated if so vast an undertaking as Canada's grain trade is considered to be a matter of purely local importance so as to prevent the Dominion from controlling it in all its aspects. Even now it is not clear how much of the present Grain Act is valid.

Again, the decision which the Supreme Court gave in reference to the development of water power in the St Lawrence shows the same uncertainty as to Dominion control over what is unquestionably a matter of the greatest national importance. The whole of Canada from the maritimes to the prairie provinces would be affected by this proposed development, and yet the constitutional questions raised by the proposal are thought by the courts to be so intricate that nobody seems to know just what parliament has the legislative power to carry the whole scheme into operation. It is quite likely that the construction of any of the necessary works might be indefinitely delayed by the opposition of a single provincial parliament.

The most recent example of the tendency is the judgment in regard to control of aerial navigation. The Fathers of Confederation gave the Dominion control of navigation and shipping; they gave it control of lines of steam or other ships, railways, canals, telegraphs and other works and undertakings connecting the provinces with any other or others of the provinces; they even gave it control of such minor things as ferries connecting two provinces. Their aim seems clear; to put interprovincial communications of all sorts under the only parliament which could effectively deal with them. And yet when the question of aerial navigation

8a [*The King* v. *Eastern Terminal Elevator Co.*, 1925 S.C.R. 434].

and flying is before the court we are told that it is primarily a matter of provincial concern. The all-embracing formula of property and civil rights is invoked without any consideration of whether or not aerial navigation has a national aspect. Apparently the question was considered settled because the Fathers were so unprophetic that they did not speak anywhere of flying. They spoke of navigation and of 'other works and undertakings'; yet, in the words of one of the judges in this case: 'Aviation, even if designated aerial navigation, is not a subject enumerated in section 91.

As was remarked previously, the Fathers gave us a living principle broad enough to cover every sort of national matter, past, present or future; the courts have made of it an exhaustive list of subjects. What would Macdonald have said to this doctrine, who remarked at the Quebec Conference: 'Our constitution should be a mere skeleton and framework that would not bind us down.'[9]

Consider the present unemployment situation as another instance. Unemployment is national in scope ... Yet both political parties agree that labour questions are a purely provincial matter, and must be left to the provinces to handle. All that Ottawa does is to vote money for the provinces to spend; the unemployed have to wait until the same matter that was thrashed out in Ottawa gets thrashed out anew in the provincial legislatures and put into the form of a provincial statute. Another example of ten parliaments having to act before a matter of the utmost national importance can be done! The present division of powers in regard to labour and social problems is particularly silly since tariffs, trade treaties, immigration, labour problems, unemployment and trade and commerce generally are so intimately connected that they cannot be divided up amongst ten legislatures without the certainty of delay, mismanagement and confusion.

There is a new problem now facing this country of the same nature as those above discussed. The Dominion can legislate so as to give effect to Empire treaties by section 132. Can she legislate equally well so as to give effect to purely Canadian treaties? It is obvious how the Fathers of Confederation would have answered this question had they conceived such a thing as a Canadian treaty to be possible. 'We are one people, not five people,' said Macdonald. Yet there are not wanting those who claim that the provincial power over property and civil rights cannot be affected by a Dominion treaty followed by Dominion legislation. In the aerial navigation case Mr Justice Cannon went so far as to argue that even where there was an Empire treaty the Dominion should not legislate until the provinces have had a chance to do so.

The above examples are merely the more striking indications of a tendency that has been going on for some forty years. The disintegration of federal power

9 Pope, *op. cit.*, p. 59.

has proceeded apace in spite of the fact that Canada's economic and social unity has increased during that same period. Every new national development tumbles into property and civil rights. The result is that the Dominion Parliament is becoming continuously less able to fulfil the function of a general parliament for which it was originally designed.

What has been the reason for this unfortunate trend of development in Canada? Why have we departed so far from the Confederation agreement? Various reasons may be suggested. One, which was foreseen by Dunkin in the Confederation Debates, is this: the distinction between matters of general, and matters of local, interest, adopted by the Fathers, is too vague to be pleasing to a court of law. When does a matter become general? Rather than commit themselves they have on the whole preferred to support legislation under some specific power, and thus the general residuary power has died of non-use. There is still no reason why it should not be revived, if only Haldane's fictitious limitations should be abandoned and the correct and sensible rule as laid down in the Liquor Reference Case adopted in its stead. This rule is to the effect that – here I quote from the judgment:

Their Lordships do not doubt that some matters, in their origin local and provincial, may attain such dimensions as to affect the body politic of the Dominion, and to justify the Canadian Parliament in passing laws for their regulation or abolition in the interest of the Dominion. But great caution must be observed in distinguishing between that which is local and provincial, and therefore within the jurisdiction of the provincial legislature, and that which has ceased to be merely local or provincial, and has become matter of national concern, in such sense as to bring it within the jurisdiction of the Parliament of Canada.

A second reason has been the not unnatural desire of the provincial legislatures to seize as much legislative power as possible, under the mistaken belief – and here I credit them with the highest motives – that they were serving the residents of their provinces best if they destroyed Dominion control. The first great 'march on Ottawa' was led by Sir Oliver Mowat, in the days of Sir John Macdonald, but he has able followers today in Premiers Ferguson and Taschereau.

Another cause of disintegration has been the attitude of the leaders of the Dominion parties of recent years. They seem to have wished to hand over as much as possible to the local legislatures. When Mr King was first asked to do something about unemployment he excused himself on the ground that it was a provincial matter. He also abandoned to the provinces the control of immigration. Mr Bennett gave way completely to the claim of Mr Ferguson that the BNA Act cannot be amended, even on matters that do not touch on provincial rights at all, without first calling a conference of all the provincial governments. We were even informed the other day by the Minister of Justice that the proposal that the Dominion should spend money in order to educate the Canadian public in regard to international relations 'was a plain contravention of both the letter and spirit of the BNA Act' – a declaration too perfect to spoil by comment.

To do the Canadian politicians justice, however, it must be admitted that their hands have been tied in many cases by legal interpretations of the BNA Act. The courts have been most to blame for what has occurred, and here the decisive influence has been that of the Privy Council. Canada today has a constitution different from that which she plainly adopted in 1867 for the simple reason that the interpretation of sections 91 and 92 has not in the last resort rested with Canadians. Early judgments of the Canadian Supreme Court show that the Canadian judges had a true conception of the Confederation agreement. But the Privy Council has seen fit to force upon our judges views which they would not have arrived at themselves. One of the most prominent members of the Judicial Committee, Lord Haldane, has himself boasted of this fact. Speaking of Lord Watson, another influential judge of the Committee, he said:

At one time, after the BNA Act was passed, the conception took hold of the Canadian courts that what was intended was to make the Dominion the centre of government in Canada, so that its statutes and its position should be superior to the statutes and position of the provincial legislatures. That went so far that there arose a great fight; and as a result of a long series of decisions Lord Watson put clothing upon the bones of the constitution, and so covered them over with living flesh that the constitution of Canada took a new form.

We have seen something of the new form which our constitution has taken under the guidance of Lords Watson and Haldane. Whether or not some Canadians are so provincially minded that they like the new arrangement, all must admit that the intentions of the Fathers of Confederation have not been followed, because their precise aim was to make the Dominion the 'centre of government in Canada' for all matters of general concern. The fact is that the Privy Council has been too handicapped by its ignorance of Canada to be able to give good judgments in Canadian constitutional law. As examples of this statement I might refer to Sir Montague Smith's dictim in Parson's case, that the Fathers of Confederation when inserting the words 'regulation of Trade and Commerce' in the constitution were doubtless thinking of a statute of Queen Anne; or to that supreme joke of Canadian constitutional law – Lord Haldane's discovery in the Lemieux Act case that the evil of intemperance at the time of the Canadian Temperance Act was 'So great and so general that at least for the period it was a menace to the national life of Canada so serious and pressing that the National Parliament was called on to intervene to protect the nation from disaster.'

No doubt in many instances the law which the Privy Council has been called upon to apply has been clear, and the decision inevitable. But in a surprisingly large number of cases carried to London the scales of legality have been so evenly balanced that the result has depended upon some personal inclination of the judges. It is precisely here that the absence of a Canadian point of view has been so seriously felt, and it is precisely here that the Privy Council for some unknown reason, has fairly consistently favoured the provinces at the expense of the Dominion.

My conclusions may be briefly stated. The first is that in the original constitution the Dominion Parliament was endowed with a general grant of power intended to enable it to meet new national needs as they arose. My second is that this general residue of power has been taken away from the Dominion and given to the provinces under the heading of property and civil rights. My third is that the new constitution is not as good as the old. Canadian federalism has developed continuously away from the original design. Constitutionally we have grown disunited, in spite of the fact that in other respects, as a result of the increased facility of communication, the rise of our international status, and the general spread of what may be called our national consciousness, we have grown more united. The Dominion Parliament does not play today the full part which the Fathers of Confederation planned for her. The evil which has been done is probably too great to be remedied by anything short of constitutional amendments, and if the provincial rights doctrine continues to be exploited by provincial politicians even this way out may prove difficult. Just at the very time when the exigencies of the economic situation call for drastic action, for increased international cooperation and for a planned internal social order, we find ourselves with cumbrous legislative machinery and outworn constitutional doctrines. The situation calls for the same intelligent and disinterested reform as that which produced the original constitution.

# III

# The Trial of the Toronto Communists

*This notorious trial was part of Prime Minister Bennett's policy of having 'no truck nor trade' with the Soviet Union, and placing 'an iron heel' on Socialism and Communism. Until the Depression years, the Communist Party had been virtually inoperative, though during the Winnipeg General Strike of 1919 some Labour leaders were erroneously labelled as members. As none of the eight convicted in Toronto had ever committed any overt act of violence, they were true political prisoners – unlike the members of the* Front de Libération du Québec *(FLQ) jailed in Quebec as a result of seven years of bombings, bank robberies, and kidnappings.*
From *Queen's Quarterly,* 39, 1932, 512–27

The trial and conviction of the eight Toronto Communists caused many Canadians to ask themselves for the first time just what our British traditions of freedom of speech and association really mean, if anything. The Communist Party is a lawful and recognized political party in almost every civilized country today. Its members are sitting in parliaments in France, Germany, and Czecho-Slovakia; it once had a member in the English House of Commons; in Canada, besides the fact that it has contested Dominion, provincial and municipal elections frequently, it was at one time represented on the Winnipeg City Council. Only in Italy, Japan, Poland and some of the more reactionary Balkan states is the party completely outlawed. By the Toronto verdict Canada has allied herself with this group of select reactionaries. She is the only country amongst them which claims to be a democracy.

The law under which this result was obtained is in itself remarkable. British countries in periods of great social danger have sometimes enacted repressive measures; the 1927 Public Safety Act of the Irish Free State is a recent example. But these laws have seldom remained long on the statute book. The common law crimes of treason, sedition, seditious conspiracy and unlawful assembly have always been considered an adequate protection for public security in any situation short of actual or impending rebellion. Yet Canada in 1919 proceeded to graft on to her criminal code a special section – the now notorious section 98 – which for permanent restriction of the rights of association, freedom of discussion, printing and distribution of literature, and for severity of punishment, is unequalled in the history of Canada and probably of any British country for centuries past. The temporary Irish statute is mild by comparison, for its maximum penalty is five years whereas the Canadian is twenty. The Canadian Act begins by defining as 'an unlawful association' any association whose purpose is to bring about governmental or economic change within Canada by the use of force, violence or injury to person or property, or which teaches or advocates these methods of securing such change. All the property of such an association is forfeit to the Crown. Every person who is an officer or member of it, who contributes money to it, or who wears any badge indicating he is associated with it,[1] is liable to twenty years' imprisonment. Any person who has even attended any of its meetings, spoken publicly in advocacy of it, or distributed its literature, is presumed to be a member of it – i.e., contrary to accepted British criminal law traditions, is presumed guilty until he proves himself innocent. Any proprietor of a hall who knowingly permits a meeting of the association 'or any subsidiary or branch thereof,' is liable to a fine of $5000. Further, any person who prints, publishes, circulates or sells any literature which advocates the use of force to effect governmental or economic change, or who mails such literature in Canada, or who imports it by any means (whether or not he is aware of its contents) is liable to twenty years; and individuals, whether members of the association or not, who advocate or defend such use of violence, are to be similarly punished. Finally, it is the duty of every Dominion civil servant, in any position, to seize such literature and send it to Ottawa where the Commissioner of the Royal Canadian Mounted Police will make up his mind as to whether Canadians should read it.

With such statutory backing for the police, one may wonder how the Communist Party ever got a footing in Canada. Yet the fact remains that the party was organized secretly in 1921, came into the open in 1924, and operated quite publicly, with conferences, demonstrations and newspapers, until the raid on the Toronto headquarters on August 11th, 1931, and the arrest of the eight leaders. Its programme, policy and general aims were well known to the authorities during all these years, for the spy of the Mounted Police, Sergeant Leopold, was a member of the party from 1921 till 1928 under the name of Comrade Esselwein,

1 At the moment of writing, a man in Montreal, Steve Koslov, is awaiting trial under section 98 for having worn a badge on his coat on May Day, 1932. If found guilty he may be imprisoned for 20 years.

and indeed appears to have been active in building up its organization and inducing workers to become members. Even after his expulsion by the Communists in 1928 no action was taken by the Canadian authorities. Not till 1931, when the economic crisis had become acute, was the move to outlaw the party made, and section 98 of the Criminal Code, which had been a dead letter for twelve years, invoked for the first time. This tacit acquiescence of the police in the continuation of the party is what makes the sentence of five years handed down by Mr Justice Wright seem so extremely harsh. The trial was a test case; the accused were first offenders; their 'crime' had been tolerated for seven years. Yet they are to be imprisoned for this length of time and then deported.

There was no particular incident, no attempt at rebellion, which moved the police to make the arrests. On the evening of August 11th, 1931, they dropped quietly down on the Toronto headquarters of the Communist Party and on the offices of the Workers' Unity League and *The Worker* (the party newspaper), and at the homes of Tim Buck, Tom Ewen and John Boychuk. Tim Buck, the Secretary of the party, and John Boychuk, a Ukrainian organizer, were arrested immediately. Mike Golinski was arrested early next morning. A.T. Hill – secretary of one of the Finnish organizations – was taken at Cochrane. Sam Carr and Malcolm Bruce – the only native-born Canadians – were brought from Vancouver. The others arrested were Tom Ewen, Tom Cacic and Mathew Popovich. Golinski was subsequently released, as it was proved he was not a member of the Communist Party but only of the Young Communist League.

The trial began in Toronto on November 2nd, 1931, before Mr Justice Wright and a jury. Not even the accused could describe the latter as 'capitalist': it was composed of two farmers, two electricians, an engraver, a draughtsman, an accountant, a watchmaker, a buffer, a salesman, a carpenter and a stockkeeper. Norman Somerville, KC, and Joseph Sedgewick appeared for the Crown; Hugh J. MacDonald and O. Brown for all the accused except Timothy Buck, who conducted his own defence. The charge was, first, that the accused in the years 1921 to 1931 in the City of Toronto and elsewhere in Ontario 'did become and continue to be members of an unlawful association, to wit, the Communist Party of Canada, section of the Communist International'; secondly, that they 'did act or profess to act as officers of an unlawful association, to wit, the Communist Party of Canada'; and thirdly, that they became parties to 'a seditious conspiracy contrary to the provisions of the Criminal Code.'

A preliminary point of law was raised by Mr MacDonald; he moved to quash the indictment on the ground that it was improperly drawn; it did not show why the Communist Party was to be regarded as 'an unlawful association.' Mr Justice Wright overruled the objection, holding that the indictment sufficiently charged the offence in the language of the statute. In this he was later upheld by the

Court of Appeal. The Crown was, however, ordered to furnish particulars of the offence.

Mr Somerville presented the evidence for the Crown under two heads: first, to show membership of the accused in the Communist Party, and, secondly, to show that the objects of the Party were such as are prohibited by the sections of the Criminal Code dealing with unlawful association and seditious conspiracy. The fact of membership need not be examined here at length, since it was amply established by evidence and admissions for all the accused except Golinski, who was released. The principal battle was about the 'objects' of the Communist Party. Were these objects to bring about 'any governmental, industrial or economic change within Canada by use of force, violence or physical injury to person or property, or threats of such injury?' Did the Party 'teach, advocate, advise or defend the use of force ... to effect such change?' Finally, was there an 'agreement between two or more persons to carry into execution a seditious intention?

The evidence submitted in regard to the unlawfulness of the Party's objects was most voluminous. It consisted principally of literature seized at the Party headquarters or elsewhere. A great part of the trial was spent in the reading to the jury of extracts from this literature. In addition to these documents, the Crown called twelve witnesses, all policemen except A.E. Smith, General Secretary of the Canadian Labour Defence League, and including the star witness and 'stool-pigeon,' Sergeant John Leopold. The testimony of all these men except Leopold (who told a great deal about the formation of the party 'underground' and its coming into the open in 1924) was concerned solely with establishing the membership of the accused, the details of arrest and the identity of documents. There was no evidence of any reliable sort to show that the party had ever committed any overt act of violence within Canada. It was admitted by some of the accused that the Party organized mass demonstrations which the police frequently broke up, but these were said to be – and it was not shown that they were not – simply for the purpose of organizing the workers and teaching them to realize their solidarity and to protest against poor wages and insufficient unemployment relief. It was shown that the party was connected with certain strikes, but not in any illegal manner. In any case, as Mr Justice Wright said, striking is not the kind of force aimed at in section 98. The accused were tried, not for past or present violence, but for membership in an organization that, it was contended, aimed at and advocated the use of violence to effect changes in Canada some time in the future.

The strength of the case for the Crown lay in the fact that it was not difficult to show that the Communist Party of Canada was merely a branch of the Communist International and bound to follow the latter's policy on all fundamental points. The connection between the Moscow parent and the Canadian child was established by Sergeant Leopold's evidence of the formation of the Canadian party in 1921 at the instigation of agents of the Pan-American Bureau, the body used by Moscow to organize the Communist Party in North America; by the fact that Canadian delegates were sent to the Congresses of the Third International and given votes; by copies of actual orders from Moscow dealing with specific Canadian problems, such as the expulsion of Jack MacDonald; and by the membership card, which applicants sign before joining the Party, and which binds them to adhere to 'the programme and statutes of the Communist International and of the Communist Party of Canada.' Tim Buck explained that there was nothing in the programme of the Communist International that could not be deviated from according to the conditions existing in any particular country; that it was a general world programme and a 'guide to action.' But the connection was established sufficiently to enable the police to put in as evidence of the objects of the Canadian Party, all the literature they had collected dealing with the Moscow body, including the Theses and Statutes of the Communist International, resolutions of Party Congresses, and even explanations of Communism by individuals such as Bucharin and Vasiliev. It was Russian documents rather than Canadian which constituted the bulk of the evidence dealing with revolution.

In these documents there are numerous passages in which the use of force to achieve the overthrow of Capitalism is advocated. It is necessary to quote from these in order to appreciate what the jury had to decide upon. The following extracts are taken from an early edition *The Communist*, June, 1921, which is interesting as being one of the few pieces of Canadian literature which directly refers to violence. It is speaking of the formation of the Party in Canada, and states:

The result of the Constituent Convention is the organization of the vanguard of the Canadian working class into the Communist Party of Canada, Section of the Communist International, with a programme of Mass-action as the vital form of proletarian activity, armed insurrection, civil war as the decisive, final form of mass-action for the destruction of the Capitalist State, proletarian dictatorship in the form of Soviet power as the lever of the Communist reconstruction of Society.

And, further, showing that the actual revolution will come in the future through a gradual intensification of the class struggle:

The revolutionary epoch upon which we have now entered forces upon the proletariat the application of militant methods, namely mass action which leads to direct collision with the bourgeois state, developing into armed insurrection and civil war. The centralized power of the capitalist class is exercised through its control of the state machinery, the army, navy, police, courts, bureaucracy, etc., by means of which it imposes its will upon the workers. Mass action is the proletarian revolt against the power and oppression of the capitalist class, and develops as the spontaneous activity of the workers massed in the large industries; the mass strike and mass demonstration being among its initial forms. In these strikes and demonstrations, large masses of workers are unified in the struggle. They develop new tactics and a new ideology ...

As these strikes grow in number and intensity, they acquire political character by coming into collision and open combat with the Capitalist State which openly employs all its machinery to break the strikes and to crush the workers' organization. This culminates in armed insurrection and civil war aimed directly at the destruction of the Capitalist State and the establishment of the proletarian dictatorship.

This article is equally explicit about the attitude of the Communists toward Parliaments. It declares:

The bourgeois parliaments, which constitute one of the most important instruments of the bourgeois state machinery, cannot be won over by the proletariat any more than can the bourgeois order in general. The task of the proletariat consists of destroying the entire machinery of the bourgeois state, including all the parliamentary institutions.

The parliamentary system of the bourgeois government of Canada, based on a Constitution, which is interrelated with and subservient to the British Imperial Government, with an apparatus of independent legislatures, courts, etc., makes the capitalist dictatorship which is screened behind the bourgeois democracy, a formidable power in the hands of the capitalist for the crushing of the working class aspiration.

Similar ideas can be found in the official Theses and Statutes of the Communist International, passed at its Second World Congress in 1920, and ratified by later Congresses. The following are some of the more outspoken paragraphs:

The working class cannot achieve a victory over the bourgeoisie by means of the general strike alone and by the policy of folded arms. The proletariat must resort to an armed uprising. Having understood this, one realizes that an organized political party is absolutely essential and that shapeless labour organizations will not suffice ...

The mass struggle means a whole system of developing activities growing ever more acute in form and logically leading to an uprising against the capitalist state. In this warfare of the masses, developing into civil war, the guiding party of the proletariat must, as a general rule, secure every and all legal positions, making them its auxiliaries in the revolutionary work and subordinating such positions to the plan of the general campaign, that of the mass struggle.

The above quotations have been given at some length because they contain certain ideas which go to the root of the offence charged. The mere desire to change the present economic order radically, to alter the nature of our governmental structure, and to vary the whole existing system of courts, is not illegal. As Mr Justice Wright said to Mr Somerville during the trial: 'It is needless and endless repetition to introduce evidence now to show that their principle is to destroy the present parliamentary system. This issue is, how they propose to do it, whether by lawful or unlawful means; that is the whole inquiry.' It is not difficult by ordinary legislation to destroy Canadian institutions. Nova Scotia recently abolished the Legislative Council – by legal means. The Dominion has set up a Court of Inquiry for deportees suspected of 'red' activities, which is not composed of judges, which holds secret trials, and from which no appeal lies save to the very Minister who appointed its members: this is as dictatorial and contrary to Canadian traditions as anything could be, yet it is apparently legal. The Canadian constitution, unlike the American, guarantees neither personal liberty, private property nor religion. Not the novelty or strangeness of Communist proposals makes them illegal, but only the manner in which it is said they must be effected. Thus in all the evidence introduced the only portions strictly relevant to the issue are those passages, like the above, which advocate the use of violence to attain the desired ends, or which evidence an agreement to carry out that elusive quantity known as a 'seditious intention.' In the same way there is no illegality in the fact that the Canadian Communist Party takes orders or even money from Moscow, so long as those orders are not illegal. Many religious bodies in Canada receive orders from external sources (e.g. The Vatican) and missionary societies receive money from abroad.

Counsel for the defence were faced with this difficulty; they had a number of their own publications before them, full of passages about violence, which to the average juryman could only mean what they appeared to mean, and which to persons steeped in Communist philosophy could be interpreted in a very different manner. Yet how explain away the written word? There is a discussion between Mr Justice Wright and Mr MacDonald which illustrates the point:

MR MACDONALD: We must make our defence from this material, by attempting to explain it and indicate that it does not mean what it appears to mean.
HIS LORDSHIP: I doubt if that will be permissible. Here are certain written statements contained in documents. How can any witness come and say that it does not mean this or that? That is for the jury.

MR MACDONALD: I may be quite frank about it now, my Lord, rather than have it come up by way of objection from time to time as I seek to put evidence in, and as I see the situation we are confronted with what is, in effect, a philosophic system which puts into practice the doctrines of Marx and Engels and Lenin.

HIS LORDSHIP: You will be confined to the system as disclosed in the evidence.

MR MACDONALD: I quite understand that, my Lord.

HIS LORDSHIP: This trial is not an enquiry into the whole system, but an inquiry based on the evidence adduced, and I am not going to allow you to travel beyond that.

The general line of argument for the defence was that the Communist Party had always conducted itself quite legally in Canada, that it was not under all circumstances bound to follow the dictates of Moscow, and that in any case the violence which was referred to in the literature was not something which it 'advocated' or 'taught' in the sense of 'aimed to bring about,' but rather was a form of violence which according to the Communist interpretation of history was inevitable and for which the Communist Party merely prepared. The first two points need only be outlined briefly. Four witnesses – all amongst the accused – appeared for the defence: Tim Buck, Thomas Ewen, A.T. Hill and Malcolm Bruce. In regard to the legality of the Party's behaviour, they showed how its members were continually running in municipal, provincial and federal elections. True, the Party had organized in an underground manner in 1921 because it feared repression, but it had come into the open in 1924 and had remained there. Its activities amongst the Finnish and Ukrainian benevolent societies were aimed at influencing these bodies in the direction of Communism, but that purpose was natural and not carried on in an illegal manner. Only a small percentage of their members were Communists. Indeed, a striking fact brought about by the evidence is that while the Party claimed 4,810 members in 1922, Moscow was blaming it for having no more than about 4,000 in 1931. It obviously was not flourishing on liberty. In regard to the orders from Moscow, the witnesses contended, as stated above, that their affiliation with the Third International left them free to adapt its programme to the particular conditions of Canada.

The main task of the defence, however, was to convey to the jury some conception of what the Communist means by revolution. Was this 'armed uprising' which was referred to, this rebellion, this resort to force, a policy which the Communist Party attempted to put into effect? Was the object of the Party to 'create' a revolution? Every one of the four accused who stepped into the box denied that it was. They based their position on the Marxian analysis of history. 'Dialectial Materialism,' said Tim Buck (and one can imagine the difficulties the jury must have experienced in attempting to understand a new system of philosophy in a day), is that Materialism which is based upon an understanding of the developments of history, which is based upon an understanding that everything which happens in history is a development from something which has happened and developed before; that the progress of the world, which does not go forward in a simple matter of steady development, is actually one long progress, although sometimes it goes very slowly, and another day it goes with revolutionary speed. Forces accumulate and there is a certain accumulation until suddenly the pressure of these forces ...

The change from Capitalism to Socialism, he contended, 'is a process, it is not an act.' There is no dogmatic assertion in Marxism that the change must be violent: it depends upon the correlation of forces at the time. If a socialist government came into power in Germany there would probably be peaceful revolutions in some of the Balkan states dependent on Germany. The following portion of Mr Buck's cross-examination makes clear his position:

MR SOMERVILLE: Now the object of the programme is to bring about Communism? A. Yes.
Q. And to bring about Communism means the destruction of the Capitalist system? A. Yes.
Q. That is what you describe as the 'Capitalist System' whatever it is? A. Yes.
Q. So that to bring about Communism involves the destruction of governmental organizations and industrial organizations as they at present exist? A. It means much more than that; destroying them would not bring in Communism.
Q. Do you mean that is the first step? A. It would be necessary to establish a new form of State and State machinery before it would be possible to eliminate private property and exploitation.
Q. And the clash would come when one attempted to destroy or do away with the present State in order to establish a new State? A. I am not prepared to prophesy exactly where the clash would come; the clash might come on some other point altogether; the clash might come on the question of the socialization of certain industries, the expropriation of certain industries, the infringement of property rights.
Q. There would have to be that clash? A. I believe the clash is inevitable.
Q. And in order to bring about that clash one organizes the masses, the proletariat? A. Pardon me. Did you say 'in order to bring about that clash?'
Q. Yes? Or rather, in order to direct that clash one brings about the organization of the masses? A. No. We organize the masses so that the masses while organizing themselves to-day, shall gain every measure that it is possible for the workers to gain under the present system, and, in gaining those measures, will prepare and

when Capitalism is in a crisis the working class will be able to take advantage of that situation, instead of allowing economy to drop into chaos.

The argument was fully elaborated in the address of Tim Buck to the jury.[2] His position may be outlined in this way: Revolutions have developed through the past ages as a result of conflicting forces. They do not come because parties make them but because society progresses from one epoch to another and because privileged classes will fight to retain their privileged position. They are part of the logic of history, which Communists cannot prevent or create any more than capitalists can. The Communist Party is thus on trial for something which it has not 'advocated' or 'taught,' since it does not 'advocate' the inevitable. The Party simply predicts that violence is coming and prepares for the inescapable day. If it is not ready when the time comes, if it does not then bring about the proletarian dictatorship, society will not come through to socialism, but will drift into complete anarchy or Fascism, and real social progress will be further postponed. The Communist intends to save the world for the worker by taking over the reins of power from the decaying Capitalist state.

Was this a fair explanation of the passages about violence in the literature presented to the jury? Evidently the jury did not think so.

Several incidents, useful as headline material for the press, marked the trial. Sergeant Leopold, 'with eyes straight ahead, his red coat making a splash of colour in the drab surroundings' (Canadian Press), was something of an event. Seven years a spy in the Party, he spoke with authority. The Hearst papers carried his picture through the United States, and the reporters of the *Toronto Star* got a long story from him during the course of the trial. This was considered 'highly improper practice' by the Judges. Some of the friends of the accused staged a demonstration outside the Court House, for which they were committed for contempt and fined. Then Ewen startled the court by admitting that in the event of a war between Canada and the Soviet Union he would look to the latter as his Fatherland, 'no matter who the aggressor against the Soviet Union is.' This admission does not seem to have much to do with bringing about changes by violence, which was the point at issue under section 98, nor has it a very clear relation to seditious conspiracy. Obviously it would not make a good impression on a jury.

Tim Buck and Mr MacDonald addressed the jury for the defence: Mr Somerville for the Crown. Mr Justice Wright summed up the evidence. The jury deliberated one hour and a half, and returned a verdict of guilty on all three counts.

2 This address, which contains an elaborate statement of the Party's views, is being distributed in pamphlet form by the Canadian Labour Defense League.

Cacic received a sentence of two years, the others five years each. In the Court of Appeal the objection of Mr MacDonald in regard to the form of the indictment was not maintained in so far as section 98 was concerned. The charge of seditious conspiracy, however, was held bad, but as the maximum penalty for this crime is two years, it did not affect the result. Discussing the merits, the Court held that on the evidence the jury had reasonable grounds for finding as they did, and therefore their verdict was not disturbed.

Thus the Communist Party of Canada has been held an 'unlawful association' by the Ontario Court. The Courts of another province might possibly hold otherwise: the case might conceivably reach the Supreme Court and be settled in some other sense. But these eventualities appear unlikely. Canada is now faced with a new social problem – how to deal with a large number of persons whose beliefs make them outlaws. The present remedy appears to be mass deportation.

Comment on political trials is somewhat of a waste of time, since there is no absolute criterion for judging the result. Nothing will convince Canadian radicals that the trial is not simply an example of the class-war, a temporarily successful attempt on the part of the privileged classes in Canada to defend their position against proletarian attack. Nothing will convince conservatives in Canada that the trial was not a perfectly reasonable enforcement of the criminal law against a lot of foreign 'reds' who had clearly broken it. So the matter must rest. Which view will prevail will depend upon which class prevails. Mr Gandhi breaks the law in India: is he a criminal? Louis Riel broke the law and was hanged; there is plenty of French-Canadian literature which tells of him as 'le martyr du Nord-Ouest.' Twelve French-Canadians who took part in the rebellion of 1837 in Lower Canada were hanged in Montreal; to-day there is a monument erected to their memory on the place of execution – now named 'Place des Patriotes' – which bears their names with the inscription *Vaincus dans la lutte, ils ont triomphé dans l'histoire*, and the statement that they died on the scaffold *Pour la liberté de leur pays.* So the process goes on. Are the Communists any less sincere than the rebels of 1837? Have they any less injustice to protest against? It is difficult to believe so. Some day there may be a monument in Toronto to the memory of Tim Buck and his fellow-accused. In the meantime one can only repeat:
*Malheur à qui fait des revolutions: heureux qui en hérite.*

# IV

# Freedom of Speech in Canada

*In Canada as elsewhere the police behaviour during the years of economic crisis brought questions of freedom of speech and association sharply to the fore. This was the picture as I saw it in 1932 in a paper read to the Annual Meeting of the Canadian Political Science Association.*
From *Papers and Proceedings*, Canadian Political Science Association 1933, 169–89

The present economic crisis has brought sharply to the front in Canada the question of freedom of speech. The individual liberties of the Canadian citizen have suddenly been discovered to have very definite and unexpected limits. On all sides we have seen men and women thrown into gaol simply for making speeches; peaceful meetings broken up by the police; street parades prohibited or dispersed; demonstrators arrested and deported after secret trials before administrative tribunals. There has been a growing censorship, exercised through the post-office, over literature imported into Canada from abroad, and a direct suppression in certain instances of papers printed here. In the narrower field of academic freedom there have been disquieting rumors of repression, and though hitherto the record of our universities has been clear, the recent incident of Professor Gordon,[1] and the frequent trouble over student publications, suggest that the problem exists there also. What is more, Canada, alone amongst British and indeed amongst parliamentary countries, has outlawed the Communist party, and has sent eight of its leaders to the penitentiary for five years merely because of their membership in it. Under these circumstances it is important to examine the nature of our right to free speech and the extent of the present restrictions upon it.

1 See Ernest Deane, 'Trying to Teach Christian Ethics,' *Canadian Forum*, June, 1933 (Vol. XIII, No. 153), p. 331.

To understand why freedom of speech should again appear in jeopardy, when it has seemed securely planted in our tradition and our practice, it is essential that the question be considered in relation to the world economic crisis. It is not mere coincidence that makes economic insecurity and repression of opinion and speech occur together. The one is the cause of the other. The economic insecurity of today induces repression for two reasons. It puts fear into the hearts of governments, and fear drives out tolerance. It operates also to make people critical both of the economic system which brings them to their unhappy condition, and of the men who control it. This critical attitude is carried further in proportion as the crisis deepens. The longer the return of capitalist prosperity is delayed, the more do the sections of the community on which depression bears heaviest absorb ideas of radical reform. Thus it is today that plans for great changes in the economic system, and even plans for replacing it by what appears to many to be a more efficient and more just system, are everywhere being put forward. The air is full of talk of reconstruction, of socialism and of communism. Freedom of speech is being demanded, not simply, as in the past, to discuss variations of policy within an accepted framework of fundamental ideas, but to question the fundamental ideas themselves. What is the proper place and degree of private property in the modern industrial state? Should the capitalist system be scrapped entirely, or can it be repaired? Can desirable changes be made by the methods of normal political action, or will they involve violence? Is violence ever justifiable? These are the sorts of question that are being asked, and for which free speech is invoked. The sixteenth and seventeenth centuries fought the issue of religious freedom; the eighteenth and nineteenth the issue of political freedom. The battle is now being waged along the economic front. The control of the machinery of the state – and thus of repression – being largely in the hands of the owners of wealth, the struggle for freedom of speech becomes, in its broad development, a fight between social classes – between those who benefit from the system and those who do not.

Let us remind ourselves what our so-called British tradition of freedom of speech has meant in the past. At bottom it is an attitude of mind rather than a set of rules. Its simplest and best expression is probably to be found in Voltaire's statement: 'I do not believe a word that you say, but I will defend with my life your right to say it.' On analysis our belief in this liberty will be seen to rest on the following propositions:

1 That the search for truth is socially useful;

2 That a greater freedom of speech assists the discovery of truth, while a lesser freedom hampers it;

3 That the legal restrictions upon this freedom, if justifiable at all, should be as few as are consistent with the preservation of orderly social change.

Put in another way, freedom of speech is to be protected because if an idea is true, we should know it; if it is not true, public discussion will most quickly destroy it; if it is partly true and partly untrue, discussion alone will separate the truth from the error. Both sides of a question must be heard before it is possible to make a fair or reliable decision upon the point at issue.

Our tradition of liberty necessarily covers more than this belief in the value of free discussion. It includes also certain allied liberties, and for its effective enjoyment it requires the existence of certain recognized conditions. It is perhaps impossible to isolate the particular safeguards for freedom of speech from the complex of institutions and practices that make up a given social environment. Freedom has well been defined as a condition under which activity takes place, and consequently is affected by all the forces – religious, political, economic – that mould the habits of a people. One might say, for instance, that education is necessary to intellectual liberty, and hence to freedom of speech. An ignorant person may be at liberty to speak, but he will have little to say. So too the individual is not free whose education has firmly riveted on his mind a fixed pattern of ideas. The enquiry here leads us into the field of psychology and other subjects alien to this paper. Again, the problem of freedom of speech, as of freedom in general, is inseparably bound up with the wider question of the distribution of wealth and the nature of the social relationships between man and man. A concentration of wealth means a concentration of freedom in the same hands. The wealthy man who speaks his mind has nothing but the law to fear – if that; the employee will fear for his job as well. There is grave danger to freedom of speech in our modern industrial society if the contract of employment can be broken at the mere whim of the employer.

Without going too deeply into these aspects of the problem, however, it is possible to single out certain essential requisites for freedom of speech. Freedom of association is obviously one. My right to talk is valueless unless I can talk to people. Speaking implies an audience. Any law, any practice, which strikes at the right to form clubs, societies and associations, or which prevents them from holding meetings, open-air or otherwise, is a direct infringement of the right to freedom of speech. The right of association includes the right to petition governing bodies of all sorts, and the right to hold parades under proper circumstances. Freedom of the press and a free circulation of books and periodicals are further essentials. Mr Walter Lippman in his *Liberty and the News* goes so far as to argue that the critical interest in the modern state, where more people read newspapers than attend meetings, is the protection of what he calls 'the stream of news.' If that stream is restricted or colored, the liberty of opinion is correspondingly destroyed. The facts will not be available on which to form valid judgments. The same reasoning applies to the public utterances of public officials. If they adopt a policy either of secrecy about matters of public importance, or of deliberate misrepresentation of the facts, they deal a blow at freedom of speech.

Finally, it is a necessary part of our tradition in this regard that the machinery of justice should be operated so as to secure to the individual the full use of his freedom. No man should be hindered in his enjoyment of liberty save for an infringement of some legal restriction upon it. This involves first of all a right to fair trial in open court, before judges sufficiently independent from the executive branch of the government to be free to defend the accused against an arbitrary exercise of power on the part of the state.[2] It involves the right to trial by jury, to counsel, to call witnesses, to be presumed innocent until proven guilty, and generally to the full protection of what we describe as British justice. It means also that the accused has a right to decent treatment at the hands of the police, that he will be allowed to keep silence if he chooses, and hence will be free from third degree methods to compel confession. It means that in the courts, in the words of the Bill of Rights, 'excessive bail ought not to be required, nor excessive fines imposed, nor cruel and unusual punishments inflicted.' It means the citizen has a right to pursue his daily activities free from the interference of spies.

So much by way of reminder of the positive content of our right to freedom of speech. The normal legal restrictions upon it may be dealt with equally briefly. Under the Canadian – as under the British – system of government there are no permanent constitutional guarantees of personal liberty, such as occur in the American and other written constitutions. The law contains no declaration of rights; it merely lays down prohibitions. Everything may therefore be lawfully said which does not come within a prohibition. The types of speech which our traditional law has considered anti-social and hence punishable may be classified under three heads, according to the interest which the law protects in each case. These are (1) crimes against the state or public order, (2) crimes against morality, and (3) crimes against individuals. To which must be added the general rule that anyone becomes a party to a crime who counsels or procures another to commit a crime which is committed.

Of the crimes which may be committed by words against the state, the most important is sedition. Minor offences, like spreading false news and libelling foreign sovereigns, may be mentioned, though they are seldom enforced, and the crimes of unlawful assembly and riot may hamper freedom of speech by affecting the right of association. Sedition, however, remains the principal restriction. It is not defined by our criminal code, the content of the crime being built up out of decided cases. It thus possesses what is, for the police authorities, a most convenient elasticity, and the only useful description one can give of it is that it includes all words which a judge or jury, in a given case, consider likely to cause people to adopt unlawful means to secure social change or to disturb the tranquillity of the

---

2 Montesquieu said: 'There is no liberty if the power of judging be not separated from the legislative and executive powers.'

state. Our code narrows the area of sedition a little by saying that no one shall be deemed to have a seditious intention only because he intends in good faith to point out errors or defects in the Canadian constitution, or to excite His Majesty's subjects to attempt to procure by lawful means the alteration of any matter in the state. In England the penalizing of seditious speeches is rare, the law not being usually enforced save where there have been overt acts of a criminal sort other than the mere uttering of words. In Canada the number of prosecutions for sedition has increased very greatly since the war; in Montreal alone during the past three years there have been at least ten cases, all connected with meetings that were admittedly peaceful.[3]

The offences against morality are indecent or obscene words or publications, and blasphemy. Our Criminal Code still contains the archaic rule that publishing instructions regarding contraceptives or cures for venereal disease is criminal unless the accused can show that the public good was served by his acts. On the other hand the Code is liberal enough to provide that blasphemy consists, not in the nature of the idea expressed, but in the manner of its expression. No one is guilty of a blasphemous libel for expressing in good faith and in decent language any opinion whatever upon any religious subject. Advocating atheism is thus no crime, if it be done in a temperate and considered manner. Defamatory libel is the only crime that can be committed against an individual by words. In general, truth and public interest are a good defence. A similar curb on freedom of speech, not part of the criminal law, is the civil action in damages to which everyone is liable who injures the reputation of another.

The rights and restrictions outlined above constitute the framework within which Canadians have been accustomed for generations past to carry on their public and private discussions. Whether or not this belief in freedom of speech is valid, whether the legal restrictions upon it are too narrow or too wide, is a question outside the scope of this paper. What is important, is the historic fact of the existence of the right of this degree of freedom. This is what is meant by our British tradition of free speech. We in Canada inherited that tradition and that law. What use have we made of it?

There are practically no reported cases of sedition or allied crimes to be found in the Canadian law reports prior to the war. This does not mean of course that there was no repression of freedom of speech in Canada. Few decided cases are reported, and many forms of repression involve no lawsuit. But it is reasonable to believe that few persons were interfered with, if only because there was no serious criticism being directed against established institutions by any organized body of opinion. When the war started, however, there was immediately trouble with the pro-German foreign element in the west. The treatment it received from

3 For an example see my note in the *Canadian Bar Review*, Vol. IV, No. 10 (December, 1931), pp. 756 ff.

the Canadian authorities was a foretaste of the latter's capacity for persecution. An Albertan judge remarked in 1916: 'There have been more prosecutions for seditious words in Alberta in the past two years than in all the history of England for over 100 years, and England has had numerous and critical wars in that time.'[4]

In this case a man was sentenced by a judge because while sitting in a drug store he expressed satisfaction at the sinking of the Lusitania. Another man was convicted of sedition by a jury in Saskatchewan because he wrote sarcastically of the people who were volunteering for active service, suggesting that they would die of fright if they saw a German soldier.[5] The prosecution was dropped later in the first case, and a new trial ordered in the second, but the two stand as monuments to the potentialities of the law of sedition.

At the close of the war Canada found herself for the first time in her history face to face with a serious movement of anti-capitalist opinion. Many demobilized soldiers, trained to organization and conscious of their strength, were restive at the discovery that the fruits of their victory were to be long hours in factories for small pay. The Russian revolution had made communism a world force, frightening the supporters of the existing system and confusing the issue between intelligent reform and violent social change. It was the period that gave notoriety to those magic words which are still able to make many worthy Canadians stop thinking: Bolshevik, Communist, Red, Socialist, Pacifist, Anarchist, to which category the word 'foreigner' seems to be a recent addition. It was the time of the One Big Union and the Winnipeg strike, when Mr Woodsworth was arrested and detained in gaol for quoting the Prophet Isaiah,[6] and to the south of us, a Vice-President of the United States was discussing in the *Delineator* the pressing problem 'Are the Reds Stalking our College Women?'[7] It was a time which England passed through with no alteration of her law regarding freedom of speech, and which Canada met by adding Section 98 as a permanent part of our Criminal Code, and by making deportation easier under the Immigration Act.

The notorious Section 98 was prepared by a committee of the House of Commons appointed on May 1st, 1919, and the bill itself was rushed through Parliament between June 27th and July 5th, 1919 – immediately after the Winnipeg strike. Its inspiration was undoubtedly the American Espionage Act and the various state statutes against criminal anarchy and criminal syndicalism.[8] Nothing like it can be found in British criminal law since the Napoleonic era. For the purposes of this discussion its provisions may be summarized as follows:

4 *Rex* v. *Trainor*, 33 Dominion Law Reports 658.
5 *Rex* v. *Giesinger*, 27 Canadian Criminal Cases 54.
6 A.V. Thomas, 'Quoting Isaiah in Winnipeg,' *Nation* (New York), Jan. 3, 1920 (Vol. CX), p.850.
7 See J.H. Robinson, *The Mind in the Making* (New York: Harpers, 1921), p. 193.
8 Mr Guthrie suggested its American origin, *House of Commons Debates* (Canada), Vol. II, 1919 (first session), p. 1956.

Subsection 1. Any association whose purpose is to bring about governmental, industrial or economic change within Canada by force or violence, or which teaches or defends such use of force or violence, is an unlawful association.

2. All property belonging or suspected to belong to an unlawful association, may be seized without warrant by any person authorized by the Commissioner of the Royal Canadian Mounted Police.

3. The following acts are crimes punishable by twenty years:

(a) Acting as an officer of an unlawful association, and

(b) Selling, writing or publishing anything as representative of it, or

(c) Becoming and continuing to be a member of it, or

(d) Wearing a badge or button indicating membership of or association with it, or

(e) Contributing to or soliciting dues for it.

4. This provides that anyone who has attended a meeting of an unlawful association, or spoken publicly in advocacy of it, or distributed literature of it shall be presumed to be a member of it in the absence of proof to the contrary.

5. The owner of any hall, who knowingly permits therein any meeting of an unlawful association or subsidiary, or of any group of persons who teach or defend the use of force, shall be liable to five years or a fine of $5000.

6 and 7 provide for search of premises and of persons and seizure of literature, by general warrant from any judge or magistrate.

8. The publishing and selling of literature in which is taught or defended the use of force to effect governmental change, etc., and the actual teaching or defending the use of such force, is punishable by twenty years.

9. Mailing such literature is a crime punishable by twenty years.

10. Importing such literature into Canada is a similar crime.

11. This makes it the duty of every Dominion civil servant to seize suspected literature and send it to the Commissioner of the Royal Canadian Mounted Police.

At the same time as this bill was passed the penalty for sedition was increased from two to twenty years, and the liberal section, narrowing the definition of seditious intention, was removed from the Code. Both these latter changes have since been repealed, but the bill to repeal Section 98 itself, though successful in five separate occasions in the Commons, was thrown out every time by the Senate – once by a majority of three votes.[9]

The particularly serious way in which Section 98 restricts freedom of speech in Canada are, firstly, the severity of the penalties. The penalty for sedition today, is two years; for unlawful assembly one year; for riot, two years. But the penalty under Section 98 is twenty years. The difference is absurd in view of the

9 In the session of 1929. [It was eventually repealed in 1936.]

similarity of the offences. The equivalent American statutes range from one to ten years[10]; even the emergency Public Safety Act of the Irish Free State in 1927 had a maximum penalty of five years and its penalty for distributing literature was six months. Secondly, subsection 4 of the section violates our traditional rule that the burden of proof of guilt rests on the Crown. Here a man who has merely attended a meeting, even unknowingly, must prove that he is not a member of an unlawful association – an almost impossible task, since no member of the association would dare to give evidence. Thirdly, the right of association of even lawfully disposed persons is seriously threatened by the severe penalties against owners of halls under subsection 5, for who is to say what is a 'subsidiary' of an unlawful association? Are we to take the totally unwarranted pronouncement of the Dominion Department of Labor, which has compiled in a document called *Labour Organization in Canada*[11] a list of subsidiaries of the Communist party? Such an example of arbitrary blacklisting is typical of the corrupting influence which this type of legislation has upon official minds. Not a vestige of proof is adduced for the inclusion of any of the named societies. Fourthly, the section creates entirely new crimes connected with the publishing, selling, distribution and importation of any literature which advocates or defends the use of force. A bookseller can be punished for selling a book the contents of which were unknown to him! A strict enforcement of the law would make the sale or importation of most of the classics of political science unlawful, since there is a large body of reputable opinion in favor of the view that revolution is morally justifiable under certain circumstances. Fifthly, the forbidding of 'industrial' change by threats of force comes perilously near to destroying the right to strike. Finally, under subsection 2 the police have power to invade premises and seize property without warrant and on mere suspicion, so that in Canada no man's home can be called his castle.

It was in virtue of Section 98 that the Communist party of Canada was declared an unlawful association by the Ontario courts in 1931.[12] What is most striking about the trial is the fact that the eight accused were in effect sentenced solely on account of their opinions, since there was no reliable evidence adduced to show that they or the party to which they belonged had actually occasioned any acts of violence in Canada. The use of force in which they and the party believed was to occur at some future date. It is also to be noted that they were found equally guilty of the crime of seditious conspiracy, which shows that our normal criminal law on these matters is quite adequate to look after the Communist par-

---

10 Z. Chafee, *Freedom of Speech* (New York: Harcourt, Brace & Co., 1920), p. 190.
11 Department of Labour, *Labour Organizations in Canada* (Ottawa: King's Printer, 1932).
12 For a review of the trial see my article 'The Trial of the Toronto Communists,' *Queen's Quarterly*, Vol. XXXIX, No. 3 (August, 1932), pp. 512 ff.

ty even without Section 98, if we wish to proceed against it. Just why it should be necessary to outlaw Communists in Canada when it is unnecessary in all civilized countries that have not turned fascist, we have never been told. Nor are we informed why the policy of persecution will have any other than the normal result of spreading the very doctrines it is designed to suppress.

Certain aspects of Section 98 are a sufficiently severe break with our traditional freedom, but the deportation provisions of the Immigration Act,[13] because they lead to exile after secret trials, and because they bear most hardly upon the friendless foreign element in Canada, are even more pernicious. Under this act, whenever any person other than a Canadian citizen advocates in Canada the overthrow by force or violence of any British government, or of constituted law and authority, or shall by word or act create or attempt to create riot or public disorder in Canada, he is to be classed as an undesirable immigrant, regardless of the length of time he has been in the country, and a written complaint of this fact must be sent to the Minister of Immigration.[14] Similar complaint can be made whenever any person other than a Canadian citizen or a person having Canadian domicile becomes a public charge.[15] At once the machinery of deportation may be set in motion.

Deportation from Canada is ordered by a board of inquiry. This consists of any three officers nominated by the Minister of Immigration, sitting at any port of entry. No qualifications, legal or otherwise, are required to be an officer, and no tenure of appointment is guaranteed. The hearing of all cases brought before the board 'shall be separate and apart from the public,' but in the presence of the immigrant 'whenever practicable.'[16] The immigrant may be represented by counsel, but none of the accepted rules of evidence apply to the conduct of the case, the board being entitled to base its finding upon any evidence considered credible or trustworthy by it.[17] From a decision of the board, which goes by a majority vote, an appeal lies to the minister who appointed it. At present he is, incidentally, also Minister of Mines and Minister of Labour, so that the time at his disposal for hearing these appeals may readily be imagined. If the minister dismisses the appeal, the person shall be deported forthwith. If he is the head of a family, the dependent members may be deported also.

The bare recital of these provisions, astonishing though they are, gives little idea of what they mean in practice. For the purpose of turning back undesirable immigrants at the moment they are seeking to enter Canada, a board of inquiry

13 *Revised Statutes of Canada, 1927*, chap. 93, as amended by 18–19 Geo. V., chap. 29.
14 *Ibid.*, sec. 41.
15 *Ibid.*, sec. 40.
16 *Ibid.*, sec. 15.
17 *Ibid.*, sec. 16.

may be both useful and necessary. For the totally different purpose of administering justice to foreigners who have committed certain crimes – for that is what these boards are doing – they are a travesty of everything we profess to believe is proper in the enforcement of criminal law. The accused does not stand a dog's chance. He is tried secretly. He may be whisked away from Winnipeg to be tried in Halifax, as happened in the case of Dan Holmes and others. He is not stated to have the right to call witnesses in his own behalf – and the right would be ineffective where long distances intervene between his home and the port of entry. He has no right to refuse to give evidence, but may be questioned. His judges are probably petty officials untrained in the interpretation of statutes and the weighing of evidence, and liable to direct pressure from above. His appeal may be even less a trial than the enquiry: the Minister is not obliged to hear counsel for the defence. And the penalty is the 'cruel and unusual punishment' of exile, as likely as not to a country where further penalties will await the radical deportee.[18]

The use to which these powers may be put for the purpose of suppressing undesired opinion may easily be imagined. Many startling instances of deportation of alleged Communists and 'reds' have been reported in the press. It is not known how many others there may be. Total deportations for 1931–32 were 7,034. In the years 1929–32 deportations as 'public charges' alone numbered 8,858. How easy to pick out ringleaders among the unemployed! Even naturalized aliens cannot feel safe, for under the Naturalization Act the Governor in Council may at any time revoke a certificate granted to a person who has 'shown himself by act or speech to be disaffected or disloyal to His Majesty,' or wherever he is satisfied that the continuance of the certificate is not 'conducive to the public good.'[19] In 1931–32, 239 certificates were revoked or annulled, as against an average of 27 or 28 for the three preceding years. No reasons are given. Naturalization thus gives no security in regard to freedom of speech; even sedition seems an exact term beside the words 'disloyalty' and 'disaffection,' and as for the clause protecting the 'public good,' what is this but straight permission to cancel certificates at will? Moreover, being of British origin with Canadian domicile, as so many of our immigrants are, though it makes a person a Canadian citizen, does not free him from danger, since Canadian domicile is lost under the Immigration Act 'by any person belonging to the prohibited or undesirable classes,'[20] and the advocacy of force to overthrow the government of Canada, and other prohibited opinions,

18 Some of the Poles detained for deportation at Halifax were even refused permission to pay their own way to the Soviet Union. See the *Citizen* (Ottawa), January 16th and 17th, 1933.
19 *Revised Statutes of Canada, 1927*, chap. 138, sec. 9.
20 *Ibid.*, sec. 2 (e) ii.

brings one within these classes.[21] Thus the only people who appear free from the danger of deportation are the British subjects born in Canada. As there were 2,307,525 immigrants in Canada according to the census of 1931, this means that some 23 per cent of the population of this country is liable to be exiled for the expression of certain types of opinion, without any protection from the ordinary law courts or any proper trial. It would be hard to find a parallel degree of bureaucratic control in any country on the face of the globe.

Star-chamber justice and Section 98 strike directly at free speech in Canada. But there are other methods of repression, less direct but equally effective, and very widely used. About these it is not easy to find reliable information, and my authority for the most of what follows is admittedly the newspapers. There are no official reports of the number of hall-owners threatened by police with cancellation of licenses if certain meetings are permitted. Yet this is a common practice in Canada today. The most flagrant instances have occurred in Toronto, where, for instance, the Fellowship of Reconciliation in 1931 found its meetings blocked in this way,[22] and where a meeting arranged by a Co-operative Commonwealth Federation Club in March, 1933, was similarly prevented. In Montreal, May 27th, 1932, an Anti-War meeting, called by the Young People's Socialist League and staged on the same night as the fashionable military tournament, was interfered with by the police and had to be postponed. The whole question of open-air meetings and parades is treated by most Canadian municipalities with the utmost disregard of lawful claims to freedom of speech. It has become a settled policy, in Montreal, for instance, that no soap-box oratory will be permitted anywhere. It is no question of traffic regulations, or of enforcing the law against sedition or unlawful assembly. The man or woman who dares to step forward is arrested or driven away before a word is said – on what legal ground it is impossible to see.[23] The use of violence in dispersing crowds – and this touches upon freedom of speech – is of common occurrence.[24] On one occasion the Montreal police, after an attempted demonstration, mounted guard over the bread lines and drove away everyone whom they considered to be a Communist.[25]

This increasing authority on the part of the police, often unwarranted by law, is a marked feature of the present depression, and is increasingly threatening our personal liberties. Evidences of it are visible on all sides. The Commissioner of the Royal Canadian Mounted Police under Section 98 of the Criminal Code, cen-

21 *Ibid.*, sec. 3 (n and o).
22 See J.F. White, 'Police Dictatorship,' *Canadian Forum*, February, 1931 (Vol. XI, No. 125), p. 167.
23 E.A. Forsey, 'Montreal is a Quiet City,' *Canadian Forum*, June, 1931 (Vol. XI, No. 129), p. 327.
24 E.g. behavior of police at the Zynchuck funeral, Montreal, March 11, 1933.
25 The *Gazette* (Montreal), February 26, 1931.

sors radical literature for us. Municipal police are given or assume the right to prohibit meetings and parades in advance. May Day is treated in most parts of the country by the police as though everyone who celebrated the occasion was a public enemy, though the holiday is simply intended as a symbol of international working-class solidarity and there is no reason in law or common sense why parades should not be permitted and protected. Third-degree methods, from which our police have hitherto been fairly free, are already beginning frequently to be charged; and now that they have publicly received the blessing of the Attorney-General for Quebec for the stated reason that they produce 'confessions,' they may be expected to develop.[26] With their adoption the traditional right to silence of the accused disappears, and public respect for 'law and order' is further destroyed. Equally deplorable is the growing use of spies, of which Sergeant Leopold is the prize example. He has been going the rounds of the boards of inquiry under the Immigration Act, lecturing the officials on the nature of Communism. He is a fit successor to the Corporal Zaneth of the same trade, who gave evidence during the trial of Russel after the Winnipeg strike, and who defended the practice of spying by declaring, 'Yes, I think Canada needs liars.'[27] Our once glorious Mounted Police are now associated with this dirty game. 'The freedom of a country,' wrote Erskine May, 'may be measured by its immunity from this baleful agency.'

Moreover, there is a growing tendency on the part of the police to excuse all arbitrary behavior by calling the persecuted persons Communists or Socialists (the two categories, distinct in law, being deliberately or ignorantly confused). When Constable Zappa of the Montreal Police Force was asked by a press reporter why he shot the unemployed Pole, Zynchuck, in the back during an eviction in Montreal, he replied with a shrug of the shoulders, 'He's a Communist.'[28] The fundamental rule that no one is a criminal until a court of law has found him so, seems incapable of appreciation by the police mind. Even if we have outlawed the Communist party, the alleged Communist is no criminal until the case is proved against him; he attends meetings, makes speeches, marches in parades, an innocent man. The police, if they have evidence, may arrest him and bring him in before a court, just as in the case of other law-breakers, but that is all they may lawfully do. Everything else is persecution.

Another favorite form of police repression is the enforcement of laws only against individuals whom they dislike. A group of unemployed in March, 1932, set out in a truck from Montreal for Quebec to present petitions to the provincial

26 An address by the Attorney-General for Quebec before Police and Fire Chiefs Association, the *Gazette* (Montreal), May 9th, 1933. The rack and thumbscrew also produced confessions from the innocent as well as the guilty.
27 J.A. Stevenson 'A Set-Back to Reaction in Canada,' the *Nation* (New York), March 6, 1920 (Vol. CX), p. 292.
28 The *Star* (Montreal), March 7th, 1933.

government. This was a valid exercise of a constitutional right. They were arrested for speeding and having dirty license plates.[29] Two members of the Young People's Socialist League of Montreal were arrested for placing posters calling an anti-war meeting on telegraph poles belonging to the Montreal Light Heat and Power Company.[30] The proceedings were legal under a city by-law, but similar cases of placarding, notably at election time, pass unnoticed. There is another Montreal by-law prohibiting the distribution of circulars or papers in the streets and public places of the city;[31] it is enforced principally against persons handing out radical notices.

No change of attitude on the part of the police, however, is likely to occur when so little respect or consideration for freedom of speech is shown by certain of our public men. They do not seem to realize that toleration means allowing the expression of unpleasant as well as pleasant ideas. Lip-service to our traditions is paid from time to time, but qualified in such a way as to show a total ignorance of what that freedom means. The following statement, which comes from the highest quarter, is typical:

This is a land of freedom, where men may think what they will and say what they will, so long as they do not attack the foundations upon which our civilization has been built. But as we have freedom, so we have justice, and it is not right nor just that now or at any other time we should permit such action by words or deeds as may tend to unsettle confidence in the institutions under which we live.[32]

Note the limitations: 'attacking the foundations of our civilization' and 'tending to unsettle confidence in our institutions.' Neither of these can be classified under any known legal restrictions upon freedom of speech. Institutions and foundations may be attacked freely so long as lawful methods of abolition or reform are urged. Mr Justice Humphreys stated the law clearly, during his summing up at the recent trial in England of four Communists charged with conspiracy to seduce soldiers from their duty, when he said:

A person in this country has liberty to say that its constitution or its religion should be changed, that there ought to be no religion at all, that there ought to be no king, that we ought to have a republic, or any other form of government. What persons cannot do is to advise that changes should be made by force or terrorism.[33]

29 The *Gazette* (Montreal), February 19, 1932.
30 This case is known to me personally.
31 No. 270.
32 *House of Commons Debates* (Canada), 1931, Vol. IV, p. 4278.
33 Cited in the *Citizen* (Ottawa), May 20th, 1933.

This failure to distinguish between the content of the idea and the manner of giving effect to it leads to the frequent but erroneous confusion between Communism and Socialism. The Socialist aims to secure political power by lawful means; the Communist expects to use violence. The two parties on this point are poles apart. It would be quite lawful to preach every communist doctrine so long as the element of violence were omitted, and socialism has never come near the edge of the law. References to the 'iron heel of ruthlessness' and similar talk,[34] create the impression that the radical is without rights – and the Constable Zappas shoot the more readily. A similar confusion is created in regard to the foreigners in our midst – 'the people with unpronounceable names': it is somehow considered a special offence for them to express disapproval of the labor conditions under which they work, or the institutions under which they are compelled to live. In the eye of the law the freedom of speech of foreigners, at any rate in so far as the Criminal Code is concerned, is identical with that of native-born Canadians. If we do not practice tolerance towards foreigners, we are not likely to practice it amongst ourselves. Freedom of speech cannot survive in a country where people's minds are filled by public men with these fixed ideas and prejudices about racial or political groups. What type of justice can be expected from a Recorder in Montreal who greets a new batch of prisoners with the words: 'Some more Communists? I believe that if they would get stiffer sentences, it would put a stop to these smart reds.'[35]

The repression of opinion manifests itself in many other ways today. The withholding of information upon matters of public importance is one. The Beauharnois investigation is suddenly stopped; the Montreal Harbor Bridge enquiry is withheld. The government consistently refuses to publish full information regarding income tax statistics in Canada, such as have been available in the United States. When enquiries are compelled in regard to penitentiaries and coal monopolies, they are held in private. Public opinion, in the expressive phrase of Mr Lippman, is thus 'blockaded.' In parliament itself the freedom of speech of members is seriously curtailed. Government business takes more and more time. The speaker of the Commons, with all his control over debate, is invariably a party nominee; in England his post is by tradition permanent. Mr Woodsworth in the session of 1932, was for a time denied even first reading of his bill to repeal Section 98.[36] During the past year discussion of an important matter of foreign policy – the Sino-Japanese situation – was choked off on the novel plea that matters under consideration by the League of Nations should not be debated in Parlia-

34 See speeches before the Ontario Conservative Association, November 9, 1932, reported in the daily press.
35 The *Gazette* (Montreal), March 19th, 1931.
36 *House of Commons Debates* (Canada), 1932, Vol. I, p. 380.

ment as they were *subjudice*,[37] a rule which if adopted generally might prevent the Canadian people from giving any authoritative voice to its opinions on pressing international affairs.

The most potent influence upon the popular mind, the press, is obviously not free in Canada from those practices which, by controlling the news, control our liberty of thought. Exceptions of course there are, but Canadian newspapers for the most part are owned by interests and make their profits from advertisers who are for economic reasons opposed to freedom of speech for radicals. The result is seen in their failure to report certain types of meeting, their totally inadequate reporting of speeches containing an unpopular point of view, and in other ways. Publicity can so easily be manipulated in favor of one side. This winter at the time of the formation of the Co-operative Commonwealth Federation Clubs in Montreal *La Presse* and *La Patrie* refused to carry a paid advertisement asking all people interested in the movement to send their names to a given address. Consistent misrepresentation of an opinion is another way of attempting to suppress it, and this is all too common a habit in certain editorial offices. The attack sometimes comes from other parts of the newspaper world. The weekly paper *Change*, first published in February, 1933, and mildly radical in its opinions, was put out of business because the distributing agencies in Toronto refused to handle it.

There is an interesting fight for freedom of speech in progress at the present moment in Montreal. The Université Ouvrière, a French-Canadian workmen's college where anti-clerical and radical economic views are taught, has been for many years a thorn in the flesh of the provincial authorities. Its headquarters were raided by a band of students from the University of Montreal in 1930, and some of its property damaged. It has now been deprived of its charter by the repeal of the Mechanics' Institute and Library Associations Act at the last session of the Quebec Legislature, compelling all associations formed under the Act to seek new charters under the Quebec Companies Act. According to the Hon. C.J. Arcand, Minister of Labour at Quebec, the University was expounding doctrines 'harmful to the public weal.'[38] Its newspaper, *Spartacus*, was seized and stopped by the police. No court action has yet established that any of its teaching was illegal, though its daring leader, Albert St Martin, is now undergoing trial on a charge of blasphemous libel. Undaunted by the attack, the University has reformed as a business firm carrying on the business of education.[39] It remains to be seen how long this device will avail to preserve it. Some 70 years ago a much more respectable French-Canadian society, L'Institut Canadien, fought for smaller rights, and lost.

One last form of repression, and one of the most powerful, must be mentioned.

---

37 *Ibid.*, (unrevised edition), November 21, 1932, pp. 1464–9.
38 The *Gazette* (Montreal), April 10, 1933.
39 *Ibid.*, May 8, 1933.

It does not lend itself to easy measurement, and may perhaps best be described in plain English by saying that there is a widespread feeling in Canada today that if a man wants to hold his job he had better not talk too much. This feeling undoubtedly exists amongst all classes of employee, both salaried and wage-earning. Its existence is a fine commentary upon the nature of our social life, implying as it does that the person who works for a living is owned body and soul by the employers, and that these are unscrupulous enough to penalise a man for his opinions. It largely explains our public apathy in the face of manifold provocations. How often we hear it said of someone that he is in favor of this or that reform, but of course he 'cannot say anything.' He cannot say anything, the other man cannot say anything – no one can say anything, except the Communist, and he is promptly deported. So the leading British Dominion drifts along in this year of grace 1933, frightened out of its all too diminutive wits. Our captains of industry are firm believers in individual initiative and private enterprise, but they are the first to deny the application of their pet principles in the field of freedom of speech. In fairness to them, however, it must be admitted that this sense of fear may equally be due to a lack of courage on the part of the employee.

'The time, it is to be hoped, has gone by' wrote John Stuart Mill, 'when any defence would be necessary of the principle of freedom of speech.' His hope was vain. The time for defending freedom never goes by. Freedom is a habit that must be kept alive by use. In times like the present, when mankind is hesitating before a bewildering choice of remedies for its afflictions, freedom of discussion is more necessary than ever. There are two ways of attempting to solve our present economic problems. One is to use the sword; this is the Communist and Fascist technique. The other is to think through the difficulties, to decide a policy, and to legislate it into existence. This is what we like to think is the Canadian technique. It cannot work without the utmost freedom of speech and discussion.

The achievement of a full degree of personal liberty must await the conquest of the economic system by the democratic principle. But much could be done immediately to widen the area of freedom of speech in Canada, and liberal minds of all parties should unite in this endeavor. In particular the repeal of Section 98, the confining of the immigration boards to their proper functions, a restriction of police control over owners of halls, a reasonable granting of permission for parades, and the setting aside in every city and town of specified localities for outdoor meetings under police supervision, are essential steps toward regaining our traditional freedom. Law and order would be more secure in this atmosphere of tolerance, because tolerance induces a respect for authority. The well-tried rules of our normal criminal law[40] would still be available to put down violence and to preserve the public peace.

40 E.g. treason, sedition, unlawful assembly, riot, etc.

# V

# Wade *v.* Egan: A Case Comment

*This case was chosen from among many others as showing certain judicial attitudes towards police behaviour when human rights are involved. The facts appear all too clearly from my comment. The judgment in question, rendered by the Manitoba Court of Appeal in a split decision, will be found in (1935) 64 Canadian Criminal Cases, p. 21.*
From the *Canadian Bar Review*, 14, 1936, 62–7

IMMIGRATION ACT – FALSE ARREST – ILLEGAL TREATMENT OF ARRESTED PERSON

Anyone interested in the growth in Canada of what is now called 'The New Despotism,' should study the case of *Wade* v. *Egan*, recently decided by the Manitoba Court of Appeal.[1] The facts disclose, in a startling manner, some of the practices which have developed in Canadian police administration, and some of the abuses to which the deportation provisions of the Immigration Act may so easily give rise. Plaintiff was a labour leader – one of that class of persons whose activities, like those of Republicans, Dissenters and Non-conformists in times past, are causing this generation to learn for the first time the nature and content of our civil liberties. Though born in Canada, he appears to have claimed to be an American citizen on more than one occasion. On December 5th, 1931, the defendant Egan, in his capacity as Deputy Minister of Immigration and Colonisation, issued an order under section 42 of the Immigration Act authorising any officer of the Royal Canadian Mounted Police to arrest plaintiff as 'a person other than a Canadian citizen who advocates in Canada the overthrow by force or violence of the Government of Great Britain or Canada, the overthrow by force or violence of constituted law and authority and by word or act creates or attempts to create

1 (1935), 64 Can. C.C. 21, on appeal from 62 Can. C.C. 260.

riot or public disorder in Canada.' This order was received by Inspector Mellor at Winnipeg on or about December 10th. It was not acted on until May 1st, 1932, after plaintiff had delivered a speech to an out-door meeting in Winnipeg, when he was arrested, taken to the barracks and searched. The next morning he was interviewed by a barrister acting for the Canadian Labour Defence League, who immediately discovered that he was a Canadian citizen and hence not liable to deportation. Inspector Mellor was asked to show the order for arrest, but declared that it was in possession of another member of the force and agreed to produce it at an appointment made for 3.00 o'clock that afternoon. Instead of keeping the appointment as promised, at which presumably the whole matter could have been cleared up, the Inspector broke his engagement, placed plaintiff and some other prisoners, handcuffed, in a car, drove them to Transcona, 8 miles out of town, put them on board the transcontinental express and sent them 2,000 miles away to Halifax. Here plaintiff was brought before a Board of Inquiry, his Canadian citizenship was established, and he had to be discharged. He was given transportation back to Winnipeg and $1.00 in cash.

Plaintiff brought an action for false arrest and imprisonment against Egan and certain officers and members of the RCMP. The trial judge dismissed the action, and this decision was confirmed on appeal by a majority of three to two. The courts, in other words, refused any redress to a Canadian citizen who had been treated in the manner described.

Before considering the legal reasons for this astonishing result, certain of the facts should be emphasized. It is often in executive behaviour rather than in the law that the real danger to civil liberty is found. In the first place, it is noteworthy that a supposedly dangerous character,[2] determined to overthrow the government of Canada by force, was allowed his freedom for five months after the warrant for his arrest had issued. Why this failure of the RCMP to carry out their duty? Were they trying for those five months to 'get their man,' or were they using discretion to arrest only if plaintiff became prominent in labour activities? No explanations were given. The delay in making the arrest, its execution after a speech to a crowd on May day, all suggest, as one of the dissenting judges pointed out,[3] that a warrant for a proceeding under the Immigration Act was used for another purpose. Instead of freeing the country of revolutionary immigrants, which is the purpose of the power to deport, the police were apparently concerned only in breaking up a working class demonstration. The proper way to do that, if the preservation of order demanded it, was by arresting for sedition or unlawful assembly. The facts indicate a clear case of what in France would be called a 'détournement de pouvoir.'

2 No evidence was given of any subversive activities.
3 Robson J.A., 64 Can. C.C. at p. 38.

Secondly, no effective inquiry was made to ascertain whether or not plaintiff was an alien. Questioned on the point Mr Egan declared that 'if we started to institute inquiries of the many hundreds of people we handle we probably would be making inquiries until doomsday.' Arrest first and question afterwards – that seemed to be Mr Egan's motto. To this, Robson JA remarked: 'Such an attitude toward personal liberty needs no comment.'[4] In view of the failure of other members of the court to award damages, such an attitude obviously needs a great deal more comment than it has so far received, if it is to be eradicated from the executive organs of our government.

Thirdly, it was not disputed that an RCMP inspector broke an appointment with a barrister and by this piece of trickery prevented the release of the prisoner. The police effectively obstructed the course of justice.

Fourthly, the Board of Inquiry before which plaintiff was taken was held at Halifax instead of Winnipeg. Winnipeg was an 'immigrant station' at which, under section 42 of the Immigration Act, the inquiry could have been held; Mr Egan admitted in evidence that in the usual course of events the Board would have met there.[5] It was where the arrest took place and where the prisoner's friends and counsel were. It was also the nearest point to the United States, to which country deportation would have to take place if justified. No good reason was shown why the venue was changed. By railroading plaintiff to Halifax his chances of establishing his rights were made infinitely more difficult, his length of imprisonment was increased, and the taxpayer had additional rail fares to pay.

Lastly, plaintiff was searched at the barracks, and handcuffed on the train without cause being shown why this force was necessary. But in face of other aspects of the case these personal indignities, though probably illegal, may seem trivial. They may be classed amongst the luxuries of freedom, which we in Canada do not appear to have achieved.[6]

In the face of these manifest injustices, why were the courts unable or unwilling to grant protection to the citizen?

The answers given by the majority of the judges are, to say the least, unsatisfactory. Montague J in the trial court, held that there was no duty on the part of Egan as Deputy Minister to inquiry into the correctness of the complaint about plaintiff on receipt of which he ordered his arrest; that he was protected by the rule applying to magistrates that when acting within their jurisdiction they are not liable for an error in judgment, but only for malice or want of *bona fides*, which were not suggested here. As to the constables, they were protected by the

---

4 *Ibid.*, p. 36.

5 *Ibid.*, p. 26.

6 Robson J.A. alone commented on these facts; *ibid.*, pp. 38–39.

warrant, valid on its face, under which they acted. Every other aspect of the case, such as the railroading to Halifax and the breaking of the appointment, was ignored.

In the Court of Appeal, Prendergast CJM simply dismissed the appeal without any reasons given. Richards JA also moved for a dismissal, on the ground that plaintiff had brought his troubles on himself by misleading statements as to his citizenship; true, the 'hasty actions' of the RCMP officers were 'greatly regretted,' but 'the evidence adduced does not establish any improper motives of such officers.' (One is tempted to ask how far the police must go in treating barristers with contempt and defeating the ends of justice before improper motives can be inferred.) Trueman JA was most outspoken in his criticism of the officials; he found that Egan knew plaintiff was being taken to Halifax; he said, in regard to the surreptitious method employed by the RCMP to checkmate plaintiff's counsel, that 'for parallel high-handed proceedings one must go back to 1667'; he pointed out that barristers no less than courts were guardians of the liberty of the subject. Yet he too, in spite of this admission that plaintiff was deeply wronged, dismissed the appeal on the highly technical ground that the action was for false arrest and imprisonment of a British subject, which point he thought was met by plaintiff's claim to be an American citizen. He intimated that had the action been for 'imprisonment and detention based on abuse of process and procedure, and the essential evidence been given that established its existence in fact and law, judgment for the plaintiff would have followed.'

Two judges only out of the six, Robson and Dennistoun, JJA, would have allowed the appeal and awarded damages. Both showed an admirable concern for the protection of personal liberty, and a firm grasp of the duty, clearly imposed on the judiciary by the nature of our constitution, to stand as guardian of the citizen against arbitrary behaviour by the state. Their statement of the nature of the action renders Trueman JA's technical difficulties somewhat hard to understand. Dennistoun JA pointed out that the action was not only for unlawful arrest, but also for 'illegal treatment after arrest.'[7] Robson JA explained[8] that plaintiff 'not only set up facts to show the original unlawfulness of the warrant but added allegations of the excessive and wrongful manner of its execution. It was evidently never suggested that this blending was either embarrassing or as a matter of pleading objectionable. Such a point was never raised either below or here.' He expressed what is surely a conservative viewpoint when he said that 'to put it at its lowest the conduct of authorities in such a case should at least be reasonable.' But he was in the minority.

7 *Ibid.*, p. 21.
8 *Ibid.*, p. 33.

The decision of the majority is no doubt correct in holding that defendant Egan would not be liable without proof of malice. It is somewhat dangerous to base this view, as did Montague J, on the authority of *Cave* v. *Mountain*,[9] a case which, as Robson JA pointed out,[10] was discussing the liability of magistrates. Egan was not a magistrate, but an ordinary administrative official exercising ministerial functions. He was protected, if in good faith, by the normal rule applying to public officers other than judges who exercise a discretionary power; they are liable for malice, but not for errors of judgment.[11] Bad faith might well have been inferred from the facts of this case; one could wish that other members of the court had supported Robson JA's view that an administrative duty whereby the liberties of individuals may be cut off was not duly discharged when approached in the routine manner adopted by Egan. But conceding this point, the other allegations of plaintiff still remain to be dealt with. To pass them by in silence is tantamount to excusing the police. For the railroading to Halifax Egan would be liable if, as head of the department responsible, he ordered it to take place or it was clearly shown to be his act.[12] And then there are the separate complaints against the police officers; the warrant, valid on its face, was certainly authority to make the arrest, but it was not authority to prevent plaintiff by trickery from obtaining his release, not, it is suggested, was it authority to keep the warrant handy for five months before making the arrest. Judgment should certainly have gone against the members of the RCMP on these grounds, unless Trueman JA's technical difficulty that the action took the wrong form is to be accepted; this was not advanced as a reason by any other judge, and was expressly repudiated by the two dissenting judges.

The case as a whole presents a striking contrast between the complete willingness of the executive to disregard all standards of fair play, and the almost complete unwillingness of the judiciary to check such behaviour. It cannot be too often pointed out that the 'rule of law,' on which our democracy so largely depends for its sanction, is no stronger or wider than the courts may care to make it, and that every decision of this character undermines the only legal safeguards under the constitution for the preservation of civil liberties. In *Rex* v. *Trainor*,[13] a sedition case decided in 1916, it was said 'There have been more prosecutions for seditious words in Alberta in the past two years than in all the history of

9 (1840), 1 Man. & G. 257.
10 64 C.C.C. at p. 37.
11 Halsbury, *Laws of England*, 1st ed., Vol. XXIII, p. 334.
12 Halsbury, *op. cit.*, p. 323.
13 33 D.L.R. 658, 666. This was the famous case where a man was charged with sedition for expressing pleasure at the news of the sinking of the Lusitania. He was convicted, but the Alberta Court of Appeal ordered the trial judge to state a case, and the Crown later withdrew.

England for over 100 years, and England has had numerous and critical wars in that time.' In the case under discussion we are told that 'For parallel high-handed proceedings one must go back to 1667.' Perhaps an ordinary citizen may be permitted to suggest that it would be more useful if, instead of merely calling attention to these marvellous Canadian records in despotic government, something effective were done to put a stop to them.

# VI

# Nationalism in French Canada

*The Liberal Party formed the government of Quebec from 1897 until the over-throw of Premier Taschereau in 1936, when it was replaced by a new party, the Union Nationale, under Maurice Duplessis. He led the province into a new era of intensified nationalism, characterized by widespread political corruption and a disregard of civil liberties.*
From *Round Table*, 27, no. 105, 1936, pp. 126–36

I THE OVERTHROW OF MR TASCHEREAU

In Canada the economic depression is lifting, but its political effects continue. The world crisis started political movements which show no signs of disappearing with the advent of better times. Social Credit is entrenching itself in Alberta and is spreading into neighbouring provinces; Mr Woodsworth's socialist party, the Co-operative Commonwealth Federation, has maintained its national organisation; for the first time, in Manitoba, a Communist has been elected to a Canadian legislature. Mr Stevens' Reconstruction party alone of the new groups seems to have ceased its activities. So far these recent movements have left the French-Canadians virtually untouched. Sheltered from English-Canadian thought by the barrier of language, educated apart in their Catholic schools and universities, they have sought for solutions to their difficulties in a way quite different from their English fellow countrymen. Whereas falling wages and unemployment made the English-Canadian turn his thoughts to economic change, they caused the French-Canadian to turn to nationalism. The political consequences are now beginning to make themselves felt. A new party, the *Union Nationale*, is in power in Quebec, and there is on foot in the province a nationalist movement that in its more extreme manifestations is vociferously secessionist.

For the first five years of the depression there was little in Quebec provincial politics to indicate what direction the underlying movements of opinion would take. The mass of the population, trained to a Catholic view of life, were at first inclined to accept unemployment, low wages and low prices much as they would accept a hard winter or a bad harvest. Pastoral letters from the bishops urged patience and warned against the dangers of radical thought. The provincial Liberal party had been in office since 1897; under the leadership of Mr Taschereau, who had been Premier since 1920, it had become so rooted in every corner of the province that it seemed inconceivable that it might be overthrown. When a certain Maurice Duplessis took over the leadership of the Conservative Opposition in 1933 he could control but 11 members in a house of 90. In the autumn of 1934, however, there emerged a new man and a new party. Paul Gouin, son of the former Premier Sir Lomer Gouin, gathered round him a group of younger Liberals dissatisfied with the Government's do-nothing policy, and formed the *Alliance Libérale Nationale*. It announced that it had two aims: the overthrow of the Taschereau régime, and the reconstruction of the economic and social life of the province in accordance with the needs of the French-Canadian masses. It met with success from the start. The discontented elements, particularly amongst the younger professional and business men, were looking for just such a rallying point, and flocked to the new standard. By an astute move Mr Gouin made an agreement with Mr Duplessis and the Conservatives just before the elections of 1935, so that all the anti-Government forces were united. When the results of that vote were made known it was found that Mr Taschereau had but 48 seats against an Opposition of 42. For the first time in forty years, Quebec was on the march.

Events from that moment moved quickly to a climax. The subsequent parliamentary session was hectic and brief. Mr Duplessis, who remained as Opposition leader in the House, succeeded in unearthing a series of political scandals by the simple method of forcing the Public Accounts to account – something that apparently had not been done in Quebec for years, save in a formal manner. For persons interested in the ethics of North American politics, the details make instructive reading. Mr Taschereau was forced to resign, and in a last-minute effort to save his party he handed over the leadership to Mr Godbout, one of the best of his younger Ministers. But repentance had come too late. New elections were held in August 1936, and not even a break between the two new leaders, which caused Mr Gouin temporarily to retire from politics, could stem the flood. Mr Duplessis, with a party re-named the *Union Nationale* after the split with Mr Gouin, was returned with a majority of 76 to 14.

Superficially the overthrow of the Liberal party may appear as the familiar collapse of a long-established Government which has had the bad fortune to meet an economic crisis. Actually, however, it is due in large part to the development

of the nationalist spirit, which made the election an event of much deeper significance than a mere party contest. The causes and nature of this new nationalism,
and the forms that it is now taking, can only be understood when seen as part of
the recent history of the relations between the French and English in Canada.

## II VISION OF LAURENTIA

Before Confederation the French-Canadians, having been conceded their religion
and their civil law, struggled principally for three constitutional rights – responsible government, representation by population, and the recognition of French
as an official language. These were all accorded in the British North America Act,
and a number of additional minority guarantees were added. Since that date the
population of Quebec has had the fullest political liberty. The provincial power
to control such matters as religion, education, property and civil rights has meant
that the French-Canadian may determine his own development in the province in
his own way. The English minority in Quebec never has more than four or five
seats in the legislature, and has no guaranteed right to any. Outside Quebec the
French minority has a right, varying somewhat in different provinces, to its separate Catholic schools, and the French language is official for proceedings in the
Dominion Parliament and in Dominion courts. Two judges out of six in the Canadian Supreme Court are always French, and Quebec is guaranteed a certain representation in the Dominion Senate and House of Commons. As the French-Canadians grow in number in the other provinces (there are now some 700,000 in the
rest of Canada) their influence naturally increases. It is next to impossible to-day
for any Canadian Government to carry through a policy to which the French-
Canadians are unitedly opposed. For these various reasons the Confederation
agreement has always been considered by the bulk of Canadians as having placed
minority rights on a secure and ample foundation. Such racial conflicts as have
arisen have never seriously threatened the bases of Confederation. Sir Wilfrid
Laurier as premier of Canada symbolised the conception of a broad Canadian nationalism unified in political expression but based on a duality of race and
culture.

While the bulk of French-Canada accepted this idea, there has long been a
minority in Quebec that has pushed the claims of nationalism much farther.
Canada's participation in the South African war stirred Henri Bourassa in 1900
to form the *Ligue Nationaliste*. The League attacked the concept of a closely
united Empire, opposed British immigration to Canada, and sought a greater control over the English commercial corporations in Quebec, but did not advocate
secession. In 1911 no less than 25 Nationalists were elected to the federal House
of Commons. This movement subsided, to revive in a new form through the stim-

ulus of Canada's entrance into the world war. Seldom has racial feeling run higher in Canada than during the attempt to enforce the Conscription Act of 1917 in Quebec; for the French-Canadian had not sufficient love for the England that had conquered him, or the France that had turned anti-clerical, to feel that their quarrels in Europe were his concern. In that year Mr Francoeur introduced into the Legislative Assembly a resolution to the effect that Quebec would accept the breaking of the Confederation pact if the other provinces felt she was a hindrance to the development of Canada. Though withdrawn without a vote, the motion crystallised an attitude. From that moment secession became openly a part of nationalist thinking. In the same year a new organisation with a newspaper, the *Action Française*, was founded to carry on educational work along nationalist lines; from its activities have come the bilingual postage stamps and currency in Canada, the celebration of St John the Baptist's day as a provincial holiday, and the growth of a number of French patriotic societies and youth movements. Its guiding spirit was the Abbé Lionel Groulx, who is still the most powerful influence amongst the nationalists to-day. Writing in 1922, one member of this group, Father Villeneuve, now Cardinal Villeneuve, said: 'We are not hurrying toward separation. We watch it coming, for it is coming toward us ... That a French Catholic state can during this century arise in the St Lawrence Valley is no longer in the minds of many a pure Utopia but an ideal worthy of ambition.' These words have become the semi-official text on which the present secessionist movement bases its propaganda.

During the era of post-war prosperity the nationalists ceased their talk of separation and concentrated on the lesser issues. They coined the term *refrancisation*, to indicate the constant fight for the elimination from French-Canadian culture, institutions and language of every element of English or American origin. Their influence penetrated into many quarters, though their actual numbers were not great. Then came the economic depression. Nationalism received a fresh stimulus, this time much greater than that given by the South African war or the world war. Not only was there renewed talk of war in Europe, which enabled the leaders to evoke the isolationist sentiment in the population in anticipation of another conflict in which they might be called on to take part. There were in addition two new circumstances to add fuel to the nationalist fire. One was the growth of communism, which, though it has little strength in Quebec, has a small but active following in Ontario and the West. Nationalism is seen by the Quebec authorities, both lay and clerical, as a useful counteracting force to the threatening danger from communist propaganda. The other stimulant was the fact that the natural resources and wealth of the province of Quebec, the water-power, forests, mines, large industries and financial institutions, had come to be almost entirely owned and controlled by English-Canadian and American capital. French-

Canadians provide the cheap labour while the English and Americans reap the large profits – and how low those wages are the recent governmental enquiries have startlingly shown. The importance of this economic control was but dimly perceived until the depression taught the public to examine the economic system under which they live.

It is this question of English economic domination that gives the nationalist movement in Quebec its particular form and strength at the present time. In the English parts of Canada the growing popular suspicion and dislike of the big trusts and monopolies that exploit so much of the country's financial and industrial life have given rise to the new radical parties. In French-Canada the same dislike has become allied with the nationalist sentiment. The principal complaint against the Taschereau régime was that it was in hand and glove with the English trusts in Quebec. *Refrancisation* in economic terms means recapturing for French-Canada the control of the sources of wealth that are now in non-French hands. It means a steady policy of lifting the French-Canadian out of his inferior position as hewer of wood and drawer of water for his English masters. As the French have little capital, this can only be done through political action. The power of the state, it is supposed, will be used to curb and eventually to destroy the stranglehold of foreign finance. There are elements here of socialism, but it will be the right-wing socialism of a Mussolini rather than the complete socialism of a Stalin. Italian fascism has had a considerable influence on the thinking in Quebec, and every nationalist is a believer in some form of the corporative state.

There are thus a number of strands that make up the new French-Canadian nationalism. Its general programme may be summed up in the words 'Quebec for the French-Canadians, both economically and politically.' This programme is to be achieved, to use Abbé Groulx's words, 'within Confederation if possible, outside if impossible.' Even if this policy may involve the abandonment of the French minorities outside Quebec, the price is one that many are willing to pay. The Abbé put the case in simple form when he recently told the *Congrès des Jeunesses Patriotes* that 'Quand on ne peut tout sauver, on sauve ce que l'on peut. Et rien ne servirait de périr tous ensemble sous prétexte de s'entraider.'

Necessarily the achievement of a French Catholic state will mean a radical change in the English position in Quebec. A wave of anti-English feeling is steadily mounting, and along with attacks on the English have gone some even more virulent forms of anti-semitism. The Jewish population in Montreal is just sufficiently large to give occasion for violent outbreaks of the fascist type, a number of which have already occurred. The nationalist movement is also anti-democratic, for it has been taught to see in parliamentary democracy not only an English institution but also a party system that sets French-Canadian against French-Canadian. It is becoming aggressively opposed to the toleration of any radical speech or activity, however mild. It is a strongly Catholic movement, most of the parish priests and many of the religious orders, particularly the Jesuits, being its chief supporters. At the opening of the new legislature last October Cardinal Villeneuve was provided with a special throne in the Council Chamber, to symbolise his equality with the representative of the Crown; the Anglican bishop was merely in attendance. In regard to foreign affairs the nationalists are complete isolationists, even those who do not advocate secession being ardent advocates of a policy of neutrality for Canada *vis-à-vis* both the League and the Commonwealth. On domestic issues they stand for a policy of decentralisation, and oppose all suggestions of amending the British North America Act or of strengthening federal powers in any way.

## III SEPARATISM AND ISOLATIONISM

Any attempt to estimate the strength of the nationalist forces at the present time is difficult for an English-Canadian to undertake. Obviously different parts of the programme receive different degrees of support. The out-and-out separatists are a small minority even of those who may be called nationalists. Their principal organ is *La Nation* of Quebec, edited by Paul Bouchard, an ex-Rhodes Scholar, but a number of other newspapers openly preach secession. 'Laurentia' has already been chosen as the name of the new state. The 'long-term' separatists who look for ultimate independence but for the moment are content to work within Confederation are a much larger number. Before the provincial elections of last August several candidates spoke of separatism as an ultimate ideal, but only one, René Chalout, included the plank in his immediate platform. Since the elections, now that the task of defeating the Liberals is complete, the more responsible leaders have been attempting to hold the extreme nationalists in check; Mr Duplessis has appealed to his followers to respect the tradition of racial toleration, while Mr Gouin and even the Abbé Groulx have recently urged that the French-Canadians must prepare themselves by study and education before they can hope to occupy the position that is rightfully theirs. The movement for economic emancipation from the domination of English capital is undoubtedly extremely widespread and will have important repercussions in the near future. The point on which there is the maximum agreement is the isolationist foreign policy; Canada could not take part in another European conflict at the moment without incurring the serious danger of a civil war.

The immediate economic consequences of Quebec nationalism will probably take the form of an attempt to control more closely certain of the large corporations in the province. The electric power companies are likely to be the first to be dealt with. A new Electricity Commission is in existence with wide powers of investigation and control, and there is strong sentiment in favour of municipal ownership of stations. The chief proponent of public ownership of electric power, Dr Hamel of Quebec, was excluded from the Duplessis Cabinet, but he has a large following in the party and may yet force the hands of his chief. The chain stores are also under suspicion; for, besides the fact that they are not French in ownership, the nationalists dislike large-scale organisations and lean toward petty industry and independent retail merchandising. In anticipation of new taxes the biggest oil companies have already abandoned the retail field and have handed over their filling stations to independent operators. Co-operative agricultural associations are favoured by the nationalists, but the genuine co-operative spirit may well find itself handicapped by too much state interference.

Independent of legislative action there is growing up a movement for the *achat chez nous*, designed to make the French-Canadians confine their purchases to their own stores. There is also a steady demand that more French-Canadians should be employed in the big English companies and in the Dominion civil services. But it is difficult to see that economic *refrancisation* can go far unless the Quebec legislature is willing to embark upon public ownership on a large scale, and it is safe to predict that this will not occur, since the Church will oppose any direct attack on the principle of private property, disliking as it would the confiscation of investments of which it holds itself no inconsiderable share. Certainly the talk of creating a 'corporative state,' in which many nationalists profess to see their salvation, is unlikely to achieve anything save the destruction of democracy.

From the wider point of view of Dominion politics the nationalist movement in Quebec is of the greatest importance. Canada's allegiance to the principle of collective security, and still more her participation in any schemes of imperial defence, are rendered that much more difficult. Mr Mackenzie King's non-committal speech at the last League Assembly was received with great approval in the province that supplied him with 54 French Liberals in the last federal elections. French-Canadian opinion supported Italy throughout the Abyssinian incident, just as it sympathises with the Spanish rebels to-day. Any plan to bring in new immigrants to Canada will meet extreme opposition from nationalists who see in the French birth-rate a promise of future domination in the Dominion. Amendments to the British North America Act will be bitterly fought; if the Privy Council does not uphold Mr Bennett's legislation on the present references from the Canadian Supreme Court, the outlook for a national system of industrial regulation is poor. Finally it is quite possible that the old party alignments will be abandoned in Quebec, and that the *Union Nationale* will enter federal politics. It is the expressed desire of the nationalists that French-Canadians should not be divided amongst themselves but should present a united front to the rest of Canada.

To direct the existing feeling in Quebec into constructive channels will require wise statesmanship from the leaders of both races. Unfortunately there is little evidence of such leadership on either side at the moment. French-Canadian liberalism, in the best sense of that word, is temporarily crushed. The voice of the extremist is most frequently heard. Until the clergy are willing to improve the education they give the people, French-Canadians can never hope to possess the technical skill and experience required by modern industry and finance. Yet all attempts to liberalise the education policy of the Catholic School Commission meet with stern opposition from the Church. English-Canadian opinion on its side is only now beginning to awake from the indifference with which it usually treats the movements of thought in Quebec. The English commercial interests, by opposing much needed social legislation, have added to the subjection of the workers and stimulated the very spirit from which they will be the first to suffer. Undoubtedly a prolonged revival of prosperity would ease the present situation, but the momentum already acquired will carry the nationalist movement far before it declines.

# VII

# The Privy Council and Mr. Bennett's 'New Deal' Legislation

*The Conservative Party under Mr Bennett replaced Mr Mackenzie King and the Liberal Party in the general election of 1930. At first the new government reacted to the economic crisis in a typically conservative way: higher tariffs, retrenchment, an attack on the Communist Party, and so on. Then in 1934 Mr Bennett, to the surprise of the country and his own party, suddenly announced a whole set of reforms which earned the name 'New Deal' because of the evident influence of President Roosevelt's policies in the United States (Mr Herridge, Canada's ambassador to Washington, was Mr Bennett's brother-in-law). When Mr King returned to power in 1935 he referred eight of the new statutes* en bloc *to the courts to test their constitutionality. The Privy Council reacted in much the same way as did the American Supreme Court when it first faced the Roosevelt New Deal. The nature of the legislation, and the effects of the judgments on future constitutional interpretation, are considered in these comments.*

From the *Canadian Journal of Economics and Political Science*, 3, 1937, 234-40; with further comments from my article 'The Consequences of the Privy Council Decisions,' in the *Canadian Bar Review*, 15, 1937, 485-92

On January 28, 1937, the Judicial Committee of the Privy Council rendered its decisions upon the constitutionality of eight of Mr Bennett's reform measures.[1] The statutes submitted for judicial review were the Weekly Rest in Industrial Undertakings Act,[2] the Minimum Wages Act,[3] the Limitation of Hours of Work Act,[4] the Natural Products Marketing Act,[5] the Employment and Social Insurance

---

1 [1937] 1 D.L.R., p. 673 *et seq.* Also reported in *Votes and Proceedings of the House of Commons*, Feb. 10, 1937, p. 108.
2 *Statutes of Canada*, 1935, c. 14.
3 *Ibid.*, c. 44.
4 *Ibid.*, c. 63.
5 *Ibid.*, 1934, c. 57, amended 1935, c. 64.

Act,[6] the Farmers' Creditors Arrangement Act,[7] the Dominion Trade and Industry Commission Act,[8] and the new section 498A of the Criminal Code dealing with unfair trade practices.[9] The general character of the legislation was discussed in an earlier volume of this journal;[10] the first three laws were based upon the Draft Conventions of the International Labour Organization dealing with those topics. Taken together the statutes constituted the principal attempt made by the Dominion Parliament to cope with the economic problems disclosed by the world depression.

As a result of the decisions the Weekly Rest in Industrial Undertakings Act, the Limitation of Hours of Work Act, the Minimum Wages Act, the Employment and Social Insurance Act, and the Natural Products Marketing Act were totally invalidated. Every Dominion power invoked in their favour was found to be inadequate. The three ILO Conventions were not treaties falling within the Dominion power under section 132 of the BNA Act or within the residuary clause; the national marketing scheme was not 'regulation of trade and commerce'; the unemployment insurance plan was not a proper use of the residuary clause or of the Dominion taxing power. In fact, all these national issues turned out to be mere matters of property and civil rights in the provinces. On the other hand, the Farmers' Creditors Arrangement Act was upheld as a valid exercise of the Dominion power over Bankruptcy and Insolvency, section 498A of the Criminal Code was considered a proper form of criminal law, and the Dominion Trade and Industry Commission Act was maintained, save for section 14, as being supported by the Dominion power to regulate trade and commerce combined with its powers ancillary to criminal law. The victory for 'provincial rights' was thus not complete, but it substantially destroyed Mr Bennett's attempt at national regulation. More important, however, than the fate of the legislation will be the effect upon the Canadian constitution of the new principles of constitutional law which were enunciated during the course of the judgments.[11]

The three statutes dealing with the weekly day of rest, limitation of hours, and minimum wages were discussed together in the courts, since each of them was a substantial reproduction of a Draft Convention of the International Labour Or-

---

6 *Ibid.*, 1935, c. 38.
7 *Ibid.*, 1934, c. 53, amended 1935, c. 20.
8 *Ibid.*, 1935, c. 59.
9 *Ibid.*, c. 56, s. 9.
10 Vol. I, p. 599.
11 The statutes were submitted to the Supreme Court of Canada on November 5, 1935, on a reference from the Governor-General-in-Council. The decisions were thus based on hypothetical argument and not on concrete cases involving private rights. The distinction, however, though made much of in certain quarters, is of little importance. The time has passed when judgments on abstract questions referred by the executive might be considered as of less binding force than those rendered in the usual manner.

ganization which the Dominion government had ratified and then implemented by legislation. Dominion jurisdiction thus appeared to be supported as part of its power to implement treaties under section 132 of the BNA Act, or alternatively under its general residuary power to make laws for the peace, order, and good government of Canada on matters – like international agreements – not assigned to the provinces. The Supreme Court judges divided equally on the question of validity,[12] the Chief Justice and Davis and Kerwin JJ upholding the Dominion jurisdiction, while Crocket J with the two Quebec judges, Rinfret and Cannon JJ, took the opposite view. If there had been no appeal to the Privy Council, the statutes would have remained in force. The Privy Council ruled the statutes *ultra vires* the Dominion. This decision is, therefore, another example of the way in which the Privy Council has compelled the adoption in Canada of an interpretation of the constitution unfavourable to a strong central government.

The new view of the treaty-making power is of such fundamental importance for the future development of Canada's international relations that it may be analysed in some detail here. Sir Lyman Duff CJ had based the Dominion jurisdiction to implement the conventions on two grounds. First, he pointed out that section 132 of the BNA Act gives the Dominion an exclusive jurisdiction for the purpose of giving effect to any treaty obligation imposed upon Canada, or any one of the provinces, by force of a treaty between the British Empire and a foreign country. Examples of the use of this jurisdiction are to be seen in the statutes created to give effect to the International Waterways Treaty of 1909,[13] to the Anglo-Japanese Treaty of 1913,[14] and to the Convention Relating to the Regulation of Aerial Navigation of 1922.[15] All these Dominion statutes implemented treaties coming within section 132, and all of them interfered with property and civil rights in the provinces. The two last-named were upheld by the Privy Council.[16] The Treaty of Versailles, he argued, is another such 'British Empire' treaty; this was given legislative effect in Canada by Dominion statute;[17] article 405 of the Treaty imposes an obligation on Canada to implement conventions adopted by the International Labour Organization. Moreover, in one instance, Dominion legislation based on a purely Canadian convention, which was not an Empire treaty and which also trenched upon property and civil rights, was upheld by the Privy Council.[18] These decisions seemed to make it clear that the provinces have

12 [1936] S.C.R. 461.
13 1911, 1–2 Geo. V, c. 28.
14 1913, 3–4 Geo. V, c. 27.
15 R.S.C. 1927, c. 3.
16 *Attorney-General for British Columbia* v. *Attorney-General for Canada*, [1924] A.C. 203; *Re Aerial Navigation*, [1932] A.C. 54.
17 Treaties of Peace Act, 1919, 10 Geo. V, c. 30.
18 *Re Regulation and Control of Radio Communication*, [1932] A.C. 304.

no power to legislate for the purposes of giving effect to any international agreement to which Canada is a party, whether it be a treaty or a convention. Secondly, even if these previous holdings did not apply, Canada has now acquired the status of an international unit as a result of the constitutional development of the last thirty years; she has power to enter into international agreements on her own authority; all such arrangements are within the exclusive competence of the Dominion whose jurisdiction over treaties not falling within section 132 is co-ordinate with those which do.

This argument was rejected by the Privy Council. The narrower view, put forward by the three opposing judges in the Supreme Court, was adopted. Lord Atkin, speaking for the Judicial Committee,[19] held that the obligations of Canada in regard to the subject matter of the conventions did not arise under the Treaty of Versailles, but only under the conventions themselves; such obligations were, therefore, not based on an Empire treaty covered by section 132. While Canadian treaties and conventions were not thought of in 1867, 'it is impossible to strain the Section (132) so as to cover the uncontemplated event.' It was therefore necessary to test the statutes by the provisions of sections 91 and 92 of the BNA Act, and when these were examined the only section dealing with the subject matter of the conventions was found to be 'Property and Civil Rights in the Province,' a field of provincial jurisdiction. No further legislative competence has been obtained by the Dominion from its accession to international status, and neither the *Aeronautics Case* nor the *Radio Case* affords a warrant for holding that legislation to perform a Canadian treaty is exclusively within the Dominion legislative power. The Dominion cannot 'merely by making promises to foreign countries,' clothe itself with legislative authority which it did not possess originally, and thus invade the provincial domain.[20] Nor were the statutes valid under the general residuary power over matters relating to the peace, order, and good government of Canada, since such legislation is justified only in 'some extraordinary peril to the national life of Canada,' in some 'abnormal circumstances' or 'epidemic of pestilence' [*sic*], and apparently the facts of the present case were very far from these conditions. The only way in which Canadian treaties dealing with provincial classes of subjects can be implemented is by 'co-operation between the Dominion and the Provinces.'

There is no room here to consider the legal merits of this interpretation of the BNA Act, nor to inquire why the doctrine of 'aspects' was totally disregarded, why the argument from possible abuse of Dominion power was accepted when the same argument used to restrain provincial power has invariably failed, why a narrow and technical interpretation of the Act was preferred to the more liberal one which has prevailed in certain recent cases, and why the judicial mentality

19 [1937] 1 D.L.R., pp. 673 ff.
20 This argument, it is scarcely necessary to point out, completely begs the question.

does not consider the world economic depression to be an 'abnormal circumstance.'[21] The effect of the interpretation is reasonably clear. There are now three categories of treaties or conventions which must be distinguished. First, 'Empire Treaties' falling under section 132: Dominion legislation implementing these is fully competent no matter how much it interferes with property and civil rights. Second, Canadian treaties or conventions whose subject matter falls within a specified head of section 91 (such as trade and commerce) or at least outside section 92 (like the Radio Convention): Dominion legislation implementing these is also valid though it interfere with property and civil rights. Third, treaties or conventions whose subject matter falls within the provincial powers enumerated in section 92: here the implementing of the treaty requires provincial legislation, and it may be that the negotiating of the treaty requires provincial executive action as well, since the Privy Council expressly refused to decide the question whether the Dominion had any authority even to perform the executive act of entering into the treaty.[22] As party to a British Empire treaty Canada is therefore a unitary state;[23] as an independent country she is composed of nine (or is it ten?) sovereign states whose assent is required before the obligations of certain treaties can be fully performed. The logical political consequence of this is that plenipotentiaries from the provinces will have to attend at the negotiating of treaties of this third category in order to insure their adoption and enforcement; which is equivalent to saying that Canada is practically incompetent to make any such treaties at all. Moreover, no one but the courts will be able to tell with certainty to what category a particular treaty belongs, and this, of course, cannot be decided until after the treaty is made. The only certainty lies in reverting to colonial status and never venturing beyond the imperial orbit; the fruits of independence are disunity and decentralization. The law of the Canadian constitution has now degenerated into this welter of confusion.

Having come to these conclusions on the major questions involved in the appeals, the Privy Council disposed of the other questions in short order. The Employment and Social Insurance Act had established a Dominion Commission with power to administer an employment service and an insurance fund collected from compulsory contributions by employees and workers. The Act was not supported

21 A discussion by various authors of these and other legal questions involved will be found in the *Canadian Bar Review* for 1937.
22 [1937] 1 D.L.R., p. 679. The provinces contended that the Dominion had no such power.
23 Lord Atkin (*ibid.*, p. 680) pointed out the distinction between 'legislative powers given to the Dominion to perform obligations imposed upon Canada as part of the Empire by an Imperial executive responsible to and controlled by the Imperial Parliament, and the legislative power of the Dominion to perform obligations created by the Dominion executive responsible to and controlled by the Dominion Parliament.' The distinction shows how far the law of the constitution is out of line with political realities, and with the spirit of the Balfour declaration of 1926.

by any treaty, but Duff CJ and Davis J in the Supreme Court had found it valid on the ground that the Dominion was empowered to raise money by any mode or system of taxation, and had full jurisdiction over the public debt and property; it might therefore, they held, dispose of its moneys for unemployment benefits in conformity with the directions of Parliament. The four other judges in the Supreme Court, however, ruled the Act invalid as mere colourable legislation, in pith and substance dealing with the contract of employment, insurance, and health matters, which are of provincial concern, and attempting to give validity to its provisions by reference to the taxing power. Nor was the Act, in the view of the majority, justified either as a regulation of trade and commerce or as part of the residuary clause. In these contentions the Privy Council agreed. Lord Atkin pointed out that this was not emergency legislation since it was intended to be permanent, and he remarked that although the Dominion has collected by means of taxation a fund, 'it by no means follows that any legislation which disposes of it is necessarily within Dominion competence.'[24] ...

## FURTHER COMMENTS

The decisions of the Judicial Committee on Mr Bennett's 'new deal' statutes will thus have very grave and far-reaching consequences ...

In the first place, the law of the Canadian constitution is affected in a number of essential respects, of which the following are the most important:
1. Canada ceases to be a single nation in the conduct of her international relations. This fact is without question the most serious consequence of the decisions. In a real sense it stultifies the whole development of Dominion status since the War. The Fathers of Confederation established Canadian unity in face of the outside world by incorporating section 132 into the British North America Act. The Dominion Parliament was given full power to give legislative effect to obligations imposed upon Canada or any province, arising under treaties between 'the Empire and foreign countries.' As this was the only kind of treaty possible at that time, it meant that the Dominion Parliament originally had jurisdiction over all international treaties relating to Canada, without restriction. No safeguards whatever were written into the Act for the protection of 'property and civil rights in the provinces' from invasion by such treaty arrangements, and the whole scheme of the Act negatives any such idea. Every other enumerated Dominion power carries with it, by virtue of the concluding paragraph of section 91, an authorized right of interference with provincial powers, even in matters merely ancillary to the enumerated head: it is scarcely to be wondered at that the Act did not place international treaties on a lower footing. The treaty-making power, for example, is at least as much a matter of national importance as Bankruptcy or Bills of Ex-

24 *Ibid.*, p. 687.

change, both of which enable the Dominion to trench upon property and civil rights. But by the interpretation now given to section 132, narrowly restricting the category of 'Empire' treaty to those treaties which are entered into on behalf of the whole Empire,[1] there has come into existence a new category of 'Canadian treaties,' apparently not provided for in the original Act. These treaties are henceforth to be dealt with quite differently from Empire treaties. The implementing of Canadian treaties is to be distributed between the Dominion and the provinces in accordance with the current judicial idea as to what is the true nature of the subject matter of the treaty. Section 92 of the British North America Act, enumerating the provincial powers, has thus a new subsection added to it, namely 'The implementing by legislation of treaties between Canada and foreign countries relating to property and civil rights in the provinces.'

Two important questions of law spring to mind as a result of this holding. The first is, Who can actually make or create the Canadian treaty or convention relating to property and civil rights? Is it the Dominion executive or is it the provincial executive? The provinces went so far as to contend in this recent reference that the Dominion executive had no authority even to enter into the Convention. In the Supreme Court Duff CJ, speaking also for Davis and Kerwin JJ, considered the Dominion competent both to create and to implement the conventions;[2] Rinfret J was of the opinion that a foreign obligation affecting matters of provincial jurisdiction 'should not be *created* or entered into before the provinces have given their consent thereto,'[3] thus, apparently, conceding the Dominion executive authority provided there has been prior authorization from the provinces; Cannon J confused the term 'ratification' with 'implementing' and is obscure on the point, though clearly leaning to the provincial point of view;[4] Crocket J agreed with the Chief Justice.[5] The majority of the Supreme Court was thus in favour of Dominion executive authority. But the Privy Council expressly refrained from answering the question,[6] which thus remains open. So long as this fundamental issue is in doubt, we do not know whether the Dominion has a right to have its representatives even go so far as to conclude negotiations with a foreign government with regard to any proposed treaty or convention, until its subject matter has been properly classified. Executive authority may be divided in

---

1 Actually the Privy Council has not yet defined what an 'Empire' treaty is. The decisions hitherto have merely decided that neither the Radio Convention nor the ILO Conventions fall within that category.
2 [1936] S.C.R. at p. 495.
3 *Ibid.*, at p. 511. Italics mine.
4 *Ibid.*, at p. 520.
5 *Ibid.*, at p. 535.
6 [1937] A.C. at p. 348; [1937] 1 D.L.R. at p. 679.

the same way as legislative jurisdiction, and we may yet live to see the provinces negotiating treaties on their own initiative. There are two possible views: either the provinces enter into and implement their own treaties, or else the Dominion executive enters into all treaties and the provinces implement those which relate to classes of subjects falling within section 92. On either interpretation, the conduct of Canada's foreign relations will henceforth be impossibly handicapped; the Dominion Cabinet and Parliament will always be in doubt as to their jurisdiction save in those increasingly rare cases when the Imperial Crown enters into treaties binding the whole Empire.

The second unanswered question is whether or not the decisions as to the ILO conventions would be applicable to a formal treaty or convention affecting Canada alone but entered into by the Imperial Crown acting – as it must always now act in such cases – on the advice of its Canadian Ministers. Such a treaty, for instance, as the Halibut Treaty of 1923. Mr Cahan, speaking in the House of Commons, expressed the opinion that the present decisions should be restricted to the particular class of convention under consideration[7] – conventions which, like the Washington agreements discussed in 1925,[8] are mere agreements between governments and not really treaties in the full sense. Crocket J appeared willing to concede this difference,[9] but the language of the Privy Council, while not expressly directed to the point, is full of loose phrases indicating that the acquisition of dominion status does not permit of any enlargement of Dominion jurisdiction, and that legislation in regard to Canadian treaties may require exercise of the 'totality of powers,' Dominion and provincial. No decision so far rendered, however, precludes the possibility that the words 'Empire treaty,' as used in section 132 of the British North America Act, may be extended, as has been suggested by Dean MacDonald and others,[10] to include a treaty between the Crown acting on behalf of Canada and the head of a foreign state. If this view were to prove correct, some of the damage done by the recent decisions would be overcome. To secure this result all we need ask from the Privy Council would be a further decision which need not even be so inconsistent with the present holdings as these latter are with the *Radio Case*.

2. A further legal consequence of the cases under discussion is that they compel us to return to Lord Haldane's conception of the 'peace, order and good government' clause as giving the Dominion merely an emergency power to be used in

7 House of Commons Debates April 5th, 1937, (unrevised edition), pp. 2775, 2778.
8 *In re Hours of Labour*, [1925] S.C.R. 505.
9 [1936] S.C.R. at p. 523.
10 V.C. MacDonald, *Canada's Power to Perform Treaty Obligations* (1933), 11 Can. Bar Rev. pp. 581, 664. See also Brooke Claxton, *Social Reform and the Constitution*, Canadian Journal of Economics and Political Science, Vol. I at p. 413 ff.

the direst circumstances. We can no longer follow the more liberal lead given in the *Aeronautics* and *Radio Cases* in regard to the residuary clause. No more striking example of judicial legislation can be found than this interpretation of section 91 of the British North America Act. It has had the effect of giving us a constitution exactly the opposite, in one vital respect, of that which we actually adopted in 1867. The United States constitution, by amendment 10, declares that 'The powers not delegated to the United States by the Constitution, nor prohibited by it to the States, are reserved to the states respectively, or to the people.'

The residue of unspecified powers was thus withheld from the federal legislature and reserved for the states or the people. The Fathers of our Confederation closely studied the American model, and stated clearly that they wished to avoid the great evil of 'states' rights' existing in the Union. As Sir John Macdonald put it,

Here we have adopted a different system. We have strengthened the general government. We have given the legislature all the great subjects of legislation. We have conferred on them, *not only specifically and in detail all the powers which are incident to sovereignty, but we have expressly declared that all subjects of general interest not distinctly and exclusively conferred upon the local governments and local legislatures, shall be conferred upon the general government and legislature.* We have thus avoided that great source of weakness which has been the cause of the disruption of the United States. [11]

In Canada the federal legislature was given a residue of matters of general interest, just as the provinces have a residue over matters 'of a merely local or private nature in the province.' Subjects unspecified in 1867 were intended to be distributed in future between the provinces or the Dominion in accordance with the test of national importance, regardless of whether property and civil rights were 'trenched upon' or not. The concluding paragraph of section 91 was obviously intended to apply to every subject specified in 91, including the general power of the residuary clause, which, though without a magic number opposite it (as it had in the Quebec Resolutions, No. 37 of Resolution 29), is nevertheless numbered amongst Dominion powers. *Russell's Case* was undoubtedly correct in its law if not on its facts. But today under the new interpretation, the Dominion residuary clause, while kept alive verbally by courtesy, is virtually non-existent, and the residue of power throughout Canada, in matters of national as well as of local importance, even in the midst of an emergency as great as that which befell us between 1929 and 1935, belongs exclusively to the provinces. For it may be contended that an emergency power which the world economic crisis does not

11 Confederation Debates, p. 33. Italics mine.

justify using is no power at all. For all practical purposes our federal legislature exercises none but enumerated powers, just as does the American Congress. Lord Haldane, having forced our constitution into the American mould, adopted his theory of 'implied' emergency powers, which he elaborated in the *Fort Frances Case*,[12] and which he undoubtedly picked up from American constitutional law. His idea of an expanding power in time of war is to be found in the American case of *Hamilton* v. *Kentucky Distilleries*.[13] That which the builders rejected has indeed become the corner stone. A well-balanced distribution of sovereignty between Dominion and provinces, giving to each residuary as well as specified powers, which was carefully planned by Canadian statesmen knowing the needs of the country, has been scrapped for an alternative theory of a severely limited Dominion but an unlimited provincial residue. None but foreign judges ignorant of the Canadian environment and none too well versed in Canadian constitutional law could have caused this constitutional revolution.

3. Another important consequence of these holdings is the doubt they cast upon the possibility of Dominion-Provincial co-operation as an escape from constitutional difficulties. Hitherto it has been thought that whatever problem there might be with regard to legislative jurisdiction, the difficulty could be overcome by joint action by all the legislatures. If the Dominion added all its powers to those already possessed by the provinces, surely, it seemed, anything and everything might be accomplished. On several occasions the Privy Council and the Supreme Court of Canada have suggested that this is a proper method of procedure. In the very decisions under review Duff CJ, discussing the Natural Products Marketing Act, quoted from the judgment in the *Board of Commerce Case*[14] and said that such a scheme of regulation as set up by the Marketing Boards was not practicable 'without the co-operation of the provincial legislatures';[15] while the Privy Council tempered their destruction of the Dominion treaty-making power with the helpful reminder that 'It must not be thought that the result of this decision is that Canada is incompetent to legislate in performance of treaty obligations. In totality of legislative powers, Dominion and Provincial together, she is fully equipped.'[16]

Nevertheless, in the judgment on the Marketing Act in the Supreme Court there was no consideration whatever of the fact that every province in Canada had co-operated with the Dominion in setting up Marketing Boards, and had en-

12 [1923] A.C. 695, 703.
13 251 U.S. 146, cited in the *Fort Frances Case, supra*, at p. 707.
14 [1922] 1 A.C. 191 at p. 201.
15 *Reference re Natural Products Marketing Act*, [1936] S.C.R. at p. 426.
16 *Re Weekly Rest in Industrial Undertakings Act, etc.*, [1937] A.C. at pp. 353–354;
   [1937] 1 D.L.R. at p. 683.

acted special legislation to provide for this co-operation. Ten legislatures in Canada had acted to attain an end unanimously desired, yet the key-statute was declared *ultra vires* and the whole structure destroyed. The Dominion Act by section 12 provided that if any parts of the Act were *ultra vires*, none of the other provisions should be inoperative on that account, but should be considered as separate enactments; and the provincial statutes were intended to supply any legislative power lacking in the Dominion.[17] In the Privy Council Lord Atkin, after repeating the empty formula that 'satisfactory results' for both Dominion and Provinces 'can only be obtained by co-operation,' went on to warn that 'the legislation will have to be very carefully framed, and will not be achieved by either party leaving its own sphere and encroaching upon that of the other. In the present case their Lordships are unable to support the Dominion legislation as it stands. They will therefore humbly advise His Majesty that this appeal should be dismissed.'[18]

Thus the courts take the view that even where there is complete co-operation between all Canadian legislatures, each one contributing its share of legislative capacity, still the scheme thus established will be destroyed, if, perchance, one legislature has made a slip in the wording of its contributory statute and has in fact included some subject matter beyond its jurisdiction. Instead of considering that this mistake is rectified by the other supporting statutes, it may be looked upon as fatal. So co-operation between the Dominion and the provinces, as in the case of the marketing legislation, may be of no use whatever in the way of overcoming constitutional difficulties, and leaves the courts as free as before to set aside legislation of which they disapprove. This legalistic straining at technicalities will do little to enhance the prestige of the courts. The Dominion Marketing Act was not an isolated statute, but was part of a national scheme and should have been interpreted as such.

Turning from the legal to the economic consequences of the decisions, it is obvious that they leave this country even more helpless than she was in 1929 to deal with the problems created by a changing economic system. The depression came, revealing gross injustices and inefficiencies in the body economic; the Stevens Committee and the Royal Commission on Price Spreads disclosed evils crying out for remedy; a considerable attempt was made to provide a system of controls and palliatives on a national scale. This attempt has failed because the constitution could not, in the hands of the judiciary at the moment interpreting it, adapt itself to the new requirements. The situation resembles that existing in

17 See Statutes of P.E.I., 1934, c. 17; New Brunswick, 1935, c. 44; Nova Scotia, 1934, c. 58; Quebec, 1934, c. 24; Ontario, 1934, c. 38; Manitoba, 1934, c. 90; Saskatchewan, 1934, c. 62; Alberta, 1934, c. 34; British Columbia, 1934, c. 38.
18 *Re Natural Products Marketing Act*, [1937] A.C. at p. 389; [1937] 1 D.L.R. at p. 695.

the United States before Mr Roosevelt's drive to modernize the Supreme Court caused its sudden change of attitude on the Wagner Labour Relations Act. Canada's 'new deal' will have to come from the federal authorities or not at all, and the net result of the Canadian constitutional developments, culminating in the decisions under review, has been very greatly to weaken the central government, and so to postpone indefinitely any further attempts at government regulation of the economy in the interests of stability and social security. If the whole trend of world developments is wrong and all government interference in economic matters is an obstacle to progress, then Canada will benefit from her constitutional impasse, but should the reverse be true, should the need of the hour be increasingly to bring an intelligent and conscious direction to economic affairs, then Canada has suffered a national set-back of grievous proportions. A federal government that cannot concern itself with questions of wages and hours and unemployment[19] in industry, whose attempts at the regulation of trade and commerce are consistently thwarted, which has no power to join its sister nations in the establishment of world living standards, and which cannot even feel on sure ground when by some political miracle it is supported in a legislative scheme by all the provinces, is a government wholly unable to direct and to control our economic development.

The history of recent cases dealing with the control of trade and commerce in Canada shows a fairly consistent attitude in the courts against control, an attitude which overrides any feeling for or against provincial autonomy. The only exception is the evolution of the criminal law in respect of combines, where for some unexplained reason a liberal interpretation has recently prevailed. Dominion control over the grain trade was successfully attacked in *King* v. *Eastern Terminal Elevators*,[20] while a provincial attempt at a compulsory wheat pool was similarly held *ultra vires*.[21] A provincial marketing scheme was set aside as interfering with interprovincial trade and commerce in the *Lawson Case*,[22] and now the Dominion Marketing act is destroyed because it interferes with provincial trade. A provincial attempt to regulate the production and prevent wastage of gas and oil in the Turner Valley fields was frustrated.[23] It would seem that even without special mention in the British North America Act, the doctrines of *laissez-faire* are in practice receiving ample protection from the courts.

19 Actually the immediate consequence of setting aside the Employment and Social Insurance Act is to prevent the substitution of 'contributory' unemployment insurance for the present noncontributory scheme which we call the dole.
20 [1925] S.C.R. 434.
21 *In re Grain Marketing Act*, [1931] 2 W.W.R. 146.
22 [1931] S.C.R. 357.
23 *Spooner Oils* v. *Turner Valley Gas Conservation Board*, [1933] S.C.R. 629.

# VIII

# Canada's Future in the British Commonwealth

*The 1930s not only made Canadians question many of their internal political and economic assumptions, but also made them re-assess their relations to the new Commonwealth whose basis was laid in the Statute of Westminster of 1931.*
From *Foreign Affairs*, 1937, 429–42

Preparations are under way for another meeting of the Imperial Conference, to take place in London while representatives from the Dominions are gathered for the coronation of George VI. This will be the first full and official meeting of the Conference since 1930[1] and the thirteenth since the original Colonial Conference was summoned to London in 1887. In view of the disturbed condition of the world and the breakdown of the League, questions of foreign policy and defense are certain to have first place on the agenda. Amid the enthusiasm stimulated by the Coronation, and faced with the threat of war, the older school of imperialists, well represented in the British Government, are likely to bring strong pressure to persuade the Dominions to tie their foreign policy more closely to that of Great Britain and to share in schemes for imperial defense. How will the Canadian delegates respond to these suggestions? What attitude will they adopt toward the various other topics that will come up for discussion? These questions are giving rise to much speculation in Canada, and in certain quarters at least to no little apprehension. For Canadians at present have very strong and very divided opinions on the subject of Canada's obligations toward the Commonwealth, and there is great uncertainty regarding the stand which the Dominion Government proposes to take.

The coming Imperial Conference will differ from all its predecessors in that for the first time the Dominions will meet on terms of legal equality with Great

1 The Imperial Economic Conference at Ottawa in 1932 discussed commercial matters only; the British Commonwealth Relations Conference at Toronto in 1933 was entirely unofficial.

Britain. The last two meetings of the Conference, held in 1926 and 1930, were primarily concerned with evolving a new political theory for the Commonwealth, and in bringing the law of the constitution into harmony with that theory. These aims have now been accomplished. The principle of equality of status and complete autonomy for the component parts of the Commonwealth in every aspect of their domestic and external affairs was enunciated in the Balfour Declaration of 1926. It became legally a fact, in so far as legislative capacity is concerned, through the adoption of the Statute of Westminster in 1931. Certain developments since then have rounded out the work of the last Conferences and clarified the meaning of the formal texts. The Union of South Africa, by legislation adopted in 1934,[2] established full internal control not only over its own constitution but also over the methods by which the royal assent may be given to statutes and other documents, thus rendering possible independent action by the Union probably even on matters of peace and war. The Irish Free State successfully contended before the Privy Council its right to disregard the restrictions imposed in the Treaty of 1922,[3] and it also has virtually full internal control over the exercise of the royal prerogative in foreign affairs. Canada's power to prevent appeals from its courts to the Privy Council by purely Canadian legislation has been upheld,[4] and though her capacity to give legislative effect to treaties has been grievously weakened by the recent decision of the Privy Council with regard to Mr Bennett's 'new deal' legislation, the power to negotiate all treaties short of those relating to separate peace and war remains somewhere in the Dominion.

The events surrounding the abdication of Edward VIII, while in one sense indicating the unity of the Commonwealth, also demonstrated the equality of status enjoyed by the Dominions, since their consent had to be obtained before the Abdication Act could be passed by the British Parliament; and they have since adopted their own Abdication Acts into the bargain. Those portions of the constitutional unity of the former British Empire which remain – and they are not inconsiderable – rest clearly on the voluntary agreement of the Dominions to retain them rather than on the absence of Dominion capacity to dispose of them. This is true even of Canada's present inability to make her own declarations of war and peace. She has not yet acquired a separate right to control these vital matters, and so in this respect is far from equality with Great Britain; yet it would appear that she could at any time follow the example of South Africa and obtain the power by making the necessary constitutional changes. In any case, the right of every Dominion to decide how far it will participate in a British war has been fully recognized by previous Conferences. The coming Imperial Confer-

2 Status of Union Act, and Royal Executive Functions and Seals Act.
3 *Moore* v. *Attorney-General for the Irish Free State*, 1935 Appeal Cases, 484.
4 *British Coal Corporation* v. *The King*, 1935 Appeal Cases, 500.

ence, then, which ought now to be renamed the 'Commonwealth Conference,'[5] will represent nations more legally independent of one another, more free to adopt separate courses of action, than at any time in their history.

These considerations alone would suffice to give the approaching meeting a special significance. It will disclose to what extent the new freedom of the Dominions will be exercised. But there is another factor which will make the Conference of particular importance, not only to the members of the Commonwealth but also to the world at large. The modern idea of the Commonwealth was evolved along with the new concepts of international behavior which found embodiment in the League of Nations. The separate Dominion membership in the League heralded the constitutional changes in the Empire. Dominion autonomy came to maturity under the aegis of Geneva, and the loosening of the legal bonds with Great Britain was peacefully arranged in a world that subscribed to the idea of collective security. If it had not been possible for the Dominions to look to the alternative protection of the League in place of the weakening Imperial guarantees, their constitutional evolution might have been very different. Today the League is powerless. Collective security can scarcely be termed even a remote ideal.

How will this change affect the policies of the Dominions? Will it drive them to seek an old security by strengthening the defenses of the Empire, thus creating a military unity to replace the constitutional autonomy? Or will they keep clear of the political implications of such a policy and look to new regional groupings dictated more by geography than sentiment? And what possibility is there of the Commonwealth nations coming forward as champions of a revivified League? These are the basic questions of the forthcoming Conference. Other matters of lesser importance, such as trade agreements, immigration, communications and shipping, will doubtless receive their share of attention. But it is the decisions on the larger political issues, whether these decisions be express or tacit, which will be of prime importance in shaping the Commonwealth's future development.

To show how completely the outlook has changed even since the informal British Commonwealth Relations Conference met in 1933, we may cite a portion of the report of the special sub-committee appointed by that Conference to go into the question of a Dominion's right to neutrality in the event of a war involving Great Britain. The all-important question was disposed of in the following manner:

It seems to us academic and unprofitable to consider legal constitutional difficulties which might arise if there were no Covenant and no Kellogg Pact. The prin-

---

5 The 'Colonial' Conference became the 'Imperial' Conference in 1907; since the Statute of Westminster, the Imperial Conference would more properly be called the 'Commonwealth' Conference.

ciples of freedom and coöperation and 'agreed anomalies' on which the Commonwealth is based, may create difficulties in many fields and we feel, therefore, that it would serve no useful purpose to try and foresee problems in one field, that of war, which we are entitled to hope are never likely to arise, and to seek to apply to them legal conceptions as to war and neutrality appropriate to the pre-League world.

Today the 'academic' question of neutrality is uppermost in the minds of Canadians, and the 'legal conceptions as to war and neutrality appropriate to the pre-League world' are precisely the ones in the light of which the obligations of the members of the Commonwealth must now be decided.

Thus the Canadian delegates to London, like those from the other Dominions, will be faced with decisions of the greatest moment. But unlike some of their colleagues, the Canadians will labor under the added difficulty of having to represent an extremely divided public opinion at home. In view of the racial and religious composition of the Canadian population, and the conflicting economic interests of different sections of the country, this division is scarcely surprising. No mistake is more common, even among Canadians, than to talk about 'Canada' as though the term represented a single people with well-defined political allegiances. Because Canadians have a white skin and a parliamentary system of government they are assumed to be a 'British' people with a natural tendency to take a British view of world affairs. An examination of the facts will give a different impression. Some 30 percent of the people are French-Canadian, and fully another 20 percent have non-British origins. At the 1931 census the Canadians of British descent amounted to only 51.8 percent of the population, and the non-British, whose natural increase is greater, are almost certainly in the majority today. In other words, Canada has ceased already to be racially British. Further, no less than 41 percent of the people in Canada are Roman Catholic (as against 6 percent in Great Britain). The fact has an increasing political significance in a world where international conflicts are taking on more and more the aspects of wars of religion. And while some 'assimilation' (which to the British-Canadian means 'anglicization') of the foreigners has taken place, while they may speak English, or a variant of it, and are accustomed to a holiday on Empire Day and the King's birthday, these factors are more than offset by the growing North American character of the political thinking of the Dominion, especially in those areas far removed from contact with any country save the United States. These racial and religious diversities are additional to the economic and geographic factors which have always divided Canada into sections, setting the industrial East against the agricultural West, and cutting off the St Lawrence Valley from the Prairies and separating the Pacific seaboard from both.[6]

6 See further on this point, 'The Social and Economic Bases of Canadian Foreign Policy,' by Professor A.R.M. Lower, in 'Canada, The Empire and the League,' Nelson, 1936, p. 100.

The inescapable social facts here briefly indicated produce conflicting attitudes within Canada. And it is her internal conflicts, not any nastiness of temperament in the Canadians, which chiefly explains why the Dominion has always been so lukewarm toward proposals for closer Imperial coöperation. Canada's real difficulty is not how to coöperate with other members of the Commonwealth, but how to secure coöperation within herself. The constitutional evolution within the Dominion during the past forty years has accentuated the internal divisions. The Privy Council, through its interpretations of the British North America Act, has steadily whittled away the authority of the federal parliament, and exaggerated, against all reason, that of the provincial legislatures; the recent decisions on Mr Bennett's legislation are the most destructive of all, virtually undoing all the work of nation-building that has gone on since the World War. The consequence is that national unity is still further delayed and both Commonwealth and international coöperation are rendered more difficult. The Privy Council has been an important factor in weakening the Imperial sentiment in Canada.

Today there are at least four important groups of Canadian opinion on foreign policy. There are, first, the pure nationalists or isolationists, who argue that as Canada has no enemies and is under no conceivable threat of invasion she should keep clear of all entanglements in the Empire, the League, or elsewhere, and devote herself to the solution of her own internal problems. The second group, closely allied in sentiment, would welcome isolation from European commitments, but would willingly see Canada join the Pan American Union in an attempt to create a regional system of security in the Americas. It is safe to say that all French-Canadians belong to one or other of these two groups of thought, as well as a great preponderance of the 20 percent of the population who are neither of French nor British origin, and a fair proportion – greatly increased in the past two years – of the Canadians of British descent. Thus a substantial majority of Canadian citizens would almost certainly be 'North American' in the prevailing temper of the country, and though they have no desire to see the British connection broken, some cause or ideal greater than mere Commonwealth solidarity would be needed to make them support the idea of active participation in European affairs. Such a cause was felt to exist in the Italo-Abyssinian affair, and the prompt application of sanctions by Mr King undoubtedly met with general approval in Canada outside Quebec; but even then the isolationist sentiment reappeared suddenly with the Government's repudiation of Dr Riddell's suggestion of the oil sanction. In the absence of a strong League and collective international action, there probably is no cause for which a preponderant number of Canadians would be willing to go to war in Europe. Certainly another appeal to save democracy would be a doubtful rallying cry.

The other two schools of opinion are still influential in Canada though their numbers are declining. One consists of the 'imperialists,' the other of League of

Nations supporters. The imperialists are still heard to say that the British Empire is the strongest bulwark of world peace, and that Canada should stand ready to answer the call of the motherland in every emergency. They want closer ties with Great Britain generally, large expenditures on Canadian defense, and more British immigrants. Mr J.W. Dafoe has recently said that this old type of imperialism 'has almost completely vanished from the minds of the people of Canada' in the years since the World War.[7] This is probably an over-statement, though it is true that the process is going steadily on. The imperialists usually occupy the more dignified positions in church and state and thus sound more numerous than they actually are. No one would deny the reality of the pro-British sentiment in Canada; but it is more and more becoming a respect for certain ideals, institutions and forms of government, and it is ceasing to include either a blind faith in the continual rightness of England's foreign policy or a tacit assumption that the Commonwealth constitutes an offensive-defensive alliance. The Englishman may see that his frontier is on the Rhine; the Canadian finds it a little difficult to believe that his is also. From this position it is only a step to the demand for the right to neutrality. Similarly, the fourth block of opinion in Canada, composed of those who believe in collective security, is important because it has representation in responsible quarters. The members of this group hope against hope that some turn of affairs may restore the prestige of the League and make possible a revival of the collective system, to which they would want to see Canada give full support. Should such a revival occur, public sympathy for the League would revive with it; but at the moment there are no signs of either event.

These groups of opinion are not always mutually exclusive, and their relative strengths vary with changes in the international situation. Only present tendencies can be analyzed; future alignments cannot be forecast too precisely. This much seems clear, however. French-Canadian opinion is steadily nationalist; most of the other Canadian opinion appears to fluctuate between support of the collective system and some form of isolationist policy. The true imperialist fares badly. Recent political changes, both in the international and in the domestic sphere, have tended to move public opinion rapidly toward isolation. The principal factor, influencing especially the English-Canadians, has been the foreign policy followed by the National Government in Great Britain since 1931. Whether the Canadian interpretation of that policy be correct need not be argued; in these matters it is not the truth of the opinion, but its acceptance, which counts. Briefly, many Canadians feel that the National Government betrayed the principles of the League over Manchuria, throwing away the chance of coöperation with the United States;[8] that its sudden use of the League in the Abyssinian incident was

---

7 *Foreign Affairs*, January 1936, p. 298.
8 The Canadian delegate at Geneva supported the British *laissez-faire* policy at the time, but his action was severely criticized on his return to Canada.

mere support of the traditional imperialist policy of protecting the sea route to the East, and not at all a defense of the Covenant, of international law or of weaker member states – the Hoare-Laval treaty being an unexpectedly abrupt dropping of the disguise; that the subsequent day-by-day conduct of British foreign relations, almost without regard to Geneva, shows an absence of vision and leadership and a frank preference for office politics of the old type; and that a government like that now in office in London will simply try to use the Commonwealth as a supplier of men and munitions for the inevitable and futile war that its policy will produce. This belief has driven many former imperialists, and many more of the League supporters, into the isolationist camp.

Other events, different in kind, have had similar consequences. The successful working of the new Reciprocity Treaty with the United States, the reëlection of President Roosevelt on a progressive program, the recent and widely publicized Pan American meeting at Buenos Aires, have convinced many Canadians that their natural and proper affiliations lie more in the Americas than in Europe. The old fear of absorption by the United States seems completely to have disappeared from the Canadian mind, due partly, no doubt, to the stronger national consciousness found in Canada today as a result of the ending of the colonial status, and partly to a greater belief in the absence of any desire for expansion in the minds of people in the United States. Canada is ceasing to feel herself a sort of semi-European visitor in the North American household. Even some of the French-Canadian newspapers have recently supported Dominion membership in the Pan American Union, and though the full implications of the idea have not yet been appreciated the idea is undoubtedly finding much favor. A North American system of security would furnish a common meeting ground for the extreme isolationist and the disappointed League supporter, each of whom finds it preferable to participation in the European armament race toward war. Those who have once tasted the larger loyalty to the League will not now, in their disillusion, revert to a narrow imperialism, whatever the guise in which it may appear – not even though it be described, in the truly ingenious phrase of an English Member of Parliament, as 'collective security within the Empire.'

Amongst the French-Canadians the most important development has been the revival of nationalism in the Province of Quebec. Never before has this movement been so vocal or so aggressive.[9] Its extreme wing is openly secessionist, aiming to create an independent French-Canadian republic on the banks of the St Lawrence. The resurgence of nationalism was the principal reason for the overthrow of Mr Taschereau and the provincial Liberal Party in August 1936, and the coming to power of Mr Duplessis at the head of a new party, the *Union Nationale.*

9 See 'Nationalism in French Canada,' *The Round Table*, December 1936 [reprinted in this volume].

The instinctive isolationist attitude of the French-Canadian is fortified by the movement, and every suggestion of closer ties with the Commonwealth is now being met with vigorous opposition. The pressure of this nationalist influence upon the 59 French-Canadian members of Mr King's Liberal Party will tend to make the Canadian Government's policy more cautious toward proposals for co-öperation in imperial defense, assistance to immigration, and kindred matters. It would be utterly impossible, in Quebec's present temper, to induce any French-Canadians to take part in another European war simply because Great Britain was engaged in it; and any attempt by the Dominion to enforce conscription for this purpose would create civil disturbance on a large scale. The knowledge of this fact has a sobering influence on the impulsive loyalties of certain imperialists in Canada.[10]

Such, in broad perspective, are the movements of Canadian opinion which Mr Mackenzie King will have to bear in mind when he sits with his colleagues around the conference table in London. The net result will be discouraging for those who expect Canada to assume further responsibilities toward the Commonwealth. Mr King himself has stated that 'Canada's first duty to the League and to the British Empire, with respect to the great issues that come up, is, if possible, to keep this country united.'[11] The impossibility of maintaining Canadian unity on a policy of rigid Commonwealth commitments should be clear to the reader. If attempts are to be made to bring the Commonwealth closer together in a political and military sense because of the League's breakdown, Canada will be inclined to draw farther away. A united move by the Commonwealth nations to restore the League would undoubtedly command wide sympathy in Canada, and would have the effect of strengthening the Imperial connection, for then the one loyalty would incorporate and give new purpose to the other. It is difficult, however, to see the initiative for such a policy coming from Mr King. He has indicated on more than one occasion that Canada must take a back seat at Geneva.[12]

The policy of promoting Canadian unity, however, will necessitate some de-

---

10 At the same time it must be remembered that the French-Canadian is first of all a Catholic, and will always support a Vatican foreign policy. He is more under the influence of Rome than the English-Canadian is of London. The French-Canadians, despite their isolationism, sent a contingent of volunteers to Rome to fight for the Pope in 1870, and might be expected to lend assistance to Great Britain if she should join the Fascist powers in an attack on the Soviet Union. The sympathy of the Quebec nationalists, which was pro-Boer in the South African War because of a fellow feeling for the small nation fighting imperialism, was completely pro-Italian in the Abyssinian war and is now strongly pro-rebel in Spain.

11 Canadian House of Commons Debates, March 23, 1936, p. 1441.

12 On this and other aspects of Mr King's foreign policy, see articles by Escott Reid in *University of Toronto Quarterly*, January 1937, and in *Canadian Journal of Economics and Political Science*, February 1937.

gree of Commonwealth cooperation on the part of Mr King in order to satisfy the imperialist sentiment. In so far as defense is concerned, the recent large increases in the Canadian defense estimates, which were explained as being required solely for Canadian purposes, are clearly intended to ease the pressure for greater military preparedness without unduly exciting the isolationists. There is not likely to be further concession to the proposals that Canada should share in the cost of British rearmament. Some English imperialists would do well to remember that any attempt to impose additional taxation on Canada for defense purposes, by veiled implications that Canadians are enjoying the privileges without the responsibilities of membership in the Commonwealth, are simply going to force Canada to consider the question whether those privileges cannot be too dearly bought. The membership dues paid by Canada between 1914–1918 amounted to some 60,000 dead and a legacy of internal debt of over four billion dollars. Moreover, it is difficult for Canadians to believe that the existence of Canada today has added one farthing to the amount which the British Government was determined to spend on rearmament in any event. England cannot solve her military problems by invoking the military aid of the Dominions to help her dominate the Continent or isolate herself from it, and in so far as the Dominions foster that illusion they are doing a disservice to the true interests of the British peoples and to Europe also.

More important even than defense is the vexed question of neutrality. This delicate issue has so far been successfully evaded by the Dominion Government, and the uncertainty continues as to what Canada's position would or could be in the event Great Britain were involved in a war. In the debate on January 25, 1936, on Mr J.S. Woodsworth's resolution supporting a policy of neutrality, Mr King and Mr Lapointe talked at length on the subject, and only added to the confusion. 'So far as participation in war is concerned,' Mr King said, 'It will be for the Parliament of Canada to decide ... It will be for this Parliament to say in a given situation whether or not we shall remain neutral.' This sounds as though Canada were free to do as she pleased, and doubtless was intended to convey such an impression. Yet the fact is that under the existing Canadian constitution a declaration of war by the Crown in Great Britain would automatically avail to make Canada at war. The royal prerogative in foreign affairs has not been fully delegated to the Dominion Governor-General. Therefore Mr King's decision in the event of such a declaration could only be a decision as to how far Canada would supply troops and materials; it could not be a decision to 'remain' neutral, since war would have begun in Canada. In his remarks in the House he has confused the right to neutrality with the right to 'passive belligerency,' and his word 'participation' is ambiguous. Such language is the language of political dodgery rather than of fact; it can only be intended to stave off an open fight on the issue, so that Mr King can carry on his government while avoiding a revelation of the wide differences of opinion which exist within his own party.

Public opinion in Canada will not long be satisfied with evasion, and already is moving to demand that the situation be clarified whether or not the coming Conference intends to deal with it frankly. The consequences of independent action in time of war are difficult to weigh.[13] But the right to neutrality will have to be granted sooner or later, and the theory of a permanent personal union under a divisible Crown expanded to meet it. Canada can never be held permanently in the Commonwealth if a mere majority party controlling the House of Commons in London is to be able at any time to involve Canadians in war. The lack of racial unity in the country, if not plain self-respect, would make the British connection impossible on those terms. The full implications of the Balfour declaration of 1926, that the Dominions are to be autonomous in *every aspect of their domestic and external affairs*, will have to be accepted very shortly, and the decision as to whether Canada will lend aid to Great Britain must be made independently by Ottawa on each occasion as it arises, free from the technical condition of belligerency which the present position automatically involves. It should be the task of this coming Conference to provide in advance a method for possible Dominion neutrality; only so can the Commonwealth avoid the confusions and recriminations that independent and unprepared action by a Dominion will inevitably entail. The right to non-participation has already been conceded; the right to neutrality is the next step ...

13 See P.E. Corbett, 'Isolation for Canada,' in *University of Toronto Quarterly*, October 1936, and Escott Reid, 'Can Canada Remain Neutral?,' *Dalhousie Review*, July 1935.

# IX

# Section 94 of the British North America Act

*The Canadian constitution contains an unusual provision in Section 94 whereby the laws relative to 'property and civil rights' – a very large category – can be rendered uniform in the Common Law provinces without recourse to formal procedures of constitutional amendment. This article examines the purpose and potentialities of the Section. In the event of Quebec acquiring some kind of independent status, it might prove of great value to the remaining provinces wishing to form a closer union.*
From the *Canadian Bar Review*, 20, 1942, 525–44

During the 1930s Canadians learned a great deal about their constitution. The economic collapse of 1929 necessitated federal recovery measures; these had to be tested in the courts; and the Privy Council judgments on Mr Bennett's 'New Deal' statutes suddenly exposed the damage wrought by decentralizing judicial interpretation. This combination of circumstances, which was the occasion for the appointment of the Royal Commission on Dominion-Provincial Relations in 1937, is familiar to us all. But in seeking ways out of the legal impasse into which the courts had led the country, very little attention has been paid to one of the most interesting clauses in the Canadian constitution. This is section 94 of the BNA Act which provides a means whereby the laws regarding property and civil rights in the common law provinces may be rendered uniform. Only the briefest mention of the section occurs in the Sirois Report[1] and it was clearly not considered to contain any idea of much value at the present time.

---

1 Vol. II, p. 73. Some briefs made reference to it; e.g. League for Social Reconstruction, p. 10; Nova Scotia, p. 22. Professor Corry in his study of *Difficulties of Divided Jurisdiction*, Appendix 7, does not mention it, but it is referred to briefly by Messrs Gouin and Claxton in *Legislative Expedients and Devices Adopted by the Dominion and the Provinces*, Appendix 8, p. 26–7.

While the advent of the war has, by bringing into play the Dominion residuary clause, overcome temporarily the juridical problems of the 1930s, nevertheless this emergency will not last forever. It may be worthwhile, therefore, to examine more fully the purpose, provisions, and potentialities of section 94. There may even be an immediate value in the investigation, since, as this analysis will attempt to show, the section may in fact be operative now in regard to certain subjects, contrary to the generally accepted view. If such is the case the Dominion will find itself endowed with a greater extent of jurisdiction than it now imagines itself to possess.

The first point that strikes us when we examine the actual provisions of the section in question is that it occurs in Part VI of the BNA Act entitled 'Distribution of Legislative Powers.' There are five sections or articles under this head. The first is entitled 'Powers of Parliament' (section 91); the second, 'Exclusive Powers of Provincial Legislatures' (section 92); the third, 'Education' (section 93); the fourth, which we are studying, is called 'Uniformity of the Laws of Ontario, Nova Scotia and New Brunswick' (section 94); and the last is 'Agriculture and Immigration' (section 95). All the articles in Part VI are of general application, extending equally to all provinces, except section 94 which refers to three provinces only. That is to say, everything in Part VI applies to all the provinces which existed or were created in 1867, except section 94 which did not apply to Quebec. Legislative power to render laws uniform was granted to the Dominion over every common-law province in the union.

Section 94 reads as follows:

Notwithstanding anything in this Act, the Parliament of Canada may make Provision for the Uniformity of all or any of the Laws relative to Property and Civil Rights in Ontario, Nova Scotia, and New Brunswick, and of the Procedure of all or any of the Courts in those Three Provinces, and from and after the passing of any Act in that Behalf the Power of the Parliament of Canada to make laws in relation to any Matter comprised in any such Act shall, notwithstanding anything in this Act, be unrestricted; but any Act of the Parliament of Canada making Provision for such Uniformity shall not have effect in any Province unless and until it is adopted and enacted as Law by the Legislature thereof.

The purpose of the section, if we leave aside for the moment the question of its geographical applicability, is quite clear. None of the writers who have considered it have been in any doubt about it. Section 92 left the subject of 'Property and Civil Rights in the province' within the exclusive jurisdiction of provincial legislatures. If the Act had stopped there, Canada would have been divided into watertight compartments which it would have been impossible to break down without going through the difficult process of amending the constitution itself.[2] The law which established federalism would itself have been an obstacle in the way of greater national unity should the desire for such unity ever arise. Now the last thing the fathers of Confederation wished to do was to prevent Canadians from becoming united. They did not believe, and still less provided, that the divisions of their day would be perpetual. The purpose of Confederation was to bring greater union, and to eradicate the exaggerated provincialism which was holding back all sections of British North America in 1867. While for various and good reasons a federation and not a legislative union was all that could be agreed upon, it was clearly understood and intended by the framers of the Act that, outside Quebec, an easy way should be left open for an even closer integration of the provinces than was provided at the beginning by the Act itself. A power of amendment, in the direction of unity, was written into the act; in this sense it is not true to say that the BNA Act cannot be amended in Canada. Quebec was excluded from this provision, because the guaranteeing of her control over her basic civil law was looked upon as part of the racial agreement implicit in the constitution.

The meaning of section 94 appears at first sight to present little difficulty. As explained in the Sirois Report, 'The Dominion was given power to make provision for uniformity of laws relating to property and civil rights in the three common-law provinces but any federal act designed to do this required adoption by the legislature of a province before it had any operative effect in such province. When the act had been thus adopted the Dominion acquired full legislative power in perpetuity to deal with its subject matter.'[3] The procedure involves, 1st, the enactment by the Dominion of an act designed to produce uniformity, 2nd, the adoption of the act by the provincial legislature. No other formality of any kind is required. From the moment the provincial law becomes effective, the subject matter of the act passes out of the provincial and into the Dominion sphere as finally as if it had actually been written into section 91 as a specified Dominion head. Thus the province abandons the field to the Dominion, and loses even the right to change its mind subsequently so as to reclaim the power transferred.

Had the hopes of the fathers of Confederation been carried out, Canada would

---

2 To read certain Privy Council decisions, one would imagine that this was in fact the purpose of the Act. See e.g. Lord Atkin's highly misleading metaphor in the *ILO Conventions Case:* 'While the ship of state now sails on larger ventures and into foreign waters she still retains the watertight compartments which are an essential part of her original structure'; [1937] A.C. 326, at 354. Such parts of the Act as sections 90, 92–10c, and 94 show how far removed this language is from reality.

3 Vol. II, p. 73.

have moved steadily toward a greater union by this means, and most of the difficulties with the constitution we have since experienced would never have arisen. When section 94 is thought of in relation to the basic principle for the division of powers, namely that matters of 'common interest to the whole country' would belong to the 'General Government' and that the 'Local Governments' would have merely 'the control of local matters in their respective sections,'[4] the full weight of the desire for national unity that underlay the constitution can be appreciated; for section 94 makes it possible to establish uniformity on matters that are otherwise of merely local interest in the provinces. Whatever may have happened to section 94 in the legal evolution of the constitution, it remains as an outstanding political idea which formed part of the plans and aspirations of the men who built the nation from coast to coast.

Shortly after Confederation a beginning was made to unify the laws of Ontario, New Brunswick, and Nova Scotia under section 94. The Hon. J.H. Gray was appointed to examine into the problem and to prepare a preliminary report. It was apparently the intention to follow this by the appointment of a Commission which would prepare a final detailed bill. The sum of $20,000 was appropriated by parliament for the expenses connected with the work. When this sum was being discussed in committee a most interesting political point was raised. Mr Mills, an Opposition member, moved an amendment to the motion for supply, to the effect that it was inexpedient to make any provision which would, if it became law, transfer the powers of legislation upon the subjects of property and civil rights from the Provincial Legislatures, where they are at present vested, to the Parliament of Canada, as any such provision would, in the opinion of this House, tend to destroy the present system of federal government.

This raised the issue squarely as to what was the intention of section 94. Did it permit the curtailment of provincial sovereignty or did it not? Was 'federalism' an essential part of the Confederation arrangement or was it not? On the vote being put the amendment was defeated by 81 votes to 33. Among the names recorded as opposed to Mr Mills' amendment we see those of Cartier, J.A. Macdonald, Tilley, Langevin, Pope, and others.[5] Neither these men nor the House of Commons itself was frightened at the idea of reducing 'federalism' in Canada, or felt that anything in the scheme of the BNA Act made it impossible.

Mr Gray presented his report in 1871.[6] It was entitled 'Preliminary Report' and was confined to 'pointing out the differences' between the laws of the three common-law provinces. He concluded however that

4 Quebec and London Resolutions, no. 2.
5 *Journals of the House of Commons*, 1869, pp. 43, 186, 268.
6 *Sessional Papers*, 1871, no. 16.

there can be no doubt that an excellent practical Code of Law, simple in its language, easily understood, expedient and economical in its administration could be formed from a judicious selection of the best laws of each of the provinces by men who were severally acquainted with each.

With that pious hope ends the first attempt to apply section 94 in the Dominion. Partly, no doubt, because of the emergence of other more pressing problems, partly because of the decline in the sentiment of national unity after Confederation, the proposal to unify the provincial laws was forgotten for a generation.

In 1902, on the motion of Dr Benjamin Russell, member for Hants county, a proposal to apply section 94 was again made in the House of Commons.[7] No vote was called, however, and discussion was not followed by action. The Minister of Justice, the Hon. Charles Fitzpatrick, vigorously opposed the motion, on the precise ground which Mr Mills had raised so ineffectually in 1869, namely that any action under section 94 would destroy the federal character of the constitution; the practical way to proceed in the matter, he interjected sarcastically, 'would be to ask the local legislatures how soon they are going to be disposed to commit suicide.'[8] The pendulum had indeed swung far away from the earlier nationalism. Since 1902 there have been no further attempts to make use of this provision in the BNA Act.

With this general background to the section we may examine in more detail some particular questions that arise. The first problem is with regard to the application of the section. In its terms it provides for uniformity of laws in three provinces only, namely Ontario, Nova Scotia, and New Brunswick. From this fact it has been argued by some that no method of establishing uniformity exists in any other provinces. That is to say, it is suggested that not only was Quebec excluded from the application of the section, but also all the other provinces that came into Confederation or were established after 1867. 'There is considerable doubt,' says the Sirois Report, 'whether the section applies to provinces other than Ontario, Nova Scotia and New Brunswick.'[9]

The solution to this problem involves a close study of the Quebec and London

7 *Debates*, House of Commons, 1902, pp. 1067 et s.
8 *Ibid.*, p. 1097.
9 Vol. II, p. 73. A note in *Canada Law Journal*, Vol. 46, p. 41, assumes that the section is confined to three provinces only. This was Dr Russell's opinion: see his article in 34 *Canada Law Journal*, 513 at 521. On the other hand Mr Eugene Lafleur seems to have assumed without examination that it applied to all other provinces except Quebec: see his *Uniformity of Laws in Canada*, Canadian Law Times, vol. 35, p. 396. Mr W.F. O'Connor does not deal with the point in his reference to section 94 in his article *Property and Civil Rights in the Province* (1940) 18 Can. Bar Rev. 331, at p. 344.

Resolutions, of the statements made by the framers of the Act, and of the statutes and orders-in-council setting forth the terms of admission of other provinces. But before we indulge in the luxury of legalistic exposition it may be well to approach the matter first from the common sense point of view. It would be very odd to discover that the constitution enabled half the state to unify its law, but not the other half. What a curious restriction on the idea of national unity! For part of Canada, the compartments of jurisdiction would be changeable; for the other part they would be perpetual. It is a little difficult to conceive that men of the intellectual calibre of Sir John Macdonald, Sir George Cartier and others would have supported any such strange proposal. The exception of Quebec is understandable for there the law itself differs in origin and character. But the exception of Prince Edward Island and the western provinces would be quite incomprehensible. The words of Lord Coleridge in *The Queen* v. *Clarence*[10] seem relevant here, and one could wish that they had been applied to the BNA Act: 'If the apparent logical construction of its language leads to results which it is impossible to believe that those who framed or those who passed the statute contemplated, and from which one's own judgment recoils, there is, in my opinion, good reason for believing that the construction which leads to such results cannot be the true construction of the statute.'

Unfortunately there are some judges who will not permit common sense to stand in the way of a legislative absurdity. They prefer the maxim *dura lex sed lex*, and when the result of what is called 'strict interpretation' is not too fantastic all they can do is to exclaim, in the words of the judicial committee of the Privy Council, that 'although the question had obviously to be decided on the terms of the statute, it is a matter of congratulation that the result arrived at seems consonant with common sense.'[11]

Setting aside, then, the temptation to any short cut solution, and turning to the Quebec Resolutions,[12] we find that the present section 94 appears in Resolution 29, no. 33, as one of the general powers allotted to the Dominion parliament. The interesting and instructive point in the resolution, however, is that it applied not only to Upper Canada, Nova Scotia, and New Brunswick but *also to Newfoundland and Prince Edward Island*. The last two provinces were obviously included because they were represented at the Quebec Conference, and the provi-

10 22 Q.B.D. 23, at p. 65. A similar rule is stated in *Rowell* v. *Pratt*, [1938] A.C. 101 at p. 105.
11 *Radio Reference*, [1932] A.C. 304, at p. 317.
12 Those authorities who hesitate or refuse to refer to the Quebec and London Resolutions when interpreting the B.N.A. Act are fortunately on the decline. The simple truth is that the constitution cannot be understood without going behind the statute – a fact which seems sufficiently well attested by frequent citations from the Resolutions in Canadian courts and at least five references to them in *Privy Council* judgments.

sion for unity was made to extend over all the provinces whom it was hoped to federate, except Quebec. In the London Resolutions the section appears as Resolution 28, no. 32, but now the provinces to which it was said to apply are only the three mentioned in the BNA Act. This was because Newfoundland and Prince Edward Island did not send delegates to London and were not included among the original confederating provinces. Thus it is a fact that at Quebec and at London the section was made applicable to every common-law province proposing to come into Confederation.

In the debates on the Quebec Resolutions Sir John Macdonald remarked that

the 33rd provision is of very great importance to the future well-being of these colonies. It commits to the General Parliament the 'rendering uniform all or any of the laws relative to property and civil rights in Upper Canada, Nova Scotia, New Brunswick, Newfoundland and Prince Edward Island, and rendering uniform the procedure of all or any of the courts in these provinces.' The great principles which govern the laws of all the provinces, with the single exception of Lower Canada, are the same, although there may be a divergence in details; and it is gratifying to find, on the part of the Lower Provinces, a general desire to join together with Upper Canada in this matter, and to procure, as soon as possible, an assimilation of the statutory laws and the procedure in the courts, of all these provinces. [13]

Further evidence of this intention will be found in a report which Macdonald, as Minister of Justice, made on December 20, 1869, on the progress of the work being done for assimilating the laws under section 94. After explaining the programme he wrote:

A Commission can then be appointed, should it be thought expedient to do so; but the undersigned would suggest that perhaps its issue had better be postponed for a time in the hope that the remaining provinces in British North America may, ere long, be added to the Dominion. *The Commissioners could then report Measures rendering uniform the laws of all the provinces and not merely of the four which now compose the Dominion.* [14]

13 *Confederation Debates*, p. 41. See similar remarks by Macdonald at p. 29 and by Cameron at p. 462–3, who refers to the five provinces; also, in the same sense, Joseph Howe, *Letters to the People of Nova Scotia*, April 20, 1871, cited O'Connor, *Report on the BNA Act*, Appendix I, p. 122–3.
14 *Sessional Papers*, 1870, no. 45. Italics mine. The reference to the 'four' provinces is interesting. Macdonald knew sections 94 did not apply to Quebec, therefore he must have been thinking of Manitoba as the 4th province. The admission of Rupert's Land had been decided at this time and a provisional government arranged by the Statutes of Canada, 1869, c. 3.

These quotations give the proper key, it is submitted, to the problem we are seeking to resolve. Certainly no historian looking at the evidence would feel any doubt about the reason for naming three provinces in section 94. The purpose of the section was to provide for further unity in 'all those provinces' which based their system of law upon the common law of England. At the Quebec Conference five provinces of this character were present; therefore Resolution 29, section 33, applied to all five. At London there were only three such provinces represented; therefore Resolution 28, section 32, applied to those three. In both cases Quebec was omitted because of its possession of the civil law. Hence the naming of three provinces in section 94 was not intended to be exhaustive, but merely to be indicative of the kind of province to which section 94 might apply.

What the fathers of Confederation intended is reasonably clear; we may now turn to the manner in which they carried out the intention. As other provinces were admitted into Confederation after 1867 or were created out of unorganized territory they were all brought under the general provisions of the BNA Act of 1867, except in so far as these might be varied by the statute or order-in-council which set forth the terms of admission. The language used in these documents of admission is unfortunately not identical and is somewhat confusing unless read in the light of what has just been said. The relevant section of the Manitoba Act, 1870 reads as follows:

On, from and after the said day on which the Order to the Queen in Council shall take effect as aforesaid, the provisions of the British North America Act, 1867, shall, except those parts thereof which are in terms made, or, by reasonable intendment, may be held to be specially applicable to, or only to affect one or more, but not the whole of the Provinces now composing the Dominion, and except so far as the same may be varied by this Act, be applicable to the Province of Manitoba, in the same way, and to the like extent as they apply to the several Provinces of Canada, and as if the Province of Manitoba had been one of the Provinces originally united by the said Act.[15]

Both the Alberta Act and the Saskatchewan Act contain a provision the relevant portion of which is similar to that contained in the Manitoba Act.[16]

In the order-in-council of 1871 admitting British Columbia the equivalent statement reads:

10. The provisions of the British North America Act, 1867, shall (except those parts thereof which are in terms made, or by reasonable intendment may be held to be specially applicable to and only affect one and not the whole of the Prov-

15  33 Vic. cap. 3, sec. 2 (Dominion).
16  Alberta Act, 1905, sec. 3; Saskatchewan Act, 1905, sec. 3.

inces now comprising the Dominion, and except so far as the same may be varied by this Minute) be applicable to British Columbia in the same way and to the like extent as they apply to the other Provinces of the Dominion, and as if the Colony of British Columbia had been one of the Provinces originally united by the said Act.

The order-in-council of 1873 admitting Prince Edward Island is so nearly identical with that for British Columbia that it can give rise to no different interpretation.

When the language of the three statutes is compared with that of the two orders-in-council, a slight variation will be noticed. In the orders-in-council, all the provisions of the BNA Act are said to be applicable, unless varied by the Order, except those portions thereof which 'may be held to be specially applicable to and only affect one and not the whole of the provinces.' Section 94 of the Act does not affect 'one and not the whole' of the provinces. It affects more than one and not the whole. It therefore would not be strictly within the exception. Hence it could be argued that on this ground section 94 was extended necessarily to British Columbia and Prince Edward Island, even if no other considerations impelled us to this conclusion. But, as we shall see, there are better grounds for so thinking.

With the language of the Manitoba, Alberta and Saskatchewan statutes there may be more difficulty. The difference here is that in these the exception refers to those parts of the BNA Act which are in terms made, or by reasonable intendment may be held to apply to 'one or more but not the whole of the provinces.' The doubt arises over the effect of the words 'or more,' which are not in the orders-in-council. Section 94 applies to more than one province but not in express terms to all those composing the Dominion; hence it appears at first sight to be within the exception and so would not apply in these three provinces.

However this interpretation, which is narrowly verbal and textual, must, it is submitted, be rejected on several grounds. It does violence to the scarcely disputable intent of the Quebec Resolutions and to the quite indisputable explanatory statements of Macdonald and others. It also creates an inexplicable inequality among the provinces. It means that three of the common-law provinces have greater powers than five others. It also lands us in other textual difficulties arising out of the wording of sections 90 and 97 of the BNA Act. Section 90 is introduced with a heading 'The Four Provinces.' These provinces were Ontario, Quebec, Nova Scotia and New Brunswick. Since four are named, the section might be considered as being intended to apply to them only. This is another section apparently applying to 'one or more but not the whole' of the provinces. Yet there is no doubt that the provisions of section 90, referring for example to disallowance of provincial acts, are made applicable to the provinces of Manitoba,

Alberta and Saskatchewan.[17] In the body of section 90, it is true, the language is less restrictive, since it speaks of the legislatures of 'the several provinces,' which is an all-embracing term. Yet the specific and limited heading to the section remains to be got over. If section 90 can be extended to post-1867 provinces, why cannot section 94? Both refer to 'one or more but not to all' the provinces.

Section 97 is even more suggestive. This provides that 'until the Laws relative to Property and Civil Rights in Ontario, Nova Scotia, and New Brunswick, and the Procedure of the Courts in those Provinces, are made uniform, the Judges of the Courts of those Provinces appointed by the Governor General shall be selected from the respective Bars of those Provinces.' If the narrow interpretation of the statutes admitting the prairie provinces is taken this section can have no applicability to them for it unquestionably refers to 'one or more but not to all' the provinces. Yet it has been standard practice for the judges in the courts of those provinces to be selected from their respective Bars. Unless all common-law provinces come under section 94, judges in Manitoba, Saskatchewan and Alberta can be appointed from anywhere. If section 97 applies on the prairies, section 94 must apply also. It could be argued that neither applies, but only again by showing great inconsistency in the constitutional plan.

If no other effect could be given to the words 'one or more but not the whole' in these statutes than to say they included section 94, a court that disregarded history might be forced to this conclusion, since otherwise they would be otiose. There are however a number of other sections in the BNA Act dealing with more than one but not all the provinces, to which the words can refer apart from section 94. For example, sections 81-7 refer only to Ontario and Quebec: section 88 refers only to Nova Scotia and New Brunswick; and section 89 refers to Ontario, Quebec, and Nova Scotia. These are sections referring to more than one and yet not to all the provinces, which clearly are not made applicable to any of the provinces which joined after 1867. These sections are within the wording of the exception of section 2 of the Manitoba Act and sections 3 of the Alberta and Saskatchewan Acts. While this in itself is no proof the words of the exception do not apply to section 94 as well, it leaves it possible to exclude 94 from their ambit without rendering these nugatory, should there be other grounds for so doing. It is submitted that, for all the reasons given above, there are compelling grounds for saying that section 94 applies to all Canada except Quebec.

The idea expressed by another phrase in all the documents admitting provinces, namely that the BNA Act was to apply to each of the new provinces as if it 'had been one of the Provinces originally united by the said Act,' confirms this interpretation. We know that if Prince Edward Island had been united by the Act she would have been included in section 94 by name, since she was mentioned in the

17 Reference re Disallowance and Reservation, (1938) S.C.R. 71.

Quebec Resolution on that point. Can anyone doubt that if the other common-law provinces had been present at the Quebec and London Conferences they would have been accorded the same treatment. The obvious intention of the statutes and orders admitting the post-1867 provinces was to put them on an equal footing with all others, except where clear provision was made for a change. The exclusion of Quebec from section 94 is the only reasonable and necessary exclusion. The inclusion of section 94 under the general heading 'Distribution of Legislative Powers,' which covers all the provinces, is also suggestive.

No direct judicial authority exists either way on the point. So far, indeed, section 94 has been referred to in the courts principally to support the notion that 'property and civil rights' in section 92 must be given a wide and comprehensive meaning. The section intended to remove provincial jurisdiction has been used to enlarge it.[18]

There is, however, a passage in Parsons case[19] which fully accepts the fact that the limitation of application of section 94 is based on the distinction between the civil and the common law. Sir Montague Smith said 'The province of Quebec is omitted from this section for the obvious reason that the law which governs property and civil rights in Quebec is in the main the French law as it existed at the time of the cession of Canada, and not the English law which prevails in the other provinces.' If this is the reason for leaving Quebec out, it is also a reason for putting all the other provinces in.

In several other cases it has been said that section 94 does not apply to Quebec. The statement, though *obiter*, occurs in the Liquor Reference of 1896,[20] and in *Boucher* v. *L'Alliance Nationale*.[21] The point is so clear as scarcely to need mention. For that reason it is difficult to see why Sir Charles Fitzpatrick thought that action under section 94 'would be a menace in so far as Quebec is concerned.'[22] No action under that section can include Quebec even if Quebec wants to be included. Quebec is constitutionally incapable of giving up her legislative powers except by a formal amendment to the BNA Act such as was adopted for unemployment insurance; in this respect she is less free than her sister provinces, who may employ section 94.

We may now consider another question concerning section 94. Has the section ever been applied?

18 See, e.g. *Citizens Insurance* v. *Parsons*, 7 App. Cas. 96, at p. 110. *Keefe* v. *McLennan*, 2 Cart. 400, at 408; *McArthur* v. *Northern & Pacific Junction Rly.*, 17 O.A.R. 86, at p. 114.
19 *Supra*, at p. 110.
20 [1896] A.C. 348 at p. 361.
21 35 R.L.N.S. 216 at p. 226. Also in *Reference re Natural Products Marketing Act*, [1936] S.C.R. 398 at p. 415.
22 Hansard, 1902, p. 1099.

It is usually said that the section has never been applied, and that the main reason for this is the unwillingness of provinces to give up jurisdiction. Thus Attorney-General MacQuarrie of Nova Scotia told the Sirois Commission that 'the reason the section has not been used' was due to the irrevocable character of the grant once made.[23] But the question deserves more attention than it has yet received. It cannot be answered without examining the conditions which are required for the application of section 94, and then discovering whether any existing statutes in fact meet those conditions.

The conditions under which section 94 comes into operation appear from and must be found in the section itself. The Parliament of Canada first makes provision for uniformity. It passes an Act 'in that Behalf.' The act may cover 'all or any' of the laws relative to property and civil rights; even a statute on one portion of such law will be acceptable.[24] Such statute is subsequently 'adopted and enacted as law' by a provincial legislature. The transfer of jurisdiction then follows automatically and irrevocably. Henceforth the power of the Parliament of Canada to *make* laws (i.e. to change or repeal the law already made) in relation to 'any matter comprised in any such act' will be 'unrestricted.'

No special procedure is required. It is doubtful if any recitation of purpose need be included in the statute, other than some indication of a desire for uniformity. There is nothing in section 94 comparable to the express declaration of intention required by section 4 of the Statute of Westminster.[25] Section 94 establishes a set of objective conditions; once they are met, the result follows. It would be no ground for denying that a transfer had occurred, to say that the province did not know, when it adopted the Dominion Act, what was the effect of the adoption. The intent to provide uniformity must exist in the Dominion; adoption must occur in the province, but it is not necessary that the province should know that through such adoption it loses all control over the subject-matter of the statute in future. The Dominion intent to render law uniform is agreed to by the province on the simple adoption of the Dominion statute. If the validity or invalidity of statutes depended on the knowledge of constitutional law possessed by legislators, federalism would be quite unworkable. The law binds the ignorant as well as the expert. We cannot read into section 94 conditions that do not exist there.

23 Evidence, p. 3875.
24 Mr W.F. O'Connor has suggested that the 'Laws' to be made were 'statute laws,' but he admits there would be nothing to prevent 'part codification of the common law.' See his *Property and Civil Rights in the Province*,' (1940) 18 Can Bar Rev. 331, at p. 345.
25 Which provides that 'No Act of Parliament of the United Kingdom passed after the commencement of this Act shall extend, or be deemed to extend, to a Dominion as part of the law of that Dominion, unless it is expressly declared in that Act that that Dominion has requested, and consented to, the enactment thereof.'

Let us see, then, whether any Dominion statutes have been adopted by provinces under the conditions required by section 94. One possible candidate for this distinction at once springs to mind. It is the Industrial Disputes Investigation Act.

The history of the statute is well known. It was passed by the Dominion Parliament in 1907, in the belief that its subject matter fell within section 91 of the BNA Act. It worked well for many years. Then its constitutionality was challenged in *Toronto Electric Commissioners* v. *Snider*. The Ontario courts upheld the statute.[26] But they were overruled by the Privy Council,[27] Lord Haldane delivering a judgment that is a classic as well for its misreading of Canadian history as for its deflection of Canadian constitutional law. To overcome some of the mischief of the judgment, and to bring back if possible a uniformity which had been lost, the Dominion Parliament amended the statute so as to limit it to matters clearly within Dominion jurisdiction, and then added a provision, not previously present, that the act should apply to 'any dispute which is within the exclusive legislative jurisdiction of any provinces and which by the legislation of the province is made subject to the provisions of this Act.'[28]

Here is clearly a provision for uniformity of some sort. It was passed by the Parliament of Canada in the hope that the provinces would adopt it. The subject matter, namely the prevention of industrial disputes, had just been described by Lord Haldane as 'concerned directly with the civil rights of both employers and employed' in the province.[29] It was therefore the type of statute that could come within section 94.[30] What happened? It was 'adopted' by every province in Canada except Prince Edward Island.[31] Is there any reason why this procedure is not exactly within section 94?

Let us examine one of the provincial statutes of adoption. We may look at Ontario, since in Ontario there is no doubt whatever that section 94 is applicable. Ontario adopted the Industrial Disputes Investigation Act in 1932, by means of a short statute the relevant part of which provides: '1. That provisions of the *Industrial Disputes Investigation Act*, being chapter 112 of the Revised Statutes of Canada, 1927, shall apply to every industrial dispute of the nature in the said Act

26 55 O.L.R. 454.
27 [1925] A.C. 396.
28 Statutes of Canada, 1925, cap. 14, s. 1.
29 *Toronto Electric Commissioners* v. *Snider, supra*, at p. 403.
30 Lord Haldane also suggested that the subject matter of the Industrial Disputes Investigation Act might be competent to the province under the head of 'Municipal Institutions in the Province,' but that could only be in so far as the Act applied to municipalities.
31 Nova Scotia, 1926, cap. 5; New Brunswick, 1926, cap. 17; Quebec, 1931–2, cap. 46; Ontario, 1932, cap. 29; Manitoba, 1926, cap. 21; Sask. 1925–26, cap. 58; Alberta, 1928, cap. 42; British Columbia, 1925, cap. 19, repealed by 1937, cap. 31, sec. 53.

defined which is within or subject to the exclusive legislative jurisdiction of the Province.'

Of this provision surely it could be said, without stretching of language, that it had 'adopted and enacted as law' an act of the Dominion Parliament passed to secure uniformity. The Ontario legislature knew of the Dominion act, and of its provision for uniformity. By subsequent provincial statute the Dominion Act was made to apply in the province to disputes which were admittedly of provincial jurisdiction. Thus a portion of the provincial law dealing with the civil and contractual rights of employers and employees was brought under the Dominion Act. The law was rendered uniform. This certainly appears close enough to section 94 to make it necessary to examine whether the section did not immediately become operative. If it did, Ontario has lost the power to repeal its adopting statute, or to make any new laws on the subjects covered by the Dominion Act.

If this should prove to be a correct analysis of what happened in Ontario, the same conclusion seems necessarily to hold in all the other provinces, except Quebec, which have adopted the Dominion Act, since their statutes are in almost identical form. It would therefore follow that British Columbia's repeal statute of 1937[32] would be *ultra vires.*

Undoubtedly strong arguments can be raised against this conclusion. To anyone unfamiliar with the purpose and history of section 94 the suggestion may seem startling. It is highly improbable that Ontario intended this result to happen. But as has been said above this of itself is not a weighty objection. The state of ignorance of legislators, it is submitted, is irrelevant if all the objective conditions of section 94 are fulfilled. An analogous situation exists under section 93(3) of the BNA Act. In matters of education, once a province establishes a system of separate schools it immediately loses the power subsequently to affect the rights of the Catholic or Protestant minority without giving rise to an appeal to the Governor-General in Council and possible Dominion legislation. It scarcely seems likely that a province could escape this provision, and withdraw privileges once granted, merely on the plea that the provincial legislators did not realize or intend that the separate school system would escape their control once it was created. If intention is irrelevant in section 93(3) it should be in section 94. Ontario at least intended that the Dominion statute should be operative in Ontario. Similarly a province cannot escape the prohibition against indirect taxation simply by declaring its intention that a tax which it introduces is to be a direct tax.[33]

Looking at the Dominion statute it might be said that there is nothing to indicate that the Dominion Parliament intended to utilize the procedure of section 94. This is true, and is a more serious objection since it is the Dominion that must

32 Chapter 31.
33 *A.G. for Manitoba* v. *A.G. for Canada*, [1925] A.C. 561.

initiate the steps of uniformity. Yet no recitation of purpose is called for, other than an enactment 'in behalf' of uniformity. We must admit that the Dominion Parliament did desire uniformity of law regarding industrial disputes and did desire the adoption of its law by provincial legislatures. This is the essence of the procedure under the section.

Another argument against the conclusion might be based on section 2 of the Ontario Act. It provides: '2. The Lieutenant-Governor in Council may by proclamation apply the provisions of any amendment to the said Act which may after the 15th day of August, 1932, be enacted by the Parliament of Canada to every industrial dispute of the nature in the said Act defined which is within or subject to the exclusive legislative jurisdiction of the Province where-upon those provisions shall apply accordingly.' This seems to indicate that Ontario imagined that any future changes in the Dominion Act would have to be adopted afresh as they were made. But if section 94 has come into play, once the Dominion Act is adopted the province loses all future control over its subject matter. As section 94 clearly says, 'from and after the passing of any Act in that Behalf the Power of the Parliament of Canada to make laws in relation to any matter comprised in any such Act shall, notwithstanding anything in this Act, be unrestricted.' Words could not be more precise. The Dominion presumably cannot increase the area of its statute without a new provincial adoption, since that would be taking away more jurisdiction than the original act covered and the province granted; but within the area transferred the Dominion may change the law at will. If section 94 governs the case, section 2 of the Ontario Act could only be left operative by considering that it is referring to such amendments by the Dominion in future as increase the field covered by the existing Dominion Act.[34]

To refrain from applying section 94 to such a situation as is created by the Industrial Disputes Investigation Act and its provincial adoptions is to say that there is another method of rendering laws uniform in Canada totally distinct from that provided in the BNA Act, though resembling it as closely as does the one under consideration. Such a conclusion is to say the least, confusing. We shall have to build a series of legal tests to distinguish cases where provinces adopt Dominion law without involving section 94 from those cases where the adoption does involve section 94. Even if a province in adopting the Dominion law expressly stated that it intended to retain control over the subject matter in the future, it might be doubtful whether section 94 still did not apply, for a province cannot alter the section by a unilateral declaration. There is clearly one other way of rendering laws uniform, not within section 94; this is for each province to pass

34 Section 3 of the Ontario statute saves 'any Commission' appointed by the Crown. This can remain operative without affecting the above argument.

identical concurrent statutes, each within the exclusive jurisdiction of their respective legislatures. In such a case the provinces would not be adopting a Dominion Statute, but would enact one of their own. The simple distinguishing feature here would be that no Dominion statute would be operative in the provinces. The uniformity would derive from the mere fact of similarity at a given moment, and would be liable to change at any time. Such a situation exists already with regard e.g. to statutes dealing with common fault and contributory negligence. By this method even Quebec law can share the uniformity. This is in fact the sole principle on which the Canadian Bar Association's efforts to secure uniformity have been based in the past. It resembles the method used in the United States, to which the citizens of that country are compelled because they have nothing comparable to our section 94.

Though the question here raised, that the adoption by the common-law provinces of the Industrial Disputes Investigation Act might be an example of the working of section 94, has not been considered by the courts, there is some slight judicial authority in support of the proposition that this type of co-operation results in the kind of uniformity provided for in that section. In 1875 the Dominion passed its first Petition of Right Act,[35] and by section 17 of that act it was provided that the word 'Court' besides meaning any Dominion court that might be set up, would mean also certain named courts in the province of Quebec, Ontario, Nova Scotia, New Brunswick, Manitoba, British Columbia and Prince Edward Island, with the following proviso: 'But no Court except such Court as is in the first subsection mentioned, shall have cognizance of any matter under this Act, unless the Legislature of the Province of which the same is a Court, shall have empowered the said Court to administer the rights by this Act conferred, in accordance with the procedure herein defined.'

In the case of *Perley et al* v. *Burpee*, Duff, J, speaking of sections 92-13 and 94 of the BNA Act, commented on the latter section in the following words:

By the latter, the Parliament of Canada is authorized to make provision for the uniformity of the laws relative to Property and Civil Rights in Ontario, Nova Scotia, and New Brunswick. Such legislation, however, would manifestly conflict with the power given to the Provincial Legislatures by sub-section 13, were it not that section 94 provides that no law making provision for such uniformity shall go into effect, in any Province, until it is adopted and enacted as a law by the Legislature thereof. *Therefore, it was, that in the Petition of Right Act (38 Vic. cap. 12) it was expressly provided that none of the Provincial Courts should have cognizance of any matter under that Act, 'unless the Legislature of the Province*

35 Statutes of Canada, 1875, c. 12.

*of which the same is a court shall have empowered the said court to administer
the rights by this Act conferred in accordance with the procedure herein defined.*'[36]

This reference to the Petition of Right Act clearly suggests that in it we have
an example of the procedure required for uniformity under section 94. The procedure under the Industrial Disputes Investigation Act is very similar.

If the alternative view is taken, that the adoption of the Industrial Disputes
Investigation Act by the provinces established a kind of uniformity not contemplated by section 94, then, as has been said, we must conclude that something
more is required than the mere adoption of a Dominion statute to bring section
94 into play. What that extra thing might be is not clear. Presumably an express
statement in the Dominion statute that it was aiming at applying the section
would conclude the matter; but why, as has been asked, introduce such a formality so long as the intention to secure uniformity is clear? That intention might appear by necessary intendment as well as by express words. However it may be
agreed that a chance or unexpected delegation of legislative power in perpetuity
from provinces to the Dominion is not to be lightly found without good reason,
and with the present general feeling that section 94 is a dead letter and has never
been operative it is not likely that the courts would apply it to the situation
created by the Industrial Disputes Investigation Act. The argument for its application has been put forward here as strongly as the writer knows how in order to
bring the question to the fore and to emphasize the importance of the constitutional ideas contained in the section.

Looking back on the co-operation that existed under the Dominion Marketing
Act of 1934[37] it would seem improbable that section 94 could have had an application there, since the provincial statutes did not 'adopt' the Dominion Act.
They merely set up their own local marketing boards and empowered them to receive authority from the Dominion Marketing Board. This seems to be a provision aiming at administrative collaboration rather than the uniformity of law and
this does not appear to be contemplated by section 94. Even so, one could wish
that the point had at least been raised in the litigation on the validity of the
Dominion Act.

Such a situation as that created by the provincial statutes adopting the Dominion Live Stock and Live Stock Products Act,[38] dealt with by the courts in *Rex* v.

---

36 Cited in Doutre, *Constitution of Canada*, p. 330. Italics mine. In the next year the Petition of Right Act of 1875 was repealed and jurisdiction over such petitions was placed
   in the newly created Exchequer Court.
37 1934, cap. 57.
38 1923, cap. 18.

*Zaslavsky,*[39] *Rex* v. *Thorsby Traders,*[40] and *Rex* v. *Brodsky,*[41] raises other questions. It is perhaps distinguishable from that created by the Industrial Disputes Investigation Act, since in the Live Stock Act, the Dominion did not provide anywhere that it should come into effect in a province on adoption by the province. The Dominion merely established general provisions which it seemed to assume were *intra vires* Dominion powers. It was not legislating 'on behalf' of uniformity, but in exercise of a power already supposed to exist in the federal Parliament. Certain provinces on their own initiative sought to remedy in advance any unwitting invasion of their field by the Dominion by providing that any portions of the Live Stock Act *ultra vires* the Dominion should have the force of law in the province. This seems to be an attempt to secure co-existing but separate identical statutes, rather than an application of section 94. As explained above, a Dominion statute enacted on the assumption that the Dominion Parliament has full legislative power itself is not the same as a statute passed under section 94 to secure uniformity. A statute passed under the latter section must be based on the assumption that the Dominion has no jurisdiction over the subject matter in so far as the provinces are concerned. Otherwise there is already the possibility of uniformity through Dominion action alone without provincial adoption of any sort. The section contemplates a permanent acquisition by the Dominion of powers it does not possess, and assumes it does not possess, under the original constitution.

What has been said of the Dominion Live Stock Act would seem to apply also to the Dominion Dairy Industry Act and to the provincial statutes enacted to support it,[42] since the type of co-operation found there is the same.

Another principle emerges from a study of section 94. Under the section the Dominion is clearly entitled to make laws relative to property and civil rights in provinces, whenever it desires uniformity. Therefore no Dominion law can be held to be invalid solely on the ground that it deals with property and civil rights. If it is also aiming at uniformity it must be allowed to remain on the statute books, awaiting possible extension province by province. A Dominion law containing provisions on property and civil rights is only invalid when the Dominion claims or assumes that the law does not in fact deal with such classes of subjects but with federal matters included under its exclusive or concurrent powers. Hence it would follow that no court could declare *ultra vires* any Dominion statute on any aspect of property and civil rights if it contained a clause like the present ad-

39 [1935] 3 D.L.R. 788.
40 [1936] 1 D.L.R. 592.
41 *Ibid.*, p. 578.
42 R.S.C. c. 45. For supporting statutes see Nova Scotia, 1923, c. 8; Sask. 1923, C. 48; British Columbia 1923, c. 63.

option clause in the Industrial Disputes Investigation Act. The courts would have to confine themselves to discovering whether any province had adopted the Act, and if none had, to confining the Act to those matters already within Dominion jurisdiction under sections of the BNA Act other than 94.

It is to be hoped that in all future attempts to secure Dominion-Provincial collaboration the existence and potentialities of section 94 will be kept in mind. We may yet reach a time in Canada when it will not be taken for granted that the provinces are the only beneficiaries of judicial interpretation of the BNA Act. We may even reach a time when Canadians of all races and creeds will decide that the original intentions of the Fathers of Confederation were good and should be carried out. When that happy time dawns section 94 will come into its own.

# X

# Etat fédéral canadien et provinces

*An address delivered to the Junior Bar Association in Quebec City on 27 November 1943, emphasizing certain lessons to be drawn from wartime planning of the economy.*
From *Revue du Barreau*, 4, 1944, 90–102

C'est avec plaisir que je m'adresse à vous de l'Association du jeune barreau de Québec et que j'exposerai quelques-unes de mes idées sur la question constitutionnelle.

Vous jugerez peut-être que je m'avance quelque peu en traitant d'un sujet aussi discuté, mais j'ai toujours cru que la difficulté d'un sujet ne devait que nous encourager à l'étudier davantage et à le serrer de plus près.

Il ne peut être question, pour nous Canadiens, d'ignorer l'Acte britannique de l'Amérique du Nord; notre présent est basé sur ce document et notre avenir en dépend. Ou bien nous le modifierons volontairement afin qu'il réponde aux besoins et aux nécessités présentes, ou nous n'y toucherons pas et ainsi nous abandonnerons aux événements le soin d'y faire face, et d'y faire de temps en temps des changements de circonstance. Il est evident que nous vivons dans un monde changeant et croyez-moi, les constitutions des peuples ne sont pas des exceptions.

Nous vivons actuellement dans un état centralisé au plus haut point; les pouvoirs du gouvernement fédéral se font sentir partout dans les provinces. Au point, qu'il est vrai de dire que les habitants du centre du Canada n'ont jamais connu une telle centralisation depuis l'Acte d'Union de 1840. Pourtant, malgré l'accroissement des pouvoirs du gouvernement fédéral depuis le début de la guerre, nous voyons les provinces survivre et même s'en très bien porter. Les provinces ont temporairement abandonné leur droit d'imposer le revenu de leurs ressortissants et les taxes des corporations, pourtant les revenus desdites provinces n'ont jamais été aussi élevés qu'ils le sont aujourd'hui. Dans le domaine ·de la législation provinciale, sur des matières comme l'éducation, les affaires municipales, le contrôle des ressources naturelles, le contrôle des compagnies d'utilités publiques et dans le domaine du droit civil, l'autorité et la juridiction provinciales demeurent substantiellement les mêmes.

Les obligations des gouvernements provinciaux, diminuées sous certains rapports, par l'intervention fédérale, semblent avoir été augmentées par ailleurs. Par exemple, il est plus facile d'observer la lente disparition des fonctions du Sénat depuis le début de la guerre, que d'observer le même phénomène dans le domaine des pouvoirs provinciaux; et si nous devons voir de l'atrophie quelque part, il semble bien que ce soit au Sénat plutôt que dans les divers organismes provinciaux.

D'ailleurs, les fonctions des organismes municipaux du Canada augmentent et les pouvoirs de nos cités et de nos villes tendent à se développer de la même manière que nos organismes provinciaux et fédéraux.

Ce que nous observons au Canada et dans les autres pays n'est pas qu'un accroissement du pouvoir central. Sans doute, il y a un accroissement du pouvoir central dans ce que nous observons; les nécessités de la guerre nous ont imposé des rigueurs dont on se serait à peine douté en 1939.

Mais de pair avec la centralisation fédérale, nous voyons que les fonctions de tous les organismes de notre pays ont augmenté et je crois qu'il serait plus juste de dire que les pouvoirs des organismes de l'Etat ont augmenté, que de croire que seuls les pouvoirs du gouvernement central ont augmenté.

Si, pour un moment, nous observons la scène internationale, nous voyons la même tendance; les commissions conjointes des [alliés] assument de vastes pouvoirs pour régir divers Etats et même plusieurs peuples à la fois. Des corps comme la Commission des approvisionnements, l'Office de la production des ressources, le Prêt-aide et d'autres corps semblables donnent des directives et posent des actes qui font partie de la politique du Canada. Car les pays du monde actuel ne seront que des provinces dans le futur ordre mondial.

Tout ceci n'est qu'une manière de dire que le monde se détache de plus en plus de la fameuse politique économique du laisser-faire. La grande philosophie capitaliste du 19e siècle décline rapidement; des esprits caustiques diraient qu'elle est morte. Pour la remplacer, une société plus cellulaire, plus organique semble se former. L'individu devient moins un être sans nom, un atome, et plus un membre agissant au sein d'un organisme bien agencé. Aujourd'hui, nous parlons moins d'un seul ouvrier et plus des unions ouvrières. Nous pensons moins en termes d'un seul cultivateur, qu'en termes de la classe agricole et des moyens de l'aider comme groupe, à atteindre un standard de vie plus élevé. Nous voyons tous les jours, le petit marchand se débattre pour ne pas tomber en faillite et nous nous intéressons aux mouvements coopératifs qui protègent leurs membres avec l'aide mutuelle. Nous parlons beaucoup d'étatiser les utilités publiques, mais nous ne suggérons jamais que des entreprises déjà étatisées soient remises à des intérêts privés. Et si l'entreprise privée est si bien adaptée à l'homme moderne, comment expliquer les tendances actuelles tournées vers le même but: c'est-à-dire, vers une société mieux contrôlée, plus étatisée.

Comme mon auditoire peut s'en douter, je ne suis pas de ceux qui craignent cette tendance. Je sais qu'il y a des dangers graves que nous rencontrerons et que nous rencontrons déjà. D'abord, il se peut que les pouvoirs de l'Etat augmentent au point de dominer et d'écraser complètement l'individu. Ensuite, il y a le danger pour les minorités que la majorité impose indûment ses volontés et ne tolère que peu de liberté pour une culture différente.

Dans un moment, je discuterai ces dangers; mais en général, je crois sincèrement que la fin de la politique du laisser-faire est une excellente chose. Personne sûrement n'appellera société démocratique ou chrétienne, une société qui n'a aucun sens de responsabilité envers l'individu. L'individualisme a été poussé trop loin. Et si je comprends bien la doctrine de l'Eglise sur ce point, j'ai bien l'impression qu'elle a toujours condamné les excès du libéralisme économique. Les autres églises les ont aussi condamnés. L'avènement d'un nouveau sens de responsabilité envers les membres moins fortunés de notre société, le désir d'établir des systèmes de sécurité qui protégeront les plus faibles et les plus malheureux me semblent être le fait d'une société plus policée et plus avancée que cette autre société dans laquelle chacun ne chercha que son avantage personnel abandonnant son frère à son triste sort et le laissant seul dans sa misère.

Vous croyez peut-être que je m'éloigne de l'Acte de l'Amérique britannique du Nord! Pas tellement, parce que d'après moi, une constitution quelle qu'elle soit, n'est pas un but par elle-même, elle n'est qu'un moyen. Les principaux organismes de l'Etat sont destinés à amener la paix, la sécurité, le bien-être à ses citoyens et leurs fonctions sont définies par un système de loi. La mesure de l'efficacité de cet appareil juridique est établie par le degré de bonheur et de liberté qu'il assure aux citoyens. Si les Canadiens s'entendent sur les principes sur lesquels ils veulent construire leur société, alors sûrement, ils s'entendront sur les grandes lignes d'une constitution nécessaire pour atteindre leurs fins; si d'un autre côté, ils sont divisé quant à leurs aspirations nationales, alors aucune discussion de la constitution n'arrivera à les faire s'accorder.

Notre premier besoin est de porter dans nos esprits et dans nos coeurs, l'image d'un Canada auquel nous désirons tous appartenir et à la grandeur duquel nous voulons tous contribuer. Mais il faut que cette image soit réaliste, il faut tenir compte des distances, des diverses nationalités et des différentes religions. Il ne saurait être question d'une constitution purement théorique; notre constitution doit être essentiellement canadienne, elle doit utiliser nos traditions passées tout en se préparant à rencontrer nos besoins futurs. Nous devons à mon avis, demeurer un Etat fédéral, bilingue et démocratique. De plus, nous devons nous préparer à prendre notre place parmi les grandes nations industrielles du monde moderne.

En 1867, nos grands-pères se sont entendus sur la constitution du Canada. Ils ont réuni plusieurs provinces en un seul Etat. Il y eut alors des dissensions – plus nombreuses dans les provinces maritimes que dans le Québec – mais en général la solution offerte à ces problèmes passés était raisonnable et si nous regardons en arrière, il n'est pas facile de voir qu'une meilleure solution ait pu être trouvée. Je crois qu'avec toutes ses imperfections, l'Acte britannique de l'Amérique du Nord fut une oeuvre constructive qui a permis aux Canadiens de langue anglaise et aux Canadiens de langue française de se mieux développer qu'ils ne l'avaient fait jusque-là.

Il est aussi évident qu'au lieu de nous diriger vers l'unification de nos deux grandes cultures, nous nous sommes dirigés de plus en plus vers la reconnaissance totale de nos deux grandes cultures respectives. J'aime à croire, qu'avec le temps nous percevrons mieux que nous sommes tous citoyens d'un même pays et que nous sommes d'abord et avant tout des Canadiens; ensuite, nous sommes membres d'un groupe ethnique et culturel. A moins que nous apprenions à nous sentir membres d'un seul pays auquel nous devons notre allégeance politique, nous ne serons jamais capables de profiter pleinement de nos opportunités et nous continuerons à perdre notre temps dans des conflits de nationalités et dans des divisions internes.

Si nous nous mettons à la tâche, par l'orgueil légitime de notre passé et avec la détermination d'envisager l'avenir avec bonne volonté, nos problèmes sont déjà à moitié résolus. Croyons-nous que des changements s'imposent dans la distribution des pouvoirs entre le gouvernement fédéral et les gouvernements provinciaux? Voilà la grande question. L'Acte britannique de l'Amérique du Nord fut conçu et rédigé à la grande période du laisser-faire; la croissance d'une société mieux intégrée et plus démocratiquement conçue postule-t-elle un changement dans une constitution faite pour une époque où l'individualisme était la règle? Avant de répondre à cette question, rappelons-nous certains faits. A cause de l'industrialisation de notre pays, la nature de nos relations dans le domaine national a beaucoup changé depuis 50 ans. De nouvelles situations nécessitant un contrôle par l'Etat se sont imposées. C'est pourquoi, notre constitution est discutée. Aujourd'hui, nous sommes forcés d'envisager la question constitutionnelle non pas tant parce que nous voulons changer notre société, mais bien parce que celle-ci a déjà changé. Notre constitution s'adapte plus ou moins par elle-même à de nouveaux besoins sociaux dérivant de sources extra-légales.

Personne en 1867 pouvait prévoir l'essor manufacturier et commercial que prendrait le Canada. A ce moment nos pères avaient des visées beaucoup plus simples. L'agriculture était la principale source de richesses. Le chômage était inconnu et lorsqu'il y en avait, on y remédiait par un retour sur les terres et par des secours de familles. La plupart des industries étaient petites, les employeurs étaient en relations étroites avec leurs employés. Les distances étaient immenses; il fallait des semaines et même des mois pour se rendre de l'Est à l'Ouest. Aujourd'hui, une grande corporation peut faire affaire dans plusieurs provinces, une seule compagnie peut avoir des usines dans toutes les parties du Canada, sous le contrôle d'un seul bureau de direction.

Les ouvriers membres d'une seule union sont capables de déclarer une grève qui peut commencer simultanément dans plusieurs provinces. Le bien-être, les salaires de milliers de Canadiens dépendent aujourd'hui de la décision de quelques individus de Montréal ou de Toronto, ou encore du prix d'un produit sur le marché mondial: par exemple, la mévente de notre blé.

Ainsi, afin que des milliers d'ouvriers du Québec, qui travaillent dans les usines ou industries de guerre, conservent leurs emplois il faudra trouver des marchés à l'extérieur pour absorber la production après la guerre. Ainsi, les emplois dans la province de Québec ne sont pas uniquement un problème restreint aux limites de la province et conséquemment ne peuvent pas être solutionnés uniquement par une loi provinciale. De plus, le taux des salaires dans Québec sera affecté par les taux de l'Ontario ou du Nouveau-Brunswick aussi bien que par les taux en vigueur aux Etats-Unis et dans les autres pays.

Nous sommes véritablement forcés de devenir citoyens d'un monde beaucoup plus grand que celui où vivaient nos pères. La marche en avant de l'industrialisme que certains craignent tant, nous oblige de nous unir et de coopérer si nous ne voulons pas crever de faim. Nous sommes obligés de voir nos relations avec les autres pays sur un plan plus large et plus grand. Londres est plus près de Québec que Montréal ne l'était il y a encore peu de temps. L'avion, le téléphone, la radio et l'auto ont réduit le Canada à de petites proportions et pour chacune des parties de notre pays, ils ont rendu l'isolement national ou international tout à fait impossible.

Lorsque nous réfléchissons à ces changements profonds, nous pouvons mieux comprendre la rapide croissance des diverses fonctions de nos gouvernements; les relations entre les individus sont devenues plus complexes et pour ainsi dire, plus dépendantes les unes des autres et cela nécessite une direction plus unifiée. Le risque d'accidents industriels, le problème des taudis, ont augmenté et sont ainsi devenus moins contrôlables individuellement. De plus en plus, nous voyons que si nous n'anticipons pas les besoins de la santé publique, du logement, de l'éducation et des emplois en général par des lois positives, bien des gens n'auront pas leur part du patrimoine national.

Durant la dernière grande crise, des centaines de milliers de chômeurs voulaient travailler et pourtant ne trouvèrent pas d'ouvrage. Le gouvernement décidant d'un vaste programme de travaux publics aurait fait plus pour créer des emplois à nos ouvriers, que des millions d'individus se cherchant chacun un emploi chez des employeurs particuliers.

Pour faire face aux exigences d'un âge industrialiste, l'Etat a dû faire de nouvelles lois et créer de nouvelles administrations à la fois, provinciales et fédérales. En fait, l'une des plus remarquables caractéristiques de l'Etat moderne est l'accroissement des agences gouvernementales et l'essor des lois administratives. Dans le domaine du droit civil, nous notons un déclin correspondant. Tous les jours, nous pouvons constater que la Législature du Québec adopte des statuts spéciaux qui régissent des sphères qui étaient autrefois du domaine du code civil. Par exemple, les lois sur les salaires minima, les contrats d'employés et d'employeurs, la loi des accidents du travail, les lois sanitaires qui prévoient l'inspection des usines, en un mot, toutes lois qui affectent et restreignent de quelque manière le régime de la propriété.

Les droits des individus sont à la baisse, tandis que les obligations sociales augmentent. Avant la guerre, et sur une même échelle, la France – une de nos mères patries – est passée par les mêmes expériences. A l'Université McGill, reconnaissant cette tendance, nous avons augmenté notre enseignement du droit public et administratif, suivant en cela, l'exemple de beaucoup d'autres facultés de droit de notre continent.

Le problème constitutionnel est un des aspects du changement général qui prend place dans nos relations sociales actuelles. L'organisme de contrôle et de régie qui régnera sur notre économie nationale croît sans cesse et si cet organisme de régie publique doit survivre, il tirera sûrement ses pouvoirs de notre constitution. Mais d'où seront-ils tirés? Découleront-ils du domaine fédéral ou du domaine provincial? Voilà toute la question. Les nécessités de la présente guerre ont amené la croissance soudaine des pouvoirs du gouvernement fédéral; ceux-ci se sont accrus plus rapidement que les pouvoirs provinciaux dans le même domaine, mais cette tendance doit-elle se continuer ou devons-nous espérer retourner à notre situation d'avant-guerre lorsque la paix sera revenue?

Entre les divers pouvoirs législatifs, nous devons faire des distinctions claires et précises. Les divers contrôles du gouvernement fédéral doivent être soigneusement analysés et nous devons savoir exactement ce en quoi ils consistent. En soi, le fameux mot « centralisation » ne veut rien dire; nous sommes intéressés au plus haut point à ce qu'il peut vouloir dire en pratique.

Tout Etat fédéral doit subir une certaine centralisation; personne je pense, ne voudrait suggérer qu'Ottawa n'ait aucun pouvoir.

Voyons alors, quelle est la véritable situation aujourd'hui. D'abord, le gouvernement central dirige et contrôle toutes les opérations militaires, navales et aériennes, recrute des soldats, les équipe et pourvoit aux fournitures de guerre. Pour fournir le matériel nécessaire, les autorités fédérales sont à toutes fins pratiques, obligées de voir à ce que leur marchandise soit produite et distribuée sur une grande échelle à nos armées. Tout près de 800 millions de dollars de l'argent des contribuables sont aujourd'hui investis dans nos industries de guerre. Cette centralisation est uniquement faite pour des fins militaires et ne peut être entreprise que par le gouvernement fédéral. Si nous voulons mettre un terme à cette centralisation, nous devons non seulement gagner la guerre mais gagner la paix qui la suivra.

Le meilleur moyen d'éviter la guerre à l'avenir est de voir à ce que le prochain ordre international soit capable de conserver la paix. De nature, un ordre militaire est un ordre centralisateur. Nous pouvons être assurés que si le Canada participe jamais à une autre guerre mondiale, nous subirons une centralisation encore plus intense et plus rigide que celle dont nous nous plaignons aujourd'hui. Lorsque la paix sera revenue, toutes ces fonctions du gouvernement fédéral reprendront leur proportion normale. Mais d'un autre côté, elles continueront d'exister pour quelque temps après la guerre, afin de permettre de trouver des emplois aux hommes qui seront licenciés et aussi pour affecter un réajustement des soldes et des pensions qu'il faudra payer.

Ensuite, Ottawa se prévaut de certains contrôles nécessaires pour éviter l'inflation et pour distribuer des marchandises et du matériel à ceux qui en ont le plus besoin. Ainsi nous subissons maintenant un contrôle des prix, un plafonnement des salaires, des priorités de toutes sortes et le rationnement des denrées et des biens de consommation. Toutes ces choses sont de nouvelles expériences pour les Canadiens et ces restrictions nous affectent tous personnellement. Observons, en passant, qu'aucun de ces pouvoirs extraordinaires ne fut jamais utilisé par les provinces, sauf en de rares cas particuliers. Avant la guerre, aucune province n'était pas prête à faire de l'économie dirigée et Ottawa, par ces mesures, a restreint les prérogatives des corporations privées beaucoup plus que celles des provinces. Auparavant, les corporations et les trusts décidaient des questions de prix, de production et de salaire, sauf dans ce dernier cas, les salaires minima. La politique du gouvernement central dans ces domaines était à prévoir; les décisions prises étaient inévitables. Il est facile de constater qu'il aurait été impossible de prévenir l'inflation au Canada par les différentes législations provinciales. Si nous nous étions fiés à ces dernières, nous aurions été témoins d'une hausse incontrôlable des prix, comme à la dernière guerre.

Lorsque la guerre finira, je crois que les pouvoirs constitutionnels du fédéral ne seront pas suffisants pour lui permettre de continuer dans ce sens: les règlements du commerce permis par le parlement fédéral sont restreints par une interprétation légale, à bien peu de chose, à l'exception du commerce national et peut-être du commerce interprovincial. Le plafonnage des prix semble bien être en dehors de la juridiction fédérale. On ne peut pas geler les prix sans contrôler les salaires puisque les salaires forment en grande partie les prix et cela aussi semble bien n'être pas du domaine fédéral en temps de paix.

A moins de modifier la constitution, ou à moins que nos cours civiles les interprètent de nouveau, nous devons nous attendre à vois Ottawa abandonner beaucoup de ses contrôles, parce que le gouvernement fédéral ne possède pas l'autorité constitutionnelle nécessaire pour continuer à les exercer après la guerre. Cela veut dire que ces contrôles retourneront aux trusts, aux banques et aux corporations privées qui les détenaient avant la guerre. Autour de 1930, nous avons appris ce qui peut résulter de cet abandon des devoirs de l'Etat aux corporations privées. Nous pourrons facilement tomber dans une autre crise parce que même nos plus puissantes corporations privées sont tout à fait incapables de contrôler effectivement une hausse générale des biens de consommation.

Il se peut très bien, que nous soyons forcés de choisir entre une centralisation ou un désastre économique en tant que certains contrôles économiques sont concernés. Personnellement, je n'ai aucune hésitation. Ces contrôles économiques qui ne peuvent pas être efficacement exercés par une province et dont notre économie entière dépend, doit appartenir au gouvernement fédéral. Autrement, nous nous dirigeons la tête la première vers l'anarchie économique.

De plus, aujourd'hui, le gouvernement fédéral exerce un contrôle financier très sévère; les provinces ont abandonné le prélèvement de l'impôt et des taxes des corporations pour la durée de la guerre. Une entreprise privée ne peut investir dans une nouvelle industrie ou même se procurer un nouvel équipement sans une licence. Devons-nous entrevoir beaucoup de cette centralisation à l'avenir? Voilà sans doute, une question assez difficile; d'abord il nous faut observer que les pouvoirs des provinces et des municipalités de taxer, demeurent entiers aujourd'hui et leur procurent des revenus considérables. De plus, si un jour, les provinces étatisent les corporations d'utilités publiques comme l'électricité et peut-être la distribution de l'essence, les revenus des provinces augmenteront énormément parce que ces étatisations rapporteront des profits.

Je me rends compte de proférer une hérésie économique en prétendant que l'Etat doit d'un côté étatiser certaines utilités publiques et d'autre part, y trouver son profit. Il ne faut pas oublier qu'en Suède, pour ne citer qu'un exemple, les pensions de vieillesse sont payées par le gouvernement à même les profits réalisés par le trust du tabac contrôlé par l'Etat.

Je ne suis pas ici pour vous exposer une théorie économique, je veux seulement vous indiquer qu'il n'est pas probable que les provinces perdent jamais les contrôles de leurs revenus. Bien au contraire, à mon sens, les revenus provinciaux augmenteront. Ainsi le contrôle fédéral dans certains domaines de la finance apparaît moins dangereux. Avec l'entente actuelle, les provinces jouiront de nouveau de l'impôt sur le revenu et des taxes de corporation après la guerre; d'un autre côté, il faut nous demander si quelqu'un profite du fait d'avoir trois différentes espèces de taxes sur le revenu au Canada au lieu d'une seule taxe? Sous l'ancien système, un contribuable payait une taxe sur son revenu à la municipalité, une à la province et une autre au Dominion. Et en autant que les provinces reçoivent une part équitable au lieu de prélever l'impôt sur le revenu, pourquoi encourir les ennuis et les dépenses de deux ou trois différentes remises de chaque contribuable?

Enfin, nous voyons l'autorité fédérale devenir de plus en plus préoccupée des problèmes de l'assurance-chômage et de l'administration ouvrière. Le degré de centralisation existant actuellement ne doit pas être exagéré. Actuellement, il ne s'agit pas du tout de savoir combien de législations sociales existent, mais combien peu!

Sous ce rapport, notre pays est arriéré et tout Canadien, le Canadien-Français comme le Canadien-Anglais, en est plus pauvre d'autant. La seule loi importante dans ce domaine, qui est centralisée, est l'assurance-chômage et les classes ouvrières du Canada ne sont pas prêtes à regretter cette modification à l'Acte britannique de l'Amérique du Nord. Les pensions de vieillesse ne sont pas réellement centralisées parce qu'aucune province n'est obligée d'accepter ces mesures. Le présent projet d'assurance-maladie, quoiqu'il soit originaire d'Ottawa, n'est pas obligatoire pour aucune province et si l'une d'elle l'adopte, elle demeure libre de l'administrer comme bon lui semble.

Dans la province de Québec, de nombreuses discussions se sont élevées au sujet des agissements du Dominion dans le domaine de la législation sociale. Je crois sincèrement que beaucoup de ces craintes sont exagérées, parce que personne n'a proposé la centralisation complète de quoi que ce soit, de ce côté. Evidemment, quant aux lois qui ont trait à la famille, à l'éducation, les allocations aux mères nécessiteuses, les pensions aux veuves et les autres questions sociales où entrent en jeu les différentes cultures, dans les différentes parties du Canada, il vaut mieux qu'elles soient passées et administrées par les provinces et même dans certains cas, après les municipalités. Dans certaines parties de l'Ouest du Canada, il existe un praticien qu'on appelle le Dr Municipal et les statistiques montrent qu'il fut un succès partout où il fut engagé. J'aimerais voir les différents services de bien-être social dans le domaine provincial, se développer et non décroître.

Mais cela ne veut pas dire que le pouvoir central n'aura absolument rien à faire dans ce domaine; au contraire, le parlement fédéral du Canada ne peut rester indifférent et demeurer inactif devant les souffrances humaines et devant les misères de nos concitoyens. Tout le monde sera d'accord pour admettre que le devoir d'encourager la santé, de procurer de bons foyers aux familles et donner la chance aux enfants de grandir et d'être élevés convenablement et hygiéniquement devrait être un devoir important, dans tout programme d'une véritable politique nationale et non seulement dans son programme provincial. Si nous sommes plus heureux, en meilleure santé et plus forts en nous servant de tous les organismes de notre gouvernement, au lieu de nous servir uniquement des organismes de notre gouvernement local, nous devrions user de tous nos moyens, tout en maintenant toujours un juste équilibre et en reconnaissant le rôle fondamental que les provinces sont appelées à jouer.

Je voudrais qu'un principe coopératif prévale dans ce domaine et que tous nos organismes gouvernementaux fassent le maximum de leurs efforts et adoptent des lois afin de faire disparaître les injustices criantes et les inégalités évidentes que nos statistiques nous montrent sans l'ombre d'un doute. Non moins évidemment, nous ne saurions tolérer une centralisation complète, parce que les gouvernements provinciaux sont plus près de leurs citoyens et ainsi connaissent mieux leurs besoins; et même dans le cas où une politique nationale relèverait d'Ottawa, comme par exemple, l'assurance-chômage, l'administration d'une telle agence nationale pourrait être décentralisée.

La législation ouvrière devrait être traitée de la même manière. N'oublions pas que si les provinces ont une grande responsabilité à assumer dans ces domaines, cela ne veut pas dire, qu'Ottawa ne doit s'occuper de rien!

Nos grandes industries, comme nos unions ont maintenant des activités nationales, c'est-à-dire, qui dépassent de beaucoup les limites de nos provinces. Il n'est que logique que le droit d'exiger et de discuter un contrat collectif de travail entre employeurs et employés soit garanti par une loi fédérale quant aux industries nationales.

En 1907, le besoin d'une législation ouvrière se fit sentir; la loi Lemieux fut votée pour être ensuite désavouée devant le Conseil privé.[1] Il n'en reste pas moins vrai que notre tradition légale a déjà reconnu la nécessité d'une loi fédérale sur les conflits industriels. D'ailleurs l'Australie et les Etats-Unis qui ont tous deux une constitution fédérale, admettent ce principe.

Nous devons aussi considérer la législation ouvrière sous un autre aspect. Aujourd'hui, la question du traitement de nos ouvriers dans les industries n'est plus une question purement provinciale. Elle a même dépassé notre plan national. Nous vivons maintenant dans un monde qui essaie de former une législation internationale pour les problèmes ouvriers et il est de connaissance publique qu'aujourd'hui, il existe un organe international qu'on appelle le Bureau international du travail. Cette organisation s'est occupée de trois questions sur lesquelles M. Bennett a légiféré; les salaires minima, les heures de travail et le jour de repos par semaine. Mais le Conseil privé déclara ces lois *ultra vires*.[2]

Je crois que le Canada devrait coopérer à cette forme de collaboration interna-

1 *Toronto Electric Commissioners* v. *Snider* [1925] A.C. 396.
2 *A.-G. for Can.* v. *A.-G. for Ont.* (Minimum Wages Act, Weekly Rest in Industrial Undertakings Act, Limitation of Hours of Works) [1936] S.C.R. 461–538 et [1937] A.C. 326, 1 D.L.R. 673, 106 L.J.P.C. 72, 156 L.T. 302, 53 T.L.R. 325.

tionale qui est un moyen pour constituer un meilleur ordre social après la guerre. Mais afin d'y coopérer, le Canada doit avoir les pouvoirs de voter à Ottawa des lois quelles que soient les recommandations suggérées par le Bureau international du travail. Et lorsque le rapport Sirois recommandait que l'Acte britannique de l'Amérique du Nord soit modifié dans ce sens, je crois qu'il était dans la bonne voie. Si nous sommes le moins du monde avertis des événements internationaux, nous devons accepter l'évidence qui nous montre que beaucoup de problèmes économiques et sociaux, sur lesquels nous discutons au Canada, deviennent de plus en plus des problèmes non seulement nationaux et fédéraux, mais internationaux.

Après cette brève analyse de la nature de la présente centralisation au Canada je me suis permis de regarder vers l'avenir et j'ai suggéré qu'il y a des domaines où nous pouvons nous attendre que notre parlement fédéral agisse et prenne de nouvelles responsabilités. J'espère sincèrement en avoir dit assez, pour éloigner de vos esprits les appréhensions et les craintes que des prophètes de malheur se plaisent à répéter, à savoir que les provinces sont appelées à disparaître.

Bien au contraire, ces changements raffermiront le rôle des provinces et nous permettront de ramener et de consolider notre sécurité économique afin que les provinces et nos autres gouvernements locaux puissent fonctionner facilement et avec efficacité. Le système fédéral ne doit pas être aboli, mais nous devons chercher à le rendre propre à nos présents besoins. Le but constant de tout système future de loi, que nous devrons adopter devrait toujours être en fin de compte la préservation des valeurs culturelles et spirituelles de nos deux grandes civilisations.

# XI

# Constitutional Adaptations to Changing Functions of Government

*An article emphasizing the remarkable flexibility of the Canadian constitution within the rigid framework of the BNA Act.*
From the *Canadian Journal of Economics and Political Science*, 11, 1945, 330-41

It is appropriate that we should be studying today the growth in the functions and powers of the state. Whether we look at our federal, our provincial, or our municipal governments, whether we look abroad at our sister democracies or toward the less democratic régimes, the same phenomenon is evident; everywhere there is occurring an enlargement of the role in society which is being played by the political organisms created by man for his security and welfare. Political man is at last resurrecting himself, and political science seems likely to challenge the erstwhile supremacy of her dismal sister, economics. As this paper is being written, a second attempt is being made to build an international organization endowed with important functions in the world society, an attempt which, if successful, will add a supra-national authority to the existing state organs on the national plane. Whatever the end result may be, it is apparent that the trend away from an individualistic and unplanned society toward one that is more integrated and organic is not only continuing but is greatly accelerating.

Such a development both within and between the nation states puts a strain upon national constitutions. New functions for the state mean new organs for the fulfilment of those functions, or new uses for old organs. New organs must be added to an existing structure, causing shifts of power and frequent disequilibriums. Legislative processes designed for a smaller sphere of state duties and a more leisurely pace of social change are found inadequate for the increased responsibilities of governments, and a rapid, sometimes alarming, expansion of administrative processes results. No type of state escapes these pains of adjustment, be it unitary or federal. But in the federal state a special aspect of the problem arises, with respect to the distribution of the new functions between the central and local governments. Many fear that a growing centralization may tend to destroy the regional autonomy which is a fundamental part of the federal idea.

Canada possesses a constitution which is now one of the older ones of the world. Most states date their basic political institutions later than 1867. We have therefore had to adapt ourselves to a particularly long period of state growth without any major revision of the fundamental law of the constitution. It is perhaps some tribute to the framers of Canadian federalism that this has been possible; that we have been able to grow from a population of three and a half to twelve million, from colonialism to sovereignty, from agriculturalism to industrialism, without revolution or civil war. But the absence of violent or sudden change does not, of course, mean the absence of all change. Judicial interpretation, no less than formal amendment, moulds the ancient concepts. The BNA Act is particularly flexible in time of war; indeed the Canada of this war has undergone the equivalent of a constitutional revolution since those days less than a decade ago when we were too poor to undertake the public works which might reduce unemployment, and too hampered by constitutional difficulties to provide federal initiative and leadership in the expansion of production and the establishment of social security. A central government which could not provide three square meals a day to the hundreds of thousands on relief, and helplessly observed the shutting down of factories and laying off of personnel, now pours its billions annually among the astonished citizens and calls forth miracles of production from old and new enterprises.

As a statistical illustration of the increase in the functions of the state, we may remember that in 1866 less than one-twentieth of the income of the population flowed through government channels, and the total expenditures amounted to less than $6.00 per capita; in 1937 total government expenditures were equal to one-quarter of the national income of $90.00 per capita; by 1944 the needs of war alone had brought them to almost half the national income and around $400 per capita. Without seeking to base any argument on war conditions, some of which will undoubtedly be temporary, it is clear that the legal framework for our society must possess considerable adaptability. It is worth examining the process of this adaptation in the principal spheres in which it has taken place.

INTERNATIONAL AFFAIRS

Perhaps the most striking constitutional change since 1867 has been the assumption by Canada of the full attributes of a sovereign state and full responsibility for the conduct of international affairs. This has been a remarkably slow growth, considering the vital democratic principle at stake, but it seems at last to be consummated. Dominion status is thus already a thing of the past, and national independence is the only term which can now be used as truly descriptive of our position. The antiquated language of section 1 of the Statute of Westminster, which places Canada and Newfoundland in the same category as 'Dominions,' must therefore be relegated to the law books; this is a rule of statutory interpretation, not a political definition. The fact is that we now admit no limit to our right to decide every question of foreign and domestic policy for ourselves, even to the extent of declarations of war and peace. The recognition of the separate right to neutrality has been won,[1] though it is to be hoped that in the future the need for such separate national rights will diminish as the measures of force necessary to maintain world peace come to be taken not by Canada alone, nor by the Commonwealth as a group of nations, but according to the decision of a world organization.

Very little change in the written constitution has been necessary to make this political transition possible. The letter of the BNA Act remains practically unaltered. Because foreign affairs are carried on under the royal prerogative, it has been possible to transfer their control to Canada by the simple process of agreeing that when the Crown acts for Canada in foreign affairs it must do so on the advice of Canadian and not of British ministers. We have, so to speak, nationalized the Crown. A notable step in this process was the Seals Act of 1939, which marked a real advance in Canadian control over the expression of the royal will. Canada's representation abroad, developing from the early agent to the full ambassador, and covering the main capitals of the world, well illustrates the march of this progress, though we have still not separated the functions of Prime Minister and Foreign Secretary. This change in international status rests on convention and on international recognition rather than on statute; Australia, for example, issued her first declaration of war, against Japan, before she had even adopted the Statute of Westminster. The Statute of Westminster did not of itself transfer the control over external affairs; what it did was to transfer the last remnants of the legislative sovereignty of the imperial Parliament to Canada in respect of everything save the amendment of the BNA Act.

This last exception serves to remind us that our constitution has not yet completed its adaptation to our new international situation. While an established convention leaves little doubt that we can amend our constitution whenever a mere majority of our Senate and House of Commons demand it (even when, as the op-

---

1 Up to 1939 the majority of Canadian authorities still believed we had no right to neutrality. But so much attention has been focussed on the separate declaration of war by Canada on September 10 and it has been used so often as proof of our freedom of choice, that it has now become generally accepted as establishing a right. Ireland is, however, the classic example.

position of Quebec to the amendment of 1943 showed, a provincial legislature opposes the change) nevertheless the practice of travelling abroad for such national legislation seems too incongruous to survive for long even among a people so constitutionally afraid of changing their constitution as are the Canadians.

A more serious delay in adaptation is seen in the continuation of the appeal to the Privy Council; more serious, since whereas the imperial Parliament has never rejected the request of our Parliament for an amendment, and probably would never do so, the Privy Council frequently rejects the opinion of our Supreme Court as to the interpretation of our laws. The one is a rubber stamp, the other an active agency of government. Other lesser matters have also not been changed; the obsolete veto power of the imperial Crown remains, Canadian citizenship has not been clearly established, and lingering relics of the ancient theory of the indivisibility of the Crown still cause confusion.[2] It is to be noticed also that our constitutional symbolism has not yet recognized the new status, and that with respect to the national flag, the national anthem, and the office of Governor-General the older practices still prevail.

It should not be forgotten when discussing our assumption of national status that we have suffered one constitutional change which diminishes rather than extends our competence. Our treaty-making power, instead of keeping pace with our international growth, has shrunk under restrictive interpretation. While all types of treaty appear to be within the executive jurisdiction of the federal government as regards negotiation and ratification, the implementation of treaties and conventions is split between Dominion and provinces in accordance with the judicial view of its subject matter under the headings of sections 91 and 92. The only time we possess full federal legislative jurisdiction over treaties, is when we are bound by a treaty between 'the Empire' and a foreign country and section 132 of the BNA Act can operate. Our provinces therefore by a sort of indirection have been endowed with international responsibilities. A new standing order of the ILO makes it possible for them to be represented at its conferences. Are they to join the Ukraine and White Russia in demanding a separate membership in the world organization? This would fit in with Lord Haldane's understanding that 'The provinces should be autonomous places as if they were autonomous Dominions.' If we sometimes are worried about national unity in Canada we should remember that Lord Haldane uttered those words in 1925.[3] The separatist theories of the Judicial Committee are the forerunners of those advanced by the Canadian advocates of provincial autonomy.

2 See, for example, the difficulty faced by the Canadian government in September, 1939, when it prohibited trading with the 'enemy' before we had declared war.
3 During argument in *Toronto Electric Commissioners* v. *Snider et al.*; see report published by Department of Labour, 1925, p. 166.

Along with national sovereignty for Canada has come a greatly increased responsibility for national and continental defence. The airplane has shifted Canada from the periphery toward the centre of world movements. The formerly boundless north now brings us close to a new and giant neighbour. A Privy Council decision gave control over aeronautics to our national Parliament, so that both civil and military aviation can now be fitted into national policy. We have adapted ourselves to ideas of continental defence by establishing with the United States the Permanent Joint Board on Defence. Under any international organization that may be established, this military regionalism is likely to continue. But it brings up once again the problem of Canada's boundaries. Are we to remain content with the present situation on our eastern shores, where 127,000 square miles of the Laurentian shield is considered part of a Labrador whose great airport was entirely constructed by Canadian engineers at Canadian expense? Was not the vision of the Fathers of Confederation with respect to the inclusion of Newfoundland more realistic and more national than our present vision? One may be permitted to hope that for once in our history we shall experience a boundary settlement that we can greet with rejoicing.

ECONOMIC REGULATION

Turning to more domestic affairs, the most striking constitutional adaptations have been made to meet the demands of the new industrialism. The present responsibility of the state for the regulation of economic activities in Canada is not new in kind but only in degree. In 1867 the 'Regulation of Trade and Commerce' was in the forefront of the specified powers of Parliament. True, this regulation was thought of in terms of assistance rather than of control in the modern sense; it was to provide the basic necessities of private business such as canals and railroads, banking and bankruptcy laws, interest and legal tender, and the other requirements of private enterprise. But it included also state operation of enterprises which private business could not or would not undertake, such as the intercolonial railway and the post office. The federal government started also with the habit of tariff regulation well ingrained, and this form of control was used first for revenue purposes and then after 1878, as part of a national economic plan to foster home industries. But the growth and enlargement of federal economic control have been much delayed owing to various decisions of the Privy Council which sharply reduced the content of the trade and commerce clause. Ottawa lost the fight to control the liquor traffic and insurance; the attempt to set up a permanent Board of Commerce after the last war was defeated, and during the great depression even such nationally important matters as unemployment insurance and inter-provincial marketing failed to escape the destructive legal concepts evolved by the courts. There is general agreement that our constitution has departed from the original concept of the trade and commerce powers as it was out-lined by the Fathers of Confederation. Only in respect of communications have the courts been disposed to enlarge federal power; the 'telegraphs' of the constitution now include telephones and radio broadcasting.

While the law of the constitution went one way, the facts of modern industrialism went the other. We have grown more and more dependent on national and international trade; provincial self-sufficiency nowhere exists. Some planning and regulating of this industrial growth was inescapable, and where the state did not act the economy rapidly developed its own legislative controls in private hands through the devious processes of monopoly and price agreement. The pitiful efforts to stem this process by the Combines Act serve only to remind us that once there was a Manchester School. Private enterprise has itself established a regulation of trade and commerce in Canada which, over certain industries and services, is more stringent than any our past governments would have dared to set up had they been armed with the most unlimited powers. But these regulations and controls are partial, not general, and they exist for private, not public purposes. In time of war such luxuries of profit-seeking self-interest could not be tolerated without a very obvious danger to the state. So we have witnessed in Canada, in two world wars, two periods of economic regulation of unprecedented magnitude, which have, for the moment at least, placed the state in a position of dominant economic leadership. Moreover this war, unlike the last, has started the state upon the actual ownership and operation of industry to the tune of some 900 millions of dollars. It is not necessary to give the details of an expansion which has been frequently described in both public and private publications, and of whose results in terms of production Canadians may be justly proud. Nor am I concerned here with the political battle over the future relationship between business and government. What concerns us is the constitutional adaptation which has made such an achievement possible.

There has been no disagreement in the courts with the legal proposition that the residuary powers of the national Parliament are operative at least in time of war. The War Measures Act thus has ample constitutional basis, even if the specific federal power over 'Militia, Military and Naval Service, and Defence' were not in itself adequate to support it. The demands of 'total war' are such that in the result Canada may almost be said to possess a unitary form of government in war-time. This all-embracing federal war-time power has been extended by a decision of our Supreme Court in 1943[4] to include not only the right of delegation to administrative agencies (which right exists both for the federal and provincial parliaments, the latter having been conceded it in 1883[5]) but even the right of sub-

4 *Reference re Validity of Chemical Regulations*, 1943 S.C.R. 1.
5 *Hodge* v. *Regina*, 9 A.C. 117.

delegation; hence Parliament may entrust to the Governor-in-Council the power to delegate to an administrative body the power to delegate to a controller the power to issue a directive having the force of law. Laws may now emerge type-written on letter-heads signed by John Smith, of which only a carbon copy is kept on file. This is adaptation with a vengeance. Let it no longer be said that totalit-arian régimes can act more expeditiously and efficiently than democracies. And though there are dangers in this situation let it not be said either that this is no different from totalitarianism. All such powers stem from Parliament, in whose jurisdiction the control ultimately rests. What Parliament gave, Parliament can take away. We have retained our ultimate parliamentary control over the adminis-tration; what we have not done is to develop administrative tribunals and a body of administrative law adequate to control the exercise of the new state powers. This is undoubtedly one of the great needs in our present stage of constitutional development.[6]

Naturally this vast economic activity of the state has required new administra-tive agencies. It is on the side of administration that the adaptability and flexibil-ity of the constitution are most apparent. Starting from the Crown's undoubted prerogative right (a) to employ as many servants as it pleases at any time and (b) to engage in any business it chooses, and adding to this the powers granted under the various war statutes, the federal government has been able to expand the civil service, add new government departments, create commissions of control, and set up Crown companies with the greatest of ease. On the financial side it has possessed since 1933 the Bank of Canada, to which has been added foreign ex-change control and, by agreements with the provinces, the exclusive right to levy income and corporation taxes. Man-power regulations and price-fixing come un-der the special war powers. Hence there has been evident a completeness of regu-lative authority such as we have never witnessed before, all of undoubted consti-tutional validity. Even Sir John Macdonald would have been satisfied with this. And while some concern has been felt by local politicians about the invasion of provincial rights, the fact remains that despite all war-time controls the provinces still exist, their income and expenditures have risen, their functions and activities are also expanding, and it would not be easy to establish that minority rights have been in any material way diminished.

Among the various techniques employed by the state the one which seems most to deserve attention is the public corporation, with its latest variant, the Crown Company. Public corporations seem to combine certain valuable features

6 The Province of Ontario is to be complimented on having adopted an Act for the central filing and publication of regulations; this is at least a step toward the publication of this new type of law. See the Regulations Act, 8 Geo. VI, c. 52.

of both public and private enterprise. Professor Dawson has suggested[7] that the Crown Company, the special type of public corporation invented by the Dominion government for certain war purposes, may have outlived its usefulness, but it seems to be well established for the duration of the war at least, and the Province of Saskatchewan has just adopted a Crown Corporations Act[8] which looks to the permanent use of this device for certain developmental purposes. Sir Henry Bunbury, KCB, writing in *Public Administration*,[9] has given it as his opinion that 'the coming years will see in Britain a considerable conversion of what has hitherto been private enterprise into public enterprise,' and he gives his reasons why the Public Corporation has already won a recognized place for this purpose in the administrative services of the modern state. These agencies are public in the sense that their capital is provided by the state and they serve public purposes, not private shareholders, but they resemble private corporations in that they are generally independent of direct political interference, engage their own personnel, keep their own accounts, and exercise a considerable degree of initiative. The Dominion Crown Companies are more closely integrated with the work of a government department – Munitions and Supply – than are the older forms of public corporations such as the Hydro-Electric Commissions or the telephone systems of the Prairie Provinces. In Canada there is nothing to prevent public corporations being set up on either the federal or provincial level. Private capital may equally well be mixed with public capital, as in the early days of the Bank of Canada. The managerial techniques of private capitalism thus find their way into the state machine.

The subject of constitutional adaptation to state economic regulation cannot be left without commenting on the grave situation that faces us at the end of this war. Put simply, the problem is this: the need for federal control will survive the war, but much of the federal power will not.[10] The trade and commerce clause, as previously indicated, has suffered from restrictive interpretations, and it is not easy to see where the courts will find the legal basis for federal legislation which will almost certainly be needed, under any political régime, in such fields as price control, wage regulation, priority allocations, interprovincial marketing, and others, during the transition to a peace economy and after. It has been suggested that even a statute so closely related to soldier rehabilitation as the Reinstatement in Civil Employment Act is beyond federal jurisdiction in peace-time. The plain truth is that a number of constitutional adaptations in Canada necessitated by (*a*) certain restrictive judicial interpretations of the constitution and (*b*) the de-

7 In *Problems of Modern Government* (Toronto, 1941), p. 32.
8 Bill no. 78 of 1945.
9 Vol. XXII, no. 3, winter no. 1944–5, p. 137.
10 I have dealt with this problem in *Canada after the War* ed. A. Brady and F.R. Scott (Toronto, 1943), chap. III.

mands of our modern industrial society for new forms of economic regulation and social security, have just not been permanently made. One of the more highly developed arts in Canada is the art of postponement. While the Sirois Report produced much understanding, it resulted in practically no change. We have a rendezvous with the BNA Act which sooner or later we must keep.

## PUBLIC WELFARE

The welfare functions of the modern state form one of its major responsibilities. In both the provincial and federal spheres in Canada the growth of these activities has continued. The process, far from slackening, is gathering momentum; indeed by comparison with many of our sister democracies we are obviously lacking in many recognized types of social insurance, and their adoption cannot be long delayed. Upon a wise apportionment of these responsibilities among our several governments much of our future happiness as well as our financial stability, will depend.

In the original constitution the general control over 'hospitals, asylums, charities and eleemosynary institutions,' as well as 'public and reformatory prisons,' was given to the provinces. The only specified welfare powers of the Dominion were marine hospitals, and penitentiaries. In the agricultural communities of that day this was a natural allocation, and the expansion of activities in these fields came normally and properly through municipal and provincial action in so far as it was not entirely left to private philanthropy. But it must not be forgotten that the word 'welfare' was used in describing the residuary powers of the Dominion in both the Quebec and London resolutions; the phrase 'peace, welfare and good government' was only replaced by 'peace, order and good government' in the drafts of the BNA Act. That the national government should concern itself with the welfare of its citizens was not an idea foreign to the founding Fathers, and even the Privy Council, in *Russell* v. *the Queen*, considered that the safeguarding of Canadian sobriety belonged in the category of matters the cure of which was a federal responsibility outside the field of property and civil rights. Later cases, which have effectively overruled this decision, have still referred to such things as 'pestilence' and 'famine' as justifying the use of federal emergency powers. Even on the narrowest view the constitution does not exclude federal welfare responsibility altogether. If one adds the federal wardship of Indians – which, by judicial interpretation, now includes Eskimos – the unlimited federal rule over the North West Territories and federal obligations to war veterans, there is a considerable area of direct obligation resting on Ottawa for welfare measures.

These constitutional powers, however, have proven quite inadequate to meet the newer needs. Two basic factors have shown the impossibility of securing to

Canadians an equality or sufficiency of protection by purely provincial action. One is the enormous cost of contemporary welfare schemes, which few, if any, provinces can pay with their limited resources and taxing powers. The other is the close relationship of social insurance to an industrial development that has now reached not only national but international magnitude. The big risks go with the big industries, and there too are to be found the chief sources of wealth which must pay for the protection. National economic policy and national insurances cannot easily be separated.

The adaptations of our constitution to this situation have been various. All governments have developed their health and welfare activities under special departments financed out of ordinary revenues. This is a simple expansion of executive functions. Some matters, notably Workmen's Compensation, have been placed by provinces in the hands of government commissions. In only one instance – unemployment insurance – has there been a direct transfer of jurisdiction to the federal government. Some of the most important developments have come about through the use of conditional grants, which have grown to unusual and perhaps dangerous proportions. Competent studies of our experience with these grants[11] in such fields as Old Age Pensions, Unemployment Relief, VD Control, and Technical Education have concluded that they are 'an inherently unsatisfactory device.' They violate the principle that governments which spend money should raise it; they involve unnecessary duplication in administration; they make it difficult to apply uniform standards. Yet since they have the political advantage of avoiding any constitutional amendment there is a tendency for them to grow. The proposed national health bill of 1944 was based on this principle.

The underlying idea in the Dominion's Family Allowances scheme is somewhat different. Here, though co-operation with provincial governments is invited, Ottawa intends to pay for and administer the plan itself. The theory is that the Crown can pay out its own money to whoever it chooses, and if it chooses to make a gift of so many dollars a month to children under sixteen, who is to say that it has violated the constitution? No province is prevented from going ahead with its own additional scheme if it wants to. Have not the citizens of a province the right to accept gifts from the Ottawa Santa Claus? There would seem to be no invasion here of any legislative power in the province, unless the provincial law were to prohibit receiving such gifts. Yet one cannot overlook the ominous dictum of the Privy Council that 'assuming that the Dominion has collected by means of taxation a fund, it by no means follows that any legislation which disposes of it is necessarily within Dominion competence.'[12]

11 E.g. J.A. Corry, 'Difficulties of Divided Jurisdiction' (Appendix 7 to Sirois Report, chap. VI); Luella Gettys, *The Administration of Canadian Conditional Grants* (Chicago, 1938).
12 In *Unemployment Insurance Reference*, 1937 A.C. at p. 366.

If one seeks a logical division between federal and provincial welfare matters, the key might be found in the word 'charities' in section 92; a charity is a gratuitous hand-out to needy persons, something totally different from a scheme of insurance in which benefits are granted as of right to all contributors. Social insurance and social assistance are two concepts whose difference is very clear to social workers, and it may be the courts will read the distinction into the law of the constitution. The Sirois Report recommended, as the simplest solution, that we should 'provide for concurrent jurisdiction in social insurance.'[13]

## DOMINION-PROVINCIAL FINANCIAL RELATIONS

One aspect of our federalism which has been under periodic review since Confederation, thus indicating a lack of balance and stability in the state structure, has been the financial relations between the national and the provincial governments. The most flexible portion of the BNA Act has been section 118, providing for federal subsidies to provinces. It has been found impossible, partly for political and partly for economic reasons, to maintain the scale of payments originally planned, and Ottawa has had to come to the aid of needy provinces just as now it is coming to the aid of needy individuals. The simple fact is that provincial functions have grown more rapidly than provincial incomes, and only the national government, with its unlimited taxing powers, can ease the strain when it becomes too great. The bold solution proposed by the Sirois Commission, for the pooling of debts, the abolition of subsidies, and the payment of national adjustment grants, having been laid aside, we are still without any certain principles or policies to guide us through the future.

The war has temporarily eased this situation by raising provincial incomes and reducing the interest rate and hence the provincial debt burden. Though the provinces have voluntarily surrendered their income and corporation taxes under the agreements of 1942, they have far higher incomes today than ever before in their histories. All of which underlines the obvious truth that a national policy of high employment and expanding production is the soundest approach for the solution of this as well as other problems. Unfortunately, we cannot assume that these conditions are permanent; the taxation agreements will terminate at the end of the Japanese war, and no amount of employment or national income will act as a substitute for national financial control if provinces revert to their former freedom of taxation and their unlimited borrowing powers. In this sphere also Canadians have merely postponed, not escaped, their constitutional adjustment.

13 Vol. II, p. 43.

LABOUR LEGISLATION

With the growth of industry since Confederation there has developed a need to protect the wages, hours of labour, holidays, vocational training, and organizational rights of industrial workers, who now form the largest group of the gainfully employed. The function of the state in this field has been grudgingly conceded, and has been hampered by the uncertain delimitation of powers. The commercial class which put through Confederation wrote into the list of specified heads in section 91 of the constitution the subjects important to capital and business, but the needs of labour were unformulated and unrepresented. Nevertheless the needs existed, and as early as 1872 the federal Parliament adopted the Trade Union Act and the Criminal Law Amendment Act to free trade unions from the common-law liability on conspiracy in restraint of trade and to provide for national registration. The subject was one believed by many people to be within federal jurisdiction; so much so that in 1873 Nova Scotia omitted from her revised statutes a provincial law of 1864 repealing the Combination Laws.[14] As late as 1882-4 a Dominion government including five Fathers of Confederation introduced three Dominion Factory Bills, and the Minister of Justice, Sir Alexander Campbell, was confident they were constitutional.[15] In 1907 came the Industrial Disputes Investigation Act, which the Canadian Parliament and appellate courts in both Quebec and Ontario considered quite properly within federal powers. In setting aside this statute, and the later ones proposed to implement ILO conventions on minimum wages, maximum hours, and the weekly day of rest, the Privy Council deprived Canadian labour of effective protection by the only government in Canada capable of defending it against the concentrated power of a private capitalism now organized on a national and international basis. The war emergency has brought the federal government back into this field more extensively than ever before, but much of this authority, notably with respect to collective bargaining and wage control, will disappear with the war emergency.

14 See *Trade Union Law in Canada* (Canada, Department of Labour, 1935), p. 18.
15 *Canada, Senate Debates*, 1882, pp. 367–70. The broad, national point of view of the Minister of Justice is well illustrated by the following quotation: 'It is because this Bill relates to subjects so important as that, subjects which go far beyond contracts between master and servant, which in their indirect effects concern the whole community and on which, to a certain extent, and so far as the population in manufacturing establishments go, the future of the country very much turns – whether we shall have a strong, healthy and moral population, likely to be creditable to the country or whether we shall have a dwarfed and immoral population and so perpetuate in Canada all the evils which this inquiry has brought out in England and which we are trying to legislate for now – I say if these subjects do not affect the peace, order and welfare of a whole community it would be hard to say what does.'

As the federal authority has declined, the provincial state activities have grown. A mass of provincial legislation now exists on wages, hours, trade-union organization, collective bargaining, extension of labour agreements, factory inspection, and the like. The adaptation of the constitution has been one of *ad hoc* and piecemeal state intervention without any comprehensive planning or logical division of function. Throughout the development, however, one can discern the emergence of the trade union as a quasi-public institution performing recognized democratic duties, and necessitating the creation of new types of administrative tribunal for the settlement of industrial disputes. Canadians are still experimenting with these matters, and a stable pattern has not yet emerged.

## PARLIAMENTARY INSTITUTIONS

Even a survey of constitutional change as brief as this would be incomplete without reference to Parliament. In our type of federal democracy parliaments are key institutions. In them state power, and the control of that power, converge. State power without parliamentary control means tyranny; an impotent state machine, even with a parliament to watch it, means confusion and anarchy. The functions and responsibility of the state have expanded. How has parliamentary control over those functions kept pace?

The answer seems to be that it has not kept pace. Parliament still has prime duties to perform, and ultimately is the legal source of state authority over most activities, but its relative importance has declined in relation to the executive functions. Without agreeing with Stephen Leacock that Members of Parliament come together merely that they may hear the latest legislation, and indulge in 'Cheers, sighs, groans, votes and other expressions of vitality,' it is generally agreed that the present situation calls for parliamentary reform. Cabinet control over parliamentary business is too great; the ordinary MP is both underpaid and underworked; the control over expenditures has lessened to a dangerous degree, large blocks of estimates being adopted in the dying days of every session. We have at last adopted the practice of appointing ministerial assistants, but the committee work of Parliament has been greatly neglected. In respect of electoral representation, our federal constitution is beginning to adapt itself to the increasing population by a procedure the reverse of democratic; the unit of representation is expanding, and as soon as we embark upon the next redistribution the size of the House of Commons will be reduced. A particular unfairness exists with respect to regional representation; if equality is desired and Quebec is to have sixty-five seats, which seems to have been the original intention under the BNA Act, then today every other province except Alberta has too many members. On democratic principle we need a new method for calculating the size of the House of Commons, and the simplest would seem to be to take some agreed unit, say 40,000 electors, and allow to each province a number of members proportionate to its units. There seems no good reason why we should fear a House of Commons somewhat larger than that which we now possess.

Since Confederation there has been a noticeable decline in the belief in second chambers. Quebec alone possesses a provincial Upper House, whose abolition has been frequently promised, and the opinion in favour of abolishing the Senate has gathered considerable strength in recent years.[16] There has been a marked reduction in the activities of the Senate during this war. The truth is that the Commons itself has become a sort of second chamber, since private Members' bills are almost extinct, and government bills are not only gone over carefully by the Cabinet and some department before presentation, but are increasingly becoming the subject of debate and discussion with extra-parliamentary bodies such as trade associations, trade unions, farm organizations, etc., before presentation to Parliament itself.[17] The chief reason in Canada, however, for the decline in Senate prestige is the belief that it has hitherto represented for the most part only two types of interest – the retired politician and big business.

Reform of Parliament cannot get very far without reform of political parties, and reform of parties cannot get very far without a greatly increased sense of responsibility in the citizen toward his political duties. The party with an overall majority has the state machine pretty well under its full control, and given present party discipline if the party machinery can be controlled from the top it means that a minority of men dominate not only the party but the state. The democratizing of party structure is therefore essential to the preservation of democracy in the state. In particular the financing of parties needs watching, for elections are not won with prayers. Canadian law in this respect is both antiquated and inadequate. The preparation of electoral lists has lent itself to grave scandals. The preparation of party programmes, the choice of candidates, and other matters within party control are aspects of our constitutional behaviour which we neglect at our peril. We may note, however, that the established practice of the CBC in allotting free network time to parties in proportion to their general strength has been a definite contribution to the democratic process, a contribution to which there is no parallel in the daily press, now almost as much under concentrated ownership as other leading Canadian industries.

16 A Gallup Poll of October 31, 1943, showed 48 per cent of Canadians in favour of abolition.
17 See note on 'Ministerial Consultations with Outside Bodies' (*Modern Law Review*, vol. VII, 1944, p. 144).

CONCLUSION

From this survey the following conclusions may be suggested. Some parts of the Canadian constitution have proved remarkably flexible in the face of new demands upon the state. The expansion of control over foreign affairs and the growth of administrative agencies are examples. Other parts of the constitution have proven inflexible, whether as a result of judicial interpretation or initial failure to specify the jurisdiction. The federal authority over trade and commerce, industrial legislation, and social insurance may be instanced. To the needs of war the constitution can adapt itself with great ease and efficiency; to the demands of a peacetime economy, especially with the new concepts of high employment and social security, no such adaptability is possible. With the advent of peace, if not before, we shall have to choose between further constitutional amendment or renewed insecurity and frustration.

# XII

# The End of Dominion Status

*The term 'Dominion Status' acquired a certain popularity after the enactment of the Statute of Westminster in 1931. By 1945 it appeared to me to have lost its usefulness.*
From the *Canadian Bar Review*, 23, 1945, 725–44\*

During the world war 1939–1945 further important changes were made in the constitutional relations existing between the members of the British Commonwealth. This was to be expected, for each great crisis has left its mark in the past. The first world war ended the purely colonial period in the history of the Dominions. Their military contributions to the Allied war effort gave them a claim to equal recognition with other small states and to a voice in the formation of policy. This claim was recognized within the Empire by the creation of the Imperial War Cabinet in 1917, and within the community of nations by Dominion signatures to the Treaty of Versailles and by separate Dominion representation in the League of Nations. In this way the 'self-governing Dominions,' as they were called, emerged as junior members of the international community. Their status defied exact analysis by both international and constitutional lawyers, but it was clear that they were no longer to be regarded simply as colonies of Great Britain. Domestic self-government they had long possessed; international relations were to be their new prerogative.

To the changed position thus acquired the name 'Dominion status' was given. It was a useful compromise term. Its main virtue was that it suggested a new and more independent rôle for the Dominions and an individual membership in the world community as well as in the British Empire. This was what the rising national sentiment in these countries demanded. Though no one knew exactly what

---

\*The substance of the present article appeared in the January 1944 issue of the *American Journal of International Law*, Vol. 38. It has been considerably re-written for its presentation here.

the new status was, or what its limits were, Great Britain began to offer it to other less favoured portions of the Empire. Ireland was to have 'Dominion status' by the Treaty of 1921;[1] India was started on the road to 'Dominion status,' making 'rapid strides towards the control of her own affairs,' as Mr Lloyd George said at the Imperial Conference of that year. Clearly colonialism was being transformed into something new and strange. To acknowledge the abandonment of old style Empire, ruled from the centre, the very name of the association was gradually changed from British Empire to British Commonwealth.[2]

All this represented a great advance in the difficult process of making an empire democratic. By long historical association, if not by definition, an empire has been a single political unit in which one group of men rules over another; usually a unit in which one race rules over other races. For this reason all democratic sentiment is strongly opposed to imperialism. The British Empire began by being just such an empire. Down to the war of 1914 not only did the white 15 per cent rule over the coloured 85 per cent of the total population of the Empire, but those members of the white race inhabiting the British Isles ruled their fellow whites in the colonies and Dominions in all important matters of foreign policy. Though some external relations, such as commercial treaties, were beginning to be taken over by the Dominions prior to 1914, decisions as to peace and war, and the major choices in international affairs, were made in London only. The nineteenth century had witnessed the transformation from pure dependency to 'self-governing colony,' but a 'self-governing' colony was still a colony in both domestic and international law despite the contradiction in terms. Even the word 'Dominion,' which had come into general use in the early part of this century (in 1907 the name 'Imperial Conference' was first substituted for the former term 'Colonial Conference') did not at first suggest anything like independence or full nationhood. The term had come into use before the devolution of control over foreign relations had gone beyond its first steps. Dominions were colonies in the stage of growing up – colonies in their teens, so to speak. They were, in law and

1 Article I of the Treaty declared 'Ireland shall have the same constitutional status in the Community of Nations known as the British Empire as the Dominion of Canada ... etc.' Mr Lloyd George speaking on the Treaty said it was 'difficult and dangerous to give a definition' of what Dominion status meant. See Wheare, *The Statute of Westminster and Dominion Status*, 2nd ed., London, 1942, p. 21.

2 The phrase 'autonomous nations of an Imperial Commonwealth' appears as early as 1917 in Resolution IX adopted by the Imperial War Conference. In the Irish Treaty cited above (note 1) the term 'Empire' had not been abandoned. The famous declaration at the 1926 Imperial Conference used both 'British Empire' and 'British Commonwealth' in the same definition – a Balfourian touch. The Statute of Westminster speaks only of the 'British Commonwealth of Nations.' The term Empire is now used more technically to include Great Britain and the non-self-governing portion of the Commonwealth under her jurisdiction. But the old term 'Imperial Conference' has not yet been changed to 'Commonwealth Conference.'

in fact, integral parts of a unitary state whose ultimate centre of sovereignty was still in London. Every Dominion 'constitution' was merely a law of the Imperial power extending to a colony, permitting greater or lesser degrees of local self-government. All constitutional lawyers in the Empire emphasized the 'indivisibility of the Crown,' as proof that the group of countries called British were a unity and not a plurality.

Thus when 'Dominion status' was recognized at Versailles in 1919 the word 'Dominion' already had a special meaning which was carried forward into the new era and which retarded the development of the new idea. The term 'Dominion' embodied two distinct notions. On the one hand it suggested a mature type of colony or dependency, in which self-government was far advanced though incomplete. On the other hand it was by implication and tradition a territory 'belonging to' somebody else – a 'possession,' in short. Dominion means a territory ruled over as well as the process of ruling. It was still true to say that the Dominions were 'British,' and that Britain was not a Dominion. An element of colonial subordination was implicit in the term itself.

Adding 'status' to a 'Dominion' did not immediately clear away this confusion. The new word suffered from its attachment to the old. At no time was there any agreement as to the end result, or any selected point at which decentralization of an old imperial sovereignty would cease. Did the changes mean that the former self-governing colonies were to attain full international freedom, like independent nations, though linked in some mystical way by a common crown? Or were they still to be on a lower international plane than the mother country, though somewhat freer than before? Or were they, perhaps, to become co-equal members with Great Britain of a group of states all of whom would be governed by a fundamental overriding law, so that some kind of confederation would emerge? No precise answer could be given and none was attempted. The weakness of the concept of 'Dominion status' was that it contained at the outset a little of all these ideas but no definable quantity of any. The ultimate relationship was left to work itself out in course of time.

Certainly to many people in the Commonwealth the subordination of the Dominions to the sovereignty of Britain was not ended by the invention of an indefinable status. In 1917 General Smuts observed: 'although in practice there is great freedom, yet in actual theory the status of the Dominions is of subject character. Whatever we may say, and whatever we may think, we are subject provinces of Great Britain.'[3] This was at the beginning of the new era. In 1921, even after the fanfare of Versailles and the founding of the League, Lloyd George could tell the British House of Commons that 'the instrument of the foreign policy of the Empire is the British Foreign Office. That had been accepted by all the Domin-

3 Quoted by Wheare, *op. cit.*, p. 23.

ions as inevitable. But they claim a voice in determining the lines of our future policy.'[4] The instrument of policy, the Foreign Office, was something well organized and definite; it was also 'inevitable.' The voice was still an unrealized 'claim' to influence 'our' (*i.e.* British) policy. Never at any time during the inter-war armistice of 1919–1939 was any Imperial organization established by which the Dominion voices would actually share in making the major political decisions. In this respect the machinery of the League of Nations gave the Dominions more practice in international government and equality of status than did the British Empire. The Imperial Conferences did not meet the need, for they rarely met;[5] they had no executive power; they could merely make recommendations. Never at any time in that period was the full international personality of the Dominions, as nations distinct from Great Britain, established beyond equivocation. This did not come until the second world war, though South Africa and Ireland had clarified their position more than the other Dominions. Being without a power of control over British policy, and yet without a fully recognized independence from the consequences of that policy, the Dominions were left during the inter-war armistice with many marks of subordination not found in the other states members of the world community. Great Britain, of course, suffered none of these limitations on her sovereignty.

This subordination was more noticeable prior to the adoption of the Statute of Westminster in 1931. Colonial status lingered on into the era of Dominion status. For example, in 1924, the year after Canada had for the first time negotiated a treaty wholly by herself,[6] the Treaty of Lausanne was made by Great Britain with Turkey on behalf of the whole Empire. Thus peace between Turkey and all the Dominions was arranged without any of the latters' representatives playing any part in the proceedings. So, too, appeals from Dominion courts continued, with few exceptions, to go to a supreme tribunal in England – the Judicial Committee of the Privy Council. All legislation for the Dominions emanating from the Imperial Legislature was legally valid regardless of their consent. Thus there was an executive, judicial, and legislative sovereignty over the whole Empire vested in British organs of government containing no representation from the Dominions. None of this sovereignty was in fact exercised against the will of the Dominions, but this natural restraint, based on common understanding, did not alter the legal relationship. The idea of the Dominions as nation states was fast crystallizing, and found formulation in the Imperial Conference Declaration of 1926, but had not yet modified the formal law.

4 Quoted in R. MacGregor Dawson, *The Development of Dominion Status*, Toronto, 1937, p. 211.
5 Imperial Conferences met in 1921, 1923, 1926, 1930, 1932 (Ottawa Economic Conference), 1937, and 1944.
6 The Halibut Fishery Treaty with the United States.

Other indications of the semi-autonomous position of the Dominions were very evident. The diplomatic unity of the Empire had only just begun to break down before 1931, and the few Dominion representatives abroad stood out as exceptions to the general rule that foreign affairs were conducted for the whole Empire through the British Foreign Office. The refusal of members of the Commonwealth (except Ireland) to register their inter-se treaties with the League or to submit their own disputes to international arbitration, like their refusal to bring imperial preferences within the scope of most-favoured-nations clauses in commercial treaties, was based on the notion that they were not separate states but members of a single political entity. None of the Dominions was considered to have any separate right to neutrality once Great Britain declared war.[7] It was therefore impossible to rank the Dominions on the same plane as fully self-governing countries like Mexico or Sweden. Writing in 1929, Prof. Berriedale Keith could say, 'It is clear from our discussion that the Dominions do not possess the unfettered exercise of the treaty power which is a mark of independent States. It is equally certain that they likewise do not possess the power to make war or peace, or to remain neutral in a British war.'[8] Not being sovereign states, they were not equal to Great Britain and the term 'Dominion status' well expressed this difference.

This situation was, of course, greatly changed by the Statute of Westminster in 1931. But there was at first no certainty as to just what had been accomplished. By sections 1 and 11 of the Statute the legal title of Canada, Australia, South Africa, the Irish Free State, New Zealand, and Newfoundland was belatedly advanced from that of 'colony' to 'Dominion' but, as we have seen, this latter term had long been in use already and had co-existed with dependency. The remainder of the Statute did not apply immediately to Australia, New Zealand and Newfoundland, since their Parliaments had to adopt it before it became operative in their territories. Hence their former status remained after 1931, no less real because it was henceforth removable. Further definite constitutional steps had to be taken by them before the alteration in their position could be measured and recognized by other states, and none of the three took these steps in the inter-war period. Canada, South Africa, and the Irish Free State were immediately affected by the statute. The extent of the effect was a matter of debate.

The most important parts of the Statute of Westminster were those which (1) gave permission to the Dominions to amend or repeal in the future any Imperial laws extending to them, and (2) declared that henceforth no Imperial law would be deemed to extend to a Dominion unless it was expressly declared in the law that the Dominion had consented to its enactment. The first provision, on a

7 See speech of Premier King in Canadian House of Commons, June 9, 1924: cited in A.B. Keith, *Speeches and Documents of the British Dominions, 1901–1934*, p. 337.
8 *The Sovereignty of the British Dominions*, p. 462.

strict and traditional interpretation, was a mere extension of existing authority rather than an irrevocable transfer of sovereignty, and the second was a self-denying ordinance establishing a rule of construction rather than a binding restriction on the future powers of the Imperial legislature. Hence the Statute of Westminster could be, and was, interpreted by many authorities as not affecting the previous indivisibility of the Crown or diminishing the legal sovereignty of the Parliament which enacted it. And the very fact that it emanated from the Imperial Parliament only, and was not, as might have been, simultaneously enacted by all the Parliaments in the Commonwealth, prevented it from symbolizing clearly the equality it purported to establish.[9] For the Imperial Parliament, representing the citizens of the British Isles alone, cannot be a true constituent assembly for the entire Commonwealth. It is legally capable of legislating for colonies and Dominions, because of its continuing possession of an ancient sovereign authority, but politically it is without representation from the other members of the group and hence lacks that democratic base which would be expected in any body possessing sovereignty over a Commonwealth composed of equals.

The Statute of Westminster was a necessary preliminary step if what remained of the legal dependency of the Dominions was to be ended. The Statute undoubtedly was an advance in the direction of legal equality, but of such a nature as to emphasize again, through its use of the Imperial Legislature only, the colonial element in Dominion status. Moreover the Statute of Westminster, as has been pointed out, did not at once apply to Australia, New Zealand, or Newfoundland, for the reason that under its provisions the Parliaments of these Dominions had to adopt it before it affected them, and down to the end of 1943 Australia alone had done this. These Dominions, therefore, remained under the old arrangements until they voted themselves into the new. Hence as late as August 1939, the Imperial Parliament can be found legislating for Australia and New Zealand in an ordinary statute just as in the old days of Empire. The Emergency Powers (Defence) Act of that year[10] contained a clause designed to give Australia and New Zealand laws extraterritorial operation for certain purposes, and it was not felt necessary to declare that this had been done at the request of those Dominions. Moreover, the fact that Newfoundland is ranked as a Dominion under the Statute of Westminster shows that the title 'Dominion' by itself gives no special international status, for Newfoundland was never a member of the League of Nations, had no ministers abroad, and could scarcely be considered a separate person in the international world. She soon lost what little autonomy she had, for in 1933 an Imperial Statute, passed with the consent of her legislature, put

9 The Dominion Parliaments all approved the Statute in advance by resolution, thus indicating consent to the enactment. But the Statute itself came from the Imperial legislature only.

10 1939 Statutes (Imperial), cap. 62, sec. 5.

an end to her self-government and reduced her once again to the position of a Crown Colony. She is still a 'Dominion' in name, however, so that she provides a clear example of the uselessness of this title as descriptive of a self-governing community.[11]

It is what has been done by most of the Dominions since the Statute of Westminster, particularly under the stress of the present war, that has freed them so fully from former legal incapacities as to make the term 'Dominion status' now inappropriate for general use. South Africa and Ireland led the others in ridding themselves of the subordination implicit in the rank of Dominion, and established for themselves the doctrine of complete national independence. South Africa in 1934 took the imaginative step of re-enacting the Statute of Westminster in the Union Parliament so as to make it a South African statute as well as an Imperial one. In addition she changed the law relating to the functions of the Governor-General so as to make it possible for the Royal assent to be given in South Africa to every kind of state act.[12] No further reference to Westminster need be made under these laws for anything the South Africans wish to do as regards their internal or external affairs and the status of South Africa as a 'sovereign independent state' (not Dominion) was openly proclaimed.[13] Ireland went even further to eliminate the symbols of a colonial past from her constitution. The Statute of Westminster had freed her from any restrictions imposed by the Treaty with Britain of 1921. In 1931 she acquired a Great Seal for her own use on international documents, and in the new constitution of 1937 not only did she proclaim herself a sovereign and independent state but changes were made by which the Crown was entirely removed from the internal government and constitution of the country. Only in external affairs does she still use the Crown for certain purposes such as diplomatic appointments and international agreements. Both South Africa and Ireland also adopted their own flag. Yet neither, it must be pointed out, seceded from the British Commonwealth and both continued quite properly to be classed as nations that were in some degree 'freely associated' with the other states in the Commonwealth group.[14] What they did was to take steps *in*

11 This may explain why Nehru, when asked by Eve Curie how he reacted to the term Dominion Status, replied 'It makes me feel slightly seasick.' See her *Journey Among Warriors*, 1943, p. 427.

12 See the *Status of the Union Act* and the *Royal Executive Functions and Seals Act, Statutes of South Africa, 1934*, Nos. 69–70.

13 In the preamble to the *Status of the Union Act*.

14 The United Kingdom government has twice indicated, during the past decade, that it considers Ireland still to be a member of the British Commonwealth; first, after the new constitution of 1937 came into effect (the text of the declaration is in The British Empire, published by RIIA, 1938, 2nd ed. p. 330), and secondly, when Mr Emrys-Evans, answering a question in the House of Commons, March 21, 1944, said 'the position of

*their own Parliaments* to convert equality of status into equality of sovereignty and to establish the principle that constitutional authority in their countries no longer derived in any way from the former Imperial source but from their own people (or – in Ireland – from God). They decided to 'sever their law from the Imperial root.'[15]

Canada, Australia, and New Zealand, on the other hand, did not develop the theory of equality so dramatically or so extensively after 1931. None of them adopted a new national flag.[16] In each the constitution remained as before, an Imperial statute, and no attempt was made to base it on the national law. Since Australia and New Zealand did not adopt the Statute of Westminster it was highly doubtful whether they even had the power possessed by all self-governing states to make laws with extra-territorial effect; hence the need for supplementary Imperial legislation in 1939. Canada suffered an actual loss of administrative capacity to fulfil international obligations in 1937 when the British Privy Council, Canada's final court of Appeal, rules that purely Canadian treaties made by the Canadian executive did not come as completely within the jurisdiction of the Canadian Parliament as treaties made by the Imperial executive on behalf of the whole Empire[17] – thus making it much more difficult for her to utilize some of the 'status' acquired since 1919.

During the visit of the King and Queen to Canada in 1939 much emphasis was placed on the fact that the King sat in the Canadian Parliament and gave his assent to nine bills personally instead of through his representative, the Governor-General. This symbolism, from one point of view, suggested the Canadianization of the Crown, if the term may be used. It exemplified the declaration already made, in the Imperial Conference of 1926, that the representative of the Crown in a Dominion holds 'in all essential respects the same position in relation to the administration of public affairs in the Dominion as is held by His Majesty the King in Great Britain.' On the other hand, the presence of a British King in Canada symbolized that Canada was 'British' and part of a single political entity. Earlier in the same session of Parliament which enjoyed the Royal presence Mr MacKenzie King had refused to accept a Bill introduced by Mr Thorson designed

Eire is anomalous. Broadly, Eire is treated by us as a member of the British Commonwealth of Nations, but is of course excluded from the benefits of all special war-time arrangements.' Hansard, Vol. 398, col. 660.

15 The phrase is borrowed from R.T.E. Latham's chapter on 'The Law and the Commonwealth,' in Hancock, *Survey of British Commonwealth Affairs*, Vol. I, at p. 526.

16 The Speech from the Throne at the opening of the Canadian Parliament on September 6, 1945, announced that a Parliamentary Committee would be set up to choose a design for a Canadian Flag.

17 See *A. G. for Canada* v. *A. G. for Ontario*, 1937 Appeal Cases, 326, and comments thereon in the *Canadian Bar Review*, June 1937.

to clear up the great confusion regarding Canada's right to neutrality,[18] and Mr Lapointe, the Minister of Justice, had outlined the various reasons why Canada did not have the legal power to be neutral in a war involving Great Britain. These two events were as much evidence of dependency as the royal presence was of sovereignty. Of more practical use in establishing full freedom of action by Canada was the adoption of a new Seals Act, giving Ottawa increased control over the various seals to be used on royal instruments. But, unlike the South African Act which it resembles in many respects, the Canadian Seals Act has no provision for using the Governor General's signature in an emergency in lieu of the Royal signature, and is thus incomplete.[19] Under the existing law it would be legally impossible for Canada to declare war if all communication with the British Isles were severed.

A crucial test of the theory of equality of status in the British Commonwealth was bound to turn on the right of the Dominions to separate action in time of war. Only if they had the same power as Great Britain to decide whether or not they would enter a war could it be said they were in any real sense her equals in international status. Ever since their territories had become part of the British Empire they had followed the parent state automatically in and out of wars. While the right of colonies to decide the extent of contribution in men and materials was well accepted before 1931, there was no colonial control whatever over (1) Imperial policy which led to war or (2) the declaration of war which resulted in the legal commitment to the status of belligerent. The obligations and the law of Empire included unity in the face of Britain's enemies, and the colonies did not select the enemies.

The question was academically debated in the 1930s whether 'Dominion status' in this regard was changed by the Statute of Westminster. Responsible leaders in Ireland and South Africa could produce good reasons for saying that their countries possessed the sovereign power of neutrality. The Irish constitution, like that of the United States, requires the consent of the legislature to a declaration of war, and the South African legislation of 1934 stood as proof of nationhood, though the issue was complicated by the agreement to allow the British fleet the use of Simonstown. Hence when Ireland decided to remain neutral in September 1939 the position – though not the policy – was accepted on all sides, and no one felt that secession from the Commonwealth had occurred. So, too, it is probable that South Africa's neutrality would have been equally respected if Premier

18 Text of the Bill is in F.H. Soward and others, *Canada in World Affairs: The Pre-War Years*, p. 286.
19 Statutes of Canada, 1939, cap. 22. Text and comment is in F.H. Soward, *op. cit.*, pp. 257, 329. [This omission was cured by the new Letters Patent constituting the Office of the Governor General of Canada, 1949.]

Hertzog's policy to that effect had not been defeated in the Union Parliament. South Africa issued her own separate declaration of war on September 6, and thus became the first British Dominion to exercise this new right.

Equally strong reasons pointed to the absence of the right to neutrality in Australia and New Zealand. They had not adopted the Statute of Westminster, and had never made an attempt either by domestic or international action to assert the right. They had adopted no legislation affecting the distribution of the royal prerogative over foreign affairs. Both these Dominions were so sure of their determination to stand beside Britain under any circumstances that they were indifferent to the element of legal subordination implicit in their position. Hence it is not surprising that on September 3, 1939, when Britain declared war on Germany, Mr Menzies said to the people of Australia 'it is my melancholy duty to announce officially that in consequence of Germany's persistence in her invasion of Poland, Britain has declared war and as a result Australia is at war also.'[20] Australia was at war 'as a result' of Britain's and not her own declaration. The same was true of New Zealand.[21] Neither country had a representative in Berlin. Unable to notify her enemy directly of the fact that she intended to make war, New Zealand requested the British Government to 'take any steps that may be necessary to indicate to the German Government that His Majesty's Government in New Zealand associate themselves in this matter with the action taken by His Majesty's Government in the United Kingdom.' South Africa and Ireland were the only Dominions which had direct representation in Berlin in 1939.

In Canada, too, the prevailing opinion at the outbreak of the war was that no neutrality was possible.[22] This was the expressed opinion of Mr Ernest Lapointe, then Minister of Justice,[23] and a number of steps taken by the Canadian Cabinet between September 3 and September 10 (the respective dates of Great Britain's and Canada's declarations of war), such as the arrest of German nationals[24] and

20 'Constitutional authorities in Australia have on the whole considered that when the King is at war all his dominions are at war. There was, therefore, no declaration of war by Australia on Germany.' Round Table, December 1939, p. 191.
21 See Robert B. Stewart, 'The British Commonwealth Goes to War,' in the American Foreign Service Journal, Vol. 16, No. 12, December 1939, p. 645 ff. A New Zealand writer has however taken the view that his country declared war herself (F.L.W. Wood, New Zealand in Crisis, 1939, p. 30) but this seems untenable.
22 See authorities listed in the present writer's Canada To-day, 2nd ed., 1939, p. 131, n. 1.
23 Speech of March 31, 1939, in House of Commons Debates for that date; the relevant portions are cited in F.H. Soward, op. cit., pp. 300 ff.
24 This action was protested in the local press by the German consul in Montreal, thus indicating his assumption that Canada was not automatically at war. A similar attitude appears to have been taken by the Consul-General in Ottawa: see F.H. Soward, op. cit., p. 256.

the prohibition of trade with the 'enemy,' clearly implied an automatic belligerency. Indeed the decision to issue a separate declaration of war was an afterthought in Canada; it was reached by Mr King and his Cabinet some time after Parliament met on September 7, which was a week after the government had begun to take steps to put Canada on an active war footing. Pressure outside the Cabinet (particularly from the Imperialist group),[25] President Roosevelt's exception of Canada from the application of the Neutrality Act and the element of confusion regarding the exact legal position of Canada made it necessary to take seriously the constitutional issue which for so long had been treated by certain Canadians as 'academic.' A formal declaration of war alone could clarify the situation. This was issued separately for Canada by the Governor-General, after telegraphic approval had been given by the King in London, and a state of war with Germany was proclaimed as from 10 September – not as from 3 September, the date of Britain's declaration. By this time Sir Neville Henderson, the British Ambassador to Germany, had of course left Berlin, so that Canada's decision was not formally transmitted to the German government.

Thus September, 1939, revealed two things about the constitution of the Commonwealth. It showed that Dominion status was a term still applied to some Dominions which could be made belligerents by the mere action of the British government, in which they had no representation. This was the surviving colonialism. But it showed also that Dominion action could end and in some cases had ended, that situation. Ireland emerged with full recognition as an independent state. An Irish chargé d'affaires, with credentials standing in the name of George VI, continued in Berlin, and the German and other Axis ministers to Ireland remained at their posts throughout the war. South Africa also, it can scarcely be doubted, was making her own decision when she chose to declare her belligerency on September 6, and was not merely deciding the degree of her participation. In Canada, belligerency of September 3 was automatically accepted by most people, and apparently at first by the government (notwithstanding Mr King's later speeches to the effect that Canada entered the war without prior commitment); but the separate declaration of war one week later was a new constitutional claim which announced to the world that the right of sovereign choice on this point was henceforth being assumed by the Canadian Government. In Australia and New Zealand there was obviously an acceptance of the fact of automatic belligerent status resulting from the British declaration. India clearly had no independent choice in the matter.

25 See E.P. Dean, 'Canada at War,' in *Foreign Affairs*, January 1940, at p. 297; *Round Table*, December 1939, at p. 177. The Imperialists wanted the Declaration so as to commit Canada irrevocably: its effect was to show the disappearance of the old legal commitment.

Hence Mr Roosevelt's careful distinction between various parts of the Commonwealth in his application of the Neutrality Act on September 5, 1939, was based on a sound knowledge of intra-imperial relations. The proclamation invoking the Act, as originally drafted for signature, treated the Commonwealth as a unit, for it referred generally to 'The United Kingdom, the British Dominions beyond the seas, and India.' All the Dominions were grouped together irrespective of their stand on the war or their constitutional position. This first draft assumed the legal unity of the Commonwealth and the indivisibility of status during war. The President with his own hand changed the proclamation to read 'The United Kingdom, India, Australia, and New Zealand.' He took care to name individually the countries to which the Act was to apply, and to leave out Ireland, South Africa, and Canada pending their separate decisions. The Neutrality Act was not in fact applied to South Africa till September 8th and to Canada till September 10th. Thus was international recognition given to the exercise of full independence in foreign policy by the Dominions which had asserted the claim to freedom of choice. In respect of Canada the President's attitude was more nationalist than that of the majority of Canadians, and it greatly assisted the taking of a positive stand on the issue.

After September 1939 the practice of separate Dominion declarations of war became more general. In most cases these were timed to coincide very closely if not exactly with a British declaration of war, but this would be expected as part of a joint war strategy. Canada's declaration of war with Japan, however, dates from December 7, 1941, one day before either Britain or the United States declared war. Australia declared war on Japan on December 9, the declaration being made retroactive to 5 p.m. on December 8. In this instance she made the 'striking constitutional innovation' of declaring war herself after specific authorization from His Majesty,[26] thus bringing herself into line with Canadian and South African practice for the first time. In declaring war on Finland, since there was no legation in Helsinki, the Australian government asked the American Embassy to forward the declaration to the Finnish foreign minister – which necessarily involves United States recognition of Australia's capacity to declare war.[27] Ireland persevered in her neutrality throughout the new conflicts. These and other instances would seem clearly to establish that the power to make war and peace is now vested in the Dominions as fully as in any independent nations. For Canada the original purpose of the Thorson Bill, which Mr King would not accept when introduced into the Canadian Parliament in 1939, appears to have been achieved. Since Canada, South Africa, Australia, and Ireland have all exercised the right of

26 *Round Table*, March, 1942, pp. 337–338.
27 See *New Zealand and the Statute of Westminster*, J.C. Beaglehole, ed., 1944, p. 73, n. 5.

defining their enemies, and since other nations have taken cognizance of the practice, the legal power can no longer be denied to any Dominion – not even to New Zealand, though she has not yet used it.[28] The common citizenship has not interfered with this freedom of choice. It is noteworthy, also, that Australia, New Zealand, and Canada have steadily increased their diplomatic services since the war began. Canada has not only sent five new High Commissioners and twelve new Ministers abroad but has begun the establishment of Consulates, as in Greenland, St Pierre-Miquelon, and New York; beginning in 1943 she also raised her Legations in Washington and elsewhere to the status of Embassies.

With regard to several of the Dominions there undoubtedly still remain relics of Imperial sovereignty. New Zealand is still bound by Imperial legislation extending to herself since, until she adopts the Statute of Westminster, the Colonial Laws Validity Act of 1865 remains part of her law; and her power of extra-territorial legislation is dubious. Canada is freer, being able to legislate extra-territorially and to repeal or amend all Imperial laws affecting her except the British North America Act, which is her Constitution. Nevertheless Canada still must use the Imperial Parliament for the process of Constitutional amendment, and she still allows appeals in non-criminal matters to go to the Privy Council in London for final settlement.[29] Such remaining traces of colonialism, however, are now of minor importance in comparison with the international status evidenced by the declarations of war and by the whole range of independent action in international as well as domestic affairs. Except for New Zealand's failure to adopt the Statute of Westminster, they are negligible reminders of a past status, and are fully governed by the understanding that they will be removed whenever the Dominions desire to do away with them. It will also be conceded that New Zealand in practice is on an equal footing with the other independent nations of the Commonwealth; she benefits from their advance. In so far as Canada resorts to the Imperial Parliament for amendments to her Constitution she is merely using an external authority as a rubber stamp to validate the changes which Ottawa has previously adopted by resolution of both Houses of Parliament.[30] For various political, sentimental and historical reasons, Canada, Australia, and New Zealand prefer for the

---

28 *Ibid.*, p. 72.
29 Canada's right to abolish the appeal has been upheld by the Supreme Court of Canada (*1940 Canada Supreme Court Reports, 49*) but the case was not carried to the Privy Council itself and hence the issue is undecided.
30 Wheare, *op. cit.*, p. 303 says: 'The legal inequalities (remaining since the Statute of Westminster) were in the nature of voluntary restrictions imposed by the Dominions themselves upon the legislative competence of their Parliaments in much the same way as any community may choose to limit the powers of its legislature in its Constitution.'

time being to leave a small part of their machinery of government in Great Britain, just as they leave their King overseas. With the right to independent action in war and peace made clear, this symbolic remnant has ceased to indicate a diminution of statehood.

It thus appears correct to say that this war has brought to completion the evolution, well under way before September, 1939, of independent national status for the Dominions. The terms 'Dominion,' and 'Dominion status,' are obsolete as descriptions of inter-Commonwealth relationships, however much they may linger in the language of the law. New Zealand alone has the word 'Dominion' as part of her official name; Australia is a Commonwealth, South Africa a Union, and Canada and Ireland are without supplementary title.[31] If Dominion status ends, as it has, in national independence, the special terminology becomes merely confusing. South Africa's reassertion of her international status as 'an independent State,' a phrase used by her in the Conciliation Treaty made with the United States and signed at Washington on April 2, 1940,[32] is further evidence of the change that has occurred, but ceases to mark her as being on a different footing from any of the other nations associated in the Commonwealth. All the former Dominions (except Newfoundland) are independent states. The common kingship within the British group today establishes a form of personal union, the members of which are legally capable of following different international policies even in time of war.[33] The relationship of England to Hanover after the accession of George I was very similar, though the analogy is not perfect since some of the Dominions, as already pointed out, have traces left of a closer relationship with Great Britain. The Commonwealth is thus no longer a group of subordinate minor powers under the sovereignty of one independent nation, but a group of six independent nations, of varying size, associated together for certain purposes and policies which any one may abandon at will but which most of them have chosen to keep parallel rather than divergent in major crises. The 'sister kingdom' theory first suggested by the Canadian delegates to the London Conference in 1866,[34] has prevailed. Empire, in the true sense, exists for Great Britain only as regards

31  Canadian plenipotentiaries have established the practice of signing international documents with the single name 'Canada.'
32  The text is in S.S. Jones and D.P. Myers, *Documents on American Foreign Relations*, Vol. III, 1940–1941, Boston, 1941, p. 387.
33  Lord Halifax, in his speech at Toronto, on January 24, 1944, pointed out that while the Head of the Commonwealth 'in his capacity as king of Great Britain might be at war with a foreign power, as king of a Dominion he might continue to enjoy friendly relations with the enemy.' Duncan Hall appears to be a lonely survivor of the ancient theory: see *The British Commonwealth at War*, Elliott and Hall, eds., 1943, p. 25.
34  See F.R. Scott, 'Political Nationalism and Confederation,' in *Canadian Journal of Economics and Political Science*, August 1942, p. 386, at 390–396.

India, Newfoundland, and the Colonies under her jurisdiction; it is already dissolved for the rest. The relationship between the independent states associated through the Commonwealth is not Imperial in form but international.

It will be noticed that the new international status of the old Dominions depended much less on the Statute of Westminster than upon the complete divisibility of the Royal Prerogative. Australia declared war on Japan, Finland, Bulgaria and Rumania before she had adopted the Statute. 'It is the habit of exercising the prerogative separately for each dominion on the advice of dominion ministers which has enabled the dominions to achieve status at international law.'[35] No aspect of the prerogative is incapable of transference to the separate governments; even a single king is not, theoretically, a necessity for continuing association of the members. Co-operation depends on consent, not on symbols. The Statute of Westminster did not deal directly with the prerogative; it affected the capacity of parliaments to legislate.

Even the common citizenship does not compel uniformity of international action among the member states since they can make a distinction in law between their own nationals and those from other parts of the Commonwealth. Canada is preparing now a new definition of her own citizenship. Irish law does not recognize the common nationality within its territory. The quality of British subject now confers no right of free movement within the Commonwealth; no exemption from deportation proceedings; no inalienable right of appeal to the 'foot of the throne'; no obligation to bear arms unless his own state is at war. It does, however, provide a basis on which the member states can erect their own system of rights, and it still entitles the bearer to the protection of British agents abroad wherever his own country has failed to provide its own diplomatic representation.

CONCLUSIONS

This analysis of the present legal relations between the members of the British Commonwealth leads therefore to the following conclusions:
1 Dominion status has evolved into complete national independence. As a term descriptive of the states members of the Commonwealth, the word 'Dominion' is therefore obsolete and confusing. It has never been applicable to Great Britain. It should be abandoned and section 1 of the Statute of Westminster ought to be amended accordingly.
2 The 'British Commonwealth of Nations' is not a state. It has no single person-

---

35 New Zealand and the Statute of Westminster, *op. cit.*, p. 74; F.R. Scott, 'Constitutional Adaptation to Changing Functions of Government,' *Canadian Journal of Economics & Political Science*, August, 1945, at p. 331.

ality either in international or municipal law and no single government capable of acting for the whole.[36] The name is merely a convenient way of referring to a particular association of nations – Great Britain, Canada, Ireland, South Africa, Australia, and New Zealand, and their respective dependencies. It belongs rather to the category of collective names as 'the Pan-American Union' or the 'The United Nations.' The term 'British Empire' should be restricted to Great Britain and her empire (India, the Colonies and Protectorates) in which case it refers to a specific entity in international law.

3 The independent nations in the Commonwealth are still 'freely associated' together by reason of their desire so to remain, and this association finds symbolic expression in their use of the common Crown for certain purposes, in their retention of an underlying common nationality, and in a number of generally accepted modes of behaviour vis-à-vis one another. A nation outside the Commonwealth is no more independent than one inside, though it is free from the results of this association.

4 Since Dominion status has been transformed into national status any offer of 'Dominion status' to a non-self-governing part of the Commonwealth (such as India) is impliedly an offer of complete independence of action. There is nothing now withheld in such a grant. The acceptance of the status would, however, imply a continued association with the other members of the Commonwealth, but only on terms defined by the member itself and terminable at its sole discretion.

5 The use of the common Crown is not an essential condition of membership in the Commonwealth. Ireland has abolished it as a part of her internal constitution. A republic could be associated with other monarchies if such were the agreement. The use of the Crown as a symbol of association does not restrict the freedom of action of the nation states within the Commonwealth, though it does sometimes confuse the citizens with regard to the entity to which they owe allegiance.

6 The oath of allegiance of public officers in each of the member nations is an oath to the Crown in relation to and as part of the constitution of that nation. It is not an oath to the Crown generally and in every aspect. Hence it is not a violation of the oath of allegiance to urge the Crown to adopt any particular policy (e.g. belligerency or neutrality) vis-à-vis the nation of which the proponent is a citizen, even if the Crown adopts the opposite policy elsewhere. Treason can only be committed against the national crown.[37]

7 The practice of excluding members of the Commonwealth from the application

36 See P.E. Corbett, 'The Status of the British Commonwealth in International Law,' in *University of Toronto Law Journal*, Vol. III, 348, 359.

37 This point arose in Montreal in September 1939. Certain members of the Bar opposed Canada's participation in the war, and Chief Justice Greenshields criticised them for having violated their oath of allegiance by so doing – an accusation clearly unfounded

of the most-favoured-nation clause in commercial treaties, originally justified on the ground that the members were not separate states, can no longer be so justified.
8 Any member of the Commonwealth may make whatever treaties, alliances, or unions it desires with any other non-British state. The offer by Great Britain of complete union with France in 1940 is an example of the freedom possessed by the individual members. There was no previous Commonwealth agreement on this action, no assent from the other members of the group. The union would not on this account have been illegal in any respect. Similarly, Canada's Joint Defence agreement with the United States of August, 1940, required no Commonwealth approval. Members of the Commonwealth, however, are by agreements of Imperial Conferences expected to inform one another of negotiations likely to be of mutual interest.
9 The High Commissioners representing the various members of the Commonwealth vis-à-vis each other should belong to the category of the diplomatic corps, and it would be logical to accord them this status. At present their rank is inferior to that of the ambassadors of the smallest states.[38]
10 Full independence of action, in war as in peace, is possessed by all members of the Commonwealth. The common underlying citizenship is no legal obstacle to partial belligerency in the Commonwealth group.
11 When the nations of the Commonwealth ratify the charter of the United Nations it would be improper for them to refuse to apply the rules of that association to themselves in their relations with one another. The *inter se* doctrine, by which the relations of members of the Commonwealth are supposed to be exempt from the principles and procedures of International Law, is now so out of line with the facts and so out of harmony with the spirit of mutual trust and dependence among peoples that it should be totally abandoned. In the past its principal consequences have been: (a) refusal to register *inter se* treaties with the World organization, (b) refusal to allow a treaty made by two or more members with a foreign power to apply between themselves, (c) refusal to submit *inter se* disputes to the World Court, (d) refusal to contemplate enforcement of sanctions against a fellow member violating the covenant. All these practices lessen the authority of the World organization.[39]

unless Canada was still a dependent colony in foreign affairs, since Canada's declaration of war had not yet been issued. See *Revue Legale*, n. s., 1939, p. 513.
38 This conclusion supports the opinion vainly urged by the Canadian Government at the time of the appointment of the first Canadian High Commissioner to London in 1880. See the correspondence in W.P.M. Kennedy, *Statutes, Treaties and Documents of the Canadian Constitution*, 2nd ed., at p. 676.
39 For the *inter se* doctrine, see discussion in R.T.E. Latham's chapter in Hancock's *Survey of British Commonwealth Affairs*, at p. 602 ff; also in P. Noel-Baker, *The British Dominions in International Law*, 1929, passim.

12 The British Commonwealth, being an association of states *sui generis*, offers to the world no model of international organisation. It is not a type on which a new world order can be built. It has been steadily applying to itself over the past century the principle of national sovereignty, which under the United Nations charter, ought to be reduced rather than extended. Its surviving institutions are a remnant of a much greater unity and not the result of an effort toward a new and closer association. It has none of the common organs of government which a world society would need. Its strength lies in its many examples of purely voluntary co-operation based on sympathy, tradition, and consent. It also provides useful examples of techniques by which dependent peoples may reach national status.

13 It would be improper, if a peace conference is held to terminate this war, for the British nations to claim the same dual representation they possessed at Versailles in 1919, when, in addition to their representation as separate states, they also were granted representation on the British Empire panel. Each should be represented by its own plenipotentiaries on the same basis as all other states.

These conclusions, it need hardly be said, are based on the law of the constitution and do not contain any implications as to future policy. It is quite possible for the law of the constitution to move, as it has, toward complete independence for the former Dominions while at the same time the practice of co-operation on matters of common interest can show a continuing growth and development. Freedom includes the right to work together as well as the right to pursue a separate path. The ending of the legal obligation puts co-operation on the only democratic basis on which it can securely rest, namely a free and willing consent to work together for high objectives. It is the same basis on which co-operation between members of the Commonwealth and other states should exist. Co-operation in the Commonwealth and co-operation outside it do not differ in kind, but only – and it is hoped, to a steadily decreasing extent as world co-operation grows – in degree.

# XIII

# The Special Nature
# of Canadian Federalism

*A plea that the Canadian constitution should be interpreted, not by some pre-conceived theories of federalism, but in the light of its history and actual words.* From the *Canadian Journal of Economics and Political Science*, 23, 1947, 13-25

Since the end of hostilities in 1945, Canada has been undergoing a rapid constitutional change. The power to make laws on many vitally important matters, which on the outbreak of war in 1939 became vested in the national Parliament either under the emergency doctrine or under the specified jurisdiction over defence, has now almost entirely passed back again to the provincial legislatures. The process of decentralization is slower than the former centralization, but it is well under way. A shift in legislative authority is thus in process, affecting such subjects as production and investment control, labour legislation, rent restriction, regulation of prices and wages, man-power distribution, and other essential elements of economic planning. The War Measures Act ceased to be in effect on January 1st, 1946, and the National Emergency Transitional Powers Act which replaced it is being continued on a purely temporary basis.[1] While further prolongation of the latter act may be sought on the theory that the war emergency is not yet over, the mere lapse of time will bring increasing doubt as to its constitutional validity. Sooner rather than later Canada will revert to all the constitutional limitations on the national government which existed in 1939; the one exception is unemployment insurance, the first and only transfer from provincial to federal legislative power made by formal amendment since 1867.[2] The various taxation

---

1 This Act as amended in 1946, expires March 31, 1947, or sixty days after the opening of the 1947 session, whichever is the earlier.
2 The Statute of Westminster enlarged federal authority in regard to both extraterritorial legislation and the repeal of British statutes affecting Canada, and thus in effect amended the BNA Act, but this was not a direct alteration of the terms of the constitution.

agreements between the central and local governments, some of which have been renegotiated on an individual basis, have not shifted the legal power to levy taxes but have merely produced a voluntary abstention on the part of some provinces in respect of certain forms of taxation.

The results of this return to constitutional 'normalcy,' this diminution of legislative power in the national Parliament, may well be extremely serious. Just how the next constitutional crisis will affect us cannot be predicted, but it is beyond reason to suppose that the inadequacies of the pre-war constitution, so tragically evident during the long period of human suffering and economic waste in the 1929-39 decade, so fully analysed in the Sirois Report, will not be even more injurious to our national life and economy in the future than they proved to be in the past. The Second World War has still further integrated the Canadian economic system, has greatly accelerated the industrialization of the country, has increased the power of monopoly, and has multiplied our relationships with the outside world. All these trends, by creating problems and obligations that reach far beyond the boundaries of even our largest provinces, have rendered more imperative than before the need for a wider federal jurisdiction and control. No matter what theories about the Canadian constitution are propounded, no matter how much politicians may cry for 'provincial autonomy' or the sacred rights of provinces, no matter how much 'centralization' may be held up as an unmitigated evil, the fact remains that the peace-time distribution of legislative powers to which we are returning has already proved incapable of producing that 'efficiency and harmony' aimed at in the constitution of 1867, because the magnitude of many social problems exceeds the boundaries of provincial jurisdiction within which they legally lie.

In the face of accumulating evidence of the need for a reasonable adaptation of the existing constitution, it may be valuable to remind ourselves of some of the basic principles of the original BNA Act. These are too easily forgotten. Only a few years ago a penetrating analysis of Canadian constitutional development since 1867, made by the parliamentary counsel to the Senate, brought him to the startling conclusion that all that was needed to make the constitution workable today was to compel the courts, and particularly the Judicial Committee of the Privy Council, to apply the BNA Act as originally drafted and to discard the fanciful interpretations which the judicial mind later introduced.[3] The advice, though couched in most respectful terms, has passed unheeded, but that it could be given shows that, to one student at least, the trouble does not lie with the Fathers of Confederation. This historical approach is perhaps more than ever necessary at the present time, when there are two streams of constitutional thought in violent

3 *Report to the Senate of Canada*, by W.F. O'Connor (Ottawa, 1939), at p. 13.

opposition, represented by the supporters of federal authority on the one hand and the advocates of the 'compact theory' on the other. To link these opposing systems in a common source, let us assume for the moment that there was a compact. It is surely obvious that the nature of the compact is to be found in the constitution of 1867. If that constitution has been departed from, or judicially repealed, as Mr O'Connor claims, then the compact is not now in force as originally intended. To insist on the compact is to invoke history.

Perhaps the fact about the 1867 constitution on which there would be the least controversy is that Canada was to have a 'federal' constitution and not a legislative union. So far so good. But from this point on, the divergencies of view begin. Whole theories are built upon the difference between federal and unitary states, and the word 'federal' is treated as though it had some precise theoretical meaning which should be read into the BNA Act regardless of what that Act itself contains. Now it is true that political scientists are in general agreement upon what constitutes a federal as distinct from a unitary state. The essence of the distinction lies in the fact that the unitary state has but one omnicompetent legislature, whether or not, like South Africa, it has subordinate provinces with defined powers. In the unitary state there can be no field of legislation which the central Parliament cannot enter. In the federal state, on the other hand, sovereignty is divided between the central or local governments so that each of them is independent of the other. Each government has a separate and co-ordinate power. If the central government can invade the provincial field at will, or the provinces can control the central government, there is no federation.

This distinction is clear among political scientists. It is another matter to say it is clear in the text of the BNA Act. One approach to the Act is to accept the political definitions, and then, assuming that Canada is a federal state as thus defined, to read them into the law. With this approach courts may even twist or interpret away those texts which do not seem to fit the theory. But such an approach is utterly wrong. It is not justified, as Professor H.F. Angus seems to think,[4] because the preamble of the Act states that the three federating provinces, have 'expressed their desire to be federally united.' It is not what comes in the preamble, but in the provisions of the statute itself, which counts. The whole Act must be examined to see what it provides, each clause being read in the light of all other clauses, and only then can the entire scheme be classified according to the accepted theory of federalism. We should not say 'A federal state requires such and such relationships between the governments, therefore we will find them in the Canadian constitution.' We should say 'This is what the Canadian constitution provides: what kind of federalism is it?'

4 See his article 'The Canadian Constitution and the United Nations Charter' (*Canadian Journal of Economics and Political Science*, vol. XII, no. 2, May, 1946, p. 127).

A recent examination of the BNA Act from this point of view, made by a most competent and impartial scholar, leads him to doubt very much whether Canada has a truly federal constitution at all. Professor K.C. Wheare, in his *Federal Government*,[5] has this to say after examining the text of the BNA Act: 'The federal principle is not completely ousted, therefore, from the Canadian constitution. It does find a place there and an important place. Yet if we confine ourselves to the strict law of the constitution, it is hard to know whether we should call it a federal constitution with considerable unitary modifications, or a unitary constitution with considerable federal modifications. It would be straining the federal principle too far, I think, to describe it as a federal constitution without adding any qualifying phrase. For this reason I prefer to say that Canada has a quasi-federal constitution.' Professor Wheare goes on to point out the distinction between a federal *constitution* and a federal *government*, and has no hesitation in concluding that in the practice of government, in the adoption of conventions and forms of behaviour, Canada acts as a federal state. A country may behave as though it is federal when in strict law it is not. But these conventions and this behaviour have grown up since 1867, and here we are discussing the nature of the original constitution to which alone the compact, if there was one, can refer.

How can it be possible to doubt whether Canada possesses a federal constitution? Professor Wheare gives three reasons. To these some others of perhaps equal importance may be added. For a truly federal constitution to exist, as has been said, there must be such a division of powers that the general and local governments are each, within their spheres, co-ordinate and independent. One should not be able to control or invade the territory of the other. Is this true of the BNA Act? Professor Wheare finds three examples of a federal right of interference in provincial affairs which cannot be made to harmonize with the federal principle. Each of these may be discussed in turn.

In the first place, the federal government in Canada has a power of veto over provincial legislation. This drastic control is subject to no restriction whatever, except that it must be exercised within one year after the adoption of the provincial statute.[6] It can be applied as much to financial as to other measures, and whether the province has kept within its authority or not. It is difficult to imagine a more unfederal principle than this, and it is not surprising that the abolition of the power was sought at the first interprovincial conference in 1887. So marked, however, has been the tendency of judicial interpretation and constitutional convention to weaken the federal authority in Canada, that by the nineteen-twenties some commentators were beginning to talk as though the power of disallowance had virtually disappeared.[7] Mr Aberhart, by a frontal attack on the citadels of

5 Toronto, 1946, at p. 20.
6 BNA Act, sec. 90.
7 See W.P.M. Kennedy, *The Constitution of Canada* (Toronto, 1922), at pp. 427 ff.

finance, happily provided the maximum incentive to a judicial restatement of the letter of the law.[8] We know that the Fathers of Confederation did not intend the provinces to have a power to act detrimentally to the nation as a whole, and entrusted the national executive with the duty of protecting the national interest against abuses of provincial jurisdiction.

The second example consists of the federal power of appointment of lieutenant-governors. It is now settled, since the Liquidator's Case, that the lieutenant-governor, though appointed by Ottawa, represents the Crown as fully for purposes of provincial government as the governor-general does for all purposes of national government. Nevertheless, the fact that he is chosen, paid, removed, and instructed by federal authority gives a power of interference in provincial affairs not consistent with the idea of provincial autonomy. The federal power of instruction is particularly important; 'in assenting to bills, withholding assent, and reserving bills for the signification of the Governor General's pleasure, he [the lieutenant-governor] exercises his discretion subject to the instructions of the Governor General.'[9] Since confederation there have been 104 cases of disallowance of provincial bills, 64 cases of reservation by lieutenant-governors, and 25 cases of outright refusal of assent,[10] so that it cannot be said that convention has rendered obsolete these forms of control. The governor-general is now by convention free from Imperial executive interference; not so the lieutenant-governor from federal executive interference. The latter was intended to be, and still is, an agency through which in certain instances the will of the federal executive can make itself felt in provincial affairs. It is for this reason that the provinces may amend their constitutions as they will, 'except as regards the office of Lieutenant-Governor.'[11]

As his third example of the unitary principle, Professor Wheare cites the rule that appointments to all the important judicial posts in the provinces are in the hands of the Dominion executive. Here again there is a departure from the strictly federal idea. Though the provinces may create courts of justice, and staff the inferior ones, the higher posts are filled with judges selected, paid, pensioned, and removed by federal authority. Appeals go from the provincial court of appeal to the national Supreme Court. There is not in Canada an independent provincial judiciary such as exists in the states of the American Union.

For these reasons Professor Wheare has his doubts about the accuracy of the term 'federal' as applied to the Canadian constitution. He might have gone further, and added other examples of the unitary principle. For instance, in both

8 *In re Disallowance and Reservation*, 1938 S.C.R. at p. 71, where it was held that the power was unrestricted.
9 *Ibid.*, at p. 77.
10 See E.A. Forsey, 'Disallowance of Provincial Acts' (*Canadian Journal of Economics and Political Science*, vol. IV, no. 1, Feb., 1938, p. 47).
11 BNA Act, sec. 92, ss. 1.

the Quebec and London Resolutions it is said that: 'In regard to all subjects over which jurisdiction belongs to both the General and Local Legislatures, the laws of the General Parliament shall control and supersede those made by the Local Legislature, and the latter shall be void so far as they are repugnant to or inconsistent with the former.'[12] Though this clause does not appear in so many words in the BNA Act, except with regard to the two subjects of immigration and agriculture in Section 95, it is the rule applied by the courts. '*Intra vires* federal legislation will override *intra vires* provincial legislation,' says Clement.[13] The idea behind the rule is that federal legislation, if truly founded upon a base of federal jurisdiction, is not to be restricted by reason of the fact that it conflicts with a valid provincial law and thus invades a provincial field. The lesser authority gives way before the greater. This is seen when the exercise of an exclusive federal power cuts away a portion of the field formerly covered by the provincial law. Thus a piece of true criminal law may declare the forfeiture of property as a penalty for the commission of a crime and may declare a contract unlawful which formerly was permitted, even though the field of 'property and civil rights' is reserved to the provinces. Theoretically this example perhaps does not illustrate the rule, since the criminal aspects of the use of property and the making of contracts never were within provincial jurisdiction; yet since the federal Parliament can make new crimes whenever it chooses, the end result is a diminution of the provincial sphere. A more correct example would be seen in the use of the 'ancillary' doctrine; a subject ancillary to a federal power, such as the contracting out of liability by federal railways, can be dealt with by Dominion legislation even though such matters come normally within provincial jurisdiction.[14] It is but a logical extension of this principle of Dominion paramountcy to say, as the Privy Council did in *In Re Silver Bros.*, that if there is a clash between two taxations, Dominion and provincial, and the question of absolute priority arises, 'the Dominion must prevail.'[15] Professor Wheare's comment on this case, as on a similar Australian one, is that 'if they are good law, then the federal principle does not appear to find a place in these constitutions so far as the taxing power is concerned.' Canadian provinces are today realizing how tenuous is their 'autonomy' in face of the federal taxing power.[16]

12 Quebec Resolutions, no. 45; London Resolutions, no. 43.
13 W.H.P. Clement, *The Law of the Canadian Constitution* (3rd ed., Toronto, 1916), p. 468.
14 *Grand Trunk Railway* v. *A.G. for Canada*, 1907, A.C. 65.
15 1932 A.C. 514 at p. 521.
16 Undaunted by the law of the constitution, Premier Duplessis has even contended that 'It is the considered opinion of the province of Quebec, it is the considered opinion of highly qualified jurists, that the fact that the constitution of 1867 specifically gives to the provinces the right of direct taxation means conclusively that the provinces have

The chief basis in the BNA Act for the modern claim by provinces to a vast autonomy rests on their jurisdiction over 'property and civil rights in the province.' The manner in which this clause has been built up by judicial decision until it has become the effective residuary clause of the constitution in peace-time need not be detailed here. It is a remarkable example of judge-made law. But the 'compact' of 1867 in regard to property and civil rights gives a quite different impression of what was intended. Both the Quebec and London Resolutions stated positively that there was to be no exclusive right in provincial legislatures over this field. In both Conferences the provincial jurisdiction over property and civil rights was qualified by the words 'excepting those portions thereof assigned to the General Parliament.'[17] Words could not be clearer that the field was divided, part going to the provinces and part to the Dominion. Therefore it does not matter whether the words property and civil rights were used in their largest sense or in some lesser sense; if the largest sense is to be taken as it has by the courts, then the portions excepted should be larger. In the BNA Act the qualifying clause was changed so that the provincial jurisdiction now covers 'Property and civil rights in the province.' This might seem a change of some importance, but it would be erroneous to think so, for the concluding words of Section 91 of the Act, giving a paramountcy to the specified Dominion powers when they conflict with a provincial field, fulfil the same purpose.[18] Though the fact is less clear in the wording of the Act than it was in the Resolutions, it is still true to say that the provinces have no exclusive jurisdiction over property and civil rights. If they had, every time there was a conflict between a Dominion power and the property and civil rights clause the latter would prevail. How then could the War Measures Act justify a control of rents (an example of Dominion residuary powers prevailing over property and civil rights in war-time), or the Bank Act control a minor's right to deposit and withdraw money (an example of a Dominion specified power prevailing over property and civil rights in peace-time); a portion of the field of what otherwise would be property and civil rights is occupied by federal law in both these cases; therefore the provinces have no exclusive authority over this class of subject.

One can easily discover other examples of Dominion powers which touch pro-

priority in the matter of direct taxation. Otherwise Confederation would be meaningless.' In *Dominion-Provincial Conference Proceedings, Plenary Session No. 5, April 29, 1946* (Ottawa, 1946), at p. 29. No authority is given for this extraordinary opinion.

17  Quebec Resolutions, no. 43, ss. 15; London Resolutions, no. 41, ss. 15.

18  This is the orthodox view. As Clement puts it (*Law of the Canadian Constitution*, p. 468) 'the exclusive authority of the provincial legislatures over the 16 enumerated classes of section 92 is weakened and, in a sense, invasion is made possible by the concluding clause of section 91.' Even if Mr O'Connor's new interpretation is accepted the same result follows.

vincial subjects. It is loosely said that the provinces have an exclusive right to control education, but this is not so. Apart from the power in the federal Parliament and executive under Section 93 of the BNA Act to interfere in educational matters, and even to make laws for a province, when certain guaranteed school rights have been violated, it is clear beyond question that no schools can teach in a manner contrary to the Criminal Code or other federal laws of like character. Sedition, blasphemy, criminal libel, spreading false news detrimental to the public interest, violating the Official Secrets Act – these matters would not be tolerated because they might occur inside a school textbook or a school building. The 'Solemnization of Matrimony' is an exclusive provincial power, but what if a province provided a ceremony whereby a man might marry two wives simultaneously? In the last resort there is little notion of 'watertight compartments'[19] under the BNA Act, except as regards the federal compartment which cannot ever be invaded by provincial law. At least in time of emergency, 'the authority of the Dominion in respect of legislation relating to the peace, order and good government of Canada may, in view of the necessities arising from the emergency, displace or overbear the authority of the provinces in relation to a vast field in which the provinces would otherwise have exclusive jurisdiction.'[20] And while in the past it has taken a war to provide us with an unquestioned emergency, this is by no means the only conceivable kind.

Let us continue the examination of the text of the Act. In Section 92-10 (c) there is a power in the federal Parliament to declare a 'Work' to be for the general advantage of Canada, or of two or more provinces, and thereby to bring it within federal control. 'Works' can thus be lifted out of provincial jurisdiction by a magical formula, before as well as after their execution. Does this power square with the federal idea? Does this suggest that the main concern of the Fathers of Confederation was to preserve the 'autonomy' of provinces? The watertight compartments are leaking badly here. Yet this is a clear text of law, and part of the 'compact.' It is possible that the courts will eventually cast a suffocating judicial mantle over this text also, finding it does not harmonize with some preconceived notion of a 'federal' state, but at the moment it stands as further evidence that Canadian federalism was to be of a very special type, fitting no theoretical definition and leaning heavily in clear intent and purpose toward a strong national government. Any interpretation or convention which departs from this intent and purpose is tearing down the original structure. Perhaps this may be desirable or inevitable, but it should not be called an adherence to the 'compact.'

The treaty clause of the constitution provides us with another example of a

19 Lord Atkin's unfortunate metaphor, used in the Labour Convention Case, 1937 A.C. 326, at p. 354.
20 Duff, CJ, in Chemicals Reference Case, 1943 S.C.R. 1 at p. 10.

federal power of invasion of the provincial field. Every kind of treaty made under Section 132 and which imposes obligations upon Canada or any province, is implemented and enforced by the national Parliament and government. Even if the treaty affects one province only, and on a matter of property and civil rights, it is still Ottawa alone which can legislate. Since in 1867 every treaty of every sort affecting Canada was an Empire treaty within Section 132, this meant that the Fathers of Confederation agreed that Ottawa alone should enforce Canada's international obligations. Examples of this form of invasion are not lacking. The Dominion statute giving effect to the Boundary Waters Treaty of 1909[21] contains the following clause: '2. The laws of Canada and of the several provinces thereof are hereby amended and altered so as to permit, authorize and sanction the performance of the obligations undertaken by His Majesty in and under the said treaty ... ' Provincial laws are being set aside to enable Canada's international obligations to be fulfilled. The Migratory Birds Convention of 1916 contained special restrictions applicable only to the Maritime Provinces, and these were made effective by a federal statute.[22] The Japanese Treaty Act of 1913 rendered invalid a British Columbia statute limiting the employments of Japanese in that province. The Aeronautics Convention of 1919 justified Dominion control of aviation. In all these cases the provincial sphere was invaded, and properly invaded, by federal statute based on treaties. Despite all that was said by the Privy Council in the Labour Conventions Case in 1937 these federal statutes are still good law since they fall within Section 132 of the BNA Act. Any treaty in the future affecting Canada and dealing with any subject would presumably give equal authority to federal legislation provided the curious test laid down by Lord Atkin for 'Empire treaties' were fulfilled, namely that their obligations should be 'imposed upon Canada as part of the Empire by an Imperial executive responsible to and controlled by the Imperial Parliament.'[23] Canada is not likely to use this device for the strengthening of her treaty-making power, but the original law of the constitution certainly made no attempt to protect the provinces from invasion through the treaty road until Lord Atkin added his contribution to the balkanization of the country in 1937.

Is it possible to conceive that the Fathers of Confederation, who did not hesitate to place in the national government a veto power over provincial laws, a control over provincial executives, a nomination to provincial courts, a right to commandeer provincial works, a right to legislate on Empire treaties, besides the general residuary power over matters concerning the peace, order, and good government of Canada – is it possible to conceive that the Fathers would have wished

21 1–2 Geo. V, c. 28.
22 1917, c. 18.
23 Labour Conventions Case, 1937 A.C., 326 at pp. 349–50.

to place on provincial legislatures the duty of legislating to give effect to another kind of treaty just because it was negotiated by Canadians instead of by Englishmen? And if seeking the intentions of the Fathers seems vain, is it consistent with the nature of the federalism established by the BNA Act to place this great new international responsibility in the hands of the kind of local legislatures established in 1867? Even 'ferries between a province and any British or foreign country' are a specified Dominion power in Section 91. These provinces to which Lord Atkin gives the power to enforce ILO Conventions, cannot run a ferry to a foreign country. The present judge-made law makes no sense at all in the light of the 'compact' of 1867.

In the Privy Council judgment on the Labour Conventions occurs this passage: 'It would be remarkable that while the Dominion could not initiate legislation, however desirable, which affected civil rights in the provinces, yet its government not responsible to the provinces nor controlled by provincial parliaments need only agree with a foreign country to enact such legislation and its parliament would be forthwith clothed with authority to affect provincial rights to the full extent of such agreement. Such a result would appear to undermine the constitutional safeguards of provincial constitutional autonomy.' This passage well illustrates the extreme lengths to which judicial misdescription may go. Cannot the Dominion initiate legislation which affects civil rights in the province? It does so at every session of Parliament. Examples have been given above. Almost all legislation under the enumerated heads of 91 'affects' the provincial sphere. In wartime – an exceptional time, it is true, but so are treaties exceptional things – it cuts huge swathes into property and civil rights. The BNA Act does not prohibit federal legislation 'affecting' civil rights; the word 'affect' nowhere appears in the Act. The federal Parliament may not make laws 'in relation to' provincial matters, but the distinction between a law affecting a civil right and a law in relation to a civil right is very clear. If the matter in relation to which the law is enacted is, for example, criminal law, then the incidental affecting of a provincial right is no obstacle to the validity of the legislation. The same is true of a use of the emergency powers under the residuary clause; the rental control now operating affects civil rights but is not in relation to them.

Lord Atkin then goes on to remark that the Dominion government, 'not responsible to the provinces,' nor 'controlled by provincial parliaments,' could affect provincial rights to the full extent of the treaty agreement if federal jurisdiction over treaties were admitted. But again we may ask a question: Is not the federal Parliament responsible to the provinces? Is it not precisely the only Parliament which is responsible to the provinces on all federal matters? Is it not elected on a proportionate basis from every province? Does it not speak for Canadians of all provinces on the matters of national concern entrusted to it? Obviously it is not controlled by provincial Parliaments; Canada is not just a confederation. And what more natural than to place this great power, as most of the other federations of the world have done,[24] in the hands of the only Parliament speaking for the whole nation? If Ottawa were to enter frivolously into a fraudulent treaty for the sole purpose of acquiring jurisdiction over a provincial matter, the courts, under the doctrine of colourable legislation, would have no difficulty in setting it aside. But the possibility that a power may be abused is no proof that it does not exist; this the Privy Council has said many times. And what about the possibility that the provinces will refuse to implement a treaty and thus leave Canada utterly incapable of fulfilling her world obligations? Why must Ottawa be the only suspect? There has never yet been a frivolous Canadian treaty, but there is today a continuing refusal by provinces to implement Canada's obligations under the three ILO Conventions ratified in 1935, which might well be regarded as frivolous.

The provisions of the BNA Act do, it is true, reserve to the provinces a jurisdiction over their local affairs which is exclusive unless some superior federal authority comes into play. In this sense, and remembering the federal controls such as the veto, there is a real provincial autonomy. But an analysis of the basic law of 1867 certainly gives no evidence that these provincial spheres were to be the untouchable and impenetrable enclosures that Lord Atkin seems to imagine. On the contrary, whenever the text of the constitution varies from the federal idea, it leans toward national unity and not toward provincial autonomy. If the provinces had wished to 'preserve their autonomy,' they would never have entered Confederation at all.

The unusual provisions of the BNA Act all suggest more and not less federal control. It therefore seems strange that Professor H.F. Angus should state that the Canadian constitution 'would cease to be federal if the government of Canada without any consultation with the provincial governments could enter into a treaty with a foreign government and by so doing could increase the legislative powers of the Canadian parliament at the expense of the provincial legislatures.'[25] Surely the American constitution has not ceased to be federal? Washington alone possesses the treaty-making power, and consultation with the Senate is not the same as consultation with state governments. Besides, what does Professor Angus mean by 'ceasing to be federal?' The BNA Act does not exactly conform to any

24 See 'The Treaty Making Power in Canada,' the League of Nations Society's brief to the Sirois Commission, Appendix II, for the treaty powers of other federal states. It is usual and normal to place the power in federal hands.

25 'The Canadian Constitution and the United Nations Charter,' p. 128. This statement begs the question: if a federal power over treaties exists, its use does not increase federal powers at provincial expense any more than does the making of a new crime.

accepted definition of federalism. It has unique modifications of its own, and these modifications, being all unfederal, harmonize better with a national power to legislate on treaties than with a provincial power over such matters. It is closer to the truth to say, not that Canada ceases to be federal if Ottawa possesses the full treaty power, but that Canada ceases to have the kind of federalism designed for her if the provinces possess it. The generation of Canadians that were already talking of a 'New Nationality' in the eighteen-sixties were not preparing to endow the local legislatures, charged only with 'the control of local matters in their respective sections,'[26] with any, let alone a prime, responsibility for the fulfilment of Canada's international obligations.

These considerations and this historical approach put a different complexion also on the vexed question of amendments to the BNA Act. The advocates of the compact theory, and indeed many others who do not accept that theory, have argued that no change should be made in the distribution of legislative powers as laid down in the original constitution without the consent of the provinces. Logically, on the compact theory, the dissent of one province should prevent any change, yet this leads to so impossible a conclusion that even such stout supporters of the theory as Mr Duplessis have seemed to qualify the demand for unanimity by admitting that the consent of the 'four pioneer provinces' might be sufficient.[27] But the compact of 1867, in so far as there was one, was a compact to set up a national government 'charged with matters of common interest to the whole country,' to quote again the second of the Quebec and London Resolutions. This is what Clement rightly calls 'The Cardinal Principle of Allotment.'[28] Is changing the constitution a matter of common interest or just of local interest? The opening words of Section 91 of the Act give the central Parliament jurisdiction over 'all matters not coming within the classes of subjects by this act assigned exclusively to the legislatures of the provinces.' Is there the slightest suggestion in Section 92, that a power to participate in amendments to the BNA Act itself is assigned to the provinces? Quite the contrary. The first head of provincial power is a power to amend 'the constitution of the province,' and even from that is excepted the office of lieutenant-governor. Since the provinces have no jurisdiction save what is expressly assigned to them, the residue being in federal hands, the amending power would logically fall into Section 91. The inclusion of the specific provincial power of amendment excludes any more general power. Only the ancient doctrine of Imperial sovereignty, which made it impossible for any colony to change an Imperial act extending to it, prevented a full power of amendment vesting in Ottawa's hands. It was not any concept of federalism or of compact which stood in the way; that is a later invention.

26 See the second of the Quebec and London Resolutions.
27 See *Dominion-Provincial Conference Proceedings*, cited above, at p. 29.
28 *Ibid.*, chap. XXII.

Now what was the traditional way by which the Imperial Parliament was induced to change its laws relating to colonial legislatures? Historically, apart from
situations created by crisis or rebellion, the process was that of a request from
the colonial legislature concerned. This had happened before in Canada, and the
Fathers of Confederation knew it would happen again. The question arose during
the debates on Confederation in 1865, and the answer made then was, quite correctly that the Charter 'can only be amended by the authority that made it,'
namely the Imperial Parliament.[29] The constitution of 1840 had been three times
amended, once in 1848 when the use of the French language was restored, and
twice in 1854 and 1856 when the Legislative Council was made elective, by just
such a method.[30] There were several amendments to the Constitutional Act of
1791. It seems impossible to doubt that Dr Skelton was right when he suggested
that this previous history explains why no general power of amendment was included in the BNA Act.[31] It was not necessary to include it; everyone understood
how amendments would be obtained if the need should ever arise. It was only
necessary to specify the provincial amending power, and this was done with the
strict limitation mentioned above.

There was another good reason why the Canadian constitution needed no
power of amendment. All future contingencies were provided for by the residuary
grant to the national Parliament. There is never any need to take away authority
from a province over a matter of purely local importance. These were the only
matters placed in provincial hands. New matters of general or national importance
were expected to fall into the residuary clause of the Dominion. In the United
States constitution an amending power is necessary, as it is for Australia, since in
both federal systems the residue is in the states or in the people. New powers that
are felt to be ripe for central control must be granted specifically by an amendment since otherwise they remain in the state's residues. But in Canada the grant
to the national Parliament from the Imperial Parliament (the Canadian provinces
granted nothing; not one of them passed or could have passed a single statute
about Confederation) was over all matters, past, present, and future, except those
local ones specified as belonging to the provinces. Every subtraction from the
federal whole was for local purposes only. Hence I view the amendment of 1940,
granting the subject of unemployment insurance to the Dominion, as effecting

29 The Honourable D'Arcy McGee, in *Parliamentary Debates on the Subject of the Confederation of the British North American Provinces* (Quebec, 1865), p. 146. See also the
remarks of Dorion at p. 263 and Cauchon at p. 701. Rankin believed that, under the
Confederation scheme, 'the Federal Parliament will possess the same power to change,
alter or amend for the whole country, as we now possess for Canada alone.' *Ibid.*, p. 918.
30 See, for example, the joint resolution requesting the 1854 amendment, in the *Journal of
the Parliament of Canada*, 1852–3, at p. 944.
31 House of Commons, Special Committee on the BNA Act, *Minutes of Proceedings*
(Ottawa, 1935), at p. 25.

no transfer from provinces to the Dominion at all; all it did was to clarify a Dominion power which the courts, by their long line of restrictive judgments, had lost the capacity of identifying. For it would be difficult to imagine a subject more obviously national in scope and importance, more surely beyond the local aspect of property and civil rights, than unemployment insurance designed to protest the national economy from the mass misery and widespread dislocation brought about by the world's greatest economic depression. The courts are forced to admit that certain crises, notably that of war, do bring the federal residuary power into full play. If they would only draw a more intelligent line, one more in conformity with the clear intentions of the Fathers as expressed in innumerable speeches at Confederation, and one more in harmony with the very words of the Act itself, they would solve the problem of amendment by rendering it superfluous. Every enumerated head of Section 91, singled out by the Fathers as a matter of national importance in 1867, sets the standard of importance that must be reached, and the only standard that need be reached in order that other future matters may be properly allotted to the federal residue, regardless of whether they incidentally affect property and civil rights. This is the only interpretation that does not 'restrict the generality' of the peace, order, and good government clause.

History provides further proof of the correctness of this approach. Immediately after 1867 the first federal amendments were made. In 1869 there was a change in the subsidies provision as regards Nova Scotia, affecting the plan established by Section 118 of the BNA Act. When Mr Holton moved that 'any disturbance of the financial arrangements respecting the several provinces provided for in the British North America Act, unless assented to by all the provinces, would be subversive of the system of government under which the Dominion was constituted,' his motion, with all its 'compact' implications was rejected by the Commons. Two years later a motion by David Mills containing the same insistence on provincial consent, was again rejected without debate; this time the amendment in question was actually increasing the legislative power of Parliament in regard to newly created provinces, and over all territories not included in any province. Such repeated action by Parliaments containing most of the Fathers of Confederation, and taken while the idea and the purpose of Confederation were still fresh in the public mind, is sufficient proof of the understanding which existed about the method of amending the BNA Act.[32]

The correct manner for seeking constitutional change was clearly set out in the same Parliament of 1871 which rejected the second attempt to impose the

---

32 These motions are cited in N. McL. Rogers's paper on 'The Compact Theory of Confederation (*Proceedings Canadian Political Science Association*, 1931, s. 205 at p. 222).

compact theory, when it accepted *without dissent* another motion by Mr Holton – this time phrased by him in proper terms – 'That no change in the provisions of the BNA Act should be sought by the Executive Government without the previous assent of the Parliament of Canada.'[33] This motion entirely accords with the whole scheme of government set out in the BNA Act, and more particularly with the clear limitation on provincial authority in Section 92 in the matter of constitutional amendments. Before Confederation the individual colonies made requests for amendments from their legislatures; after Confederation the national Parliament took over that office under its exclusive authority to speak for the country on all matters of national importance. The Imperial authorities were therefore acting quite constitutionally when they totally ignored the request for changes in the Act of 1867 emanating from the five provinces (Quebec, Ontario, Manitoba, Nova Scotia, and New Brunswick) who held an inter-provincial conference in 1887 without Dominion participation or approval.

It is not the purpose of this article to argue for or against any particular proposal for a new process of amending the BNA Act. The author has done this elsewhere.[34] Many things have happened since 1867. The Canadian provinces today possess powers, resulting from judicial interpretation, considerably larger than they were thought to possess in 1867. It may be we shall never get back to the original 'compact.' But we should at least be sufficiently aware of our own history not to be misled into thinking that the maintenance of an enlarged provincial autonomy is part of an original agreement or treaty between the confederating provinces. We should realize that its acceptance means a definite departure from the clear intentions of the Fathers. We should also avoid being misled by the word 'federal,' which has a meaning in political theory which it does not have in Canadian constitutional law. The technical meaning never hampered the framers of Canada's federal system in their purpose of creating a strong national government free from the doctrine of 'states' rights' which had so largely contributed to the American Civil War. While we have fortunately avoided any armed conflict between federal and provincial authorities, we have not avoided and we are entering again upon, the frustrations and dissensions which a wrong understanding of our own type of federalism in both the courts and in sections of the public perpetuates and foments.

33 Cited by Dr Skelton, Special Committee on BNA Act, *Minutes of Proceedings*, at p. 27.
34 Before the House of Commons Special Committee on the BNA Act. See *Minutes of Proceedings*, at pp. 86 ff.

# XIV

# The Deportation of the Japanese Canadians
## An Open Letter to the Press

*There are few blacker pages in the history of the struggle for human rights in Canada than the story of the treatment of the Japanese Canadians during and after the second world war. The deportation Orders of December 1945 covered even some Japanese who were Canadian citizens by birth. Even today Canadians have no constitutional protection against the punishment of exile once the War Measures Act has been proclaimed, for by Section 6(5) of that Act anything done under it shall not be deemed to be an infringement of any right or freedom recognized by the Canadian Bill of Rights.*
Sent to fifty-five newspapers in Canada, 4 January 1946; published in eleven.

To the Editor,

The Canadian government is about to deport from this country some 10,000 men, women and children mostly Canadian citizens, for no other crime except that they have a particular racial origin. They are being sent to a land which most of them have never seen, which is too devastated by war to receive them, and where their future is hopeless. Not since the expulsion of the Acadians has such severe treatment been accorded to any social group within our frontiers, and there was at least some military justification for that deportation whereas there is none for this.

I refer, of course, to the government's decision to deport the Japanese Canadians, which is now being carried out. The first point to note about this policy is that it solves no problem whatever, since at least 14,000 of the total 24,000 Japanese in Canada will be left behind. Only about 10,000 are being sent away. Therefore every social and political difficulty caused by the existence of Japanese within Canada remains after deportation as it was before. The problem of what to do with them and where they may live is unsolved. It is not being suggested that we can absorb 14,000 in the future, but not 24,000.

The next point that strikes one is the complacency – hypocrisy would not be too strong a term – with which the policy is justified before the Canadian people. It is pretended that only those are being sent who have asked to go, or who are shown to be disloyal. This is superficially true, but it hides the real situation. If there are any Canadian Japanese who genuinely wish to return to Japan I would certainly let them go. I hope every Canadian is free to go wherever he wants, whenever he wants to. So are Italians free to go back to Italy, or Germans to Germany, so far as our law is concerned. But we did not put Germans and Italians into a concentration camp when the war broke out, seize all their property and sell it, thus destroying their economic life, and then force them to state whether they wished to leave Canada. Why do we single out the Japanese among all the enemy races for this treatment? The Italian colony in Montreal was rife with fascism before the war, yet it was not dealt with in this manner. Mr King stated in Parliament on August 4th, 1944, that 'no person of Japanese race born in Canada has been charged with any act of sabotage or disloyalty during the years of the war.' Yet we refused them the right to enlist (with only trivial exceptions) or to work in war plants, whereas in the United States the famous 100th battalion, entirely composed of Japanese, fought with distinction and gallantry in the Italian campaign.

Thus the trick or device – for that is what it was – of asking the Japanese throughout Canada to sign repatriation forms while the war was still on cannot deceive anyone who knows the facts. It is like offering a condemned man a pistol so that he may choose swift suicide to a public hanging. Is his death voluntary? Perhaps no one was 'forced' to choose repatriation, but the whole Canadian policy, the extreme racial hatred in British Columbia, the refusal of other provinces to co-operate in resettlement, the long history of deprivation of citizens' rights to people who were Canadian born British subjects, the statement of the Hon. Ian Mackenzie that they could never return to the coast – all this was the compulsion. Not unless the Japanese wanted to go back to Japan *after* we had set in motion our plans for their rehabilitation and *after* we had done something to make their citizenship equal that of other Canadians could it be said that their choice was free. At that moment certainly we should let all go who wish to go; it would be wrong to keep them. But to base plans for deportation on choices made under 1945 conditions, or to accuse the signers of disloyalty, is grossly unfair. Moreover, for the naturalized Japanese the right to change their mind has been arbitrarily taken away as from September 1st, 1945. Has not any man a right to change such a decision when circumstances change?

At the very moment when Parliament is trying to give some secure status to Canadian citizens by the Citizenship Bill, we should not treat fellow citizens in this fashion. It makes a farce of citizenship. We are all immigrants in Canada, except the Indians and Eskimos, and no citizen's right can be greater than that of the least protected group. Every Canadian is attacked in his fundamental civil liberties by this policy. To find it sponsored by a government bearing the name Liberal and not objected to by vigorous public protest, warns us how far our standards have sunk during these past years, despite our military victory over Nazism.

The real problem we have to solve in Canada has nothing directly to do with the Japanese at all: it is the problem of racial intolerance. This problem is only aggravated by the deportations. They mean a victory for intolerance and bigotry. We should be generous to this harmless minority whom we previously admitted to our shores, and apply fully to them the principle that race, religion and colour are no bar to full citizenship in this democracy.

# XV

# Duplessis *versus* Jehovah

*On 4 December, 1946, Mr Duplessis, then Prime Minister of Quebec, ordered the liquor license of Frank Roncarelli to be cancelled by the Quebec Liquor Commission because he persisted in giving bail for his co-religionists, the Witnesses of Jehovah, in the Montreal courts. The long saga of his fight for justice, ending thirteen years later in the Supreme Court of Canada, provides an important affirmation of the Rule of Law in Canadian jurisprudence. (See* Frank Roncarelli and The Honourable Maurice Duplessis *(1959), Supreme Court of Canada Reports, 129.) But though Roncarelli established a great legal principle, his restaurant was closed, his social status in Montreal undermined, and he was obliged to earn his living elsewhere. The Witnesses of Jehovah, however, now practise their religion unimpeded by the Quebec police.*
From the *Canadian Forum*, 26, 1947, 222–223.

Mr Duplessis, having helped Mr Drew to wreck the Dominion-Provincial Conference in the name of 'provincial autonomy,' seems now about to wreck all civil liberty in Quebec in the name of 'law and order.' On December 4 [1946] he cancelled the liquor license of Frank Roncarelli, owner of a well-known and highly respectable restaurant in Montreal, because Mr Roncarelli was continuing to put up bail for Jehovah's Witnesses as fast as Mr Duplessis continued to arrest them. And plenty have been arrested: some 800 cases are pending in Montreal.

This reminds us of Blair Fraser's article in *Maclean's Magazine* of Nov. 15, 1945, showing how Mr Duplessis cancels the licenses of people who do not contribute to the Union Nationale party funds. Mr Duplessis thinks nothing of using his authority as Premier and Attorney-General of the Province to take away the means of livelihood of people whose only crime is that they do not agree with his political views or dare to oppose his policies in a lawful manner. His violent attacks recently upon certain labor leaders, and his issuing instructions to the courts to refuse them bail, are all in keeping with the recent persecution of the Witnesses and of Mr Roncarelli. Add to this general picture the deal with the Hollinger Mining Company, by which immense resources, possibly containing the richest iron ore on the continent, were bartered away for a mere pittance to a private corporation, and some idea of the character of this man who so dearly loves 'provincial autonomy' may be perceived. Quebec is being 'saved' from 'centralization' and 'communism' in order that exploitation by big monopolies and suppression of all opposition may continue unchecked.

It is to be hoped that the Roncarelli affair will provide a rallying point for responsible and organized protest. The issue rises above religious and party lines. It is not often that papers like the *Montreal Star, The Gazette*, and *The Canadian Register* (organ of the English-speaking Catholics) are to be found voicing a common criticism, yet on this issue they are in general agreement. Similar criticism has been expressed in certain sections of the French press, though the fact that the Witnesses direct their chief attacks – and frequently very scurrilous attacks – upon the Catholic Church confuses the issue for many people and prevents them from protesting the arbitrary action of Mr Duplessis for fear of being thought to sympathize with the ideas which the Witnesses disseminate. No doubt Mr Duplessis is relying on this confusion to confine the protest to insignificant proportions, just as he probably imagines that the cancelling of the license will not raise an outcry from the Protestant clergy, many of which are unaccustomed to defending a man's right to sell liquor. Fortunately he seems to have underestimated the number of people who will not be fooled by such tactics. Had he confined himself to laying charges against individual Witnesses the volume of protest would not have been anything like as great as it is now that the larger issue has been raised by the action taken against Mr Roncarelli.

Perhaps the most amazing aspect of this affair is Mr Duplessis' stated reasons for the step. This is how it is reported in the *Montreal Gazette* of December 5: Turning to Roncarelli's case, Mr Duplessis stated that: 'A certain Mr Roncarelli has supplied bail for hundreds of Witnesses of Jehovah. The sympathy which this man has shown for the Witnesses in such an evident, repeated and audacious manner, is a provocation to public order, to the administration of justice and is definitely contrary to the aims of justice. He does not act, in this case, as a person posting bail for another person, but as the mass supplier of bails, whose great number by itself is most reprehensible.'

Was there ever a more astonishing statement from a Canadian Attorney-General? Mr Roncarelli is a member of Jehovah's Witnesses, and his 'audacious sympathy' for his co-religionists is to be justification for taking away his livelihood! He was not himself distributing pamphlets; he was merely giving bail. And what is bail? Bail is the security given by or on behalf of an accused person to ensure that he will appear to stand trial. Bail aids the administration of justice, and is a traditional part of it. It is for the courts, and the courts alone, to decide whether or not bail should be allowed, and in these cases they had permitted it. Mr Roncarelli was guaranteeing that the Witnesses would duly appear to be tried. What a 'provocation to public order!' For the exercise of this legal right and this ancient guarantee of human liberty Mr Roncarelli has his license cancelled and his restaurant raided by a gang of policemen who, incidentally, carried away his entire stock of liquor.

What Mr Roncarelli really did was not to promote disorder, but to check Mr Duplessis' mass persecution of the Witnesses. Because while the laying of a charge – in this case of peddling literature without a license – is not necessarily persecution, it becomes so when we learn that the number arrested reaches many hundreds, and particularly when Mr Duplessis tries to deny the accused the normal right of every citizen to bail. At the present moment, under a pretence of legal process, and in Mr Roncarelli's case without even a pretence, a small religious sect is being persecuted and indeed martyred in many parts of Quebec.

When the first storm of protest broke, Mr Duplessis immediately changed his ground and issued a new statement. This time he argued that since Mr Roncarelli held his license as a privilege – not as a right – from the Province, and since he was engaged in arranging bail for a mass of people deliberately committing 'illegal acts,' then the Province, from which he drew his funds, became a party to his proceedings. 'To allow him to continue to have that privilege, and, because of that privilege, secure the means of encouraging acts leading to public disorder would have been, in effect, to make the Attorney-General an accomplice.' On the same basis of reasoning, of course, the City of Montreal is an accomplice because it allows him water, the Quebec Hydro because it supplies electricity and gas, the Bell Telephone Company because it provides him with a telephone, and every diner who eats a meal aids and abets the horrible crime. Yet curiously enough Mr Duplessis does not dare lay any charge of any sort against this man who is such a dreadful menace to our national society. Mr Roncarelli is even allowed to continue in possession of his license to manage a restaurant. Can it be that the restaurant license is continued because to cancel it Mr Duplessis would have to show cause in a court of law, whereas, under the dictatorial powers of the Alcoholic Liquor Act, cancellation can be imposed at the mere whim of the Premier? Such excuses as Mr Duplessis gives are an insult to the intelligence.

Several important issues stand out clearly from this incident. One is the need for active civil liberties associations in this country. The recently formed Montreal Civil Liberties Association, composed of representatives of all the principal races and groups in Montreal, is taking up the matter, but the principles at stake concern every Canadian. Certainly the most Catholic province in Canada should hesitate before it officially supports the idea of religious persecution, even under the provocation which the Witnesses undoubtedly give. There are too many people who might be persuaded that persecution is a good policy, and it might be difficult to confine it to Quebec. Another issue to be faced is the need for judicial review of administrative acts. Mr Roncarelli should be able to appeal the cancellation to an impartial tribunal. There is none in Quebec, and other provinces may find the same lack in their laws. And lastly it may be worth warning too zealous defenders of civil liberties against using this incident as an excuse for another attack upon Quebec. The most serious breach of civil liberties in this country is British Columbia's – and the federal government's – treatment of Canadian citizens of Japanese origin. Beside it the case of Jehovah's Witnesses in Quebec is less reprehensible. For the Japanese-Canadians do not insult their fellow citizens by calling them evil names in widely distributed pamphlets.

# XVI

# Canada, Quebec, and Bilingualism

*The language question has always been a major ingredient in English-French relations in Canada; since the growth in the nationalist sentiment in Quebec and the development of the 'two nations theory' it has come to be more important than the religious factor. This article deals with a typical argument used against the acceptance of French as an official language.*
From *Queen's Quarterly*, 54, 1947, 1-7.

A recent letter to the editor of a Canadian weekly journal contained the following declaration: 'Just because French is the mother tongue of three million people in the province of Quebec, we have no desire to become a bilingual country. English is the official language of the rest of Canada, and of 130 million people in the United States.'

The writer of this letter lives in British Columbia. Safe behind the rampart of the Rockies, he must feel himself secure in his cultural nest. Perhaps he did not notice that he had used bilingual coins to buy the bilingual stamp which he stuck on the envelope as he posted his protest. Quebec was, in his view, an exception to the general pattern of Canada, a remote and peculiar province whose claim of equality for the French language must not be allowed to prevail. No doubt in voicing this opinion he expressed the views of many people who live outside Quebec.

Yet British Columbia is already, in an important respect, a bilingual province. So are all the other common-law provinces. English is not 'the official language of the rest of Canada,' if by that is meant the only official language. Throughout the whole country, and not only in Quebec, the French language has an official status. True, it has an additional use and position in Quebec, for purely provincial purposes, that are not found elsewhere, but the federal use of the language is surely more important than the provincial use. Canada is a bilingual country, and British Columbia can truthfully be called a bilingual province.

It is surprising that it should be necessary to make this point clear, so many years after the principle was laid down in the British North America Act. It is well known that Section 133 of that Act contains a guarantee for the two languages. The terms of the Section, however, apparently need to be emphasized. They read as follows:

Either the English or the French Language may be used by any Person in the Debates of the Houses of the Parliament of Canada and of the Houses of the Legislature of Quebec and both those languages shall be used in the respective Records and Journals of those Houses; and either of those languages may be used by any Person or in any Pleading or Process in or issuing from any court of Canada, established under this Act, and in or from all or any of the Courts of Quebec.

The acts of the Parliament of Canada and of the Legislature of Quebec shall be printed and published in both Languages.

This last sentence is particularly important. It means that every piece of federal legislation is published in the two official languages. Since federal legislation operates everywhere in Canada as much as in Quebec, the French version of the federal laws has the same authority in British Columbia as it has in Quebec. All the law of the common law provinces that is enacted by the federal Parliament is written just as officially in the French language as in the English.

Now there is a great deal of federal law to-day. Not only are there the four volumes of the *Revised Statutes of Canada*, with many additional statutes, but there are the innumerable Orders-in-Council which are promulgated under the authority of these laws. It is said that some 90,000 Orders-in-Council were issued by Ottawa during the past war. Most of these applied throughout the country, and they were – or should have been – published in the two official languages. More and more of the law in force in the English-speaking provinces in being written in French as well as in English. Thus the actions, rights and duties of Canadians, in British Columbia as elsewhere, are just as much governed and regulated by the French version of the federal law as they are by the English. In practice, since not many Canadians outside Quebec speak French, the English version may be the only one consulted, but this does not give it any greater validity. There is no rule of interpretation which says that if the French version is different from the English, the English must prevail. It may be the French version that will prevail over the English, even in British Columbia. In a recent case in the Exchequer Court dealing with the registration of trade-marks Mr Justice Thorson preferred the English text, but only because it gave a more reasonable rule.

An interesting example of the use of the French language as an aid in interpreting a federal statute arose in a case which went to the Supreme Court of Canada in 1935. It came from the Province of Ontario, but the French language is no more and no less official in Ontario than in any other common-law province. An automobile belonging to the Government of Canada, used by the Radio Branch of the Department of Marine, was involved in an accident in which a private citizen was killed. A question arose whether the automobile was a 'public work' within the meaning of the Exchequer Court Act. If it was, the Government had to pay; if it was not, the Government was free from liability. The Supreme Court held that the automobile was not a public work. But the point of interest is that Chief Justice Duff in his judgement referred specifically to the French version of the Exchequer Court Act, where the phrase 'chantier public' excluded any notion of public employment which might have been found in the 'public work' of the English version. In part because French was an official language in this provision of the law in force in Ontario, the plaintiff lost his case.

In the course of his judgement Chief Justice Duff made the following comment: 'Before calling attention to the effect of this language, it is right to mention, first of all, that the statutes of the Parliament of Canada in their French version pass through the two Houses of Parliament and receive the assent of His Majesty at the same time and according to the same procedure as those statutes in their English version. The enactment quoted is an enactment of the Parliament of Canada just as the enactments of the section, expressed in English, are.' These remarks apply as much to the province of British Columbia as they do to Ontario.

The barrister in a common-law province advising his client on any point of federal law would do well to consult the French version of the law as well as the English. He may find something there to his advantage. The courts of all the provinces are bound by the decisions of the Supreme Court of Canada, and this latter court will certainly not hesitate to consult a French text. Sometimes, indeed, a judgement will be rendered entirely in the French language on some point of federal law – a judgement binding on the lower courts everywhere in Canada.

This, however, is only part of the story. There is another way in which French is an official language in every English-speaking province. We find another provision in Section 133 of the British North America Act. It says that either French or English 'may be used by any Person or in any Pleading or Process in or issuing from any Court of Canada established under this Act.'

What are the 'courts of Canada' established under the British North America Act? They include such federal courts as the Supreme Court of Canada, the Exchequer Court, the Admiralty Court, and Courts Martial or Military Courts. Any person in any province can plead in these courts in either language. He could not be prevented from using French in Vancouver or Halifax. It may not be practical or reasonable to use a language which none of the court officials can understand, but there can be no question of the right to use either language. If the Dominion government should establish additional courts, the same rule should apply. The Labour Boards set up under federal labour legislation would probably not come under this rule, since they are not strictly 'courts,' but it would be fair and reasonable to treat them as if they were, and the practice has been to admit the use of the French language in their proceedings.

Since, then, the French language has an official status in a large part of the law in every province outside Quebec, and also in certain courts that exist in these provinces, it is surely not straining language to say that these provinces are already bilingual. Two languages are officially recognized by their law. It is true that they are not completely bilingual, since in their own provincial legislatures, statutes and courts only English may be used, but certainly they are in a different position from English-speaking countries where English is the only official language.

It may also be pointed out that a federal member of Parliament from a common-law province has a right to the use of the French language when speaking in the House and he has a right, as have all people in Canada, to the French version of Hansard. It seems logically to follow from this that he can speak to his constituency in French, whether from the platform or over the radio.

Just why so many people in Canada should resist the idea that French should be officially recognized it is difficult to understand. Quite apart from the erroneous view it represents of the actual situation, plain democratic justice and common-sense would seem to indicate that the mother-tongue of one-third of the population of any country has a claim to recognition which cannot be denied. We are at the point where we should consider whether another province, namely New Brunswick, is not ready for bilingualism even in the provincial field, since 35 per cent of the population are of French origin.

There is an added reason to-day why every Canadian should write and speak both languages. They are the two 'working languages' among the five official languages of the United Nations. They are also the only two official languages of the International Court of Justice. Article 39 of the Statute of the International Court says: 'The official languages of the Court shall be French and English.' Canada has subscribed to the Charter of the United Nations and is a member of the new Court. If every Canadian could be brought to realize that the possession of these two languages is a great national and international asset and not a liability, not only would we have more national unity in this country, but our delegates to international conferences would be better equipped.

There is a considerable movement on foot to-day to establish an International Bill of the Rights of Man. Various private legal bodies, including the American Bar Association, have made studies of the project and have prepared drafts. The Division on Human Rights of the United Nations Secretariat is preparing a Year-book of Human Rights in which will be reported all the provisions dealing with human rights in the various national constitutions. Besides showing the protection for individual liberties, the volume will also contain the clauses covering minority rights. Many people in Canada who would ardently support the individual civil liberties hesitate to accept the extension of the idea of liberty to the racial and linguistic group. On the other hand, it is probably fair to say that the French-speaking minority in Canada has always shown more concern for minority rights than for individual liberties. What is needed is a blending of the two correlative ideas. Canada has already made some contribution to the solution of minority problems, but there is plenty of room for improvement, as the plight of the Japanese-Canadians – to take but one example – only too clearly shows. The insertion of a Bill of Rights in our own Constitution, and support for the proposal of an International Bill of Rights, seem to be logical parts of a good domestic and foreign policy for Canada. Perhaps a growing recognition of the international importance of cultural liberty for minorities will help us to reduce our internal conflicts over such issues.

# XVII

# The British North America (no. 2) Act, 1949

*Canada emerged from the second world war as a completely independent nation state. The right to make her own declarations of war had been exercised against Germany in 1939 and Japan in 1941; full control over all aspects of the Royal prerogative affecting Canada was conceded in the new Letters Patent of 1947; the right to repeal or amend all British statutes relating to Canada, with the important exception of the British North America Acts 1867-1930, had been granted in the Statute of Westminster, 1931. There remained the final step in constitutional 'patriation'; the transference of the full amending power so as to render any further reference to the United Kingdom Parliament unnecessary. Pending agreement with the provinces as to how this should be done, Mr St-Laurent, then prime minister, took the bold step of securing the enactment of the above statute giving the federal Parliament power to change all parts of the constitution which did not impinge upon provincial jurisdiction. It was adopted despite the unanimous opposition of the Quebec legislature, whose agreement was considered unnecessary. As all the Dominion-Provincial conferences called to deal with the wider question have failed to reach agreement, this is how the matter remains today. (The No. 1 Act of 1949 provided for the admission of Newfoundland to the Confederation.)* From the *University of Toronto Law Journal*, 18, 1949, 201-7.

Canada has now embarked upon the difficult process of bringing to her shores that ultimate legislative authority which, in spite of her complete political autonomy, has continued to rest in the Parliament of the United Kingdom, and which has from time to time been invoked for the purpose of amending the British North America Act. When that Act was adopted in 1867 no amending procedure was included; the practice of making constitutional changes by petitioning for special enactments in London, already established before 1867, was continued; and section 7 of the Statute of Westminster, 1931 preserved this anomalous situation at the request of Canada. On October 17, 1949 Prime Minister St-Laurent, employing the customary procedure, moved the adoption of a joint address praying His Majesty to cause a measure to be laid before the Parliament of the United Kingdom for the enactment of certain provisions granting a limited power of amendment of the Canadian constitution to the Parliament of Canada. After approval of this joint address by the House of Commons on October 27 and by the Senate on November 9, a bill incorporating its provisions, with minor verbal changes,[1] was introduced into the British Parliament and adopted by the House of Lords on November 22 and by the House of Commons on December 2, under the title of the British North America (No. 2) Act, 1949. Royal assent was given on December 16. Thus was completed, in short order, the first stage in the transfer of the amending power; the further steps necessary to complete the process were referred to a Dominion-provincial conference called to meet in Ottawa on January 10th, 1950.

The operative section of the new Act gives to the Parliament of Canada, as the first of its enumerated heads under section 91 of the British North America Act of 1867, power to legislate regarding:

1. The amendment from time to time of the Constitution of Canada, except as regards matters coming within the classes of subjects by this Act assigned exclusively to the Legislatures of the provinces, or as regards rights or privileges by this or any other Constitutional Act granted or secured to the Legislature or the Government of a province, or to any class of persons with respect to schools or as regards the use of the English or the French language or as regards the requirements that there shall be a session of the Parliament of Canada at least once each year, and that no House of Commons shall continue for more than five years from the day of the return of the Writs for choosing the House; provided, however, that a House of Commons may in time of real or apprehended war, invasion or insurrection be continued by the Parliament of Canada if such continuation is not opposed by the votes of more than one-third of the members of such House.

The technique of amendment here provided is expressed in the simple form of a general federal power, subject to certain defined exceptions. The ordinary process of legislation is all that is required; that is to say, a bill approved by both Houses of Parliament and assented to by the governor-general. This will allow debate in committee, which is not possible on a joint address. Despite this simplicity, the adoption of the section raises many interesting points.

It is clear that the refusal of the Canadian government to consult with the provinces before the adoption of the amendment, as urged by the Conservative

---

1 Though these changes were verbal and not substantial, the fact that any changes were made at all is a little surprising. They were not approved by the Canadian Parliament.

party and by several provincial premiers, indicates its rejection of the compact theory of Confederation. Mr St-Laurent in effect admitted this in his opening speech on the joint address,[2] though he stressed that his proposal involved no change except a change of the venue where the amendments can be made, since only matters 'within the exclusive concern of the federal authorities' were being dealt with. As no one knows, however, just what such matters may be, and as the provinces might take a different view from that of the Canadian government, or even of the Supreme Court were the question referred to it, we must consider this unilateral action by the federal Parliament as further evidence against the claims of those who would treat the constitution as a compact, either in law or in political theory. Nevertheless, the calling of the Dominion-provincial confer-ence in January, 1950, to consider the proper technique for amendment of those parts of the constitution of joint concern to Ottawa and the provinces, recognizes, as was to be expected, a constituent role in the provincial legislatures. It is im-portant to note that in Canada, as in the United States, the participation by prov-inces or states in the process of amendment does not necessarily indicate that the constitution is a compact. The American constitution is not so considered.

In the first line of the amending clause occurs the expression 'The Constitu-tion of Canada,' and in the fifth line there are the words 'Constitutional Act.' These are, in technical language, novel phrases. Hitherto they have been terms of political science rather than of Canadian constitutional law. In law we have spoken of the British North America Acts, 1867 to 1949. Some important constitutional statutes are not included in such a description. For instance, the Ruperts' Land Act of 1868, the Canada (Ontario Boundary) Act, 1889, the Canadian Speaker (Appointment of Deputy) Act, 1895, the Statute of Westminster, 1931, and others are already part of the constitution of Canada though not among the Bri-tish North America Acts. By using the broader phrase the amending power is made to cover all statutes, orders-in-council, treaties, or judicial decisions which might be considered part of the total constitution. But, as Professor Clokie has pointed out, it is not easy to say where the Canadian constitution begins or ends.[3]

As already noted, the federal amending power is an all-inclusive power, the 'amendment from time to time of the Constitution of Canada,' subject to certain exceptions. The phrase 'the Constitution of Canada' includes the provincial con-stitutions. There is no separate 'federal' constitution; the constitution is a single body of law setting up and apportioning authority to different organs of the state, some federal and some provincial. If the section had stopped there, it would

2 Canada, House of Commons, *Debates* (unrevised ed.), Oct. 17, 1949, at p. 835.
3 H. McD. Clokie, 'Basic Problems of the Canadian Constitution,' in (1942) 8 *Canadian Journal of Economics and Political Science* 1.

have crystallized into law the present practice by which, through the joint address, Ottawa can secure any amendment it desires from the Parliament of the United Kingdom. But the section goes on to subtract from the generality of the opening words, and stipulates that the federal power of amendment shall not extend over: (*i*) Matters coming within the classes of subjects by this Act assigned exclusively to the Legislature of the provinces; (*ii*) rights or privileges by this or any other Constitutional Act granted or secured to the Legislature or the Government of a province; (*iii*) or to any class of persons with respect to schools; (*iv*) or as regards the use of the English or the French language; (*v*) or as regards the requirements as to the annual session of Parliament and the five-year term (provided that the House of Commons may extend that term under the prescribed conditions).

In thus limiting its amending powers the federal Parliament has indicated its willingness to give a protection to provincial and minority rights which did not formerly exist. Formerly, only convention restrained Parliament from requesting any amendment – even one affecting so fundamental a right as that to the two official languages in section 133 of the British North America Act. Now Parliament has withdrawn certain defined classes of matters from its competence, leaving them to be amended by a process to be agreed upon at the Dominion-provincial conference. Thus it has voluntarily retreated, so to speak, from the position which, by subjecting the legal supremacy of the Parliament of the United Kingdom to the conventional control of the Canadian Parliament, had accidentally resulted in giving Canada a federal constitution as flexible as the English constitution itself. However should there be a failure to achieve agreement on the amending procedure for matters falling within any of the excepted classes (*i*) to (*v*) above, then presumably the former conventional method of amendment in London after a joint address from Ottawa will continue. This would indeed create an anomalous situation, since Ottawa would then possess both processes of amendment itself – one, over exclusively federal matters, by its own legislation, and the other, over all other matters, by joint address that Westminster cannot refuse to implement. In either case a mere majority vote in both Houses is sufficient for the adoption of the amendment. There may be political wisdom in consulting with the provinces before adopting a joint address requesting an amendment affecting provincial rights, but there is certainly no legal necessity for so doing.

In strict legal theory, of course, the Parliament of the United Kingdom would still have a ghostly legal authority over Canada even when full power to amend the constitution has been provided, since the British North America Acts will still remain British statutes, and the sovereign Parliament which gave Canada the amending procedures might later change them or repeal them. This point seems to have been appreciated by Mr St-Laurent, for when he was asked by Mr Fleming what there was to prevent the Parliament of Canada from disregarding the requirement of the two-thirds vote for a continuation of the life of Parliament beyond five years, and proceeding by mere majority vote to adopt an address asking the Parliament of the United Kingdom to suspend these sections of the constitution, the Prime Minister replied: 'There would be nothing but the sense of responsibility that would have developed in the Canadian nation by exercising at home its control over its own affairs. There would be no other thing than that.'[4] He went on to say that it would be 'distasteful' to members of Parliament to ask another parliament to take such a step. Perhaps he could have gone further and suggested that the Parliament of the United Kingdom might well refuse to follow the request contained in a joint address, if another procedure had already been provided for the particular amendment required. In other words, the concept of legal sovereignty in the British Parliament, the Kelsenian *grundnorm* of the whole Canadian constitution, may well be considered to have disappeared once the amending procedures are finally determined. This will be even more evident if a process for amending the amending clauses is also adopted, and if at the same time there is a statutory renunciation by the Parliament of the United Kingdom of its authority over Canada. The ancient doctrine of the sovereignty of that Parliament has not disappeared by the mere enactment of the British North America (No. 2) Act, 1949.

An examination of the five classes of matters excepted from the federal amending power ( (*i*) to (*v*) above) raises a number of questions. Unlike the procedure for amendment suggested by the sub-committee of the Dominion-provincial conference of 1935,[5] in which the method for changing each specific article or group of articles of the British North America Act was carefully detailed, the method here enacted does not mention the sections by number but only by general content. Mr St-Laurent stated to the House of Commons that 'Care has been taken to avoid making any declaration as to where the dividing line might strike matters which are of provincial jurisdiction, those which are of federal jurisdiction, and those which are of joint concern to federal and provincial authorities.'[6] He pointed out that if, after this amendment, the Parliament of Canada were to do anything which anyone felt impinged on any of the rights or privileges guaranteed to the provinces, or on any educational or linguistic rights, the legislation could be challenged before the courts who would then decide whether or not the matter was within the jurisdiction of Parliament. In other words, litigation might

4 Canada, House of Commons, *Debates*, Oct. 20, 1949, at p. 959. See also Mr Fleming's comments, *ibid.*, Oct. 27, 1949, at p. 1206.
5 The report of this sub-committee has never been published, but reference to its work is contained in Mr St-Laurent's opening speech: *ibid.*, Oct. 17, 1949, at p. 833.
6 *Ibid.*, at p. 834.

precede, or follow, the political agitation needed to secure an amendment. The courts may thus select the procedure required for any particular constitutional change. This creates another element of rigidity, opens the door to many uncertainties, and thrusts upon the courts a novel duty seldom, if ever, found in federal states.

It is perhaps not difficult to identify specifically what sections of the constitution are intended by the phrase 'as regards the use of the English or the French language' – it refers to section 133 of the British North America Act, 1867, and to section 23 of The Manitoba Act,[7] where alone such rights are given. The exception regarding educational privileges presumably refers to section 93 of the Act of 1867, and to those sections of the Manitoba, Saskatchewan and Alberta Acts which deal with this subject, as well as to the recent provisions in the schedule to the British North America Act of 1949 relating to education in Newfoundland. But the matters excepted in classes (i) and (ii) above do not lend themselves to easy identification. Matters 'coming within the classes of subjects by this Act assigned exclusively to the Legislatures of the provinces' would seem to include all the sub-heads of section 92; it would therefore not be possible for Parliament alone to alter the provincial power of amendment of the provincial constitution in head 1 of section 92, though it would seem to follow that Parliament could alone change the office of the lieutenant-governor since this is denied to the provinces. Ottawa cannot subtract from 'property and civil rights' by unilateral action, since these matters are exclusively provincial. Thus far no difficulty is evident.

What, however, are we to say of the amendment of section 95 of the British North America Act, which gives a concurrent power to both Ottawa and the provinces over agriculture and immigration? These matters certainly are not 'exclusively' assigned to the provinces. They are therefore not protected by this exception from federal amendment. They appear to be, however, 'rights or privileges by this ... Act secured to the Legislature ... of a province,' and so must be protected from federal intervention under this wording. Provinces now have a right to make laws on these two subjects, even though they may have to give way to valid federal laws on the same subjects; such a right can therefore not be destroyed or changed by Parliament alone. It would seem that the same answer would have to be given to the question of amendment of section 132 dealing with treaties. To implement Empire treaties is now an exclusive federal power, but should Ottawa change the word 'Empire' to 'Canadian' – an amendment not

7 Although this section was changed by the Legislature of Manitoba so as to make English the exclusive language of the Legislative Assembly (see Revised Statutes of Manitoba, 1940, c. 152), the validity of the change has never been tested in the courts, and the better view would seem to be that it was beyond provincial jurisdiction.

apparently dealing with a provincial matter – the effect would be to subtract from the property and civil rights clause a power to implement Canadian treaties which has been placed there by judicial interpretation, thus again bringing the amendment within one or other of the exceptions. Such an amendment would therefore, on this analysis, be beyond the power of Parliament. These tentative answers to hypothetical questions are given merely to indicate some of the problems which immediately spring to mind and to which no authoritative answer can be given. Others may easily be imagined.

An interesting possibility arises that the Parliament of Canada may have power to bind its successors by the adoption of the 1949 amendment. By section 7 of the Statute of Westminster the Colonial Laws Validity Act continues to apply to the British North America Acts; by section 5 of the Colonial Laws Validity Act a colonial legislature may alter its constitution provided it follows such procedures as 'may from time to time be required by any Act of Parliament ... or colonial law for the time being in force in the colony.' Hence a Dominion statute requiring the powers conferred by the 1949 Act to be exercised at all times by, say, a two-thirds vote, would be binding on all future sessions of the federal Parliament.

It may be premature to anticipate at this stage the meaning and effect of this new federal power of amendment. Perhaps it will never be used, for Mr St-Laurent has indicated his willingness to seek its withdrawal if a satisfactory overall method of amendment can be devised.[8] One thing is clear; the techniques for changing the Canadian constitution within Canada appear likely to contain much complexity. Until now, when we have had no power to amend in Canada, convention has given us the simplest form, hesitant though we were to use it where provincial jurisdiction was affected; now that legal rules are being substituted for conventional practice, complicated forms are being adopted. One is inclined to think back, rather wistfully, to the remark Sir John A. Macdonald made during the Quebec Conference: 'It [our constitution] should be a mere skeleton and framework that would not bind us down. We have now all the elasticity which has kept England together.'[9]

8 See *Constitutional Conference of Federal and Provincial Governments* (Ottawa, 1950), pp. 54–5, 68.
9 J. Pope (ed.), *Confederation: Being a Series of Hitherto Unpublished Documents Bearing on the British North America Act* (Toronto, 1895), at p. 59.

# XVIII

# Dominion Jurisdiction over Human Rights and Fundamental Freedoms

*As the pressure mounted during the 1930s and 1940s for new laws to protect human rights in Canada, the question whether it was Parliament or the provincial legislatures which had the jurisdiction was increasingly debated. I set out some of my views in this article.*
From the *Canadian Bar Review*, 27, 1949, 497-536

I THE PRESENT SITUATION

To define and protect the rights of individuals is a prime purpose of the constitution in a democratic state. In Canada today many people are feeling that this purpose is not being adequately achieved. Examples of a disregard of fundamental freedoms have been frequent enough to raise doubts as to the sufficiency of our existing guarantees of personal liberty. We live under a constitution that permits the deportation of citizens born in Canada; under which persons have been denied the vote solely on grounds of race; that, in Quebec, enables an administrative official to padlock a man's house for propagating communism before he has been found guilty in a court of law and, in Prince Edward Island, has forbidden trade unions to affiliate with any bodies outside their province. While these infringements of elementary rights have existed at home, our delegates to international gatherings have taken part in the formulation of the fundamental freedoms which all members of the United Nations are pledged by the Charter to uphold. Public discussion of these issues has caused a healthy awakening of interest in the basic ideas underlying the Canadian constitution,[1] and it is not surprising that natural law concepts are being re-examined and put forward in the form of a Bill of

---

1 See W. Glen How, The Case for a Canadian Bill of Rights (1948) 26 *Can. Bar Rev.* 759; speech of Mr J.G. Diefenbaker, May 16th, 1947, *Hansard* (Daily ed.) p. 3194.

Rights for Canada, designed to shield the individual from abuses of governmental power, while at the same time a more positive rôle for the state in securing the economic basis for personal freedom is also being stressed.

During the year 1948 several important international conventions and declarations have brought these questions out of the realm of abstract discussion into the arena of more practical politics. Three draft conventions, on the gathering and international transmission of news, on freedom of information and on an international right of correction, were proposed by the World Conference on Freedom of Information held at Geneva in April 1948. The International Labour Organisation adopted a Convention on Freedom of Association at San Francisco in July.[2] A conference at Brussels in June 1948 revised the Berne Convention for the protection of literary and artistic works.[3] Most recent and most comprehensive of all, the Universal Declaration of Human Rights was approved by the United Nations Assembly in Paris on December 10th.[4] On each of these instruments Canadian delegates were obliged to vote (or to abstain from voting) and our Parliament and legislatures will now or later come under an obligation, moral if not legal, to bring our domestic laws into line with these formal statements. International action thus impels us toward national legislation. Preliminary steps to 'consider the question of human rights and fundamental freedoms, and the manner in which those obligations accepted by all members of the United Nations may best be implemented' have been taken by the federal Parliament through the establishment, during the sessions of 1947 and 1947-8, of a Joint Committee of the Senate and House of Commons, and the Committee has considered and reported upon various proposals for the addition of a Bill of Rights to the British North America Act.[5]

So far, however, more effort has been spent on the formulation of principles of individual rights and freedoms than on an examination of the division of federal-provincial jurisdiction over them. The time has arrived when the question of jurisdiction would seem to be a matter of the first importance for Canadians. The

2 See H.W. Macdonnell, Freedom of Occupational Association and Human Rights (1948), 26 *Can. Bar Rev.* 683 for preliminary texts. The final text is in the Report of the Canadian Government Delegates to the 31st Session of the International Labour Conference (Ottawa, King's Printer, 1949) p. 61.
3 The text is in the Copyright Bulletin of UNESCO, Vol. I, No. 2, Dec. 1948, p. 10.
4 For preliminary drafts and final text see (1948), 26 *Can. Bar Rev.* 548, 1106, and (1949), 27 *Can. Bar Rev.* 203.
5 *Minutes of Proceedings and Evidence*, King's Printer, Ottawa (hereinafter referred to as *Proceedings*). The Committee in a somewhat vague and inconclusive final report (*Proceedings* 1947-48, p. 207) recommended against the adoption of either a Bill of Rights for Canada by federal statute or by amendment to the constitution 'without a great deal of further study.'

great principles have achieved wide recognition; the problem now is to distribute the duty of enforcement. We cannot fulfil our international obligations until we have decided which government may act. This is an essential prerequisite to the implementation by Canada of any international agreement. Without a clear apportionment of responsibility we are all too likely to reach the same kind of deadlock in this as in so many other fields of Dominion-provincial relations.

Unfortunately grave doubt has been cast on the power of Parliament to legislate effectively in regard to human rights and fundamental freedoms. The impression has gone abroad that this subject is almost wholly embraced with the words 'property and civil rights,' and hence is a provincial matter. The Joint Committee in 1947 invited the attorneys-general of the provinces and the deans of Canadian law schools to express their views on 'the power of the Parliament of Canada to enact a comprehensive Bill of Rights applicable to all of Canada,' and the tenor of the replies was contrary to the existence of such a power.[6] Since the Committee did not define the word 'comprehensive,' however, the answers were of little help; obviously Ottawa has some, but not all, the responsibility, and the only useful inquiry would have been one directed to finding out how much rested with the national parliament. The Rt Hon. J.L. Ilsley, then Minister of Justice, stressed the importance of provincial jurisdiction in the House of Commons on May 19th of that year, and Mr Pearson's cautious attitude at the Paris meeting of the United Nations in 1948[7] emphasized the doubt. The Joint Parliamentary Committee was authorized in 1947-8 to recommend that a draft Bill of Rights be referred to the Supreme Court of Canada for a determination of the jurisdiction of Parliament, but no such step has yet been taken. Although something could be said for this proposal, it suggests that so much uncertainty surrounds the subject that no legislation should be attempted until the courts have first been asked to delimit the respective areas of legislative capacity, and the courts are likely to give vague answers to what can only be vague and hypothetical questions.

This whole approach, it is submitted, is unnecessarily dilatory and hesitant. There is always a temptation to refer to courts the questions that should be decided by governments and to use constitutional references as an excuse for political delays. The Canadian Parliament has a great many powers under the present constitution which can be used to expand our rights and freedoms, about which there exists no shadow of legal doubt whatever. Indeed it may be stated at once that there does not seem to be a single article in the Universal Declaration of Human Rights of 1948 on which Ottawa may not take some positive action if the

---

6 Sessional Paper No. 150A, Feb. 17th, 1948. The only replies worth reprinting are in an article entitled 'The Joint Committee on Human Rights and Fundamental Freedoms' (1948), 26 *Can. Bar Rev.* 706.

7 See official statement in External Affairs, Jan. 1949, p. 23.

government so wishes; and it seems equally true to say that some federal law already exists touching each article in some degree. There is, of course, an important field for provincial action as well, but this in no way hinders the exercise of federal powers. For example, because each province may decide who votes in provincial elections is no reason why racial discrimination should exist in the federal Election Act. It is the purpose of this paper to examine what these undeniable federal powers are and to suggest various ways in which they might be employed. It should also be pointed out that we are not tied to other people's apronstrings; it is not necessary for us to restrict ourselves to the minimum level attainable in an international Declaration. Canada can give leadership in matters that did not pass the international committees and, whether or not we may wish to amend our constitution in the future, it is desirable that Parliament should exercise its present powers in such vital matters to the fullest extent.

## II PROPOSALS FOR A BILL OF RIGHTS

The term 'Bill of Rights' is generally used to express the idea of a single charter or statute in which the principal liberties of the citizens are set out. The French Declaration of the Rights of Man of 1791, and the Bill of Rights in the United States constitution, are notable examples. There has been a considerable demand for the adoption of a Bill of Rights by our federal Parliament. There are two ways in which such a Bill could be given the force of law. It could either be written into the BNA Act by a constitutional amendment, or it could be enacted as a solemn statute by the Canadian Parliament alone. The first would require action by the United Kingdom Parliament after a joint address requesting the change had been adopted by the Senate and House of Commons; the second would require the same procedure as for the enactment of an ordinary federal statute. Some confusion seems to have arisen owing to a failure to appreciate the differences between these two proposals. Further confusion has arisen owing to a general unawareness that the BNA Act already contains the elements of a Bill of Rights, however incomplete they may be. To assist in clarifying these various ideas it may be well to restate certain general principles of Canadian constitutional law.

The BNA Act contains two basic notions which are somewhat contradictory. One is the principle, inherited from the United Kingdom, of the sovereignty of Parliament; the other is the acceptance of specific limitations on this sovereignty. In England no court may declare an act of Parliament ultra vires, no matter to what degree it destroys the cherished liberties of the subject, or violates the fundamental rights of man. The King in Parliament is legally supreme, and his laws can never be invalid. The great documents of English constitutional history, such as Magna Carta, the Habeas Corpus Act, and the Bill of Rights of 1689, can be repealed or amended by a mere majority vote in the Lords and Commons. These charters of liberty protect the citizen against arbitrary action by the Crown or executive, but not against the legislature itself. In a certain sense, they are not worth the paper they are written on, since they can always be set aside at the will of Parliament. It is a legal impossibility for the British to write an untouchable charter of liberties into their present constitution. On the other hand, the vitality and enduring influence of these great English statutes prove their value as a protection for individual rights.

Canada has adopted, but in part only, the principle of parliamentary sovereignty. We have adopted it to this extent, that within the spheres of jurisdiction assigned to them under the BNA Act, and with some important exceptions to be noted immediately, our Parliament and provincial legislatures are supreme. No acts of any parliament in Canada can be held ultra vires just because they punish a man without trial, for instance, like the Quebec Padlock Act, or because they confiscate his property without compensation or interfere with his private contracts. We can create ex post facto crimes, we can prescribe cruel and unusual punishments, and can do many things which are denied to American legislatures. It follows that if we enact a Bill of Rights by federal statute, in the second manner suggested, we can repeal it at will. What Parliament gives it has the legal power to take away. The courts are only called upon to see that the boundaries of Dominion and provincial jurisdiction are not crossed, and may not decide upon the morality or justice of the law. Their sole function is to ensure that the law in question has been enacted by the proper legislature. This is the general rule.

### III FUNDAMENTAL RIGHTS IN THE BNA ACT

It is the exceptions to this rule, however which are important for our present discussion. For there are some absolute limitations on the principle of parliamentary sovereignty in Canada, and these occur precisely in order to guarantee certain political and minority rights. There is no Bill of Rights in the BNA Act in the sense of a single article or section listing all the freedoms which are safeguarded from legislative invasion, but there are a number of specific rules which no laws, federal or provincial, can repeal. Added together, these make the beginnings of a Bill of Rights. Thus the use of the English and French languages is guaranteed by section 133; the right to separate schools by section 93; the right to an annual session of Parliament by section 20; the right to a new Parliament every five years by section 50; the right to representation by population by section 51; the right to an independent judiciary by section 99. Every one of these rules protects a fundamental freedom, and every one is a limitation on the sovereignty of either the Dominion Parliament or the provincial legislatures, or both. It has also been held by the courts, though perhaps not finally, that other implied limitations on legislative supremacy exist. Thus the right of the citizen to have access to the courts in order to test the constitutionality of a statute has been protected from provincial violation,[8] and a principle of freedom of the press has been deduced from the use of the word 'Parliament' in the text of the BNA Act – a 'Parliament' obviously being a legislative body surrounded by supporting rights such as free speech, a free press and freedom of assembly.[9] If this view prevails, the declaration in section 17 of the BNA Act that 'there shall be one Parliament for Canada' will effectively secure certain basic civil liberties against provincial interference, though not against federal legislation.

Our notions of parliamentary sovereignty are therefore strictly limited in Canada and the addition of a formal Bill of Rights to the constitution, to extend the protections that now exist, would in no way change the nature of the constitution. It seems necessary to emphasize this point, since so eminent an authority as Mr J.L. Ilsley has stated that 'the adoption of the other system, the system of constitutional limitations upon the powers of parliament, would be a radical departure from principles which have heretofore applied'[10] and Mr F.P. Varcoe, Deputy Minister of Justice, in his evidence before the Joint Committee suggested that it was a 'retrograde step' to take away from Parliament a sovereign power and to return it to the source from which it came, namely the United Kingdom Parliament.[11] The difference is one of degree and not of kind; we have no absolutely sovereign parliaments in Canada.

The addition of a new section to the BNA Act containing a list of further rights, entitled a Bill of Rights, should therefore be looked upon as something which would carry forward and enlarge upon rules already formulated in our constitution. Whether or not we should take this step is a matter of policy. It would have the advantage of making the prescribed rights more secure against legislative repeal. Any rights enumerated in the BNA Act operate as restrictions on the jurisdiction of legislatures and enable the courts to set aside any later statutes invading the protected area. If freedom of association is guaranteed, laws taking away this freedom would be unconstitutional where today they are not. One purpose of a Bill of Rights is to protect the citizens against the tyranny of legislative majorities, and to substitute the sovereignty of the people for the sovereignty of Parliament. On the other hand an inescapable effect is to shift the burden of defining the protected rights from our elected representatives to our nominated judges. Ultimately the question narrows down to a choice between a faith in the courts

8 *Ottawa Valley Power Co.* v. *A.G. Ontario*, [1936] 4 D.L.R. 594; *Independent Order of Foresters* v. *Lethbridge*, [1938] 3 D.L.R. 89; *Reference re Legal Proceedings Suspension Act*, [1942] 3 D.L.R. 318.

9 *Reference re Alberta Statutes*, [1938] S.C.R. 100.

10 *House of Commons Debates*, May 19th, 1947, *Hansard* (Daily ed.) p. 3263.

11 Proceedings, 1947, p. 84; 1947–8, p. 202; and in his reply cited *supra* (1948), 26 *Can. Bar Rev.* at p. 710. Also Senator Gouin, *Proceedings*, 1947–8, p. 180.

and a faith in legislatures. History has shown that either may become the enemy of freedom.

Moreover the mere enunciation of rights, important though it is, has little practical value unless it is backed up by adequate enforcement machinery. *Ubi remedium, ibi jus*; where you have a remedy, there only have you an effective right. The Russian constitution of 1936, like those of the American Southern States, contains a greater list of fundamental freedoms than are to be found in the BNA Act. Yet these countries are not the best examples of free societies. They have the principles, but are deficient in practice. From these examples we may learn the lesson that the work of protecting our freedoms only begins when they have been formulated; the next and equally important duty arises of providing cheap and effective remedies to the individuals whose rights are violated. This usually means protecting persons who are weak and unpopular against those who are strong and respectable.

## IV A BILL OF RIGHTS WITHOUT AMENDMENT TO THE BNA ACT

A Bill of Rights written into the constitution, then, would provide certain guarantees for fundamental freedoms by limiting the power of legislatures to enact laws to the contrary. It would also raise the problems that have been mentioned. What about a Bill of Rights of the second kind, a federal statute setting out, like the English Bill of Rights of 1689, certain fundamental rights of Canadian citizens? What would be its nature, and what might it accomplish?

We have seen that such a Bill of Rights would not bind future parliaments. It could always be amended or abrogated by a mere majority vote, or even by a later statute which contradicted it without expressly amending it. It might be protected from inadvertent amendment by making a new rule of interpretation to the effect that no subsequent statute would prevail over the Bill of Rights unless the intention to do so was clearly indicated by Parliament. This would be analogous to the rule that no statute can affect the rights of the Crown unless they are specially mentioned. Such a practice was adopted in Quebec to preserve the Civil Code from casual changes,[12] but it provides only a limited protection. Judges already have rules of interpretation which justify them in reading very strictly any statute limiting the rights of the subject. The chief value of such a Bill resides in the solemnity of the occasion on which it is adopted and the symbolic nature of its provisions. It might become almost a sacred legend, like Magna Carta, impressing by its moral force rather than by its inviolability.

The Bill could not, of course, affect in any way the rights of the provinces. It

12 See 41 Vict., c. 7, referred to in *Diva Shoe* v. *Gagnon* (1941), 70 K.B. (Que.) 411.

could have effect only within the federal area of jurisdiction. Ottawa cannot acquire any new powers under the BNA Act simply by using the magic term 'Bill of Rights.' But the federal area of jurisdiction in this field, as will be indicated later, is very wide, and the operation of the Bill would extend to all persons in Canada in a large degree and to particular groups of persons in still larger degree. Although not binding future parliaments, it could be made binding on the executive branch of the federal government; one might cite as an example the provision in the War Measures Act requiring the payment of compensation whenever any property is appropriated or used for war purposes. It could also contain sanctions for its infringement which would protect the citizen from interference by other citizens in the exercise of his rights. The Criminal Law power of the federal parliament has by no means been exhausted as a protection for the fundamental freedoms of the individual, and were it to be applied with some more imaginative recognition of democratic objectives a number of evil practices might be stopped that are now permitted. A great deal of good might reasonably be expected from a federal Bill of Rights of this second type.

## V REVISION OF EXISTING FEDERAL LAWS

Even if the federal Parliament were to decide to do nothing about the adoption of a Bill of Rights, either by way of amendment of the BNA Act or by special statute, much could be done to fulfil Canada's international obligations and to strengthen fundamental freedoms by action that would be less spectacular but perhaps more useful. It would be quite a simple matter, though it would take time, to revise all the existing federal laws which touch upon or affect human rights, and to change and where necessary supplement them so as to bring them up to the desired standards. No doubt most of these laws are already up to the level prevailing in other countries calling themselves democratic, but there are obviously a number that are not. In others the protection for the individual or for minorities could be improved if it were the duty of some revising committee to read the statutes with this purpose in view and to make recommendations to Parliament. The current revision of the Canadian Criminal Code – a development that is long overdue – offers a special opportunity for this kind of law amendment. The work could be done simultaneously with the preparation of the next Revised Statutes of Canada, publication of which might be delayed until the needed amendments and additions had been approved by Parliament.

## VI FREEDOMS AND RIGHTS: SOME DISTINCTIONS

In his evidence before the Parliamentary Joint Committee Mr Varcoe made a sharp distinction between a freedom and a right. He said:

The distinction which is given in these two matters may be stated as follows:

A right, according to this view, connotes a corresponding duty in some other person or the state towards the person holding the right. If, for example, a person has the right to education, there is a corresponding duty upon the state to provide it.

Now, freedom on the other hand, or liberty, is a benefit or advantage which a person derives from the absence of legal duties imposed upon him. They are the things which a person may do without being prevented by law. You will note that in the charter the words are, 'Human Rights and Fundamental Freedoms.' I take it that the draftsmen of the charter had in mind this distinction between, on the one hand, rights, and on the other hand, freedoms. I give you a list of some of the so-called rights on the one hand and freedoms on the other. There is the right to own property; the right to social security. There are many others, but those are just examples. On the other hand, you have freedom of the person; freedom of speech; freedom of the press; freedom of assembly and freedom of religion. Those are examples of the freedoms. I mention those distinctions here because there is a radical difference between those two groups when you come to look at them from a legal or constitutional point of view. Human Rights, as I say, are those things which connote an obligation on some person or the state to implement a corresponding duty towards the person holding the right. When you decide what rights you want to have, then you have to proceed to create them by legislative action ...

When you come to look at the other side of the coin, the freedoms which a person is entitled to enjoy, you might say that instead of requiring the enactment of legislation these require the repeal of legislation. If you had no statutory law or any regulations at all to control a person, you would have, theoretically at any rate, a state of absolute freedom. It might not last very long.[13]

A full discussion of this distinction would lead far into the field of jurisprudence and legal theory. Suffice it to say that it is of doubtful utility for the purpose of apportioning jurisdiction under the BNA Act, and is perhaps a distinction without any real difference in law. There is no freedom where there is no right. It may be true that freedom of speech involves the absence of restraint upon the person enjoying the freedom, but it must also involve a legal restraint upon all persons who would interfere with that freedom, and these legal restraints come either from the common law or from positive legislation. Positive legislation may be almost as much needed in the case of the 'freedoms' as in the case of rights. Freedom of religion, for instance, is protected by the section of the Criminal Code which prohibits any interference with religious ceremonies. There is a well-known distinction, if difficult to define, between rights *in rem* and rights *in per-*

13 *Proceedings* 1947, p. 69.

*sonam*, and the basic freedoms belong to the former category. They are good against all the world. They are none the less rights. Mr Varcoe seems to have disregarded his own distinction when he presented to the Committee a draft federal Bill which would have been positive legislation designed to protect freedom of religion, of peaceful assembly, of the press and of communication.[14]

There is however a less technical distinction, arising out of the historical evolution of our thinking on these matters, between 'fundamental freedoms' and 'human rights.' In the older language the expression 'civil liberties' was in more general use to describe the basic political rights in a free society. Freedom of speech, association, the press and religion, and similar rights, were standard examples of civil liberties. In the United States the American Civil Liberties Union, and in England the National Council on Civil Liberties, have a long record of voluntary service in this field; in the past fifteen years in Canada there have been a number of societies using this name. More recently the term civil liberties has tended to give way to the alternative and synonymous expression 'fundamental freedoms' which the United Nations has adopted in Article 1, paragraph 3 of the Charter.

'Human Rights,' on the other hand, embodies the idea of economic rights and claims to welfare services such as the modern state is being increasingly asked to provide. We are more aware today of the foolishness of pretending that a man is 'free' when he is unemployed and without income through no fault of his own, or when he cannot pay for good health or good education for his children. Thus we hear today that a man has a 'right' to a job or to maintenance when out of work, that children have a 'right' to education and health; and President Roosevelt was true to his age when he included in his four 'freedoms' the freedom from fear and from want. Although 'human rights' thus suggests the new concepts of the claims of the individual upon society, the term as used in the United Nations Declaration, where it stands alone, embraces all the various kinds of rights together – political, religious, economic and social.

What, then, are we to include in the term 'civil rights' as used in the phrase 'Property and Civil Rights in the Province?' Are the 'civil rights' of section 92 of the BNA Act the same as 'civil liberties' and 'fundamental freedoms?' The words 'Property and Civil Rights' have received a very liberal – many would say a too liberal – interpretation from the courts. Nevertheless even in their widest sense they refer, with few exceptions, to the field of private law, not to public law. When the old French law on property and civil rights was restored by the Quebec Act in 1774 it was certainly not the public law of the old regime which was reintroduced; the public law, including the criminal law, remained English. The Quebec Act itself qualifies the restoration of the civil rights by declaring that they are granted to the Canadian subjects in such manner 'as may consist with

14 *Ibid.*, 1947–8, p. 174.

their allegiance to His Majesty, and subjection to the Crown and Parliament of Great Britain.' All the civil liberties which belong to the field of public and constitutional law are therefore quite distinct from the civil rights which derive from private law. The Civil Code of Quebec contains many civil rights but no civil liberties. This is not to say that the private civil rights have no relation to civil liberties: they do relate in many ways, and may in fact restrict the free exercise of the civil liberties. Freedom of speech is limited by the civil action in damages for defamation. Yet freedom of speech as a general right belongs not to 'civil rights' but to the public law and is, as such, regulated by the criminal law.

This distinction becomes clear when we examine the phrase 'Property and Civil Rights' in its context in section 92. It is only one among 16 heads of jurisdiction, and it is an established principle of interpretation that what is included in the other 15 subsections cannot be included also in the words 'property and civil rights.' The right to vote in a Province, for example, is not a 'civil right' within 92-13, but a constitutional right which the province may define by reason of its power to amend its own constitution under 92-1. This has been held by the Privy Council in the case of *Cunningham* v. *Tomey Homma*.[15] All the civil liberties or fundamental freedoms that relate to the provincial government – voting, nomination of provincial candidates, privileges of members of legislatures, etc. – are outside the 'Property and Civil Rights' clause though within provincial jurisdiction. Similarly all these rights in respect of the federal government are outside the clause and are within federal jurisdiction. The rights of municipal residents toward their municipal government are not 'civil rights' but part of the provincial jurisdiction over municipal institutions under section 92-8. The rights of provincial civil servants are not civil rights but part of provincial jurisdiction over 'the Establishment and Tenure of Provincial Offices' under 92-4. The rights of shareholders of companies with provincial objects are not 'civil rights' but part of the provincial jurisdiction under 92-11. These examples make clear the fact that the civil rights of 92-13 do not include the general concept of civil liberties and fundamental freedoms even in so far as the province itself is concerned; *a fortiori* they have nothing to do with the civil liberties and fundamental freedoms of Canadians as citizens of the Canadian nation. And even the provincial jurisdiction over the provincial constitution is subordinate to federal criminal law; for example, it is just as much a crime for a provincial public servant to take a bribe, or to disclose an official secret, as for a federal servant to do so, and if certain forms of racial discrimination in employment or in public places were made criminal, as they are in many of the American States, the federal law would bind the civil services of provinces as much as the federal civil service.

Property and civil rights include all those parts of private law which relate to

15 [1903] A.C. 151.

property and its uses, to successions, contracts, delicts or torts, status of persons, commercial matters and the like. From this general field of course must be subtracted the special matters of private law assigned to the federal Parliament under section 91. To the provincial field has been added by judicial interpretation a number of subjects like labour relations, control of local trade within the province and of social services. But political rights under the national Parliament, and general freedoms such as freedom of speech, of the press, of association and of religion, remain outside the provincial sphere. The field of criminal law contains the basic individual freedoms even though it may not define them. 'Laws of this nature,' said the Privy Council in *Russell* v. *the Queen*, referring to the Canada Temperance Act, 'designed for the promotion of public order, safety and morals, and which subject those who contravene them to criminal procedure and punishment belong to the subject of public wrongs rather than to that of civil rights.' This was quoted with approval by Chief Justice Sir Charles Fitzpatrick in *Ouimet* v. *Bazin*,[16] where the Supreme Court of Canada held that a province could not prohibit theatrical performances on Sunday, since Sunday observance was a matter within the field of criminal law.

This distinction between 'civil rights' and 'civil liberties' makes clear the prime federal responsibility for the latter, but it does not mean that the provinces have little concern with the general topic. It has been shown that a number of constitutional rights vis-à-vis provincial and municipal governments, though not 'civil rights,' are yet within the provinces' control. In the true sphere of 'civil rights' itself are such matters as the ownership and use of property, the right to contract, the civil rights of married women, and many other rights which must be based on principles of freedom if the legal order is to be democratic. The provinces have a wide, though not exclusive jurisdiction over labour relations, except for the general right of association. And although the criminal law, with its broad coverage of civil liberties, is federal in origin, its administration is mostly provincial, and the administration is as important as the definition of a law for the purpose of safeguarding freedom. How provincial and municipal police behave in enforcing the federal criminal law is very important to our civil liberties, and their behaviour is determined by the province. There can be no full protection for individual liberty in Canada without provincial co-operation both legislative and administrative. For this reason the province of Saskatchewan has given a helpful lead by its enactment of the Bill of Rights Act of 1947. Since this paper is concerned with federal rather than with provincial jurisdiction, however, nothing further will be said by way of outlining the area of provincial responsibility over fundamental freedoms and human rights.

It is at the 'human rights' end of the liberty scale that provincial responsibili-

16 (1912), 46 S.C.R. 502.

ties become more important, though they are by no means exclusive. The field of social legislation is divided in Canada between Ottawa and the provinces, with the provinces having a wide jurisdiction. But even where Ottawa has no direct legislative capacity there is nothing to prevent it giving financial aid to provinces or to people in provinces. The purpose for which federal subsidies were originally given at Confederation was to enable provinces to balance their budgets, their revenues from direct taxation alone not being sufficient even then; if today Ottawa grants larger subsidies to meet much larger provincial budgets, or makes agreements for the use of grants in aid, or even makes direct payments to individuals as with family allowances, there is no invasion of provincial autonomy or violation of any constitutional principle. We are apt to forget that Ottawa is already paying about 76% of the cost of all social services in Canada, with only 16% spent by provinces and 8% by municipalities.[17]

There is a further distinction that needs to be made in defining fundamental freedoms. Traditionally these freedoms have been individual freedoms. There are however certain group freedoms that a democratic society will recognize. Actually the Canadian constitution has more definite protections for groups – minorities – than it has for individuals. The guarantee for the use of the two languages, for instance, and for denominational schools, are group freedoms. There is no 'race' element in the BNA Act at all, outside of federal jurisdiction over Indians: the only minority rights mentioned are linguistic and religious. The Declaration of Human Rights of the United Nations is almost entirely concerned with individual rights, though in barring discrimination based on race, colour, creed or sex it is protecting groups as well as individuals.

VII AREAS OF FEDERAL JURISDICTION

With these preliminary observations in mind, we may now approach the very practical question of federal jurisdiction in the field. The problem here is to discover what authority Ottawa possesses under the present constitution, and without any amendment to the BNA Act, to legislate for the protection of individual or group freedoms and rights. Over this entire field, when it has been delimited, Parliament may make laws and the federal executive may take administrative steps to strengthen the democratic order.

Before discussing the individual branches of federal power it may be useful to set out the general picture by way of a series of titles and subsections. The classification here adopted has of course no legal significance and has been arranged for convenience only.

17 See Joseph Willard, Public Welfare Expenditures in Canada, *Canadian Welfare*, Vol. 23, March 1948.

*Chart of Federal Powers Over Human Rights and Fundamental Freedoms*

1 Regions under exclusive federal control
    a/ North West Territories
    b/ Extra-territorial legislation
2 Persons under federal control
    a/ Armed forces
    b/ Veterans
    c/ Indians and Eskimo
    d/ Federal Civil Servants
    e/ Employees of federal services and agencies
    f/ Immigrants
    g/ Aliens
3 Constitutional rights in relation to the national government
    a/ Citizenship, its acquisition and loss
    b/ Right to hold federal public office
    c/ Privileges of Parliament and of its members
    d/ Electoral rights: franchise, parties, secret ballot, etc.
    e/ Administrative procedures: right to judicial review and to actions against federal Crown and its agencies
4 Freedoms deriving from the Criminal Law
    a/ Basic freedoms – speech, press, religion, association, etc.
    b/ Combines and freedom of trade
    c/ Sunday legislation
    d/ Habeas Corpus
    e/ Power to create new crimes protecting freedoms
    f/ Criminal procedures and punishments
    g/ Pure foods and standards
    h/ RCMP training and activities
    i/ Penal reform policies
5 Freedom of communication
    a/ Post Office
    b/ Radio broadcasting
    c/ Telegraph and telephone
    d/ Customs censorship of books
    e/ International Conventions on freedom of information
6 Federal laws touching family rights and welfare services
    a/ Old age pensions
    b/ Family allowances
    c/ Health measures
    d/ Housing

e/ Marriage and divorce
7 Federal government and education
  a/ North West Territories
  b/ Protection of denominational rights
  c/ Scholarships
  d/ Assistance to provinces
8 Federal cultural services
  a/ The National Gallery
  b/ National Film Board
  c/ Canadian Broadcasting Corporation
  d/ Copyright
  e/ National Library
  f/ National Arts Board – UNESCO
  g/ Customs regulations re books, paintings, artists' materials, etc.
9 Federal government policies protecting the right to a job
  a/ Unemployment insurance
  b/ Employment exchanges
  c/ Full employment policies
  d/ Interest rates, etc.
10 Federal contracts and licences
  a/ Stipulations in favour of fundamental freedoms
11 Disallowance of provincial laws
  a/ Its use for protection of freedoms
12 Federal treaty power
  a/ Ratification of all treaties
  b/ Territories and treaties
  c/ Legislation implementing treaties within federal power
13 Peace, order and good government
  a/ Possible value as authority for federal Bill of Rights
  b/ Emergency powers.

## VIII SURVEY OF PARTICULAR FEDERAL POWERS

A federal Bill of Rights, of whatever variety, which provided adequate protection for civil liberties and human rights in all these branches of the law might properly be described as comprehensive. Certainly a very wide field of human activity is comprehended and not a single Canadian man, woman or child would be unaffected. To attempt to write a single bill or statute dealing with all these matters, however, would be quite impossible. Too much would have to be included. An amendment to the BNA Act containing defined freedoms, or a federally enacted

Bill of Rights, would only cover a small portion of this total field and would inevitably be concerned more with the 'fundamental freedoms' than with the 'human rights,' if by the latter phrase is meant the rights to a job and to social security. The concept of a Bill of Rights is the static one of protection, not the dynamic one of positive assistance by governments. To understand what action might be taken in these various fields, it will be important to analyse a little more fully the nature of Dominion jurisdiction in each of them.

### 1 Regions under exclusive federal control

It is sometimes forgotten that the federal Parliament has complete and unlimited jurisdiction over all the Territories of Canada which are not erected into any province. This still amounts to about 40% of the total area of Canada, though containing at present only a tiny fraction of the population. Canada enjoys a legislative union as well as a federal system under the BNA Act; section 4 of the BNA Act of 1871 provides that 'The Parliament of Canada may from time to time make provision for the administration, peace, order, and good government of any territory not for the time being included in any Province.' The smallness of the population of these areas should not blind us to the importance of the constitutional principle involved. For in the existence of this unitary portion of our country lies the right of Ottawa to legislate on all aspects of property and civil rights, education, and other matters usually reserved exclusively to the provinces, and to ratify and implement all treaties and international conventions whatever their content may be. Further, in these territories the federal Parliament may put in force all laws which have been declared ultra vires in so far as the provinces are concerned. Moreover the rapid development of the natural resources of our northland is bringing and will bring more settlers into the region, and its strategic importance in an age of air travel and atomic energy makes it increasingly a part of our national planning and policy. Here is a part of Canada free from the conflict over jurisdiction, and in which the federal Parliament may well set an example of legislation for the protection of fundamental freedoms and human rights.

Ottawa possesses a similar unlimited power to legislate with extra-territorial effect. All provincial legislation is confined to matters 'within the province'; it is only 'the Parliament of a Dominion' which by section 3 of the Statute of Westminster is declared to have full power to make laws having extra-territorial operation. This power is not in extensive use, but in so far as Canadian legislation applies to aircraft, to ships and to members of the armed forces in foreign countries it can and should take due account of the fundamental rights of the individual.

### 2 Persons under federal control

A number of specified heads of federal jurisdiction under section 91 of the BNA

Act allow Parliament to legislate exclusively with respect to particular classes of persons. The power over 'Militia, Military and Naval Service and Defence' brings under federal responsibility all the body of law relating to service in the armed forces, as well as the federal provision for the welfare of veterans. Here must be considered such matters as language rights, absence of racial discrimination, procedure before military tribunals, pensions and discharge. The educational plans necessary to train a modern fighting force also are included. The word 'Defence' clearly embraces the economic measures required to maintain supplies of war material, and with that goes a federal power to regulate labour relations in war industry as was done during the last war. Defence also reaches out into the field of censorship in wartime, and to problems of arrest and detention of persons interfering with the war effort; hence the federal responsibility for applying the Defence of Canada Regulations, with its attendant problems of civil liberties in wartime and the use of Habeas Corpus. The production of atomic materials and energy is so intimately connected with defence that all mines and undertakings of this character are within federal jurisdiction, a point made doubly sure by their declaration as works for the general advantage of Canada by the Atomic Energy Control Act of 1946.[18]

Canada's two colonial peoples, the Indian and the Eskimo, come directly under the authority of Ottawa. To maintain these groups in their present status of subordinate citizenship seems to be contrary to a number of articles in the Declaration of Human Rights. Their education and training so that they may take their place in the life of the community on equal terms with other Canadians is a matter that creates no constitutional difficulties. So too federal laws relating to immigrants, and aliens, particularly with respect to questions of indentureship, admission and deportation, call for the application of many principles in the charter of human rights. Some startling examples of judicial and administrative failure to respect these rights of immigrants are to be found in the law reports, perhaps the most extreme being the holding of the Supreme Court of Canada that it was permissible to exercise the prerogative of 'mercy' in order to secure the deportation of a man who was serving a prison sentence – thus 'pardoning' in order to punish more severely.[19]

The whole field of the federal civil service and the federal agencies of government bring the rights of another large group of Canadians within the protection of Ottawa. The federal government is the largest single employer of labour in the country. As such it can set an example for other employers in the way of fair em-

18 C. 37, s. 18.
19 See *Reference re Effect of Exercise of Royal Prerogative of Mercy on Deportation Proceedings*, [1933] S.C.R. 269. For another example, see *Wade* v. *Egan*, 64 C.C.C. 21 (Essay V above) and my note in (1936), 14 *Can. Bar Rev.* 62.

ployment practices, absence of discrimination of all sorts, protection for the right to form trade unions and to bargain collectively, holidays with pay, pensions and other related matters. The groups affected here are by no means all civil servants; some belong to the category of employees of publicly owned corporations such as the Canadian National Railways or Trans Canada Airlines. In addition to these public employees of both types there are the workers in all the private enterprises which come under federal jurisdiction, such as inter-provincial railways, shipping companies, air lines, radio stations, telephone companies, banks and so forth, who depend upon federal law for their labour relations. The several hundreds of thousands of workers in these categories involve Parliament in the application of numerous articles in the Declaration of Human Rights, and justify the adoption of every ILO Convention which lays down standard working conditions. The federal legislation ruled ultra vires by the Privy Council in 1937, based upon the three Conventions dealing with Minimum Wages, Maximum Hours and the Weekly Day of Rest, is fully competent to Parliament in so far as the North West Territories and all the workers in the above-named enterprises are concerned. Whether or not the federal Parliament has an additional jurisdiction over workers in ordinary companies holding a federal charter has never been determined because it has never been attempted; it may well be that, although the basic provincial laws will apply to such workers, standards higher than the provincial can be imposed by Parliament whenever this does not cause a conflict with provincial regulations. To take an example, when provincial law sets a minimum wage, federal companies might be obliged to pay a higher minimum as a condition of holding the privilege of doing business throughout the country. They might also be required to observe fair labour practices generally.

Then the whole question of federal control over inter-provincial trade, and the power to attach conditions to such trade, needs much greater examination than it has yet received; the right to ship goods interprovincially on federal railways is surely one subject to federal restriction in the interests of the whole country and, if dangerous and explosive goods can be prohibited, as they now are under sections 349–350 of the Railway Act, it seems reasonable to suppose that goods manufactured under such conditions as to threaten living standards and wage structures can also be prohibited. Certainly this must be true of goods entering into international trade, the exclusive control over which is in federal hands. If the nations of the world agree through the ILO that certain standards are to be aimed at by all member states, Canada should insist that no goods enter the stream of international commerce that have not been produced under conditions that meet such standards. But such has never been the approach of Ottawa; the regulations it imposes are concerned with the grading and quality of the goods themselves, not of the labour that goes into their manufacture. Yet a parcel of goods upon the markets of the world carries not only its physical qualities with it, but also its whole labour background. No province is permitted to enter the international field at all, and unless there is a gap in our sovereignty the jurisdiction in question must be in federal hands. The right to trade abroad from Canadian shores, it is suggested, could be made subject to the obligation to observe human rights in the manufacture of the goods to be exported ...

### 3 Constitutional rights under the jurisdiction of Parliament

Every Canadian, by birth or by naturalisation, acquires rights in and duties towards our national government. Its laws are made by his representatives in Parliament, and bind him directly whether he lives in or outside a province. Ottawa possesses the only geographically complete government in the country; all others are local governments. This central government requires a complete state apparatus – legislative, executive and administrative, and judicial. The general structure of this government is established in the BNA Act and cannot be changed by Canadian law; even some detailed rules, such as the holding of annual Parliaments and of general elections within each five years, are in the fundamental law. But there is a vast body of federal law which defines the rights of Canadian citizens in relation to this state structure and which can be changed or repealed by mere majority vote in the Senate and House of Commons. Since all this federal constitutional law touches upon the fundamental freedoms and human rights of every Canadian in a most direct and comprehensive manner, it is essential that it should be measured by the highest democratic standards.

Broadly speaking, the law and custom of our federal government is democratic in character and measures up to generally accepted principles of political liberty. Canadian citizenship is now clearly defined in the Act adopted in 1946. No race or creed is barred. The franchise is widely extended, without distinction of sex or requirement of property, and it is encouraging to note that most of the racial discrimination which for so long disfigured our federal Elections Act was removed in 1948; only the special cases of the Doukhobors and the native Indians remain.[20] Public office is open to all. New political parties can be founded at will, and no limit is placed upon the kind of programme which candidates are permitted to put forward. In the absence of federal prohibitions in the Election Act, it must follow that no province can ban a federal party or prevent the exercise of federal citizenship rights, for this would be an invasion of the federal field and would prevent the functioning of the national Parliament which the BNA Act establishes.

20 Doukhobors are still denied the federal vote in any province where they are denied the provincial vote (Dom. Elections Act, 1938, s. 14(2) (j) ) and Indians on reservations are denied the vote unless they served in the armed forces in either world war (*ibid.*, as amended by 1948 c. 46, s. 6).

Another aspect of this federal constitutional law, rather technical in character but none the less important in its effect on human rights, has to do with the citizens' rights of action against the federal Crown and other governmental agencies. Only slowly and grudgingly has Canadian administrative law granted redress for grievances suffered by the citizen when the injury was caused by some administrative official or body. Actions against the Crown and many government Boards and Commissions are still hedged about with procedural difficulties if they are not barred altogether. Both Great Britain and the United States have recently revised their law to permit a greater protection for the individual whose rights are interfered with by the state, and there is need in Canada for a clarification and simplification of our judicial processes in this regard if adequate remedies are to be provided for a disregard of fundamental freedoms by government officials, *Ubi remedium, ibi jus.*

### 4 Freedoms deriving from the Criminal Law

The Criminal Law is usually thought of as something which tells you what you may not do, and in a large sense this is true. Crimes are prohibitions sanctioned by penalties; each one is a limitation upon human action or behaviour. But the class of subject called 'The Criminal Law' is a field of legislation exclusively reserved to the federal Parliament, which no provincial legislation may invade. Only a portion of the field is covered by federal criminal law at any given time. The area between the outer boundary, which no province may cross, and the inner boundary marking prohibitions of the existing criminal law is territory free from any prohibition. In this area lie many fundamental freedoms.

Let us take as example the freedom of religion. The relations between churches and the state have always been and are matters of public law. They have never been included under the heading of 'property and civil rights.' The permission to practise the Roman Catholic religion in Canada was first granted in the Treaty of Paris of 1763 and was later confirmed by the Quebec Act of 1774. In the Quebec Act the section restoring the French law over property and civil rights is distinct from and additional to the section safeguarding the freedom for Catholics, thus showing that the two concepts are disjunctive. Had there been any other religions guaranteed, they too would have been established as part of the public law. Neither the Treaty of Paris nor the Quebec Act was restricted in its application to any existing provincial boundaries, for the Quebec of 1774 extended out to Ohio. At Confederation the only religious matters mentioned in the BNA Act are to be found in section 93 securing certain denominational rights to separate schools against provincial change, though provincial laws relating to property and taxation will affect the churches in many ways. The general right to practise the religion of one's choice in Canada must rest on the fact that no religion is made criminal, as some have been in our past history. Hence we find the Criminal Code dealing with religion by prohibiting blasphemy in section 198, but at the same time protecting the freedom of religious thought by providing that no one commits a blasphemous libel who expresses in good faith and in decent language 'any opinion whatever upon any religious subject.' Freedom of worship exists because no province could prevent it and the federal Parliament has not made any religion a crime.

Many other fundamental rights are likewise in federal keeping. Freedom of association is a public right within the ambit of the criminal law; by defining seditious conspiracies and unlawful assemblies the Criminal Code permits all kinds of associations which do not come within the prohibitions. No province could validly legislate to prevent any type of associations from forming, or meetings from assembling. This statement is not contradicted by the fact that provinces may legitimately regulate, directly or through municipalities, the use of parks and public places so as to avoid nuisances and preserve order. Freedom of speech and of the press belong likewise in this category, even though a province may legitimately protect the individual's character against defamation. The whole federal constitution would become inoperative if a province could pass laws which took away from citizens of that province the rights which they hold in their national Parliament under the BNA Act. And since no legislature is permitted to do indirectly what it may not do directly, provincial laws designed to destroy fundamental public rights but disguised as property laws or otherwise coloured to escape constitutional limitations are clearly void.[21] The federal government, through its exclusive jurisdiction over Criminal Law, has a major responsibility for the preservation of the most fundamental rights of Canadian citizens.

The use of the Criminal Law power extends into many portions of the field not included in the Criminal Code. Legislation designed to safeguard the use of Sunday as a day of rest from business occupations is within federal jurisdiction. The investigation and punishment of practices restricting competition and trade belong to Ottawa. The degree to which officials may disclose secrets, and the penalties for unlawful disclosures, are federal matters, binding also provincial civil servants. And with the criminal law goes the whole of criminal procedure with all its basic principles regarding presumptions of innocence, public trials and

---

21 In this category I would place the Padlock Act of Quebec and the Prince Edward Island Trade Union Act of 1948. Greenshields J. held the Padlock Act valid in *Fineberg* v. *Taub*, 77 S.C. (Que.) 233, but he declared he could find no interference with freedom of speech in the Act! The weakness of his judicial vision can be estimated by noting that section 3 prohibits the propagation of 'communism or bolshevism' in any building and section 12 prohibits the publishing and circulating of any literature which even 'tends' to propagate these undefined ideas.

freedom from cruel and unusual punishments. In Ottawa's hands lies the duty to define a proper policy for the punishment and reformation of criminals; like all other citizens the law breaker has his rights. And the character training and behaviour of the RCMP, the chief federal law enforcement agency, are important aspects of this responsibility, for nothing so rapidly destroys a faith in justice and democratic government as evil or brutal behaviour in the police of a nation.

Where the criminal law power is but little used today, and where it might be better used for the protection of freedoms, is in regard to the creation of new crimes against freedom itself. It is a crime to disturb a religious ceremony, but it is not a crime, or at least as precisely defined a crime, to disturb a public meeting or to prevent the distribution of literature. It is a crime for employers to discharge an employee for trade union activities, but it is not a crime for them to use labour spies. It is a crime to libel an individual but not a crime to libel a group or race. It is a crime to hit any man over the head with a stick but it is not a crime to refuse to serve him a meal in a public restaurant or to refuse him a room in a hotel because of his race or religion. It is a crime for any public official, whether federal or provincial, to take a bribe, but not a crime for him to discriminate against races or creeds in granting licences or franchises. It would be wrong to imagine that freedom can be created merely by adding new crimes to the Criminal Code, but this is not to say that certain practices which violate human rights ought not to be made criminal where now they give rise only to a personal action in damages if there be an action at all. The law can buttress moral principles, and make the path of the wicked more difficult. Thus there seems to be good sense in the suggestion of Mr Varcoe to the Joint Committee of Parliament, that a new section to be added to the Criminal Code setting forth new prohibitions against interference with human rights.[22]

There seems to have been some misapprehension in the Joint Committee regarding the effect of such a creation of new crimes upon the rights of the provinces.[23] But there is no difficulty here; and no conflict of any kind. No right is taken away from any province when a new crime is defined by Parliament, since the jurisdiction over crimes is exclusively federal. The power to create new crimes is unlimited, save by the colourable doctrine which forbids the use of the criminal law in an indirect attempt to control a matter wholly assigned to the provinces. The creation of new crimes designed to safeguard fundamental freedoms proclaimed in the Declaration of Human Rights could scarcely be considered as a disguised attempt by Parliament to invade the provincial sphere. Of course the

22 Proceedings, 1947–8, p. 174, gives the draft of this Bill, which was in a very tentative form.
23 Ibid., per Mr Varcoe and the Chairman, pp. 174–5.

prohibition of an act previously lawful takes away the rights of individuals; when the firing of workers for trade union activities was made criminal in 1939 the employers lost a right, but it cannot be said that the provinces lost any jurisdiction since they could not have enacted this rule *as a matter of criminal law*. To some extent there is an overlapping of provincial and federal jurisdictions in the field of penal law, since Parliament can make crimes while the provinces can impose penalties for the infringement of provincial laws, but there cannot truly be a conflict since the two kinds of jurisdiction are quite distinct in origin. Should there be an apparent conflict the federal law will prevail since the BNA Act gives it this paramountcy. Besides enunciating new crimes, the Code might well enunciate new areas of freedom from crime, as it does with respect to blasphemy, sedition and some other matters. Sections 198 and 133A make it clear that certain ideas in regard to religion and to the state do *not* constitute the crimes in question. So too a right to peaceful picketing was safeguarded, when the crime of watching and besetting was defined as not covering pickets who are merely imparting information, by an amendment to section 501. There may be other areas where similar declarations of freedom of action might be made. It seems doubtful, however, whether the criminal law can be used to declare, as is done with respect to prosecutions for common assault, that the taking of a criminal action bars any subsequent suit for damages under provincial law. [24]

*5 Freedom of communication*

The right of free access to information, through any media and regardless of frontiers, is today considered a major privilege of citizens in a democracy. It is referred to in the Universal Declaration of Human Rights, as well as in the three Draft Conventions of 1948. The protection of this fundamental right devolves primarily upon the federal government. Again the criminal law comes into play. Many sections of the Code expressly permit the publishing of fair reports of public meetings, and fair comments on public persons, as well as of the proceedings in Parliament and the courts. Section 136 of the Code declares it to be a crime for anyone knowingly to publish false news 'whereby injury or mischief is or is likely to be occasioned to any public interest.' This little used section of the Code might well be brought to the attention of certain editors. [25] The posting of immoral literature is a crime. The control of the mails gives Ottawa further responsibility for securing freedom of communication and protecting fundamental rights. Newspapers obtain special postage rates from the Post Office, and there

---

24 See note by G.V.V. Nicholls in (1948), 26 *Can. Bar Rev.* 1001.
25 For example, the Protocols of Zion, a notoriously spurious document, were published in the Quebec newspaper *Vers Demain* in 1946. If this was not a knowing publication of false news likely to injure a public interest it was an act equally harmful.

would be every justification for the withholding of this privilege from any paper which does not meet the standards required by law or by the 'non-official organization of persons employed in the dissemination of information to the public' whose formation in each state is envisaged by the 1948 Draft Convention. Ottawa should not subsidise, with public money, persons who violate the freedoms which the law aims to protect. The federal government has also power to make regulations for the use of inter-provincial telephone and telegraph services, both of which are important parts of the mass communication system. And Ottawa alone will have the responsibility of ratifying the Conventions on Freedom of Information when they are adopted, and of guaranteeing the rights of foreign correspondents in Canada, the international right of correction of false or distorted news, and the free transmission of information within and across its borders.

There are two other federal agencies which affect freedom of information. One is the radio. Here Ottawa's responsibility is clear, both for what goes over the publicly owned system and for the standards to be observed in the private stations. The radio today is probably more important than the whole of the press as a means of mass communication, and too much attention cannot be paid to the method on which it is operated. From the point of view of fairness and freedom of use, it may be said that the present CBC regulations granting free network time to national political parties in proportion to their strength in the country, and the refusal to sell it to private individuals, are far ahead of any equivalent standards which the private newspapers impose upon themselves. The power of money, so threatening to freedom of the press, is happily absent from the radio, though it is creeping up through the increasing strength of the private stations and through the effectiveness of their propaganda. Canadians interested in freedom of information will have to give vigilant support to the Canadian Broadcasting Commission to preserve this vital agency from any outside dictatorship whether of a political party or of private interests.

The other federal agency is the Customs. Through the customs must pass all printed matter coming from abroad. There is today a censorship of books and journals in Canada exercised through the customs branch, a censorship which is secret, continuous and seemingly unchecked by any independent authority.[26] This would appear to be an appropriate time for the federal government to bring out into the open, and to establish upon known and sound principles, any use it is making of the customs power to deprive Canadians of access to the thought of the world. And in addition to clarifying the censorship regulations, there is need

26 See the discussion initiated by J.S. Woodsworth in the House of Commons: *Hansard*, 1935, vol. II, pp. 1652 ff. There is an 'examiner of publications' who decides what we may or may not read.

also to revise the tax rates imposed upon literature, for it is the law today that no books can be imported from abroad, with few exceptions, without payment of taxes. In this whole field of freedom of communication, the federal government is thus seen to have a prime responsibility, and ample constitutional authority, to take whatever positive action may be necessary to make the rights effective. Some portion of the field needs provincial protection as well, notably in the censorship of moving pictures, but this does not hinder the carrying out of a sound national policy.

### 6 Federal laws touching family rights and welfare services

Social security is one of the rights proclaimed in the United Nations' Declaration as belonging to everyone as a member of society. The obligation of the state to provide it is now widely accepted. This obligation rests primarily upon the federal government in Canada since it alone has the financial resources to make the right effective. Parliament has already given some leadership in this field; as has been said, it is today contributing much more than all the provinces together. Old age pensions and family allowances came first from Ottawa. Hospital insurance was initiated by Saskatchewan in January 1947, but the federal government put forward a national plan in 1945 and has made preliminary grants towards hospital construction in the provinces. It will clearly have to assume the major part of the cost of any national scheme of health insurance that may be introduced. No constitutional barriers stand in the way of further developments of this sort on the basis of grants in aid. It is true that a province may not agree to co-operate with a proposed scheme, as Quebec refused for ten years to accept old age pensions, but this neither makes a national social security plan unworkable nor relieves Parliament of its obligations. Public pressures make it impossible for a particular provincial government to bar its people for long from participating in a scheme beneficial to themselves, particularly as the administration of such schemes is customarily left in provincial hands. These measures do not take away any legislative powers from provinces nor interfere with their control over property and civil rights; a person receiving financial aid from Ottawa is just as subject to provincial law afterwards as before his income was thus increased.

There are several new fields of social security which though still controversial are much in demand and would require federal initiative and financial aid. The present old age pension plan, which is modest in amount and subject to a means test, could be replaced by old age insurance covering every citizen and available as of right on the attainment of a prescribed age. One form of this was in fact proposed by Ottawa at the federal-provincial conference of 1945, though if it is to be contributory there may be some doubt as to Ottawa's power to enact it without amending the BNA Act. The existing pensions for the blind could be extended to cover all disabilities. If there is need for a national housing plan to relieve the serious shortage throughout the country, to provide for the progressive elimination of sub-standard dwellings and slums, and thus to give security and decency to family surroundings throughout the country, it is less constitutional law than political hesitancy which prevents it. Without arguing for any particular plan or policy, it is evident that the field of social security offers wide opportunities for the federal government to fulfill its responsibilities as a signatory to the Declaration of Human Rights. It is not to be forgotten either that the subjects of marriage and divorce, with their attendant implications upon family life, are exclusively within federal jurisdiction.

## 7  The Federal Government and education

It is sometimes overlooked that the federal government has two specific kinds of jurisdiction over education under the BNA Act. Education is not an exclusively provincial matter, though the provinces have the primary jurisdiction. In the first place, all the education provided for the North West Territories is governed by federal law. In the second place, a duty to protect the minority rights guaranteed in section 93 is placed in federal hands and if these rights are infringed the national Parliament may itself make remedial laws on education for the preservation of the separate schools. Such federal laws on education would prevail over any contrary provincial laws. Thus Ottawa possesses an ultimate jurisdiction over provinces as a guardian of these minority rights.

There are some other Dominion functions, such as military training, agricultural training, technical training for the unemployed and radio programmes which indirectly deal with educational matters. Financial assistance to individual students wishing to pursue higher studies has already been established both in regard to war veterans and under the National Research Council. The Sirois Report, while hesitating to recommend direct financial aid to provinces for purposes of primary and secondary education, did suggest 'relatively small grants' from federal funds by way of assistance to universities.[27] And while there is much concern in some quarters over any proposal that Parliament should finance provincial schools, the example of grants for the building of hospitals, which all provinces have accepted, is one that might well make such assistance possible without in any way weakening the existing control over education which the provinces possess. In a technological age, in a country with widely differing provincial incomes, the national government cannot remain indifferent to the problem of educational standards and opportunities. There is scarcely a provincial institution of note that has not received generous help from American foundations like the Rockefeller

27 Vol. II, pp. 51–2.

and Carnegie; it would seem odd to imagine that they were inhibited in accepting similar aid from our national Parliament. Certainly no constitutional principle prevents the federal government from evolving and initiating educational plans of this type. For such plans do not mean federal legislation on the subject of education itself, but rather the formulation of methods of financial assistance to existing forms of provincial education. The control over the organization of schools and the choice of curricula remains provincial.

## 8 Federal cultural services

Article 27 of the Declaration of Human Rights states that 'everyone has the right freely to participate in the cultural life of the community, to enjoy the arts and to share in scientific advancement and its benefits.' That the state has an important rôle to play in fostering the arts and in developing cultural activities in the community is now beyond dispute. This is clearly a field where both the federal and the provincial governments can operate without any conflict of interest or jurisdiction. Four federal agencies already exist which are promoting different forms of cultural activity in Canada: the National Gallery, the Royal Canadian Academy, the National Film Board and the Canadian Broadcasting Corporation. Other agencies are working in related fields. The National Research Council undertakes various forms of theoretical and applied research in the realm of science. The Dominion Physical Fitness Council is engaged in assisting recreational work in provincial centres, and is interested in cultural recreation. What might be done through all these agencies to stimulate public interest in the arts awaits, not the removal of constitutional barriers, but simply the formulation and adoption of a more vigourous policy. The appointment of the Royal Commission to survey the whole range of federal cultural activities will, it is hoped, result in proposals for such a policy and in the delimitation of appropriate spheres of federal action. The demand for a National Library and for a National Arts Board has already been vigourously pressed by many organisations, while a National Commission or some equivalent body is in fact expected of Canada as a member of UNESCO.

Two other specific federal powers can be used for the benefit of the arts. The copyright law of Canada is exclusively federal, and its provisions for the protection of artistic and intellectual property have an important effect upon the status and income of the artist. The present law is inadequate in many respects to give the artist the security he deserves. It could be thoroughly revised to meet new policies and the new problems which modern forms of reproduction present: some revision will have to take place anyway to meet the terms of the revised Berne Convention. Similarly the customs laws and regulations, dealing with materials required by artists which have to be imported and with travelling exhibitions and the like, can greatly hamper or assist artists generally, as well as public galleries and museums, depending on whether the cultural factors present in this form of cultural exchange are properly considered.

## 9 *Federal policies protecting the right to work*
The right to work, which is included in the Declaration of Human Rights, is a relatively new concept. It has evolved out of the fact that in an industrial society there is an ever present risk of unemployment. Through no fault of the individual, a man's income and that of his family may be suddenly cut off, leaving him legally 'free' but enslaved by want and insecurity. The formulation of a right to work means the recognition of a responsibility in society, through the agency of the state, to care for such persons until they can be usefully absorbed back into employment. It also implies a duty on the state to adopt policies which will eliminate mass unemployment. These responsibilities in Canada are primarily federal. Immediate relief for unemployed employables is provided in the Unemployment Insurance Act, and the administration of this service also enables the federal government to operate the nation-wide employment exchange offices that are so valuable a part of the scheme. Beyond unemployment insurance lies the problem of assistance to those whose benefits have run out and who are still unemployed.

A special aspect of any employment service is the placing in useful jobs of workers who are partially disabled. Left to the mercy of the labour market such individuals are certain to be discriminated against and to become public charges in large numbers. A beginning has been made by the Department of Labour at Ottawa to place such individuals, but Canada has not adopted legislation similar to that in England whereby firms employing large numbers of workers must assume responsibility for employing a certain proportion of disabled persons. Such legislation would be within Dominion jurisdiction for all industries under its direct control, and could quite possibly be made binding on private companies as a condition of receiving or holding any privileges under a Dominion charter of incorporation. There is a similar need to assist the older employees in securing employment, particularly in firms that have their own pension plans.

The federal government's responsibility for the adoption of national trade policies designed to maintain high employment levels is too clear to need emphasis. Public finance, taxation, banking, interest, currency, tariffs and international trade programmes are all components of such policies. Cyclical budgeting theories play their part. If the periodic crises of private capitalism are to be ironed out by national economic planning, and the security of individual employment to be thereby safeguarded, it is to Ottawa and to Ottawa alone that we must look for the major decisions.

### 10 Federal contracts and licences

The Dominion government expends vast sums of public money every year on public works of all kinds. Most of the work is performed by private contractors. In the writing of these contracts it is possible to stipulate that certain fundamental freedoms and rights must be observed. Already such contracts are governed by the Fair Wages and Hours of Labour Act of 1935. This Act could be extended to cover what are now regarded as fair employment practices, providing for the absence of racial discrimination, equal pay for equal work, and other human rights.[28] Wherever federal licences are granted they may have similar conditions attached. It is surely not too much to expect that a government which has signed the Declaration of Human Rights will insist upon the observance of these rights in every sphere of activity in which its authority runs, and will not allow payments to be made from the public treasury to any persons who violate these rules of public policy.

### 11 Federal disallowance of provincial laws

The federal power of disallowance, which is part of the formal law of the constitution, was intended to be used, has at times been used and should in future be used to protect fundamental freedoms. It could hardly be contended that these are not matters of concern to the whole of Canada. The stated purpose of the BNA Act was to create a constitution similar in principle to that of Great Britain; the principles of political liberty were part of the law and custom of the constitution before Confederation, and were intended to be continued. Violations of those principles by any province are violations of the basic agreement underlying the constitution, which it is the duty of the federal government to uphold. There is ample recognition, in the Confederation Debates, of the possible use of the veto power to protect basic freedoms against violation by the provinces; for example, the following discussion took place during the argument on the Quebec Resolutions.[29]

Hon. Mr Rose: As I read the resolutions, if the Local Legislature exercised its powers in any such unjust manner [i.e. by apportioning the electoral districts so that no English-speaking member can be returned to the Legislature] it would be competent for the General Government to veto its action and thus prevent the

---

28 This is the practice in the United States, where 'all government contracts contain a provision whereby the contractor agrees not to discriminate against any person by reason of race, colour or national origin': address by Frank E. Holman in *American Bar Association Journal*, Nov. 1948, at p. 1079.

29 Confederation Debates, pp. 407–8. See also Eugene A. Forsey, The Prince Edward Island Trade Union Act (1948), 26 *Can. Bar Rev.* at pp. 1168 ff.

intention of the Local Legislature being carried into effect – even though the power be one which is declared to be absolutely vested in the Local Government and delegated to it as one of the articles of its constitution.

Hon. Atty Gen. Cartier: There is not the least doubt that if the Local Legislature of Lower Canada should apportion the electoral districts in such a way as to do injustice to the English-speaking population, the General Government will have the right to veto any law it might pass to this effect and set it at nought.

Hon. Mr Holton: Would you advise it?

Hon. Atty Gen. Cartier: Yes, I would recommend it myself in case of injustice. (Hear, hear.)

Hon. Mr Rose: I am quite sure my hon. friend would do it rather than have an injustice perpetrated.

Other examples of the federal duty of vetoing unjust or discriminatory legislation will be found in the speeches of George Brown, Sir E.P. Taché, Sir Narcisse Belleau, and are quoted in the Department of Justice memorandum on the *Dominion Power of Disallowance of Provincial Legislation.*[30] The reasons given for the disallowance of provincial statutes after Confederation have also frequently included such concepts as that the laws were unconstitutional, abusive or contrary to justice and natural equity. There could be nothing more unconstitutional in Canada than a law which violates the fundamental freedoms implicit in the constitution, even though such law should not be technically *ultra vires* of the province which enacts it. The adoption of the Declaration of Human Rights and its signature by Canada provide future federal governments with a set of standards by which to judge whether to use the veto power in any given case. The same is true also of the Conventions on Freedom of Communication when these reach their final and official form. The Dominion power of disallowance is not a power which can create new freedoms, but it can prevent some of those we already have from being weakened or destroyed by provincial action.

*12 The federal treaty power*

Ottawa alone has the power under our constitution to conduct diplomatic negotiations with foreign states and to place the signature of Canada upon international treaties and conventions. The executive act of ratifying the document is also in federal hands. When it comes to enacting legislation to give effect to the treaty, however, without which private rights cannot be made subject to its provisions, the jurisdiction, ever since the Privy Council decision of 1937,[31] has been

30 (1937), at pp. 47 ff.
31 [1937] A.C. 326.

divided. For matters within federal jurisdiction Parliament is competent; for matters within provincial jurisdiction the provinces must adopt the necessary legislation. We have seen how broad the federal field turns out to be in respect of fundamental freedoms and human rights; any treaty dealing with these subjects can be implemented by federal legislation covering all the aspects which are included in any part of that field. The treaty of itself does not permit any invasion of the provincial area, but it may be ratified and enforced for the whole of the federal area. Take, for example, the ILO convention of the Weekly Day of Rest; just because some industries come exclusively under provincial jurisdiction in this regard is no reason why it should not be made to apply to all federal industries and services, as well as in the North West Territories. The failure of the provinces to assume their responsibilities, if there be a failure, cannot excuse inaction on the part of the Dominion. There is seldom any necessity for the two legislations to be simultaneous and concurrent. At the present moment the actual number of ILO conventions which Ottawa has both ratified and implemented is comparatively small; there seems no good reason why it should not be greatly enlarged. Even though existing laws be fully up to the international standards the fact of ratification is a positive support to the principle of international solidarity which these conventions seek to achieve.

### 13 The 'peace, order and good government' clause

It has been suggested in some quarters that the Dominion Parliament might have jurisdiction to enact a statute dealing with fundamental freedoms and human rights under the 'peace, order and good government' clause of section 91 of the BNA Act. The argument would be that the subject matter of such a statute, taking it in its broad sense, is not properly included under any of the heads of section 92 on which provincial jurisdiction alone rests, nor is it included within any single specific head of 91; it therefore must fall within the residuary power of the Dominion to make laws for 'the peace, order and good government of Canada in relation to all matters not coming within the classes of subjects by this Act assigned exclusively to the legislatures of the provinces.' Had the process of judicial interpretation not reduced the residuary clause almost to the vanishing point, and overlaid the whole of it with a theory of 'emergency' which the Privy Council itself seems unable to exorcise,[32] there might have been considerable weight to this

---

32 Despite the clear statement by Viscount Simon in the Temperance Reference of 1946 (A.C. 193, at p. 206) that 'it is the nature of the legislation itself, and not the existence of emergency, that must determine whether it is valid or not,' the emergency theory still casts its baleful influence over later judgments. See *e.g.* the *Japanese Canadian Reference*, [1947] A.C. 87, at p. 101) or the margarine decision in the Supreme Court of Canada, [1949] 1 D.L.R. 433.

reasoning. The aspect of the matters dealt with in a statute guaranteeing fundamental freedoms, at least for those which are political in character, would not be within the private law concepts of property and civil rights, nor would it be a matter merely of local or private importance in the province, but would in truth and essence be a definition of the public rights of all Canadian citizens everywhere. As such it could not possibly be embraced within any defined provincial powers even though it incidentally affected those powers. The distinction between laws which are 'in relation to' a particular matter, and laws which merely affect or touch upon that matter, is well known in the constitutional law though very unequally applied by the courts. The validity of a given law must depend, not upon whether it affects a provincial head of jurisdiction, but on whether it is passed 'in relation to' that head; if it is not, the incidental affecting is immaterial. Whether it is 'in relation to' a subject depends in turn upon its true nature, its pith and substance, consideration being given to the aspect of the matter which is primarily dealt with. In this estimation, the courts have a wide area of unfettered discretion. It is often quite impossible to predict which among several competing aspects will be selected as the dominant one which gives the whole statute its character and thus determines the jurisdiction. Experience with attempts to use the peace, order and good government clause in the past do not suggest that it would be likely, in the present current of judicial interpretation, to be a safe base on which to rest Dominion jurisdiction even over so great a matter as the definition of fundamental liberties must always be. The argument for including certain fundamental freedoms under this clause, however, is a strong one and should not be lightly dismissed. And in so far as an emergency such as war expands federal jurisdiction under this head, it expands also the responsibility for maintaining and protecting human rights.

## IX SOME PRACTICAL SUGGESTIONS

The outline of Dominion jurisdiction that has been given should make one thing clear. There is no constitutional difficulty in Canada to a comprehensive and positive programme of action by the federal Parliament and government in defence of our fundamental freedoms. Indeed, the difficulty is not that there is too little ground for Dominion jurisdiction, but that there is so much. To carry out a programme of action in all the fields where an unquestioned Dominion authority exists would require much time and thought. In certain fields certain things can be done immediately, without the slightest difficulty. To remove all traces of racial discrimination from the federal Election Act, for instance, would seem to be the least Canada should do to honour her signature to the Universal Declaration of 1948. In other fields, as in that of cultural rights or social security, where the fulfilment of the obligation to protect the right requires the development of a programme of federal services, more time will be required and more alternatives offer themselves. First things, however, should be done first.

There may be a danger of total inaction on the part of the federal authorities if the implementing of the United Nations Declaration is thought of only in terms of some Bill of Rights, some single magnificent statute, which will suddenly achieve a solution to a majority of our problems. The more spectacular the Bill, the more difficult it will be to secure its adoption. It is submitted that the writing of a new section into the BNA Act, guaranteeing certain basic freedoms which are now liable to violation by Canadian legislatures, would be a desirable thing. It would crystallise and make positive the widespread desire for more adequate safeguards against totalitarian tendencies. But even if it were to be adopted, it could not possibly cover all the field or suffice in itself to bring about the continuing development of those 'wider freedoms' which we aim to achieve. Freedom is not just a static thing to be defended by a Bill of Rights, but an expanding programme of action. A Bill of Rights, of any kind, is a shield for defence. There is need also of a sword for attack. There must be an attack upon those social evils, such as unemployment, bad housing, poor education and health, which corrupt or weaken the individual and deny him his equal right to the full development of his personality. There must be an attack upon those individuals who persistently violate the basic freedoms of others, and who now are unrestrained. To supplement the prohibitions of the law there should be the constructive work of government aimed at widening and deepening the actual content of the democratic rights.

Under our system of government the responsibility for national decisions on matters of policy rests on Parliament and on the Cabinet which is answerable to Parliament. If a programme in defence of fundamental freedoms is to be undertaken then Parliament must make the decision. In this regard there are three practical steps that might be suggested.

In the first place it would seem highly appropriate for Parliament to endorse officially the Universal Declaration of Human Rights, thus putting itself on record as supporting the general principles therein set forth. Such endorsation, which could be by way of a resolution adopted in the Senate and the Commons, would no more infringe on provincial rights than did the signing of the Declaration itself. No single Canadian law would be changed by this act alone, but there would be a commitment of Parliament to an official statement of beliefs. It would make the carrying out of the principles a matter of public policy. It might even influence the decisions of courts having to decide whether private contracts were contrary or not to public order and good morals.[39] It would make the Declaration some-

39 As in *Re Drummond Wren*, [1945] 4 D.L.R. 674.

thing that had been voted on at Ottawa and not just something voted on in Paris. And if the federal parliamentary approval were to be followed by the approval of provincial legislatures, we should really feel that Canada had taken her stand fully and firmly on behalf of these fundamental freedoms.

Secondly, the present Joint Committee of the Senate and House of Commons might be constituted into a standing committee of Parliament. The work of such a committee is never finished. The 'eternal vigilance' necessary to maintain liberty is better sustained if organised. At the present moment there are only two standing Joint Committees at Ottawa – on the Library and on Printing. Fundamental freedoms, their preservation and extension in Canada, might perhaps claim an importance equal to these weighty subjects. The function of such a committee would be to survey the situation in Canada from year to year regarding the observance of freedoms, to supervise all federal laws and orders in council from this point of view, to make recommendations for amendments or new legislation to Parliament, and generally to keep alive the interest of members and of the public in the subject. The steady work of such a committee over the years, the accumulation of records and experience, the regular publication of reports, would make the issue of freedom and human rights matters of national concern to the annual sessions of Parliament.

Finally, the experience of the United States may suggest a course of action which could be followed with profit here. In 1939, Attorney-General Frank Murphy established a Civil Rights Section in the Department of Justice at Washington. Its purpose was to encourage more vigourous use of federal laws protecting human rights and to centralise responsibility for their enforcement. When the President's Committee on Civil Rights reported in 1947, it declared that 'the Section's record is a remarkable one'[34] and recommended that the federal civil rights enforcement machinery should be greatly strengthened. There are of course differences in the Canadian constitution which must be taken into account, but since the Criminal Law in Canada is federal in origin it seems true to say that our Parliament has a greater responsibility for maintaining fundamental freedoms than has the American Congress. The duty of such a Section would be by no means entirely punitive. It could investigate complaints about the violation of civil liberties, and could serve as a centre for all the administrative aspects of the programme. Acting in co-operation with a Joint Parliamentary Committee, it could provide secretarial assistance on a permanent basis for the committee and could thus improve the quality of its deliberations.

34 To secure these rights: *The Report of the President's Committee on Civil Rights*, p. 114.

X CHANGING CONCEPTS OF THE RÔLE OF THE STATE IN RELATION TO FUNDAMENTAL FREEDOMS AND HUMAN RIGHTS

Speaking at the Lincoln Memorial in Washington in June 1947, President Truman gave expression to an important change that has taken place with regard to the function of the federal government as a guardian of fundamental rights. His words are not inappropriate to the situation in Canada. He said:

We must make the Federal Government a friendly, vigilant defender of the rights and equalities of all Americans .. Our National Government must show the way ... We cannot be content with a civil liberties program which emphasises only the need of protection against the possibility of tyranny by the Government ... We must keep moving forward, with new concepts of civil rights to safeguard our heritage. The extension of civil rights today means not protection of the people against the Government, but protection of the people by the Government.

It is this positive rôle which today calls for our attention as fully as the need – also urgent – to safeguard the citizen against arbitrary state power. In the battle to preserve freedom 'the role of government inevitably changes from oppressor to protector.'[35] Preventing the state from taking away liberties does not help the man whose freedom is attacked by a fellow citizen, or whose liberty is destroyed by poverty. Defence against the state and protection by the state are two correlative functions, not contradictory but complementary. There is no freedom save under a system of laws safeguarded by a constitution, and the prime function of governments under a democracy, while keeping themselves within their constitutional framework, is to protect and advance the fundamental freedoms and human rights of every individual by all the legislative measures that seem appropriate.

35 Robert K. Carr, *Federal Protection of Civil Rights*, p. 14.

# XIX

# The Redistribution of Imperial Sovereignty

*A paper read at the Annual Meeting of the Royal Society of Canada, 1950, discussing the problem of transforming a unified British Empire with an all powerful United Kingdom Parliament into a Commonwealth composed of co-equal independent nation states.*
From the *Transactions of the Royal Society of Canada*, 44, Series III, June 1950, 27–34

In the evolution of Commonwealth relations, the pace of legal change has varied greatly. Tennyson's concept of 'freedom slowly broadening down' is truer of England's internal development than of the complex struggle for colonial independence. Precedent in colonial history has played its part, but so too have revolution, civil war, and world wars. Too slow an adaptation in the law has generally resulted in stresses and strains that have left deep scars where they did not cause secessions. The American colonies were lost to Britain in the eighteenth century because a constitutional relationship that is a commonplace today was not then accepted. Ireland was lost (I use the term in no theological sense) through an even more protracted refusal to grant home rule. On the other hand the offer of responsible government to South Africa in 1909 was an act of forward-looking statesmanship which not even the resignation of that nation from the Commonwealth, if it should in future occur, would retroactively invalidate. This example, however, operated in the field of convention rather than strict law. Not till after World War I was the first attempt made to deal with the central problem of Commonwealth legal relations, namely, the doctrine of the legal sovereignty of the Imperial Parliament. In consequence, as R.T.E. Latham has said in a brilliant essay,[1] the British Commonwealth 'took the law by surprise.' When the Empire

---

1 See 'The Law and the Commonwealth,' in W.K. Hancock, *Survey of British Commonwealth Affairs*, I (Oxford University Press, 1937), 513.

adopted its newer and more democratic title of Commonwealth its fundamental law was still in all substantial respects the law of George III – the law which lost the American colonies.

What was this basic principle, this fundamental rule, which showed such remarkable tenacity? Dicey first made it a widely understood idea. The opening sentence of chapter I of his *Law of the Constitution* declares simply that 'The sovereignty of Parliament is (from the legal point of view) the dominant characteristic of our political institutions.' This principle means, he continues, that Parliament (i.e. the United Kingdom Parliament) has the right to make or unmake any law whatever, and further that no person or body is recognized by the law of England as having a right to override or set aside the legislation of Parliament. Hence it follows that the constitutions of the various Dominions and colonies, created by laws enacted in this Parliament, are binding upon the courts and people of the territory covered by them, and can only be 'made or unmade' by the same authority which first gave them the force of law.

Of course if the Dominion or colonial constitution contains a permission to the local legislature to amend at will, the power to change the English statute exists and may be exercised. But the reason why local amendments are then possible is that the superior legislature has specifically allowed it, and there is always present the possibility that the permission might be withdrawn. The Colonial Laws Validity Act of 1865 contained a general power of amendment for all colonial constitutions, subject to any restrictions from time to time imposed by the legislatures themselves. The two federal systems established by English statute, in Canada and Australia, created central and local legislatures which were confined strictly to their prescribed spheres of action by the binding force of the doctrine of Imperial sovereignty. The federal Parliament in Canada cannot invade the provincial sphere, nor a provincial legislature that of Parliament, because the United Kingdom Parliament says it cannot and the United Kingdom Parliament must be obeyed. The recently acquired power of the federal Parliament to amend certain portions of the constitution has not altered this relationship.

Convention has long since tempered the rigidity of this fundamental doctrine, and the Statute of Westminster of 1931 made some breaches in the actual law. Convention provides that the unlimited law-making power of the United Kingdom Parliament is a ritual or process to be employed at the request of any Dominion for the giving of legal validity to decisions already arrived at in that Dominion. When Canada wishes to amend the BNA Act (leaving aside the 1949 procedure) her Parliament simply adopts a joint address requesting the United Kingdom Parliament to make the necessary change, and the amendment is promptly made. Hence Canada possesses, by convention, a most flexible constitution, though new conventions calling for provincial consent are struggling for acceptance. The Statute of Westminster enables Canadian legislatures to amend any

British statutes extending to Canada, other than the BNA Acts, by ordinary legislation without the need of invoking the aid of the United Kingdom Parliament. This system has worked well enough until now, but obviously leaves in existence the ancient doctrine of Imperial sovereignty. The inequality of the relationship has become more and more apparent as the international status of the Dominion has risen. While the active interference of British governments in Canadian affairs has withered away, the hard core of legal dependence has been unconscionably slow in dying, and is not yet dead. The incorporation of Newfoundland into Confederation required the enactment of a British statute.

Starting after World War I, and greatly accelerating since the end of World War II, however, a new phase of constitutional evolution has begun, which bids fair to remove at last the doctrine of the legal supremacy of the United Kingdom Parliament from the fundamental role it has played for centuries in Imperial relations. The process is no less than the redistribution of Imperial sovereignty among the constituent parts of the Commonwealth. For the United Kingdom this means not the abolition of Parliamentary sovereignty, but a restriction of the area over which it can operate; for the other members it means the removal of a limitation, express or implied, upon their national sovereignty. It will involve the finding of a local and national root for the municipal law of each member state other than Britain, and the severance of a legal link which tied the local constitutions to the legal theory of the parent state. The process can be described more technically by saying that whereas till now we have had but one *Grundnorm*, one fundamental law, for the Commonwealth, namely the ultimate proposition that all laws emanating from the United Kingdom Parliament must be obeyed in all the courts of the Commonwealth, in future we shall have many totally distinct systems of law each with its own *Grundnorm*, which may well vary from country to country. To borrow another analogy from the well-known eastern myth, we may say that until now all legal rules in Canada, from municipal bylaws to whole codes of law like the Quebec Civil Code or the Criminal Code, have derived their validity from the elephant of the BNA Act, which stood firmly upon the turtle of the sovereignty of the United Kingdom Parliament. Beneath the turtle nothing further has existed to support a stable universe. Now the various Dominions are getting their own turtles, and we are looking for a Canadian turtle.

Already the process has gone very far. Ireland acquired her own national sovereignty, in its legal form, through a series of measures stretching from the treaty of 1921 through the Statute of Westminster down to the new constitution of 1936; the final link with Britain was cut by the repeal of the External Relations Act in 1948, which took effect April 18, 1949. Ireland is now a sovereign independent republic, and Irish courts obey none but Irish laws. This legal independence would not change were Ireland to re-enter the Commonwealth, any more than France would have become subject to Imperial sovereignty had she accepted Mr Churchill's offer to join the Commonwealth in 1940. It seems true also to say that South Africa's legal system is equally independent, though she is a member state. For South Africa took advantage of the lead given by the Statute of Westminster to assert her own sovereign independence by the Status of the Union Act of 1934, section 2 of which declares that 'The Parliament of the Union shall be the sovereign legislative power in and over the Union.' Moreover the same statute declared that the Statute of Westminster itself 'shall be deemed to be an Act of the Parliament of the Union, and shall be construed accordingly.' Thus in South Africa the Statute of Westminster is not an English statute but a South African statute; hence to the hypothetical question, 'What would happen if the United Kingdom Parliament repealed the Statute of Westminster?' the answer in so far as that country is concerned is 'Nothing.' The constitutional law of South Africa now belongs entirely to herself, though its English sources are clear.[2]

Ireland and South Africa were in this respect the advanced Dominions before the last war. Today only four Commonwealth members, of whom Canada is one, remain tied to the ancient legal theory of the sovereignty of Parliament. Burma, of course, though never a Dominion, became an independent country outside the Commonwealth by the enactment of the Burma Independence Act in 1947 (11 Geo. VI, c. 3). India and Pakistan obtained their independence by the Indian Independence Act of the same year (10 & 11 Geo. VI, c. 30), and Ceylon by the Ceylon Independence Act (11 Geo. VI, c. 7). The use of the word 'independence' in the title of these statutes indicates how far we have travelled. These three new nation states, while retaining their membership in the Commonwealth, have all celebrated their independence days. In so far as the question under discussion is concerned, however, we must perhaps distinguish between India and Pakistan on the one hand and Ceylon on the other. The two former states have followed the example of South Africa, and have declared that no future act of the United Kingdom Parliament shall extend to them unless it is adopted by their own legislatures. This means that they do not recognize in any degree the supremacy of the Parliament at Westminster. Their systems of law are thus severed from the Imperial root. Ceylon on the other hand has been content with the wording of the Statute of Westminster which enables Parliament to legislate for a Dominion if that Dominion has requested and consented thereto. She is therefore in the same position as Canada, Australia, and New Zealand – standing on the old turtle.

Some people may feel impatient with this analysis of a legal theory that appears to have little practical importance. Does it make any difference whether a

2 H.J. May, *The South African Constitution* (2nd ed., Capetown, 1949), p. 383.

British statute can extend to Canada whenever the preamble says Canada has requested it, or whether no such statute can have the force of law unless it has been enacted in identical terms by the Canadian Parliament? Surely a moment's reflection will show that there is a great difference. It is all the difference between the theory that the American constitution rests on the sovereignty of the people – the American people, and the theory that the Canadian constitution rests on the sovereignty of Parliament – the British Parliament. It is all the difference between having a constitution that is your own and a constitution that belongs to somebody else. It is even more practical than that. Suppose Canada takes to herself a power to amend the BNA Act, by procuring in London the addition of a clause describing how amendments may be adopted. What is to prevent a future British Parliament amending the Act on Canadian request by a separate statute which pays no attention to the amending procedures? Since the procedure rests on a British statute, the procedure itself can in future be amended in Britain. We should have no certainty or stability, unless the entire constitution were to become a Canadian constitution, binding on all future Canadian legislatures, and incapable of being altered save by a process which derives its validity from the will of the Canadian people alone.

Hence it is not surprising that at the constitutional conference which met in Ottawa in January, 1950 to discuss the amendment of the BNA Act, the larger question of sovereignty was raised. The idea that we should go beyond the adoption of a mere technique of amendment, and transmute the BNA Act into a purely Canadian document by some legal alchemy, was widely accepted. Premier McNair said: 'I feel that the final step in this work should be the divesting of the United Kingdom parliament of any authority over the constitutional affairs of Canada. I believe this is vital to the whole situation.'[3] Premier Duplessis spoke of 'the desirability of having a Canadian constitution, made in Canada by Canadians for Canada.'[4] The Premiers of Saskatchewan, Alberta, and Newfoundland spoke in a similar vein. No conclusion was arrived at on this matter, since agreement on amending procedures must precede the transfer of sovereignty if we are to avoid complete rigidity for the future. But sooner or later the transfer will have to be made, and Canadian law will then have come to rest upon a Canadian *Grundnorm*, and will be in no way subject to any action of the United Kingdom Parliament.

What will the theory be on which our constitution will then rest? What kind of a turtle shall we choose? Will it be a divine turtle, deriving its authority from God; or a provincial autonomy turtle, calling itself the compact theory; or an Anglo-French turtle, calling itself a treaty between races; or will it be a popular

---

3 *Proceedings of the Constitutional Conference of Federal and Provincial Governments* (Ottawa, 1950), p. 63.
4 *Ibid.*, p. 71.

turtle, labelled 'We, the People.' These turtles live in the preambles of constitutions, those opening sentences, bright with political foliage, which mean so little in the day to day working of governmental institutions and so much in times of great social change. The new draft constitution of India, following the example of the United States, begins 'We, the people of India, having solemnly resolved to constitute India into a Sovereign Democratic Republic ... do hereby adopt, enact, and give to ourselves this constitution.' It is a gift from the people to themselves. Ireland makes the best of both worlds, human and divine, for her constitution opens in this way: 'In the name of the Most Holy Trinity, from Whom is all authority and to Whom, as our final end, all actions both of men and states must be referred,' and then, for greater certainty no doubt, goes on to add that 'We, the people of Eire ... do hereby adopt, enact, and give to ourselves this constitution.' The gift is a self-gift, but in the divine name.

Countries like India and Ireland, however, have a history so unlike that of Canada as to be of little help to us in finding our proper formula. Our whole tradition is a royal and parliamentary one. Government is carried on in the name of a king advised by ministers and legislative bodies. In fact the King in his Canadian legislatures and on the advice of the appropriate Canadian ministers can perform every act required for the administration of the Canadian state, save only the amending of certain parts of the constitution. While in theory the courts in Canada exercise the power of judicial review of legislation on the principle of Imperial sovereignty, holding any statute *ultra vires* which exceeds the powers granted in the BNA Act, in fact they are acting exactly as do the courts in the United States where the constitution is entirely national. All we need do in Canada is to change the legal principle without changing in any way the legal behaviour. We must pull out the old turtle and slip a new one in its place, so that not even a tremor need be felt in the superstructure.

How is this to be done? So long as we all know what we are doing and agree on it, the procedure is not very important. A procedure was, in fact, suggested at the 1937 Dominion-provincial conference, but it was never carried through. The proposal was to replace section 7 of the Statute of Westminster (the section which preserves the BNA Act from amendment in Canada) with a new section empowering the Parliament of Canada to enact a federal constitution for the country by consolidating all existing constitutional rules into a single document. To this would then be added the method of amendment as worked out in Canada. On the coming into force of this Canadian constitution, which would simply be the old BNA Acts rehashed, the latter would be repealed. Hence for the future we should have a Canadian constitution which we could amend in all respects ourselves without ever going to the Mother of our Parliaments.

In my view this kind of procedure still suffers from its relationship to the

Statute of Westminster, which is an exclusively United Kingdom statute. The Canadian constitution thus created would seem to depend upon the sovereignty of Parliament as of old. While the Statute of Westminster was intended to free the former colonies from certain legal fetters, it nevertheless preserved the law-making power of the United Kingdom Parliament over the very nations it was attempting to free. Like the Colonial Laws Validity Act, it has served its turn. None of the three new Asian members of the Commonwealth utilized the Statute of Westminster to secure their independence, though Ceylon copied section 4 into her Independence Act, and some other sections reappear in both the Indian and the Ceylon Acts.[5] If Canada is to achieve the type of Canadian constitution suggested at the constitutional conference, and is to end once and for all this legal dependence, then there should be enacted a Canada independence act, under whatever title may be selected, to establish once and for all the solid fact of Canada's legal sovereignty vis-à-vis Great Britain. Premier McNair suggested this should be done by treaty, but a special United Kingdom statute at Canada's request would seem to be sufficient. In the statute would be a declaration that, as from the 'appointed day' (which might well be July 1 so as to coincide with an existing national holiday) the new constitution of Canada would take effect, and thereafter all jurisdiction heretofore vested in the Parliament of the United Kingdom in and over Canada would cease. The constitution itself would contain a declaration of sovereignty in the Canadian people, and a provision that no United Kingdom statutes would in future have the force of law in Canada unless adopted by the Canadian Parliament. Such a statute would not, of course, make any change in Canada's membership in the Commonwealth, nor alter the position of the Crown, any more than it has done in the case of Ceylon or South Africa. It would simply bring the legal theory at last in to line with political realities. It would give us our own turtle. On this firm foundation, Canada could then work out whatever future changes were required in her own constitution, conscious that her destiny is wholly in her own hands. The Crown as a symbol of Commonwealth relations would alone remain, for as long as we may wish to preserve it.

5 See K.C. Wheare, 'Recent Constitutional Developments in the British Commonwealth,' *Journal of Comparative Legislation*, 3rd series, XXX (1948), 75.

# XX

# Centralization and Decentralization in Canadian Federalism

*Discusses in relation to Canada the central problem facing all federations. It shows the support in Canada for the thesis that the constitution of 1867 provided a better distribution of powers than resulted from later judicial interpretation, and suggests that amendments to correct the imbalance would not involve drastic changes. Since the publication of this article, in 1951 and 1964, Section 94A was added to clarify federal authority in respect of old age pensions and supplementary benefits.*
From the *Canadian Bar Review*, 29, 1951, 1095–1125

The Canadian constitution cannot be understood if it is approached with some preconceived theory of what federalism is or should be. The British North America Act of 1867 was not made to fit a theoretical pattern, but grew out of a peculiar set of historical traditions, experiences and necessities. There is little evidence that its creators, outside perhaps of Macdonald himself, had made any serious study of federalism in general or even of American federalism,[1] though this model was frequently referred to during the pre-Confederation conferences and debates. The essential material for the new nation state was in the people themselves and in their already considerable experiments with different constitutional devices.

The constitution which emerged in 1867 is remarkable as much for its continuity with the past as for its introduction of federal forms. The central position of the Crown, the relations of cabinet to legislature, the legal supremacy of the Parliament of the United Kingdom, the central power of disallowance of local laws, the single court of final appeal for all provinces, the belief in a strong central government, were not sacrificed on any altar of federalism. The purpose of Confederation was not to create more autonomy for the British North American

1 See Trotter, *Canadian Federation* (1924) p. 104.

provinces (subject to what is said later regarding Quebec and Ontario) but to unite them in a federal state: that is to say, to take away from local governments many of their existing powers and to place over them a new national government endowed with a wide general jurisdiction extending territorially over the whole country. The post-Confederation provinces therefore started with their previous autonomy much reduced, but with the residue guaranteed against federal invasion and, subject to the power of disallowance, placed on an independent basis.

The legal analysis does not apply in the same fashion to the old Province of Canada. True, its legislature, like those of the other provinces, used to make every kind of law, civil and criminal, subject only to a very infrequent Imperial control. No province today has such wide powers. Yet Confederation brought about a change in central Canada that was unlike what occurred elsewhere. The Province of Canada was composed of the union in 1841 of the still earlier provinces of Upper Canada and Lower Canada. It was separated in 1867 into its two historic parts, renamed Quebec and Ontario. Confederation thus re-created the legal entity called Quebec, and by so doing provided for French Canada a degree of autonomy which it had never previously known, not even under the French regime when colonial freedom was minimal. It similarly provided for Ontario a freedom from the restraints imposed in the constitution of 1841, but this relief was not comparable to that felt in Quebec, since the English element had always possessed a majority of votes in the Union Parliament. Hence, to Quebec, Confederation represented a partial escape from centralized control, whereas to all other provinces Confederation represented an acceptance of a measure of centralized control. It is small wonder that Quebec has always insisted the most strongly that the constitution was designed to secure autonomy to the provinces. This was peculiarly her experience. It was not the same for the other parts of Canada.

It is nevertheless an historical fact that the French law and language, and the Roman Catholic religion, won the battle of *la survivance* under a regime of centralization and not under one of provincial autonomy. The interval from 1763 to 1867, from the Cession to Confederation, is longer than the period from 1867 to 1951; yet during that first century under British rule, when the French population grew from some 70,000 to 1,000,000, when the Catholic religion was guaranteed and the French language made an official language, the constitutions under which the French were successively governed placed complete jurisdiction over property and civil rights, education and religion in governments controlled by British Protestants. That was true of the conciliar governments that prevailed from 1763 to 1792, of the Lower Canadian constitution that lasted from 1792 to 1838, of the Special Council which governed from 1838 to 1841, and of the Act of Union of 1841, which deliberately secured an English speaking majority in the legislature. The Quebec Civil Code became law by enactment of a legislature of which the French were a minority, and the same legislature was the first to introduce separate schools in Ontario. If Quebec's 'way of life' had depended upon a constitution which gave her full control of the precious subjects that form the basis of a culture, there would be none of it to-day. Such a constitution did not exist until 1867.

To suggest that 'centralization' is a matter of life and death for Quebec's culture is therefore a view that lacks historical perspective. On the other hand, merely because centralization would not necessarily be a danger to fundamental values in Quebec is no proof that in a given instance it is desirable. It might become a danger, say, to the way of life in some other province, or to the democratic way of life common to all provinces. The problem of centralization is not just a problem of Quebec versus the rest of Canada. It would exist as a problem were Canada all French or all British.

## WHAT DOES 'CENTRALIZATION' MEAN?

Centralization is a currently popular term used to describe the prevailing trend toward an increase in the powers of central governments as opposed to regional and local governments. Its antonym is decentralization, the reverse process, more in evidence to-day than is generally supposed, through the delegation of state power to subordinate agencies. The problem of centralization raises the age-old question of deciding how authority should be distributed as between various levels of government. This is a vital question for all states, whether unitary or federal. Unitary states possess a single central legislature, usually with unlimited jurisdiction, but they decentralize through the use of municipal, county and regional administrations, and by delegating functions to various governmental agencies which stand in a greater or lesser degree of independence from the parent body. Even the private corporation is a state creature granted authority and personality to perform certain economic and social functions, and exercising powers differing only in some respects from those possessed by other decentralized 'little governments.' Within the private enterprise sector of the Canadian economy, centralized authority is very apparent.[2]

In federal states the problem of centralization is structurally more complicated but in essence the same. There is the primary division of legislative powers between the central and local governments – in Canada, between Ottawa and the

2 An authoritative analysis of this centralization will be found in Lloyd G. Reynolds, *The Control of Competition in Canada* (1940). See also *Report of Royal Commission on Price Spreads*, 1935, and *Canada and International Cartels*, published by the Department of Labour, Ottawa, 1945.

provinces – each of which is independent of the others and of co-ordinate authority within its own sphere; the word 'centralization' in this context means granting more jurisdiction to the central and less to the local legislatures. Yet each type of government is then free to delegate its powers to other bodies if it so desires, though apparently inter-governmental delegation is forbidden in Canada. Thus in Quebec in recent years there is evident a tendency to centralize the powers formerly exercised by municipalities and school boards in the hands of provincial departments or commissions, and similar trends are seen elsewhere.

The distribution of legislative power as between Parliament and provincial legislatures is one thing; that between Parliament and legislatures, on the one hand, and subordinate instrumentalities, on the other, is a quite separate thing. Sometimes, too, administration is decentralized where jurisdiction is centralized. The outstanding example of this in Canada is the criminal law, the enactment of which is federal and the enforcement, for the most part, provincial. The discussion in this paper is primarily directed to centralization in its federal sense, that is to say, to a discussion of the distribution of legislative powers between Ottawa and the provinces.

In Canada the contemporary discussion of this problem meets special difficulties. Some of these are semantic, arising from the connotations of the word itself; others are real, lying deep in the nature of Canadian life. Semantic difficulties exist because the term 'centralization' has an ugly sound. It conjures up the vision of a horde of bureaucrats (another loaded word) ruling by decree. It implies totalitarianism. To certain sections of the population it carries a particular menace; for most Quebecers it suggests the loss of their provincial autonomy to Ottawa, centre of British influence and Protestant majorities, while for the business community, fearful of an expanding welfare state with its increased taxation and controls, the word seems a signpost on the road to serfdom. Thus an objective analysis of the reasons for and against any proposed change in the distribution of legislative powers is not easy to achieve, particularly when, as so often happens in this centralizing age, the proposal involves an increase in federal power.

To these semantic difficulties must be added the real difficulties in distributing legislative powers, when the word 'centralization' is stripped of its emotional overtones. Canada's physical characteristics alone would make federalism difficult to apply, even were her population homogeneous. What division of powers is appropriate for a country where 90% of the people live in a narrow ribbon of settlement, broken in the middle, stretching 4,000 miles across the continent, and now including the detached island province of Newfoundland, particularly when the principal regions vary so widely in their economic activities? The wheat economy of the west, even though broadened by new industrial growth, would make an uneasy companion for the manufacturing central provinces under any form of government.

Add to this the cultural differences within Canada and the picture becomes the more complicated. In Quebec and Ontario, and to an increasing extent in other provinces, the British-Protestant and French-Catholic groups create a bicultural community whose special claims the constitution must recognize. Already the expansion of the French-speaking element in New Brunswick is pressing hard upon the limitations of section 133 of the BNA Act, which, while making French an official language in the federal Parliament and federal courts, leaves Quebec as the only officially bilingual province;[3] and Catholic demands for separate school rights are being heard in provinces not now obliged to maintain them by the educational guarantees of section 93.[4] Governmental 'efficiency' cannot be the only criterion where a large section of the population is more concerned with protecting its special French and Catholic way of life than with easing the headaches of federal administrators. Nor are the cultural problems solely related to the historic situation of Quebec within the confederation. Canada possesses minorities within minorities – Protestants in Quebec, Catholics and French elsewhere, Eskimos and Indians – who claim consideration. In the western provinces a special need exists, that of assimilating into some general Canadian pattern the new Canadians of most divergent races and creeds, many of whom hive off into colonies which set up claims to minority rights not imagined in the BNA Act.

Competing with these regional and cultural factors to-day are the insistent requirements of economic regulation and national defence in a time of inflationary pressures and world unrest. These push heavily toward centralization, but they are relative newcomers to the federal scene and, perhaps in our innocence, we tend to regard them as emergency problems to which the Constitution need not permanently adapt itself. The older factors touch deeper roots of national consciousness, and some of these make for centralization, others for decentralization. Statesmanship of a high order is demanded of Canadians if they would bring these conflicting forces into harmonious federal balance. But of one thing we can be sure if Canada is to remain a federal state, neither breaking up into separate pieces nor marching to unification under a single government: a rigid attitude either for or against centralization is quite indefensible. The problems faced by

---

3 The Manitoba Act of 1870, section 23, gave the French language an official status in the province, but this was repealed by the legislature of Manitoba. See R.S.M., 1940, c. 152. The French constitute approximately 35% of the population of New Brunswick.

4 The right to separate schools supported by state funds is guaranteed in some only of the Canadian provinces.

governments have to be assessed, and the distribution of authority determined, not only in relation to cultural guarantees, but also and in some instances primarily in relation to social need. To refuse centralization where the evil to be met is beyond provincial control is to court anarchy or to suffer the unchecked domination of private interests; to rush into centralization when the matter is not of serious national concern is to risk creating an overmighty state and depriving the people of their local democratic control.

## UNITARY PRINCIPLES IN THE BNA ACT

All the debates and discussions about the Canadian Constitution at the time of its adoption emphasized the high degree of central authority which it was to provide. Friend and foe alike agreed on this characteristic.[5] The text of the BNA Act impresses one by its apparent preference for unitary principles as opposed to provincial sovereignty. At every important point provincial freedom is hedged with federal controls, many of which no strict theory of federalism can ever justify. These are evident in the legislative, executive and judicial spheres.

Provincial legislative autonomy, for example, is subject to several restraints. No provincial bill can become law without the assent of a federal appointee, the Lieutenant-Governor. He may legally withhold that assent, or he may reserve the bill for Ottawa's acceptance or rejection. Even after it has become law it may be disallowed by the federal executive within one year, a power which in fact has been frequently exercised.[6] In cases of conflict between an *intra vires* federal law and an *intra vires* provincial law, in matters of concurrent jurisdiction, the federal law always prevails.[7] What is of greater significance, the residue of unallocated subjects is centralized by the opening words of section 91, thus contrasting sharply with the principle underlying the American constitution. Even the laws relative to 'property and Civil Rights' were intended to be progressively centralized for the common law provinces by section 94. Provincial executive autonomy is restrained by the fact that the head of the executive is the same Lieutenant-Governor who is appointed, paid, instructed and removed by Ottawa. The constitution does not require him to be a native or resident of the province. Provincial judicial

---

5 Some of these comments are collected in my article, Political Nationalism and Confederation (1942), 8 *Canadian Journal of Economics and Political Science* 386, at pp. 399 ff. (Essay I above).

6 BNA Act, ss. 58, 90; Forsey, Disallowance of Provincial Acts, Reservation of Provincial Bills, and Refusal of Assent by Lieutenant-Governors since 1867 (1938), 4 *Can. J. Econ. & Pol. Sc.* 47.

7 BNA Act, s. 95.

autonomy is restrained by the fact that the judges of provincial superior courts are federally appointed and paid; the province may appoint judicial officers to minor courts only.[8] In addition, the Supreme Court of Canada, whose members are also federally appointed, is the final court of appeal for all questions of provincial as well as federal law, thus making it a truly national court and not merely, as is the Supreme Court of the United States, a federal court.[9] Even in the delicate matter of denominational schools the federal Parliament is given an ultimate power by section 93 to make remedial laws, in defined circumstances, which will override provincial legislation. Moreover the provincial representatives in the Canadian Senate are neither elected by provinces nor chosen by provincial governments, but are nominated for life by the federal executive.[10] Provincial financial autonomy is restrained by the fact that the power of the provinces to tax is limited to the imposition of direct taxes,[11] and provincial governments are subsidized by federal grants.[12]

If one turns from what may be called the political structure of the constitution to its distribution of economic powers, a similar centralization is noticeable. What were the chief economic activities of the population of the various provinces at the time of Confederation? An answer which listed Trade and Commerce, Agriculture, Fishing, Navigation and Shipping, Railways and Canals would not be far wrong, and would not leave many classes of workers uncovered. Every one of these subjects is allotted by the Constitution to the national Parliament. Trade and Commerce, Seacoast and Inland Fisheries, and Navigation and Shipping, are exclusive federal powers;[13] Agriculture is a concurrent power, with federal laws paramount;[14] Railways and Canals are exclusively federal if interprovincial,[15] and if not, can be made exclusively federal at any time by a simple declaration by Parliament that they are for the general advantage. Any other local 'works' can be similarly removed from provincial autonomy by this form of declaration.[16] True, provinces were left with the ownership of their natural resources in such things as lands, mines, forests and water-powers,[17] but once these became developed their products would enter the stream of trade and commerce, generally

8 *Ibid.*, s. 96.
9 *Ibid.*, s. 101.
10 *Ibid.*, ss. 24, 29.
11 *Ibid.*, s. 92, head 2.
12 *Ibid.*, s. 118, as amended.
13 *Ibid.*, s. 91, heads 2, 10, 12.
14 *Ibid.*, s. 95.
15 *Ibid.*, s. 92, head 10(a).
16 *Ibid.*, s. 92, head 10(c).
17 *Ibid.*, s. 109.

using inter-provincial services, and would thus come within federal jurisdiction. Naturally the subjects concomitant to Trade and Commerce, such as Banks, Legal Tender, Interest, Weights and Measures, were exclusively federal.[18] To cap it all, provincial tariffs were prohibited, and customs and excise laws were given to Ottawa.[19] Thus the BNA Act appears to have provided beyond question for a central authority over the economic life of Canada, and to have safeguarded us against any reappearance of the provincial economic autonomy which had so stifled progress and development among the pre-Confederation colonies. In the words of a leading authority on Canadian government, 'The federation was thus intended to depart radically from the pure federal form in which the component local units are of equal or co-ordinate rank with the central government.'[20]

It will be noted that every federal power mentioned in the two preceding paragraphs is derived, not from judicial interpretation, and not from mere surmises or inferences, but from some positive text of the Constitution itself. It would be tedious to quote all the leading Fathers of Confederation who spoke in support of the idea of Parliament's predominant position, and impossible to quote any against. The compact of Confederation, in so far as it existed, was an agreement to prefer national power to provincial autonomy on all matters of general or national concern, leaving the provinces control over their local affairs only, but with guarantees as to language and separate schools. This basic contrast between 'general' and 'local' matters, which Clement has rightly called 'The Cardinal Principle of Allotment,'[21] is explicitly stated in the second of the Quebec Resolutions of 1864 and of the London Resolutions of 1866. The relevant portion of the London Resolution reads as follows:

In the Confederation of the British North American provinces the system of government best adapted under existing circumstances to protect the diversified interests of the several provinces and secure efficiency, harmony and permanency in the working of the Union is a General Government charged with matters of common interest to the whole country and Local Governments for each of the Canadas, and for the provinces of Nova Scotia and New Brunswick, charged with the control of local matters in their respective sections ...

Words could not be clearer to show that the line of demarcation between what was to be centralized and what was to be decentralized ran along the division be-

18 *Ibid.*, s. 91, heads 15, 20, 19, 17.
19 *Ibid.*, ss. 121, 122.
20 Dawson, *The Government of Canada* (1947) p. 36.
21 Clement, *The Law of the Canadian Constitution* (3rd ed.) Chap. 32.

tween matters of general or national concern and matters of local concern ('of a merely local or private Nature in the Province,' to borrow words from section 92, head 16). Enumerated heads of jurisdiction under section 91 were examples of general matters, all other general matters being thought of as contained in the federal residue; enumerated heads of 92 were examples of local matters. Education received special treatment in section 93, and Immigration and Agriculture in section 95. It was a sensible arrangement, seemingly forever free from the kind of exaggerated local sovereignty which had disrupted the United States by civil war, and which served as so clear an object lesson to the men of both races who drafted the agreements at Quebec and London.

## THE CONSTITUTIONAL REVOLUTION

Everyone familiar with Canadian constitutional history knows that the original constitution is far from representing the realities of Canadian law and politics today. The whole emphasis has now changed. Since 1867 the jurisdiction of the central government has relatively decreased, and that of the provinces increased, to such an extent that in the opinion of many authorities the intentions of the Fathers of Confederation have been frustrated. Despite the wording of the Constitution, and despite her growth in international prestige and importance, Canada is now, eighty-five years after Confederation, troubled with such a trend toward 'States Rights' (to use Macdonald's name for it) that the federal government must rely more and more on a new legal doctrine of 'national emergency' in order to legislate on matters of unquestioned national importance, and the national Parliament is increasingly obliged to defer to agreements made in a kind of General Assembly of Sovereign Provinces called a Dominion-Provincial Conference, where each government possesses a veto over decisions. This outcome is indeed a commentary on the impossibility of directing the course of history by even the most carefully drawn constitutional provisions.

To attempt an explanation of how this change occurred would be a long story. Influences making for the end result, however, would not be difficult to identify. A major one would be found in the cumulative work of the courts, particularly of the Judicial Committee of the Privy Council, now vanishing as a final court of appeal for Canada but still a powerful factor in Canadian politics as long as the doctrine of *stare decisis* remains.[22] In the United States, a looser federalism was unified by the judgments of a Marshall, while in Canada a stronger union was decentralized by a Watson and a Haldane. Other influences would be found in the

22 Cf. Laskin, The Supreme Court of Canada (1951), 29 *Can. Bar Rev.* 1038.

political, economic and social forces that form the climate in which the constitution must work. The world-wide depression that began in 1873 forced the federal government to reduce its programme of national development, and compelled Canadians to turn to 'the older and more obvious realities of provincial and local community life.'[23] An increasingly influential factor to be noted is the growing political and economic strength of French Canada, whose people have won for themselves, by their tenacity, productivity and ability, a far wider recognition of their distinctive cultural rights than was accepted in 1867. Though now past their first struggles for mere *survivance*, and with about one-quarter of their people living in other provinces, most French-speaking Canadians are generally persuaded that every limitation on Ottawa's constitutional powers means more strength in their 'citadel' of Quebec and hence more autonomy for the French-speaking element. In other regions, notably the Maritime provinces, a tradition of autonomy is also strong. Of perhaps equal importance to-day are the prevailing notions of 'free enterprise' held by wide and powerful sections of the community whose political philosophy inclines to a provincial autonomy from which they have little interference to fear, and whose influence on public opinion through agencies of mass communication and through direct party support it is difficult to exaggerate. *Le Devoir* and the Montreal *Gazette*, apt spokesmen for Quebec Nationalists and powerful business interests respectively, share many constitutional opinions.

Counter influences making for centralization are found chiefly in claims for protection for special groups such as organized labour and farmers, in the growing demands for social insurances, and in the ever insistent pressures of defence planning and international collaboration. The growing industrialization tends towards centralization, despite what autonomists may say, though at the same time it increases the duties of local governments as well. Time, as Professor Angus once said, is running against the provinces,[24] but in Canada time seems often to move at the speed of a glacier. It is the law of the constitution which will be emphasized here, and the law of the constitution, in so far as the distribution of legislative powers is concerned, is now in certain respects out of line with the facts of modern Canadian life.

JUDICIAL PREFERENCE FOR DECENTRALIZATION

The decentralizing influence of judicial interpretation resulted from a piecemeal whittling away of certain important clauses allocating legislative powers to the

23 *Sirois Report*, Vol. I, p. 47.
24 Angus, The Canadian Constitution and the United Nations Charter (1946), *Can. J. Econ. & Pol. Sc.* 127, at p. 135.

Parliament of Canada. The story is not, of course, totally one-sided; a few notable decisions favoured Dominion jurisdiction. Some of these affected executive and judicial functions rather than legislative powers. For instance, the federal power of disallowance of provincial laws and the Lieutenant-Governor's power to reserve bills were upheld in the *Reference re the Power of Disallowance and Reservation.*[25] The right of the Parliament of Canada to abolish appeals from all Canadian courts to the Judicial Committee of the Privy Council in England, and to establish the Supreme Court of Canada as the final court of appeal, was upheld in *A.-G. for Ontario* v. *A.-G. for Canada.*[26] The very unfederal power of Parliament to declare local 'works' to be for the general advantage of Canada, and thus to transfer them from provincial into federal jurisdiction, has survived many tests.[27] The federal appointment of judges has not been questioned in the courts, though the definition of what constitutes a 'Superior, District or County Court,' whose members under the constitution must be appointed by Ottawa, has been reasonably framed so as to exclude various types of provincial administrative tribunal, thus leaving the provinces a freer hand in the development of their governmental services.[28] Under the 'emergency' doctrine, the full authority of Parliament to legislate for the 'Peace, Order and good Government of Canada,' which was originally thought to be an ample residuary power covering new peacetime matters of 'general interest' as well as emergency situations, has prevailed, so that Canadians know they can at least engage in wars without constitutional difficulties.[29]

These are examples of some significant Dominion successes in the law courts on matters of broad constitutional principle. Their effect was rather to stem the drift toward decentralization than to open new fields to Dominion jurisdiction. The two most important decisions since 1867 enlarging federal legislative power were the References which held that the subjects of radio broadcasting and aeronautics belonged to the Dominion sphere.[30] These judgments are scarcely surprising; the notion of local governments attempting separate control of flying and broadcasting within a single country is difficult to imagine. Yet even so the chief ground on which aeronautics was attributed to Ottawa was that an 'Empire treaty' existed (the Aeronautics Convention of 1919) binding on Canada, and hence section 132 of the constitution could be applied. Aerial navigation was not held to

25 [1938] S.C.R. 71.
26 [1947] A.C. 127.
27 See discussion in *Dominion Law Annotations, Revised*, Vol. III (1951), p. 206.
28 For a recent discussion of this problem, see Shumiatcher, Section 96 of the British North America Act Re-examined (1949), 27 *Can. Bar Rev.* 131.
29 *Infra*, footnote 39.
30 The *Radio Reference* is in [1932] A.C. 304 and the *Aeronautics Reference*, [1932] A.C. 54.

fall within the enumerated head of 'Navigation and Shipping.' Just what might be Ottawa's position if there were no treaty it is hard to say, since the question has not been decided; already doubts have been raised in *Johannesson* v. *West St Paul* as to the federal right to choose the location of aerodromes for peacetime commercial aviation.[31]

Over against these decisions we must set the series of leading cases on particular words and phrases in sections 91, 92 and 132 of the BNA Act, and particularly on the opening words of section 91, which reshaped Canada's federal system. Very few of the federal heads of jurisdiction, other than perhaps Banks and Banking, the Criminal Law, Interest and Telegraphs, have received anything but the narrowest interpretation, while the provincial powers, notably Property and Civil Rights, have received a broad and liberal one. The federal residuary power, surely one of the most important powers to distribute in a federal state, has been reduced to an 'emergency' doctrine, virtually useless in normal circumstances, the provincial jurisdiction over 'Property and Civil Rights' being the effective residue. The turning point of this line of cases came with the *Ontario Liquor License* case of 1896,[32] which Lord Haldane himself described as 'the watershed.'[33] Here it was said by Lord Watson that

the exercise of legislative power by the Parliament of Canada, in regard to all matters not enumerated in s. 91, ought to be strictly confined to such matters as are unquestionably of Canadian interest and importance, and ought not to trench upon provincial legislation with respect to any of the classes of subjects enumerated in s. 92. To attach any other construction to the general power which, in supplement of its enumerated powers, is conferred upon the Parliament of Canada by s. 91, would, in their Lordship's opinion, not only be contrary to the intendment of the Act, but would practically destroy the autonomy of the provinces.[34]

The phrase 'ought not to trench upon provincial legislation,' meaning ought not to 'affect' or 'interfere with' the provincial laws, departs radically from the opening words of section 91 where the only limit upon the residuary power is that laws based on it must not be 'coming within the classes of subjects by this Act assigned exclusively to the Legislatures of the Provinces.' A law on Banking may

31 [1950] 3 D.L.R. 101.
32 [1896] A.C. 348.
33 In report of argument in the *Snider* case, Department of Labour, Ottawa, 1925, p. 111.
34 *Ibid.*, at pp. 360–1.

affect, trench upon and interfere with 'Property and Civil Rights,' but it does not 'come within' that subject; so too it was intended to be with laws on the new subjects of equivalent national importance such as trade unions and unemployment insurance. The weakness in the present position, from the governmental point of view, lies in the dependence upon an 'emergency' situation for the validity of a federal law on almost all unenumerated subjects, and, while the courts in the most recent case seemed to suggest that they would not look behind a declaration of Parliament that an emergency existed, 'unless the contrary were very clear,' thus making of the emergency power almost a second declaratory power similar to that existing for local works,[35] the jurisdiction thus possessed is no substitute for a plain, untrammelled residuary power over matters of genuine interprovincial concern, such as was in the original constitution. War emergencies are only one form of 'general interest,' but they are the only form the courts seem willing to accept, though 'pestilence' has been quaintly hinted at as equally justifying central authority under the residuary clause.[36] Nothing in the great economic crisis of the 1930s, not even mass unemployment and disrupted agricultural markets, was an emergency. A recent attempt has been made by Lord Simon, in the *Canada Temperance Federation* case,[37] to bring Canadian law on this point back to its source in the Constitution, but his admirable logic and common sense seems about to suffer the same polite dismissal that was previously accorded a similar statement of the law made in *Russell* v. *The Queen* back in 1883.[38]

The whole story of this major constitutional amendment is too familiar to need repetition,[39] but it may be pointed up by comparing these words of Macdonald, spoken during the Confederation Debates:

We have strengthened the General Government. We have given the General Legislature all the great subjects of legislation. We have conferred on them, not only specifically and in detail, all the powers which are incident to sovereignty, but we have expressly declared that all subjects of general interest not distinctly and exclusively conferred upon the local governments and local legislatures, shall be conferred upon the General Government and Legislature.[40]

35 *Reference as to the Validity of the Wartime Leasehold Regulations*, [1950] S.C.R. 124.
36 *Toronto Electric Commissioners* v. *Snider*, [1925] A.C. 396, at p. 412.
37 [1946] A.C. 193.
38 See remarks of Lord Morton in *Canadian Federation of Agriculture* v. *A.-G. for Quebec*, [1951] A.C. 179, at p. 197.
39 For a thorough recent discussion see Laskin, 'Peace, Order and Good Government' Reexamined (1947), 25 *Can. Bar Rev.* 1054.
40 At p. 33.

and those of Lord Carnarvon in the House of Lords discussion on the BNA Act:

It will be seen, under the 91st clause, that the classification is not intended 'to restrict the generality' of the powers previously given to the central parliament, and that those powers extend to all laws made 'for the peace, order and good government' of the Confederation, terms which, according to all precedents, will, I understand, carry with them an ample measure of legislative authority.[41]

with those which a distinguished Canadian barrister could publish in 1940:

Clearly there is in the Act no such thing as a general power to make laws for peace, order and good government. The very words of the clause itself (without even a comma to separate them) exclude from such general power everything that falls within sec. 92. It has been therefore the duty of the courts first to determine the limits of the powers conferred upon the Provincial Legislature, and only when these powers have been exhausted is the general power of the Dominion open for consideration.[42]

Obviously something drastic has occurred between 1867 and 1940. The Sirois Report muddied the historical waters by contending, with a fine appearance of impartiality, that there are grave doubts about the fundamental ideas of the Fathers, and that little light can be gained from a resort to history.[43] It cited five authorities on the side here maintained and two on the other. It might have cited a great many more than the five, but few more than the two.[44] The point imme-

---

41 *Hansard, Parliamentary Debates*, 3rd Series, Vol. 185, col. 566.
42 McWilliams, Letter in (1940), 18 *Can. Bar Rev.* 516.
43 Vol. I, pp. 32 ff.
44 The following authorities have emphasized the degree to which the courts have departed from the original intention of the constitution: Smith, H.A., The Residue of Power in Canada (1926), 4 *Can. Bar Rev.* 432; Claxton, Brooke, The Amendment of the BNA Act, in Supplement to *McGill News*, June 1929, p. 8, at p. 16; Kennedy, W.P.M., Law and Custom in the Canadian Constitution in (1929), 20 *Round Table* pp. 143 ff., and in *The Constitution of Canada* (2nd ed.) pp. 488 ff, also The Interpretation of the BNA Act (1943), 8 *Camb. L.J.* 146; Scott, F.R., The Privy Council and Minority Rights (1930), 37 *Queen's Quarterly* at p. 677, and The Development of Canadian Federalism, *Proceedings Can. Pol. Sci. Ass.* (1931), Vol. III, p. 231; Ewart, J.S., *ibid.*, Comments, pp. 248, 252; Brady, A., *Canada* (1932) pp. 45 ff, and in Innis and Plumptre (eds.), *The Canadian Economy and Its Problems* (1934), p. 475, also in *Democracy in the Dominions*, pp. 44 ff; Goldenberg, H. Carl, Social and Economic Problems in Canadian Federalism (1934), 12 *Can. Bar Rev.* 422; MacKenzie, N.A.M., The Federal Problem and the BNA Act, in *Canadian Problems*, p. 247; Skelton, O.D., evidence before Special Committee on the BNA Act, 1935, at p. 23; MacDonald, V.C., Judicial Interpretation of the

diately at issue is not whether there should be more or less centralization to-day, and not whether the BNA Act is a compact, but solely whether the Fathers of Confederation thought they had created a federal state with a general power to make laws outside the enumerated heads, and with a leaning toward centralization rather than toward provincial autonomy. On this there can be no serious debate. The courts have virtually eliminated the general power and have created a leaning toward provincial autonomy.

Next to suffer reduction after the residuary clause was another equally significant federal power, namely the 'Regulation of Trade and Commerce.' An intention clearly enunciated at Confederation, and on which much was said, was that the new Dominion of Canada was to be freed from the petty provincial economic policies and barriers to trade which bedevilled the first half of 19th century Canadian history. Hence the Constitution did not reserve to the provinces intra-provincial trade, as the United States Constitution reserved intra-state commerce. However, this provincial reservation, omitted in the law, was supplied by a line of decisions beginning with *Parson's* case.[45] On the merits that case appears sound, since

Canadian Constitution (1935–6), 1 *U. of Toronto L. J.* 260, at p. 281; Forsey, E.A., in (1936), 2 *Can. J. Econ. & Pol. Sc.* at pp. 595–6; Cahan, C.H., address to Canadian Club of Toronto, Sept. 15th, 1937, and in *House of Commons Debates*, April 5th, 1937, pp. 2574 ff, and *ibid*. April 8th, 1938, p. 2157; Thorson, J.T., *ibid*. April 5th, 1937, p. 2582; Bennett, R.B., *ibid*. pp. 2587 ff; Hugessen, A.-K., address to Junior Board of Trade, Montreal, reported in Montreal Gazette, Oct. 20th, 1937; Coyne, J.B., Canadian Neutrality (1938) pp. 30 ff; Underhill, F.H., Edward Blake, The Supreme Court Act, and the Appeal to the Privy Council 1875–6 (1938), 19 *Can. Hist. Rev.* at p. 261; Burchell, C.J., in *The Canadian Constitution* (1938) at pp. 124–5; Creighton, D.G., British North America at Confederation, Appendix 2 of *Sirois Report*, pp. 49 ff (on the intentions of the Fathers); Cronkite, F.C., Comment on the O'Connor Report (1939), 5 *Can. J. Econ. & Pol. Sc.* at p. 507; O'Connor, W.F., *Report on the BNA Act* (1939) *passim*, and Property and Civil Rights in the Province (1940), 18 *Can. Bar Rev.* 331; Clark, E.R., The Privy Council and the Constitution (1939), 19 *Dalhousie Review* 65; Richard, Réné, Peace, Order and Good Government (1940), 18 *Can. Bar Rev.* 243, at p. 259; Hanson, R.B., *House of Commons Debates*, Nov. 12th, 1940, p. 40; Tuck, Raphael, Canada and the Judicial Committee (1941–2), 4 *U. of Toronto L. J.* 33, at pp. 34, 64; Lower, A.R.M., *From Colony to Nation* (1946) p. 334; Laskin, Bora, *supra* footnote 39. Similar views will be found in the briefs to the Sirois Commission presented by the Province of Manitoba, The Native Sons of Canada, and The League for Social Reconstruction. This list is exhausting but not exhaustive. On the other side of the debate, besides the two authorities cited in the Sirois Report, Vol. I, p. 35, n. 37, will be found McWilliams, R.F., *supra* footnote 42, and in The Privy Council and the Constitution (1939), 17 *Can.Bar Rev.* 579. As long ago as 1884 Mr Justice Loranger was arguing that the residue of powers in Canada was in provincial hands: *Letters upon the Interpretation of the Federal Constitution Known as the British North America Act, 1867* (Quebec, 1884) p. 46.

45 *Citizens Insurance* v. *Parsons* (1881), 7 App. Cas. 96.

it merely held that the ordinary contracts relating to a trade were matters of property and civil rights – a proposition difficult to quarrel with. It was the *dicta* in that case, now firmly established as law, which did the damage, particularly the rule excluding particular trades (later extended to cover groups of trades[46]) from federal regulation unless expressly mentioned in section 91 outside the Trade and Commerce clause. This rule was clinched in the Insurance cases.[47] It may make sense according to the narrowest rules of interpretation for ordinary statutes, but it makes little sense in a national constitution. The historian sees the problem differently: 'The enumeration of these definite powers did not exhaust the trade and commerce clause anymore than the trade and commerce clause exhausted the economic powers implied in the general authority to make laws for the peace, order and good government of Canada.'[48] The judicial view, besides refusing to see the enumerated heads as mere examples of the general power, assumes that the drafters of the Constitution wished for no federal authority over any individual trade other than the only one specially mentioned, namely Banking, regardless of the size it might assume or the degree of dependence of the whole economy upon it. This does not harmonize with the concept of 'general interest' as a source of federal power. Hence even so major a trade as that in wheat has had to have its legal base in federal law bolstered by the clumsy device of declaring all grain elevators in the prairies to be works for the general advantage of Canada.[49] Add to this the later judicial holding that the word 'regulation' excluded prohibition,[50] so that the prohibition of production and trading (for example, in margarine[51]) is a provincial matter, and the hollowness of federal authority over this all important and highly emphasized subject is evident. Even the federal control of prices is of dubious validity in peacetime,[52] though it is not easy to see how ten local governments can control prices in a country with internal free trade. True, federal trade policies through credit control, international trade agreements, tariffs and the criminal law are of great importance, but the direct reliance upon the words 'Regulation of Trade and Commerce' is of little use.

Dominion regulation of Agriculture and Fisheries has received similar treatment. The federal law protecting the dairy industry by prohibiting the produc-

46 *The Natural Products Marketing* case, [1937] A.C. 377.
47 Particularly the *Reference* case in [1916] 1 A.C. 588.
48 Creighton, British North America at Confederation, p. 55.
49 To overcome the effect of *The King* v. *Eastern Terminal Elevator Co.* [1925] S.C.R. 434. See 3 Geo. VI, 1939, c. 36, s. 68.
50 In the *Ontario Liquor License* case, [1896] A.C. 348, at p. 363.
51 [1951] A.C. 179
52 Since the *Board of Commerce* case, [1922] 1 A.C. 191.

tion of margarine,[53] and the federal Wheat Act itself,[54] were not considered laws relating to Agriculture, nor was the Natural Products Marketing Act of 1934.[55] The all embracing Property and Civil Rights clause prevailed in these fields also. The Dominion's 'exclusive' power to regulate fisheries has long since ceased to be exclusive. Moreover, 'Fisheries' does not include putting fish in cans or in refrigerating cars.[56] Once a potato or a codfish comes to be packed, processed, shipped and sold it is Trade and Commerce, not Agriculture or Fisheries, and if confined to intra-provincial trade falls under provincial control. Under a constitution the text of which gives exclusive jurisdiction over the Regulation of Trade and Commerce, and over Seacoast and Inland Fisheries, to the central government, as well as concurrent jurisdiction over Agriculture, a provincial Natural Products Marketing Act covering the following extensive operations was held to be a matter of 'Property and Civil Rights': 'The control and regulation in any or all respects of the transportation, packing, storage and marketing of natural products within the Province, including the prohibition of such transportation, packing, storage and marketing in whole or in part,' a natural product being defined as any product of 'agriculture, or of the forest, sea, lake or river, and any article of food or drink wholly or partly manufactured or derived from any such product.'[57] A federal Marketing Act of similar scope has been held to be invalid as trenching on the provincial field.[58] The enlargement of provincial control of trade and commerce was crowned by Lord Haldane, overruling the Supreme Court, when he held that companies created by a province had the capacity to do business anywhere across provincial boundaries, if granted permission from the outside authority.[59] Hence nation-wide trade and commerce can be carried on by a provincial creature.

Treaty legislation is a matter of growing import to all states, both federal and unitary, in a shrinking world. Goods manufactured in and exported from a Canadian province, if produced under working standards and conditions below those of the country of import, carry with them a dangerous power to destroy the higher standards. Provincial legislation or its absence may thus affect vitally the lives of people in foreign countries. Any treaty binding Canada or even one province of Canada, if between the Empire and a foreign country, can be implemented exclusively by Ottawa under section 132 of the Constitution. But by defining an

53 *Supra* footnote 51.
54 *Supra* footnote 49.
55 *Supra* footnote 46.
56 *A.-G. for Canada* v. *A.-G. for B.C.,* [1930] A.C. 111.
57 The British Columbia statute of 1936, held *intra vires* in *Shannon* v. *Lower Mainland Dairy Products Board*, [1938] A.C. 708.
58 *Supra* footnote 46.
59 *Bonanza Creek Gold Mining Co.* v. *The King*, [1916] 1 A.C. 566.

Empire treaty as one made by the King on the advice of an Imperial executive, excluding those made on the advice also of the Canadian executive, the courts removed the Canadian-made treaty from section 132; and, after stating in the *Radio* case[60] that it would therefore fall in the Dominion residue under peace, order and good government, changed their minds in the ILO Conventions reference and held such legislation to be within the competence of whichever legislature had jurisdiction over the subject matter of the treaty under sections 91 and 92.[61] Thus the only single treaty-enforcing power was in effect removed from the Constitution, since Empire treaties have vanished with the Empire. To-day the fact that a subject of legislation becomes of such international importance as to reach treaty formulation does not necessarily endow Ottawa with legislative jurisdiction over it. The question of jurisdiction is tested by the courts as if there were no treaty at all. The fact that is all-important becomes non-existent. Canadian provinces, which under the BNA Act are specifically deprived of jurisdiction even over a ferry connecting them with a foreign country,[62] have full jurisdiction over the implementation of conventions treating of wages, hours of labour, and other matters otherwise within section 92, even though made between Canada and many foreign countries.

Admittedly the treaty-making power is a difficult one to distribute in a federal state. Recognition of this fact is seen in the special provisions in the Charter of the International Labour Organization on the implementation of its conventions by countries whose powers are subject to limitations. There is an inescapable dilemma: either the central government has jurisdiction over all treaties, in which case the local governments are no longer sure of their autonomous powers, since at any moment a treaty may be made which will remove its subject matter from their competence, or else the central government, which alone may make and ratify the treaty, must defer to local governments for the implementation of some or all of them, in which case the freedom of the state to assist in building international co-operation is sharply curtailed. A choice must be made between the two values, one of local sovereignty, the other of world peace.

The subject is too wide for full treatment here, but some comment is relevant to the problem of centralization in Canada. The question is, 'Which attribution of jurisdiction is the more consistent with Canada's type of federalism?' If the argument is sound, as used by the Privy Council in the *ILO Conventions* case, that to give Ottawa the same jurisdiction over Canadian treaties as it unquestionably has over 'Empire' treaties, would 'undermine the constitutional safeguards

60 [1932] A.C. 304
61 [1937] A.C. 326.
62 BNA Act, s. 91, head 13.

of provincial constitutional autonomy,' one is tempted to ask why this argument did not prevent the Fathers of Confederation from placing in Ottawa's hands those numerous powers (disallowance, Empire treaties, declaratory power for local works, etc.) which more seriously threaten that autonomy. Provincial autonomy is expressly limited to matters 'in the province,' while the essence of a treaty is that its subject matter is of international significance. The *Radio* decision put the problem in a truer light when it pointed out that a Canadian convention, though not a treaty within section 132, 'came to the same thing,' because, as their Lordships said:

This idea of Canada as a Dominion being bound by a convention equivalent to a treaty with foreign powers was quite unthought of in 1867. It is the outcome of the gradual development of the position of Canada vis-à-vis to the mother country, Great Britain, which is found in these later days expressed in the Statute of Westminster. It is not, therefore, to be expected that such a matter should be dealt with in explicit words in either s. 91 or s. 92. The only class of treaty which would bind Canada was thought of as a treaty by Great Britain, and that was provided for by s. 132. Being, therefore, not mentioned explicitly in either s. 91 or s. 92, such legislation falls within the general words at the opening of s. 91 which assign to the Government of the Dominion the power to make laws,
'for the peace, order, and good government of Canada in relation to all matters not coming within the classes of subjects by this Act assigned exclusively to the legislatures of the Provinces.'
In fine, though agreeing that the Convention was not such a treaty as is defined in s. 132, their Lordships think that it comes to the same thing.

And further: 'The result is in their Lordships' opinion clear. It is Canada as a whole which is amenable to the other powers for the proper carrying out of the convention; and to prevent individuals in Canada infringing the stipulations of the convention it is necessary that the Dominion should pass legislation which should apply to all the dwellers in Canada.'[63]

It is difficult not to believe that this view harmonizes better with the whole intent and spirit of the BNA Act than the opposite view adopted only five years later by a Judicial Committee whose personnel was totally different from that which decided the *Radio* case. And if the fanciful notion exists that Ottawa might use the treaty power as a device to extend its jurisdiction unwarrantably at provincial expense, the firm rule that colourable legislation – the attempt to dress up *ultra vires* statutes in some pretended constitutional form – is prohibited is

63 [1932] A.C. 304, at pp. 312–3.

available to the courts to prevent the invasion. No doubt other principles of control would be found if the necessity were to arise – for example, that the special and exceptional provision for federal remedial legislation in educational matters under section 93 precludes any other form of federal legislation such as might occur in implementing a treaty touching on education.

In the result, whereas up to 1937 the federal Parliament was able to legislate on all treaties and conventions binding on Canada, and had in fact so legislated so as to override provincial authority in four instances,[64] after 1937 the treaty-enforcing power in Canada was decentralized and Ottawa was deprived of a power held effectively for seventy years. A major constitutional limitation in international affairs was imposed on the Canadian nation in the very decade in which she finally achieved full national status. No other federal state in the world is so restricted, and in an age desperately seeking new bases for international co-operation such national weaknesses become something more than domestic problems. The Sirois Report recommended that Parliament be given power to implement ILO conventions, but this seems but a partial solution. Many other international organizations besides the ILO are engaged in important international work which Canada should be free to assist. The only way out now, short of further judicial interpretations and distinctions, would seem to be by amendment to the BNA Act granting Ottawa a treaty power hedged with defined safeguards against its possible use to overthrow the existing minority rights which everyone in Canada is agreed should be protected.

When a court declares that Ottawa is incapable of legislating on a certain subject it nearly always follows that the provinces have the jurisdiction. What is not centralized is decentralized. This is not always true, since some matters are withheld altogether from Canadian legislative competence and can only be dealt with through constitutional amendment adopted in the United Kingdom Parliament. For example, there is a prohibition in section 125 against taxing Crown lands, which applies to both Parliament and the provinces, and in 122 against establishing interprovincial tariffs. Then too a particular statute, as distinct from a 'class of subjects,' may be held *ultra vires* because it contains two or more matters which are unseverable, some of which are legitimate to Parliament and others

---

64 The four examples are (i) the Japanese Treaty Act of 1913 overrode a British Columbia statute applying to employment of Japanese, *Brooks-Bidlake and Whittall Ltd*. v. *A.-G. for B.C.*, [1923] A.C. 450; (ii) the Migratory Birds Convention Act of 1917 overrode a contrary provision in the Game Protection Act of Manitoba, *Rex* v. *Stuart*, [1924] 3 W.W.R. 648; (iii) the Radio Convention of 1927 upheld the Dominion jurisdiction over broadcasting, though a second ground was found in s. 92, head 10(a) of the BNA Act, *Radio Reference*, [1932] A.C. 304; (iv) the Aeronautics Convention of 1919 gave validity to Dominion regulations based upon it, *Aeronautics Reference*, [1932] A.C. 54.

not. But in general the denial of a specific power to the central government is the same as attributing it to the local governments.

Hence, in the process of judicial interpretation narrowing federal powers, large accretions of jurisdiction have come into provincial hands. The regulation of intra-provincial trade and commerce, including trade in the products of fisheries and agriculture, is no mean power for provinces the size of several in Canada, especially when it includes control of production. The jurisdiction over industrial disputes, even when between nation-wide industries and nation-wide trade unions, is a truly vast extension of the concept of 'Property and Civil Rights in the Province,' yet the Privy Council overruled Canadian courts which had held the federal Industrial Disputes Investigation Act to be a matter of Regulation of Trade and Commerce, for the protection of national peace, order and good government, and Criminal Law.[65] A national scheme of unemployment insurance of a type usual today was also held beyond federal jurisdiction,[66] and now it is generally assumed that any contributory health or pension scheme is a provincial matter except where constitutional amendment has changed the original law. A whole range of international conventions relating to wages, hours of labour, weekly day of rest and employment of women and children, even after Canada has ratified them, must be made law in ten provincial legislatures before they take effect, which is another way of saying that no Canadian legislature ever sees them. Provincial control of marketing is so wide that a carefully drawn federal statute on the same subject, attempting to steer clear of the provincial field, was upset in the courts, even though every provincial legislature in Canada had passed supporting legislation so that for once legislative consent was unanimous that the federal law was needed. Just as in the United States, until the spirit of the New Deal had transformed public opinion and with it judicial opinion, the courts were adverse to new forms of social legislation, so in Canada they appear to have built the same constitutional barriers to social change, with this difference that whereas between 1937 and 1947 the United States Supreme Court, recognizing the inevitable, overruled its previous decisions 32 times,[67] the courts of last resort in Canada have shown no equivalent flexibility. Whenever the Privy Council has attempted a more liberal approach, as in the *Radio* and *Temperance Act* cases, a later Board has restored the judicial *status quo*.[68]

Besides these decisions affecting the distribution of powers as between sections 91 and 92, the provinces also benefitted by the two leading cases which (a) established their possession not of delegated but of sovereign powers within their

65 *Toronto Electric Commissioners* v. *Snider*, [1925] A.C. 396.
66 *Employment Insurance Reference*, [1937] A.C. 355.
67 See Pritchett, The Roosevelt Court (1948) p. 57.
68 As in the *ILO Conventions* and *Margarine References, supra* footnotes 61 and 51.

spheres, including the power of delegation to subordinate agencies,[69] and (b) defined the position of Lieutenant-Governor as the direct representative of the Crown, possessed of the attendant royal prerogatives.[70] While these decisions did not greatly enlarge the provincial sphere of jurisdiction, they added much prestige to the claims of provincial autonomists. Well might J.B. Haldane, as he then was, write as far back as 1899 of the work of Lord Watson, whose provincial leanings he so flattered by later imitation:

[Watson] made the business of laying down the new law that was necessary his own. He completely altered the tendency of the decisions of the Supreme Court, and established in the first place the sovereignty (subject to the power to interfere of the Imperial Parliament alone) of the legislatures of Ontario, Quebec and the other Provinces. He then worked out as a principle the direct relation, in point of exercise of the prerogative, of the Lieutenant-Governors to the Crown. In a series of masterly judgments he expounded and established the real constitution of Canada. The liquor laws, the Indian reserve lands, the title to regalia, including the precious metals, were brought before a Judicial Committee, in which he took the leading part, for consideration as to which of the rival claims to legislate ought to prevail. Nowhere is his memory likely to be more gratefully preserved than in those distant Canadian provinces whose rights of self-government he placed on a basis that was both intelligible and firm.[71]

Years later he repeated the same idea, remarking how under Lord Watson 'The, constitution of Canada took a new form.'[72] This avowal of the political rôle of the Privy Council at least does not lack frankness.

CENTRALIZATION BY AMENDMENT

The trend to decentralization in the law of the Canadian constitution has had less damaging results on national policy than otherwise would inevitably have occurred, because the advent of war in 1939 brought the 'emergency' doctrine into play. Instantly provincial autonomy gave way, to the extent considered necessary by Ottawa to overcome the emergency. No single federal wartime control of any importance met constitutional difficulties. When the war ended, a theory of transitional emergency operated, and such continuing measures as survived the policy of 'orderly de-control,' like rent control, were upheld in the courts as late

69 *Hodge* v. *Regina* (1883), 9 App. Cas. 117.
70 *Liquidators of the Maritime Bank* v. *Receiver General of New Brunswick* [1892] A.C. 437.
71 (1899), 2 Juridical Review at pp. 279–80.
72 From the *Cambridge Law Journal* of 1922, cited (1930), 8 *Can. Bar Rev.* at p. 439.

as 1950 on the ground that the emergency had not ceased.[73] Now a 'cold war' exists which might easily (who knows?) be a new emergency of indefinite duration. Certainly the notion of what constitutes 'Defence' has greatly enlarged, and with it federal authority. It is possible that much of the law of the constitution discussed here will never again see the light of day because of world events, and that the centralization issue will be settled outside the law courts and outside Canada. But this notion, like the fear of world destruction in an atomic war, is scarcely one on which life can be planned.

Despite war emergency powers, the Canadian people have found it desirable to overcome some of the effects of judicial interpretation by constitutional amendment. In 1940 the subject of unemployment insurance was made an exclusive federal power, becoming section 91, clause 2A, thus doing away with the effects of the 1937 *Reference* decision. Then in 1951 the Parliament of Canada was given power to legislate for old age pensions, by the addition of section 94A to the BNA Act. These are the only two changes in the distribution of legislative power between Ottawa and the provinces by direct amendment to the BNA Act since 1867. Both have made for a further degree of centralization.

The latest amendment, however, has introduced an entirely new principle to Canadian constitutional law. Hitherto all legislative power in Canada has been definable as either exclusive, that is to say exerciseable by either Parliament or the legislatures alone, or concurrent, as in the case of Agriculture and Immigration under section 95, exerciseable by either authority but with the federal law always prevailing. Judicial interpretation had evolved a notion of overlapping powers, but here again federal law was paramount. The wording of the recent pensions amendment is quite different. It states that any federal law 'shall not affect the operation of any law, present or future, of a provincial legislature in relation to old age pensions.' In other words, the attribution of the pensions power to Ottawa is subject to the condition that it must not affect the provinces' right to establish any provincial pension plan they desire at any time. If there is a conflict, present or future, between the two systems, national and local (which is an improbable but not impossible eventuality), the national must give way. Thus for the first time in Canadian constitutional history a matter within federal competence has been rendered subordinate to provincial law. Whereas the Quebec and London Resolutions each provided that, 'In regard to all subjects over which jurisdiction belongs to both the General and Local Legislatures, the laws of the General Parliament shall control and supersede those made by the Local Legislature, and the latter shall be void so far as they are repugnant to or inconsistent

73 *Supra*, footnote 35.

with the former,'[74] the trend to decentralization in Canada has changed the compact of Confederation and introduced the opposite principle. Canada now has the American doctrine of nullification, that is, the right of a State to set aside national laws, written into this part of her constitution. She seems almost ready for the Hayne-Webster debate that took place in the United States Senate in 1830.[75]

THE PRESENT SITUATION

To say that judicial interpretation has whittled down federal powers, to such an extent as to alter the original balance of the constitution, is not the same as saying that it has, as a political fact, enlarged provincial powers to an equivalent extent. Provinces have much more status and legal authority now than they started with – that is obvious. But this is not the same thing as saying that provincial governments can exercise their jurisdiction. Many considerations may prevent or render ineffective the exercise of a constitutional power. Not a single Canadian province has directly implemented an ILO convention. Since they do not take part in the international processes by which the conventions are drawn up and adopted, and since no one province can be sure the others will follow its lead if it sets an example, they are not likely to. Provinces now have the power to protect their dairy industries by prohibiting the production and sale of margarine, and Quebec, for example, has done so. But Quebec's dairy farmers are not in fact protected by Quebec law, since margarine production elsewhere in Canada directly affects the Quebec butter price. Only the fact that Ottawa puts a floor price under butter helps the Quebec farmers. Similarly the control of labour relations outside the limited Dominion field, even in many nation-wide industries organized by a single trade union, comes within provincial jurisdiction. Yet provincial law may be quite powerless to control the situation that develops when a whole industry is struck by that one union, as the history of the Canada-wide Packinghouse Workers strike in 1947 clearly showed. The helplessness of the national government in that situation, and the pathetic attempts of several provincial premiers to settle the dispute by provincial action, were a sufficient commentary on false notions of provincial autonomy. This autonomy is equally hollow in face of the present challenge of inflation. If to these examples are added the numerous types of social insurance where the financing of legislative schemes is far beyond the resources of some if not all the provinces, the natural limits of a policy of decentralization are readily seen. Provincial autonomy becomes national inactivity.

74 Q.R. 45; L.R. 44.
75 On nullification and its history see *e.g.* Swisher, *American Constitutional Development* (1943) pp. 234 ff.

When governments are incapable of acting, private interests have a freer hand, and since within the private enterprise sphere a high degree of centralized control has developed, this in turn means that decentralization in provincial hands protects centralization in private hands. Thus centralization is not avoided by provincial autonomy, but is encouraged in another form – one over which the French Canadian element has far less influence than it has at Ottawa. A discussion of the social consequences of this situation is not relevant to the subject of this paper, but should the Canadian people desire a larger measure of economic control and social security than they now possess, they will find their path bristling with legal obstacles. The constitutional problem is not always a valid excuse for Ottawa's inaction, but it constantly appears as an almost insuperable barrier to the adoption of certain kinds of national policy.

A solution frequently put forward by provincial leaders, particularly those from the wealthier provinces, is that the provinces should be granted wider powers of taxation by direct constitutional amendment, by increased federal grants, or by the withdrawal of Ottawa from existing provincial fields like the income tax so as to allow of provincial increases. A proposal to give provinces limited powers of indirect taxation was close to adoption both in 1936 and at the time of the recent pensions amendment. With more income, it is argued, provinces could finance more of their own services, and the dangers of centralization could be avoided. Up to a point this argument has force. There is no doubt that the financial arrangement at Confederation, which confined provinces to 'Direct Taxation within the Province,' supplemented by limited federal subsidies, is quite unsuited to the new responsibilities provincial governments must assume as a result of judicial interpretation and growing industrialisation. Public finance and constitutional law cannot be based on two opposing theories of federalism, without a serious decrease in governmental efficiency and an increase in social tensions.

The Sirois Report gave one answer to this problem. Its proposals, however, were not adopted. Wartime taxation agreements with all provinces took their place, and post-war agreements of similar type with all provinces but Ontario and Quebec enabled Canada to carry on. The refusal of the two central provinces to accept the post-war agreements was the reason given by Ottawa for its inability to proceed with the social security provisions offered in 1945.[76] The social cost of reliance on unanimous provincial consent was thus made very evident. While the case for more permanent provincial income is strong, certain objections to it are equally plain. The disparity in wealth between economic regions in Canada means that too great a reliance on a provincial tax base produces marked inequal-

76 The story of these arrangements will be found in Buck, *Financing Canadian Government* (1949) chaps. 9–10. See also Eggleston, *The Road to Nationhood* (1946.)

ity of social services in different provinces. The accident of birth means the difference between good health, education and opportunity for Canadian children in more developed provinces and severe handicaps in the poorer ones. Production and industrial location are adversely affected by varying tax burdens, and low standard areas threaten the stability of achievements in the more advanced provinces. These differences create political tensions and perpetuate conflicts between regions. Under-developed provinces within Canada cause the same kind of unrest as under-developed countries create in the international world.

Other ways around the problem, short of outright amendment, are being tried. *Ad hoc* arrangements worked out at Dominion-Provincial conferences seem the order of the day. They provide no certainty of solution, and at best only a temporary stability. No province can be compelled to agree, no law prevents provinces repudiating any agreement when made. In any event, the matters on which agreement can be reached are mostly confined to financial relations. It is impossible in such a conference to agree on an inter-governmental delegation of responsibility, since that kind of delegation is prohibited.[77] Hence, unless there is agreement to amend the constitution, no such problem as is presented by Dominion lack of jurisdiction over price-control, or marketing of agricultural produce, or industrial relations in nation-wide industries, can be faced. If the result is merely to augment Ottawa's payments to provinces, leaving them free to spend the money as they will, then a dangerous gulf between the tax gathering and expending authorities is created, with provincial governments becoming dependent on federal largesse.

In so far as the conferences attempt to develop into constituent assemblies for the amendment of the Constitution, as they did with respect to the pensions amendment of 1951 and during the discussions seeking to find a new procedure for amendment in 1950, they suffer from two serious defects – first, the requirement of unanimity, so that, for example, the province of Prince Edward Island, with 0.7% of the population, can frustrate the will of the rest of the country, and, secondly, the unrepresentative character of the conferences, which speak for the political party in power at the moment in the Dominion and in each province and not for the opposition parties as well. It is generally recognized in Canada that the present constitutional state of affairs is unsatisfactory, and particularly that a method for amending the constitution of the country inside Canada must be found. So strong is the fear of centralization, however, particularly in Quebec, that the constitutional conference summoned in 1950 adjourned at the end of the year *sine die*.[78]

77 *A.-G. for Canada* v. *A.-G. for Nova Scotia*, [1951] S.C.R. 31, now in appeal.
78 See the two volumes published by the King's Printer, Ottawa, 1950, entitled, respective-

The most important political factor in the problem of centralization, as in so many other Canadian matters, lies in the power relations existing between Quebec and Ottawa, which in turn reflect the basic racial factors in Canadian life. This at the moment is a more difficult relationship to bring into satisfactory balance than is the other great factor, the power relationship between business and government. The consolidation of Quebec as a bastion of the French Canadian race is a firm policy of every Quebec government, made more explicit in recent years under the Union Nationale party of Premier Duplessis. Centralization appears to threaten this bastion, therefore it must be opposed in principle. This does not mean that Quebec will oppose every suggestion of an increase of federal powers, but that it will look at each proposal on its merits and decide for itself whether it is desirable or not. Quebec wishes to retain the right of veto which as a matter of recent constitutional convention she appears to have achieved. Hence the difficulty of attaining any general method of amending the Constitution by which the Parliament of Canada and a majority of provinces could impose a change not acceptable to Quebec. So far the willingness of all other provinces to surround the minority rights in the constitution with special safeguards against amendment by majority vote has not brought the parties to agreement.

In so far as the original constitution is concerned, it is significant that the BNA Act protects Quebec's rights in respect of language, denominational schools and the civil law, but not in respect of those other forms of centralized authority referred to. Quebec's lieutenant-governor, her senators and judges are selected by the same centralized power of appointment as is provided for the other provinces. There were no special political privileges accorded Quebec in the Constitution, only cultural ones. Politically, all Canadians are on an equal footing, except the Indians. Quebec laws are subject to the same disallowance as other provincial laws. What then is threatened in Quebec's special position by the advance of federal jurisdiction in matters of national concern? Not language rights, since federal laws and courts must use the two languages. Indeed an extension of federal control means an extension of the two official languages throughout Canada. It is unlikely that there would be French radio stations on the prairies today if radio broadcasting had been held to be provincial. As regards educational matters, it is difficult to take seriously the fear that the school rights defined in section 93 are threatened by an extension of federal power, since all groups in Canada are agreed that these rights must be entrenched against amendment without unanimous vote of all provinces. The question whether Ottawa should make grants to provinces for educational purposes is thus quite separate from the question whether there

ly, *Constitutional Conference of Federal and Provincial Governments, Ottawa Jan. 10–12, 1950*, and *do. Quebec, Sept. 25–28, 1950.*

should be a shift in legislative powers; Ottawa could make and has recently made such grants without any constitutional amendment, since no province is obliged to accept them and no legislative jurisdiction is changed. It is the third of Quebec's guarantees, her jurisdiction over 'Property and Civil Rights in the Province,' and hence over her civil law, which seems to be most affected by centralization. A federal control of rents, for example, does affect the civil law contract of lease and hire, and no one could pretend the contrary.

Yet the history of the survival of the civil law suggests that it has much the same kind of change to fear from provincial autonomy as it has from centralization. In either case the civil law, like all systems of private law, is going through constant adaptation to new social needs. We can observe that since 1867 the legislature of Quebec in the exercise of its autonomy has adopted a truly formidable list of statutes which have superimposed upon the civil law a body of new rules affecting or restraining its application. Many of these rules are barely distinguishable from the statutes of common law provinces on the same subjects. Laws dealing with corporations, workmen's compensation, minimum wages, hours of labour, industrial standards, pensions, public health, traffic regulation, collective bargaining, rent control, and so forth, have a common content throughout Canada because they confront a common social and economic situation. The more Quebec becomes industrialized, the more this will be true. As Professor Keirstead has said:

Quebec cannot maintain its cultural values intact by attempting to maintain a separate economy and distinct political entity, for the provincial area is inadequate for proper economic controls and the Quebec economy would continue to reflect the exploitation and instability of the national economy. Even if Quebec were an independent state the process of exploitation of the French worker, the gradual denudation of the countryside, the gradual undermining of the small-town, small-scale French-Canadian entrepreneur would continue with the consequent corruption of French-Canadian culture. The only salvation for Quebec as a cultural entity, we hope to show, must be in common effort with all Canadians to resolve economic conflict and establish economic stability on a national scale.[79]

What is happening, and what nothing can prevent, is the emergence of new aspects of property and civil rights, which have to be dealt with on new principles not found in either the civil or the common law. Most of these new aspects the courts have classified as belonging to the old category of property and civil rights, and hence have placed under provincial jurisdiction. It is only in these fringe sub-

79 In Brady and Scott, *Canada After the War* (1943) pp. 17–18.

jects, that is to say subjects of recent development, that there is any need or desire for centralization, and only for some of them which clearly are of national scope and.importance. No federal government is ever going to attempt to enact a general body of private law which could become a code for all Canada, replacing the Civil Code of Quebec. In these fringe subjects, there is little that is purely cultural. The problem created by a provincial truck when competing with a federal railway can scarcely be classed as a cultural one, yet the national railway system and freight rate structure is today being undermined by the absence of a national control over highway trucking.

Too much centralization invites tyranny, too little creates anarchy. Both tyranny and anarchy are a threat to the cultural survival of both the British and French traditions in Canada. The argument here submitted is that although there is an increasing pressure for some further centralization of authority in Canada, notably in relation to economic regulation, insurance against calculable risks of modern society such as old age and ill health, and international obligations, this development is not in conflict with the basic principles of Canadian federalism but on the contrary is their proper expression in this day and age. It is submitted also that the cultural values of Quebec in particular, and of other regions also, are in less danger of being crushed out by this limited degree of centralization than they would be if it did not take place. It may be that the constitutional issue is already settled in favour of much greater centralization than is here contemplated, because we are in the midst of a period of such prolonged international unrest as to make the 'emergency' in effect permanent.[80] It may be that the one word 'Defence' in section 91 will grow to be a new residuary clause in the Constitution. We can but hope that this will not prove true. Already it has made the federal government the biggest employer, the biggest landlord and the biggest contractor in the country. Defence needs, however, do not give Canadians social security, and do not settle the vexed question of the proper procedure for constitutional amendment. There is still need for agreement on the basic issues here raised. A plea for adherence to the original concepts of Canadian federalism wisely embodied in the Constitution of 1867 may not be out of order. Under that constitution we can all be Canadians without ceasing to enjoy our political and cultural freedoms.

80 See for example the remarkable degree of centralization provided in the Emergency Powers Act and the Defence Production Act adopted by the Parliament of Canada in 1951.

# XXI

# Canada et Canada français

*Here I discuss the 'double miracle,' the survival of French Canada as against the whole continent, and the survival of the Canadian nation as against the southern part of it.*

From the Paris journal *Esprit*, août–sept. 1952, 178–89

Il y a deux miracles dans l'histoire du Canada. Le premier c'est la survivance du Canada français, et le second, la survivance du Canada.

La cession de 1763 coupait le Canada françsis de tout contact avec la France. Les gouverneurs et administrateurs français rentrèrent chez eux, abandonnant à la seule direction de leurs prêtes et de quelques [notaires] soixante-cinq milles habitants. La colonie se vit donc séparée du tronc maternel alors que ses racines n'étaient pas encore solidement ancrées au sol. Quoique homogène, la population vivait dans des communautés dispersées le long du Saint-Laurent ; le transport et les communications étaient extrêmement difficiles ; le nouveau gouvernement était formé d'Anglais protestants habitués à considérer les Français et les catholiques comme des ennemis traditionnels ; le commercialisme nord-américain allait, en se développant, pousser ses tentacules autour et à l'intérieur des seigneuries. Aucun historien au courant de ces faits n'aurait été étonné de voir les Canadiens-français subir sur ce continent la même évolution que plusieurs autres groupes raciaux. Les Canadiens-français auraient pu adopter graduellement le mode de vie et les moeurs de leur entourage ; ils auraient pu, comme les Français de la Louisiane, ne conserver que des reliques de culture, quelques lois anciennes et des célébrations nostalgiques. Bien au contraire, ils sont restés fermement attachés à leur religion, à leur langue et à leurs lois civiles. Aux forces étrangères, ils ont offert un front uni, ils ont survécu, formant une communauté distincte qui possède plusieurs des caractéristiques d'une nation à part. Voilà le premier miracle.

Le Canada, cependant, ne se limite pas au Québec. C'est, aujourd'hui, un pays plus vaste que les États-Unis, avec une population de 14,000,000, qui augmente rapidement au rythme du développement de ressources presque illimitées. C'est une nation qui a déjà de l'influence dans les affaires mondiales, et qui est destinée à en avoir encore davantage. Nous sommes cependant portés à oublier que cette croissance d'un État unique, distinct des États-Unis, fut longtemps compromise. Le Canada français était menacé d'assimilation culturelle, de même que le Canada tout entier était menacé d'assimilation politique. Après 1763, la domination britannique en Amérique s'étendait de l'océan Arctique au golfe du Mexique. Cette unité politique eût pu se perpétuer. Le Québec fût alors devenu un autre État de l'Union. Mais à la suite d'événements dont le Canada ne fut pas responsable, l'Angleterre perdit ses colonies américaines, moins celles du nord, notamment la Nouvelle-Écosse et le Québec. Elle conserva celles-ci grâce à sa puissance navale ; et aussi parce que les Français refusèrent la proposition que leur adressa, en 1774, le Congrès continental, d'unir leurs destinées à celles des colonies du sud. Le continent nord-américain fut donc divisé une fois de plus, et la frontière canado-américaine commença de se dessiner.

Il fallait encore surmonter de grandes difficultés avant que les « arpents de neige » pussent d'abord être peuplés, puis rassemblés sous un même gouvernement. Pendant nombre d'années, l'Amérique, dont la « destinée manifeste » était de s'étendre vers le nord jusqu'au pôle, regarda d'un oeil envieux les dernières possessions britanniques. Des armées américaines envahirent le Canada en 1775 et au cours de la guerre de 1812-14 ; à plusieurs reprises, à l'occasion de disputes de frontière, Washington présenta d'extravagantes réclamations de territoire canadien ; après 1850, les plaines de l'ouest faillirent être englouties par le flux des colons américains. La géographie semblait faire du Canada une partie intégrante de l'économie américaine. Et pourtant, il existe aujourd'hui une nation canadienne, plus décidée que jamais à demeurer politiquement indépendante. Voilà le second miracle.

Tout événement historique a des causes ; parler d'un miracle, en histoire, c'est tout simplement exprimer son étonnement devant des résultats inattendus. Il existe des causes tangibles à la survivance du Canada français. La première, c'est le désir de survivre du peuple lui-même et de ses chefs. Le sens d'une « mission », d'un devoir, celui de protéger la culture français et catholique en Amérique contre toute influence qui eût pu la détruire, a donné aux Canadiens français une direction, un but qui les a grandement aidés à conserver leur identité. Le cataclysme que fut le changement d'allégeance, en 1763, a replié le peuple sur lui-même et l'a contraint de ne compter que sur ses propres ressources, tout en augmentant son attachement à sa terre d'adoption. C'est ainsi que le Canada français a acquis le sens du canadianisme avant les colons britanniques, qui ne furent jamais coupés de leur mère-patrie ; il fut difficile à ceux-ci de décider s'ils formaient un pays nouveau ou n'étaient qu'une extension du vieux pays.

Le désir de survivre ne saurait pourtant suffire à assurer la survivance dans des conditions extérieures trop pénibles. Heureusement pour les Canadiens-français, deux facteurs extérieurs les aidèrent dans leur lutte pour la survivance. Le premier, c'est que l'Angleterre, devenue leur tête politique, était déjà habituée à l'idée qu'il fallait accorder à ses coloniaux des gouvernements représentatifs. La loi publique anglaise établissait un principe d'autonomie coloniale, beaucoup plus large que tout ce qu'avait connu jusque-là la Nouvelle-France ; les nouveaux sujets du roi anglais pouvaient utiliser ce principe comme une échelle pour atteindre à une plus vaste liberté politique. En 1763, ce principe était étroitement limité ; et cependant, la première Proclamation royale au sujet du Québec, qui date de cette année-là, ordonne au gouverneur « de convoquer et d'appeler des assemblées générales », et d'établir des lois « avec les Représentants du Peuple ». La Révolution américaine retarda de trente ans une telle Assemblée ; mais quand celle-ci se réunit pour la première fois à Québec, en 1792, elle présente une majorité de membres de langue française. Elle n'a aucun pouvoir de décisions, mais possède une voix puissante dans l'administration. La cession de la Nouvelle-France à l'Angleterre s'étant produite avant et non après la Révolution française, c'est de l'Angleterre et non de la France que le Québec reçut ses institutions politiques démocratiques.

Il restait à livrer une longue lutte, jusqu'à la Confédération de 1867, avant que la Province de Québec actuelle n'émergeât avec sa propre législature démocratiquement élue, possédant le contrôle effectif du pouvoir exécutif ainsi qu'une large juridiction sur les affaires locales. Dans cette lutte, la loi et la pratique constitutionnelles anglaises fournirent des armes utiles, que les nationalistes du Québec furent prompts à saisir. Les droits des Anglais furent invoqués pour justifier les réclamations des Français catholiques, et le gouvernement anglais fut pressé de justifier son refus de concéder à ses nouveaux sujets les libertés dont ses anciens jouissaient depuis longtemps. Dans ce mouvement démocratique, les Français trouvèrent chez les réformistes et les libéraux des provinces anglaises des alliés qui désiraient aussi, mais pour d'autres raisons, un gouvernement populaire. Plusieurs de ces derniers avaient appris la démocratie avant de venir au Canada, dans les États de la Nouvelle-Angleterre. En un sens, les Américains avaient raison de dire, dans leur invitation de 1774 aux Canadiens-français, que leur peuple avait été « conquis à la liberté ».

La Révolution américaine fut l'autre facteur heureux pour le Canada français. La révolte des colonies américaines, nouvelle menace pour le pouvoir anglais en Amérique, força l'Angleterre à rechercher des alliés sur place, et lui fit concéder à ses nouveaux sujets de langue française des droits et des garanties qu'en d'autres circonstances ils n'eussent pas obtenus aussi rapidement, si jamais ils les eussent obtenus. L'Acte de Québec (1774) rétablit au Canada la loi civile française pour toutes les questions relatives aux « droits de propriété et aux droits civils » , et renforça la position de l'Église catholique en réimposant la dime comme obligation légale pour les catholiques. Un amendement au Serment d'Allégeance permit aux catholiques d'occuper, sous un roi protestant, des postes publics et des sièges à la législature – ce qui resta interdit aux catholiques d'Angleterre jusqu'au siècle suivant. L'Acte de Québec fut une sorte de Concordat pour le catholicisme canadien. A la première session de la première législature, qui se réunit à Québec en 1792, la langue française fut placée sur un pied d'égalité légale avec la langue anglaise.

Ainsi donc, dès cette première période des relations entre les deux races au Canada, on rejeta la politique d'assimilation pour assurer la politique de la double culture. Plus d'un homme d'état anglais ou canadien, particulièrement Lord Durham, espérait qu'éventuellement les Français accepteraient la langue, les lois et peut-être la religion anglaises. Cependant, une seule fois on a tenté d'établir l'anglais comme seule langue officielle ; l'incident se situe immédiatement après les soulèvements de 1837–38 et fut de courte durée. Le principe du bilinguisme fut rétabli en 1848 et inscrit dans la constitution de 1867, tant pour le Québec que pour le Parlement et les cours fédérales. Toutefois, ce principe était soumis à des limites géographiques que l'expansion des établissements français hors du Québec ne tarda pas à rendre évidentes ; dès lors, elles furent une source de conflit qui ne s'est pas encore tarie. Le Québec est la seule province où les deux langues aient un statut officiel pour les questions provinciales ; le Manitoba est revenu à l'usage de l'anglais en 1890, alors qu'une forte vague de colons de toutes les parties du monde transforma le sentiment populaire.

De même que certains facteurs externes ont facilité la survivance de la culture française au Canada, ainsi la survivance du Canada lui-même, face aux États-Unis, s'est appuyée sur certaines forces extérieures. La première en importance fut la puissance militaire et navale de l'Angleterre. Sans elle, on n'aurait pu garder la moitié septentrionale du continent. Même si occasionnellement on sacrifia les intérêts canadiens dans le règlement de différends anglo-américains, Washington savait que pour annexer le territoire qui est aujourd'hui le Canada, il fallait attaquer un empire mondial trop puissant pour céder aisément. Quand les États-Unis se trouvèrent de taille à gagner une guerre pareille (à supposer qu'ils eussent souhaité s'y engager) l'expansionnisme américain avait décliné et ils se contentèrent de développer leurs propres ressources. Le Canada émergea donc comme État et nation sous l'égide de la Grande-Bretagne. Par l'appropriation et l'extension de la démocratie parlementaire britannique, il parvint à l'indépendance nationale sans avoir jamais dû rompre ses relations avec l'*Empire-Commonwealth*.

Le développement national du Canada bénéficia, en outre de l'assistance de l'Angleterre, de l'existence du Canada français. Les Canadiens de toute race ont menè, au cours du dernier siècle et demi, une double bataille, qui touche heureusement à sa fin. Il y eut la bataille du gouvernement autonome, menée contre la domination de Londres, et la bataille de la sécurité nationale, menée contre Washington. Dans ces deux luttes, l'élément français fut d'un puissant secours aux Canadiens-anglais. Le Québec répugnait naturellement à être dirigé par des gouverneurs anglais, et détestait l'idée que le Canada fût impliqué dans des guerres pour la défense de l'Empire. En certaines occasions, le Québec a senti que, mieux que la majorité anglaise au Parlement fédéral, les autorités de Londres protégeraient ses droits minoritaires ; néanmoins, l'influence du Québec appuyait fortement le droit du Canada à poursuivre sa propre politique, aussi bien internationale que nationale.

C'est donc au Canada, et au Canada central, là où Français et Anglais vinrent en contact étroit, que fut menée et gagnée, vers 1848 la grande bataille pour le gouvernement responsable, qui rendait le Gouverneur responsable devant la majorité de la législature. Le Canada apporta la première contribution à l'élaboration d'idées qui firent du vieil Empire le nouveau Commonwealth. Le Québec fournit plusieurs de ces idées.

Le Québec fut également un rempart contre les influences et les visées américaines. Des régiments canadiens-français combattirent aux côtés des Anglais contre les Américains en 1775-76 et en 1812-14. Le Québec a vu dans plusieurs aspects de la vie américaine des dangers pour ses propres idéaux, plus graves que ceux qu'il pouvait craindre de la majorité anglaise du Canada. La Constitution canadienne contient des garanties pour la langue française et les écoles catholiques. Aux termes de la Constitution américaine, le français n'est pas reconnu, et les écoles confessionnelles ne peuvent recevoir d'aide de l'État. Les Canadiens français constituent environ 30% de la population canadienne ; ils ne constituent pas plus de 4% de la population nord-américaine. Il est dans l'intérêt du Québec que le Canada soit indépendant.

Ainsi, dans l'évolution du Canada comme nation-état, les Canadiens anglais ont également joui d'heureuses associations historiques. Ils ne doivent pas leur survivance à leurs seuls efforts. L'histoire serait pourtant incomplète si l'on n'accordait crédit à certaines formes d'influence américaine qui ont aussi joué leur rôle dans la formation des institutions canadiennes. Pour le Canada, les États-Unis n'ont pas été qu'une menace occasionnelle. Ils lui ont aussi fourni plusieurs idées démocratiques. A l'observateur superficiel, ils ne semblent révéler dans le monde international actuel que le pouvoir du capitalisme américain. Mais l'Amérique possède aussi des traditions démocratiques très vivaces ; les forces réactionnaires et progressives s'y livrent une lutte continuelle. L'une des causes de la lutte que mena le Canada au sein de l'Empire britannique, pour le *self-government* réside en ceci que plusieurs colons venus des États-Unis au Canada après la Révolution américaine, insistèrent pour obtenir au Canada, sous la domination anglaise, autant de *self-government* qu'ils en avaient connu dans les colonies de la Nouvelle-Angleterre. L'Amérique leur avait enseigné une liberté qu'ils ne voulaient pas perdre au Canada. Les syndicats ouvriers américains, plus que les syndicats britanniques, contribuèrent à la fondation du mouvement ouvrier au Canada et dans le Québec. Les syndicats catholiques ne furent guère organisés dans le Québec avant 1921 ; même aujourd'hui, on compte plus de travailleurs du Québec dans les syndicats d'origine américaine que dans les syndicats catholiques. Dans la décade de 1930, le *New Deal* de Roosevelt eut une influence importante sur la législation canadienne. Les corporations américaines contribuèrent aussi grandement au développement des ressources canadiennes – à un point tel que, selon l'opinion de plusieurs, le Canada risque de perdre, par ses liens financiers avec les États-Unis, l'indépendance qu'il a réussi à maintenir dans les questions politiques. Sous ce rapport, le Québec ne diffère pas des autres provinces, car il a bien accueilli le capital américain qui augmente rapidement, aujourd'hui, ses placements à travers la Province. La révolution industrielle du Québec, actuellement en plein essor, est, pour une large part, menée des États-Unis.

Dans la vaste perspective de l'histoire, nous voyons qu'après la cession de 1763 l'idée d'une nation indépendante appelée Canada s'est développée graduellement, grâce aux échanges mutuels entre Anglais et Français, et à leurs relations avec le monde extérieur. En même temps, les deux cultures continuèrent de croître, chacune selon son mode propre, et à s'influencer l'une l'autre sans s'absorber. Le Canada d'aujourd'hui est le fruit d'un mariage arrangé par les parents plutôt que fondé sur l'amour des conjoints, mais c'est un mariage qui exclut toute possibilité de divorce. Quelques nationalistes du Québec ont, il est vrai, rêvé d'un état indépendant appelé « Laurentie », sur les rives du Saint-Laurent, où leurs aspirations seraient satisfaites sans subir les restrictions d'une constitution fédérale qui les prive d'une large part de leur souveraineté ; mais un tel projet s'avère de jour en jour moins réalisable. Dans le monde international, tout comme sur le plan national, l'individualisme politique se meurt, et pour les mêmes raisons. La production massive, l'énergie atomique, les communications rapides et la stratégie globale enlèvent de l'importance aux petites frontières nationales, et forcent l'intégration à un niveau plus élevé. Le contraste entre les conditions de vie de l'Amérique du Nord et celles de l'Amérique du Sud démontre amplement quels avantages offre l'établissement de gouvernements assez vastes pour s'occuper des problèmes communs à des nations voisines. Et nul n'en a mieux pris conscience que Simon Bolivar lui-même ; nombreux sont les monuments qui commémorent son nom et son plan d'Union de l'Amérique latine, mais rares sont les essais de réalisations. En un certain sens, un État fédéral est un gouvernement international, qui unit, pour des fins communes, des pays par ailleurs indépendants. Si le Canada cessait d'exister, les provinces qui le constituent ne deviendraient pas indépendantes, mais seraient inévitablement rattachées à l'Union américaine. Il sera peut-être difficile d'éviter ce dénouement, même si le Canada demeure uni comme il l'est présentement.

Que la grande majorité des Canadiens accepte le fédéralisme bi-culturel qui existe au Canada ne signifie pas que les idées maîtresses du Canada anglais et du Canada français soient similaires. Les deux groupes diffèrent d'opinions sur plusieurs questions importantes ; sur d'autres, ils arrivent aux mêmes conclusions pour des raisons différentes. Le fédéralisme permet au sein du même état de grandes divergences d'opinions. Il n'est donc pas facile de parler d'idées « canadiennes ». Quelques idées sont communes à toutes les parties du Canada ; par exemple, la haine du communisme, et une préférence pour le fédéralisme, par opposition à l'État unitaire. Les deux structures culturelles de base elles-mêmes, l'anglo-protestante et la franco-catholique, bien qu'elles soient nettement distinctes de plusieurs façons, dérivent toutes deux du même corps idéologique que l'on est aujourd'hui convenu d'appeler la civilisation occidentale. Pour un Chinois ou un Arabe, les ressemblances entre les deux cultures du Canada peuvent sembler tout aussi apparentes que leurs différences. Même le visiteur d'Angleterre ou de France découvre, aussi bien dans le Québec que dans l'Ontario, certaines caractéristiques nord-américaines. Et cependant, sur un grand nombre de questions, il n'y a pas au Canada un seul point de vue, mais bien deux attitudes générales dont l'une prévaut dans le Canada français et l'autre dans le Canada anglais. D'une façon ou d'une autre, la politique canadienne doit toujours chercher un équilibre ou un compromis entre ces deux pôles.

Prenons pour exemple l'idée de démocratie. Le Canadien anglais voit dans la démocratie une forme de gouvernement où la volonté populaire s'exprime par un Parlement périodiquement élu. Il croit au suffrage, aux droits égaux des hommes et des femmes, au principe de la liberté d'expression et d'association, à la presse libre et à la tolérance religieuse. La démocratie est pour lui un processus plutôt qu'un ordre social donné. C'est une méthode par laquelle la société peut être constamment changée et améliorée. Il discerne au Canada, et dans nombre de pays dits démocratiques, plusieurs éléments anti-démocratiques qu'il veut faire disparaître. Si ses droits ne sont pas détruits, il croit qu'il pourra éventuellement vaincre ces éléments. La tradition libérale du XIX$^e$ siècle lui a légué une croyance fondamentale aux libertés civiles. Cette attitude procède d'une profonde méfiance à l'égard de l'autorité ecclésiastique ou séculière.

Le Canadien-français possède de la démocratie une tout autre expérience. Il n'en connaissait rien sous l'ancien régime ; ce qu'il en a appris vient de ses rapports avec les Anglais ; ainsi, pour lui, la démocratie s'est tout de suite identifiée à la lutte pour ses droits religieux et linguistiques. Il s'est servi de la démocratie plutôt qu'il n'y a adhéré comme à une doctrine. Son éducation catholique le rend plus conscient des devoirs et des obligations de l'individu que de ses droits personnels, et plus prêt à accepter un ordre hiérarchique. Il insiste donc plus fortement sur les droits des groupes, appelés au Canada droits minoritaires, que sur les libertés individuelles. Il est plus enclin à identifier l'ordre social total de l'Amérique du Nord, y compris le capitalisme contemporain, avec la démocratie, et comme cet ordre ne se conforme pas aisément à son idée d'une société vraiment catholique, il est parfois porté à se méfier de la démocratie elle-même. Ce sentiment est tout particulièrement sensible dès qu'on lui demande de participer à quelque guerre lointaine pour « sauver la démocratie ». Il s'est habitué à la démocratie politique dont il jouit au Canada, et ne voudra probablement pas la supprimer ; mais le mot « démocratie » signifiera d'abord pour lui le droit du Québec à se gouverner lui-même, par opposition à la centralisation du pouvoir à Ottawa, et, en second lieu seulement, le droit qu'a chaque individu de différer d'avis avec ses concitoyens sur les questions de foi, de morale ou de politique. Il se méfie d'une liberté politique qui s'étendrait à un parti communiste, et d'une tolérance religieuse qui permettrait aux Églises protestantes d'exercer leur prosélytisme dans les villages de langue française.

Ces expériences et ces points de vue différents produisent des attitudes différentes devant le fédéralisme canadien. Pour les Canadiens anglais, le système fédéral est d'abord destiné, non à conférer l'autonomie aux provinces, mais à les unir en un seul État. Le Parlement national à Ottawa est donc pour lui le véritable symbole de la nationalité canadienne. C'est un Parlement bilingue, où sont également représentées toutes les parties du Canada, et qui est donc la seule législature du pays qui exprime vraiment l'idée canadienne. Le fait que la population anglaise détienne actuellement la majorité des sièges est heureux pour lui, mais ne lui semble pas pour autant essentiel à la structure fédérale ; le nombre des sujets d'origine britannique n'atteint pas la moitié de la population totale, et les éléments non britanniques augmentent plus rapidement par l'immigration (qui n'est pas surtout britannique) et la plus haute natalité des autres races. Le Canadien anglais ne craint pas la croissance du pouvoir aux mains d'Ottawa, pourvu qu'elle ne dépasse pas des limites raisonnables ; il est plutôt porté à croire que les provinces ont trop de pouvoir et que cela empêche l'adoption de mesures nationales désirables. Il accepte le fait bi-culturel au Canada, mais n'a jamais pensé qu'il faille l'appliquer également dans chaque province ; par exemple, l'idée qu'il faille étendre au delà des Rocheuses les droits accordés dans le Québec aux écoles séparées et à la langue française semble absurde en Colombie-

Britannique. Cette province, étant complètement anglaise quand elle se joignit à la Confédération, juge une telle proposition contraire aux termes de son adhésion. La population de la Colombie-Britannique, sauf une très petite minorité de catholiques, croit à l'autonomie provinciale sur ce point. On trouverait des attitudes semblables dans les autres provinces de langue anglaise.

Le Québec voit ces questions d'un autre oeil. Il croit qu'un pays bi-culturel doit être partout bi-culturel. Il se sent lésé dans ses droits quand il les voit limités par des barrières provinciales. Pour lui, la Confédération n'est pas une simple redistribution de pouvoirs entre gouvernements, mais une sorte de traité entre les deux races, dont le premier but était d'accorder plus de liberté au Québec, et donc de sauvegarder, voire d'augmenter l'autonomie provinciale. Il craint les tendances centralisatrices si évidentes dans l'État industriel moderne. Pour lui, l'accroissement des pouvoirs d'Ottawa ne signifie pas une occasion d'exercer plus largement son influence au Canada, mais ouvre dans les murailles de sa citadelle une brèche par où des forces étrangères envahiront le Québec et corrompront son mode de vie. Pour des raisons que comprennent difficilement les Canadiens anglais, le Québec redoute Ottawa plus que le capitalisme américain. Le gouvernement du Québec défend d'une main la province contre les empiétements du fédéral, et de l'autre main invite de puissantes corporations américaines à développer ses ressources. De ce fait, semble-t-il, le Québec s'attire des transformations de son mode de vie beaucoup plus importantes que celles qui lui pourraient venir du Parlement fédéral. La transformation d'une société agricole en une société industrielle amène une révolution sociale plus profonde que l'acceptation d'un système fédéral d'assurances sociales ou qu'une réglementation fédérale du commerce et de l'industrie. Un jour, peut-être, le Québec partagera l'opinion d'un grand nombre de Canadiens de langue anglaise, qui estiment que seul un gouvernement national est assez puissant pour lutter avec succès contre l'américanisation totale ; qu'une telle résistance est impossible aux dix gouvernements locaux, et qu'une autonomie provinciale exagérée ne peut qu'affaiblir la nation devant un danger croissant.

Il va de soi que sur plusieurs autres questions le point de vue général des Canadiens de langue française soit différent de celui de leurs concitoyens de langue anglaise. Les nouvelles fonctions de l'État, qui consistent à fournir des services sociaux, sont acceptées beaucoup plus facilement dans la communauté anglaise que chez les Français, où l'Église les a si longtemps assumées elle-même. Les ouvriers canadiens-anglais se sont aisément accommodés du syndicalisme américain dans ses grandes lignes ; les ouvriers du Québec, guidés par leurs prêtes, ont été amenés à former, en plus, des syndicats catholiques. Les deux vieux partis politiques, les Libéraux et les Conservateurs, ont tous deux des sections de langue française et de langue anglaise, mais les deux ailes des partis traduisent les intérêts et les points de vue régionaux de leurs membres. Le parti CCF (*Cooperative Commonwealth Federation*), formé plus récemment, est un parti socialiste démocratique du genre anglais ou scandinave, bien établi dans la plupart des autres provinces. Dans le Québec, il lui a été presque impossible de progresser, d'une part, à cause de la méfiance catholique à l'endroit du socialisme sous toutes ses formes et, d'autre part, de la suspicion nationaliste qui pèse sur tout mouvement d'origine anglaise ; cependant, le Québec est un paradis pour les capitalistes et les monopoles privés. Inutile de dire que les causes de ces différences domestiques produisent également des attitudes toutes différentes devant les affaires internationales. Le Canada français est traditionnellement hostile aux complications internationales, et désire laisser le reste du monde vaquer à ses propres affaires ; les institutions internationales, surtout celles où les États-Unis jouent un rôle dominant, ne lui inspirent manifestement pas confiance. A cause de ses attaches britanniques, le Canada anglais a depuis toujours l'habitude de participer aux affaires internationales, y compris les guerres. Il croit plus volontiers à la nécessité du gouvernement international, en dépit des risques d'échec. Nous pourrions peut-être dire que le Canada français est profondément conscient de la faiblesse des entreprises humaines et de la tragédie inéluctable de la vie, alors que les Anglo-Saxons, plus pragmatiques et moins philosophiques, croient que l'intelligence humaine peut, par les moyens politiques et économiques appropriés, accélérer considérablement le rythme du « progrès ».

Toutes les généralisations sur les races et les nations sont dangereuses, y compris celles de cette analyse. Il est dangereux de postuler une seule personnalité qu'on appelle la race, la classe ou la nation, et de lui attribuer des caractères humains. Le Canada français et le Canada anglais d'aujourd'hui sont différents de ce qu'ils étaient hier et de ce qu'ils seront demain. L'industrialisation croissante du Canada révèle de nouveaux phénomènes sociaux qui changeront sans aucun doute les structures raciales du passé. Avec qui l'ouvrier canadien-français d'une corporation américaine géante a-t-il le plus en commun ? Avec ses confrères de langue anglaise dans d'autres usines de la même corporation ? Ou avec les capitalistes canadiens-français qui détiennent des parts dans la corporation ? La race prévaut-elle sur la division des classes ? La religion peut-elle les supplanter toutes deux ? Nous ne pouvons donner une réponse certaine à ces questions. Une race minoritaire qui se croit opprimée comme race accorde une suprême importance à son unité de sang et de langue. Quand les tensions raciales se relâchent, d'autres divisions apparaissent à la surface. Les intérêts et les sentiments des hommes évoluent en même temps que les structures sociales. La solidarité ouvrière n'est pas encore assez forte pour unir tous les ouvriers canadiens au sein du même mouvement syndical, à la grande satisfaction des capitalistes de toute race. Les employeurs canadiens-français (ils sont nombreux) ne paient pas de plus hauts salaires aux ouvriers de leur propre race que les employeurs anglais ou américains ; au contraire, leurs entreprises étant souvent plus petites, ils paient souvent moins.

Les tensions raciales ne sont pas graves au Canada d'aujourd'hui, et tout indique qu'elles se relâchent. Les Canadiens anglais sont plus conscients de l'existence et des problèmes du Canada français : à preuve le nombre croissant des études et des publications sur le sujet. Le pouvoir déclinant de l'Angleterre cède le pas à une politique canadienne plus nationale, moins coloniale, à la grande joie du Québec. En s'industrialisant, le Québec se voit aux prises avec des problèmes communs aux autres provinces ; et l'isolation devient pour lui une position de plus en plus difficile à conserver. Le Canada est promis à un grand avenir : tous ses peuples peuvent y participer, et ils y contribueront tous. Devant les dangers croissants du monde extérieur, en particulier la montée du communisme et les incertitudes de la politique américaine, on tend à une conception commune de la politique nationale. La contribution croissante de Canadiens de toute race aux arts n'est pas la moindre des influences qui jouent en faveur de la bonne entente. En musique, en peinture, en sculpture et en littérature, un réveil culturel se manifeste dans plusieurs parties du pays, et particulièrement dans le Québec. Tout laisse prévoir qu'on réussira à bâtir une nation canadienne qui s'épanouira ; que le Canada procurera le bonheur à tout son peuple et donnera au monde un exemple de stabilité et de modération. Cela, à condition que les Canadiens soient suffisamment unis pour conserver intacte leur structure politique, et qu'ils croient suffisamment à la diversité pour que leur double culture puisse croître en liberté.

[Translated by Pauline and Réginald Boisvert]

# XXII

# The Constitutional Background of Taxation Agreements

*The changing financial relations between Ottawa and the provinces are here set within the rigid framework of the distribution of legislative powers in the constitution.*
From the *McGill Law Journal*, 2, 1955, 1-10

The financial relations between Ottawa and the provincial governments form one of the most complex and changing aspects of Canadian federalism. Within two years after Confederation the original terms of Union, set out in Section 118 of the BNA Act, were varied to accommodate the claims of Nova Scotia, and since then no constitutional provision or political agreement has endured for long, whether it has been declared in the law of the constitution, as in 1867, to be 'in full and final settlement,' or whether, as in 1907, this firm intention was prudently withdrawn from the text of the amendment, at the request of British Columbia. Indeed, the new form of these financial arrangements that was adopted after World War II, based on the tax rental idea and renewable every five years, was the first serious attempt ever made in Canada to discover a method by which some order and stability might be introduced into a relationship which otherwise changes in an erratic and unplanned manner. The Sirois Report proposed another solution, but this was rejected in 1940. That the recent attempt has been only partially successful is evident from the fact that no general formula was found acceptable to all the provinces.

At a time when new financial terms are being negotiated in Canada, it may be useful to examine the law of the constitution within which any revised arrangements will have to operate. This law could, of course, be changed by constitutional amendment, as in 1907, but it is doubtful if such a course will be followed. Amending the constitution is one of those complexes in the Canadian psyche which we prefer to thrust down deep into our political subconscious, and no sofa has yet been devised on which we seem able to liberate our internal conflicts. Any new tax agreements we adopt are therefore likely to have to be fitted into the old law. This leaves a very wide area where solutions can be found based on consent, since the legal rules are relatively few. Nevertheless consent cannot be given contrary to the law, nor can it rest on foundations more secure than those which the federal framework provides. It is to these basic constitutional rules, therefore, that attention will be turned.

## TAXING POWERS IN THE BNA ACT

Leaving aside minor variations, the principle ideas in the BNA Act regarding the financial powers and the fiscal relations of the federal and provincial governments may be stated simply. The Parliament of Canada may adopt any mode or system of taxation it chooses, be it direct or indirect, progressive or regressive, fair or discriminatory. The provinces are limited to direct taxation within the province for the raising of revenue for provincial purposes, and in addition have a general licensing power for the same purposes. Provinces may also gather the royalties and income from the sale and development of their natural resources (s. 109). All provinces were granted subsidies in 1867, at so much per head of population, calculated at an amount enabling provincial budgets to be balanced with the then existing provincial responsibilities. All provincial debts were assumed by Ottawa so that every provincial government started its federal life debt free. But provinces were given power to borrow on the sole credit of the province (s. 92-3) and no restriction was placed upon the total amount that might be raised in this manner, nor upon the location of the lender. Hence provinces may incur international debts. It was not believed in 1867 that the needs of local government would be great, or that there was any danger of provincial fiscal policies endangering national economic plans. Jurisdiction over credit generally, through banks, currency and the issue of paper money, was in federal hands, along with control of interest. Both Parliament and the legislatures were prohibited from imposing any tax on Crown property (s. 125).

It is clear from these initial provisions of the constitution that the concept of provincial autonomy prevailing at Confederation was subject to two important financial restrictions; first in being limited to direct taxation, and secondly in being dependent on subsidies. On the other hand, the taxing powers of Parliament appeared unlimited. This is the reverse of the situation found in the American constitution, where the States may impose direct or indirect taxes, and where there were limitations on the right of Congress to tax which necessitated the XVIth amendment authorising federal income taxes. The notion of subsidies, substantial in relation to the original provincial budgets, which was basic to the Canadian scheme, is all the more surprising in view of the sound parliamentary tradition with us that the government which spends public money should be compelled to raise it.[1] In the United States as well as in Switzerland and Australia, however, though no subsidies were provided in the constitution, it has since been found necessary for the central government to make voluntary grants to the states in proportions comparable to those paid in Canada under the tax agreements.[2]

## VARIATIONS IN FINANCIAL STATUS OF PROVINCES

While in general the taxing powers of all provinces are equal, it was found impossible from the first to apply uniform rules across Canada. By s. 124 of the BNA Act New Brunswick was permitted to levy lumber dues not allowed to other provinces. The natural resources of the western provinces were handed back in 1930 subject to limitations from which the other provinces were free. As the Privy Council said in 1953, when holding that Saskatchewan was prevented by its constitution from taxing CPR properties, 'There was thus no set pattern of 'a Province' in the Act of 1867,'[3] a remark which does not quite square with Mr St-Laurent's comment at his Reform Club speech in the autumn of 1952 that Quebec was 'a province like other provinces.' There are very few provinces exactly like other provinces in their constitutional position, though it is true that the taxing powers of the four original provinces were the same with the one exception for New Brunswick already noted.

Thus it is not surprising to find that when the taxation agreements were negotiated in 1942 and 1947 there were two options available, and in 1953 three options, later increased to four to accommodate Quebec's income tax. Perhaps when we reach ten options we shall achieve a truly Canadian unanimity. How far these variations are compatible with the maintenance of something we can call national fiscal policy designed to maintain high employment it is not for the constitutional lawyer to say, but it is clear that the present constitution does not give Ottawa the legal power to implement a policy that controls provincial taxing powers, except with provincial consent.

## RESULTS OF CONSTITUTIONAL INTERPRETATIONS

The results of judicial decisions on the tax clauses of the BNA Act may perhaps be summarized without serious inaccuracy by saying that the courts have somewhat reduced the wide taxing powers of Parliament, and have permitted some ex-

1 See comment Sirois Report, Book II, p. 126.
2 Wheare, *Federal Govt.* 3rd ed. pp. 115-6.
3 *A.-G. for Sask.* v. *Canadian Pacific Rly. Co.* [1953] A.C. 594 at p. 613. Saskatchewan and Alberta are compelled by their constitutions to accord the CPR a degree of fiscal respect elsewhere reserved for royalty.

tensions of the limited powers of the provinces but not enough to keep pace with the vastly increased costs of provincial government.

Federal power has been diminished by the application of the doctrine that particular words override more general ones and operate by way of exception to them. Hence Ottawa cannot impose a direct tax within a province in order to the raising of a revenue for provincial purposes.[4] It can, however, impose a direct tax in order to raise a revenue for a federal purpose. What then is a provincial purpose? Curiously enough this term has never been authoritatively defined by the courts; if it means merely 'for the exclusive disposition of the legislature,' as Duff CJ said it meant in the Unemployment Insurance Reference,[5] then indeed the Dominion and Provincial powers of taxation are on different planes and cannot come into conflict. However, there was an obscure remark in the Privy Council judgment in the same case indicating that just because the Dominion has collected a fund by means of taxation, it by no means follows that any legislation which disposes of it is necessarily valid. The first unemployment insurance act, which raised such a fund, was unconstitutional, but chiefly on the ground that it interfered with the contract of employment. Obviously, not every federal statute is valid just because it authorizes the expenditure of public funds, which is all the Privy Council has actually said, but the manner of their saying it has raised some doubt as to the validity of social insurance schemes paid for out of federal revenues. It should be noted, however, that the legal doctrine referred to which limits federal powers by excepting from them specific provincial powers, only applies to direct taxes; indirect taxes escape its application, since the provinces cannot impose them at all.

Turning to the provincial taxing powers, it is evident that once the courts had classified sales taxes as direct taxes when they were based on the device of making the vendor a tax collector, a wide new field for taxation was open to provincial governments. This is a strange result in a country where excise taxes are reserved to the central government, since both types of tax have much the same economic effect on consumption. In New Brunswick a man who opens in his own home a package of cigarettes imported from another province is supposed immediately to pay his New Brunswick tax.[6] British Columbia succeeded in imposing a tax on consumers of fuel oil which was in fact being imported free into the province.[7] Thus in effect the provinces can impose a custom barrier around themselves despite the explicit reservation of customs to Ottawa in s. 122 of the constitution. The courts also approved provincial taxes on banks, federal civil servants and

4 *Caron v. The King* [1924] A.C. 999.
5 *Unemployment Insurance Reference* [1936] S.C.R. at p. 434.
6 *Atlantic Smoke Shops v. Conlon* [1943] A.C. 550.
7 *A.-G. for B.C. v. Kingcome Navigation Co.* [1934] A.C. 45; see also my comment in (1934), 12 *Can. Bar Rev.* 303.

judges, thus rejecting for Canada any doctrine of the 'immunity of instrumentalities.' On the other hand, the courts did not allow provinces to breach the tariff wall by the simple process of taking ownership of the imports in the name of the Crown and claiming exemption under s. 125. Had the reverse ruling obtained, socialism for fiscal purposes might have developed at the provincial level much more rapidly.

Despite these enlarged interpretations of their powers, provinces have had great difficulty in increasing their revenues as fast as their enlarged governmental functions, also due in part to judicial interpretation, have accumulated. This explains why, of the three formal amendments to legislative powers in the BNA Act since 1867, two have concerned costly social insurances, namely unemployment insurance (1940) and old age pensions (1951). (The third was the 1949 addition of the federal amending clause). Health insurance would be another very costly undertaking, and while, it is submitted, it could be established without an amendment, by a system of grants in aid financed through income tax and general revenue, federal administrators would no doubt feel happier with some agreed transfer of jurisdiction.

LEGAL NATURE OF TAXATION AGREEMENTS

The Parliament of Canada and provincial legislatures, being sovereign in their own spheres and incapable of binding their successors, cannot place taxation schemes on any but a 'gentlemen's agreement' basis. Despite the concurrent statutes giving effect to the agreements, nobody is really bound in law to maintain them. Hence no loss of sovereignty takes place when a province enters an agreement, any more than it takes place when a province leases natural resources to an American corporation. The restraint imposed comes from the economics, not the law of the situation. British Columbia was held to be able to impose a tax on the Vancouver Island railway belt even though it had passed a self-denying statute in 1883 as part of a scheme for aiding railway construction.[8] Quebec's acceptance of the Wartime Agreements in 1942 did not prevent her refusing the subsequent ones in 1947 and 1952.

The most startling proof of the purely voluntary nature of taxation agreements, however, was furnished by the federal government itself, when in January, 1945 it suddenly refused to pay to Saskatchewan the monies promised under the Wartime Tax Agreement of 1942 because of an unsettled claim on the seed grain debt, though repayment of that debt by Saskatchewan was never made a condition of the Agreement. It is true that the CCF Party defeated the Liberal Party in Saskatchewan in 1944, but to a constitutional lawyer no significance can be at-

8 *A.-G. for B.C.* v. *E. & N. Rly.* [1950] A.C. 87.

tributed to this event. Yet even to a constitutional lawyer it would seem that gentlemen's agreements ought to be carried out in a gentlemanly way, and that where strict law ends good faith must continue. This is particularly necessary in a federal system as complex and delicate as our own, and it does not seem an adequate answer to say, as did the Arbitration Board appointed to hear the seed grain dispute, that there was nothing illegal in Ottawa's behaviour.[9] Money promised in the Agreement suddenly ceased to be paid, upsetting provincial plans and revealing the tenuous nature of the legal obligations created.

Because taxation agreements are based on consent and not on constitutional obligation, it follows that special deals with particular provinces are legally unassailable. We have no requirement that taxation must be undiscriminatory, or equal as between the provinces. If national policy requires that wealth shall be taken from the richer and given to the poorer regions, the manner of its distribution is a matter of politics and not of law. Hence the abstention of some provinces does not preclude the possibility of agreements with others, as past practice makes abundantly clear.

## THE SPENDING POWER OF GOVERNMENTS

All public monies that fall into the Consolidated Revenue Funds of the federal and provincial governments belong to the Crown. The Crown is a person capable of making gifts or contracts like any other person, to whomsoever it chooses to benefit. The recipient may be another government, or private individuals. The only constitutional requirement for Crown gifts is that they must have the approval of Parliament or legislature. This being obtained the Prince may distribute his largesse at will. Such gifts, of course, do not need to be accepted; the donee is always as free to reject as the donor to offer. Moreover, the Crown may attach conditions to the gift, failure to observe which will cause its discontinuance. These simple but significant powers exist in our constitutional law though no mention of them be found in the BNA Acts. They derive from doctrines of the Royal Prerogative and the common law. They operate equally for the Crown in right of provinces as well as for the Crown in right of the Dominion. It would be as lawful for provinces to subsidize Ottawa as for Ottawa to subsidize provinces; the only difference is that Ottawa is obliged by the constitution to pay certain statutory sums.

These rules explain several interesting practices inherent in Canadian federalism. They explain why no amendment was necessary to the BNA Act in 1869 when the amount guaranteed to Nova Scotia was increased; if the federal Crown

9 The Board was divided in its opinion: see [1946] W.W.R. p. 257.

is obliged to give x dollars to a province, it does not violate its promise by giving x plus y dollars. It may excite the cupidity of other provinces by so doing, but that is not a legal matter. So too these rules explain how it has been possible for Ottawa to set in motion a variety of welfare projects, such as family allowances and grants to universities, through the method of the grant in aid. It explains how Canadian Government annuities were established. And not only Ottawa employs this method. The Province of Quebec, which has been most insistent on provincial autonomy in education, does not hesitate to make grants of public money to colleges in other provinces. According to Mason Wade[10] the redoubtable Mercier, as staunch a defender of Quebec's rights as the present premier of Quebec, even gave $10,000 to the University of Toronto after it had suffered in a bad fire. This was indeed a *beau geste*. But what is the difference, one may ask, between giving to a university after a fire and giving annually without regard to conflagrations? If Ottawa's gift to Quebec universities is an invasion of Quebec's rights, why is not Quebec's gift to Toronto, or to the University of Ottawa, an invasion of Ontario's rights? The true answer is that none of these gifts is an invasion of anybody's rights in so far as constitutional law is concerned. Generosity in Canada is not unconstitutional. If the grants are undesirable, it must be for non-legal reasons.

Making a gift is not the same as making a law. Because one type of government alone has jurisdiction over a class of subject under the BNA Act, does not mean that the other may not make gifts to persons whose activities fall within that class. A province, for example, may not make laws having extra-territorial operation, but it may make gifts having such operation. Quebec made a gift of $35,000.00 for flood relief in Europe in 1953. Gifts from American Foundations to Canadian universities are not 'laws in relation to education.' No more are gifts from the Crown, even though such gifts must be approved in an Appropriation Act before the payment is lawful. Tying all this to taxation agreements, it is quite lawful for Ottawa to entice provinces into agreements by offering to pay them more for surrendering certain taxes than would be received by them through those taxes. Call it a gift or a 'tax rental,' it is equally within the discretion of the Crown, if Parliament approves.

THE QUESTION OF PRIORITIES

In the recent debate between Ottawa and Quebec regarding income taxes, a claim was put forward in high provincial places, and indeed was written into the preamble of the Quebec statute imposing its income tax,[11] that the Canadian consti-

10 *The French Canadians*, p. 428.
11 2–3 Eliz. 11, cap. 17.

tution recognized provincial priority in the matter of direct taxation. This part of the statute was repealed after Ottawa agreed to allow certain deductions for the Quebec taxpayers. What is the law on the point?

If by priority is meant that every time a province enters the income tax field the federal government must evacuate it, there is obviously no such priority. As already said, the exclusive provincial jurisdiction over direct taxation is only for the raising of revenues for provincial purposes; direct taxation for federal purposes is exclusively a federal power. As was said by Lord Macmillan in the Forbes case,[12] 'Both income taxes (federal and provincial) may co-exist and be enforced without clashing. The Dominion reaps part of the field of the Manitoba citizen's income. The Province reaps another part of it.' But what happens if the poor Manitoba citizen is reaped right down to his bare stubble? Suppose the taxpayer has not enough money to pay both taxes, who then is paid first? This is the only case where conflict between the taxes exists in the legal sense.

To this question the Privy Council has already given the answer. In Silver's case,[13] where a bankrupt company owed taxes both to Quebec and to Ottawa, Viscount Dunedin, while holding that on the statutes before him the two claims ranked *pari passu*, went on to say that either under head 21 of 91 (bankruptcy) or under head 3 of 91 (taxation) it would have been competent for Ottawa to have made its claim prevail over that of the province if it so wished: 'The two taxations, Dominion and Provincial, can stand side by side without interfering with each other, but as soon as you come to the concomitant privileges of absolute priority they cannot stand side by side and must clash; consequently the Dominion must prevail.' This is because of the well-established rule that where there is a concurrent field of legislation neither the federal nor the provincial laws are ultra vires if they do not conflict, but once they do the federal law prevails. The only exception to this rule seems to be in regard to the old age pensions amendment of 1951. Prof. K.C. Wheare, in his *Federal Government*,[14] seems to think that this ruling has destroyed the federal principle in Canada in so far as the taxing power is concerned. To which my reply is that the Canadian constitution was never expected to operate on strictly federal principles as the political scientist understands them; we adopted, for what seemed good reasons, a constitution leaning toward a strong central authority whose power might offset in some degree the centrifugal forces which are always present in the body politic.[15] Let it not be forgotten that the first attempt to escape from Confederation was

12 [1937] A.C. 260.
13 [1932] A.C. 514.
14 3rd ed. pp. 110–114.
15 I have expanded this argument in 'The Special Nature of Canadian Federalism', (1947) C.J.E.P.S. pp. 13 ff. (Essay XIII above).

made by Nova Scotia within eight months of the coming into force of the BNA Act.

## THE SYMBOLISM OF TAXATION AGREEMENTS

The dry bones of constitutional law are not the living flesh of Canadian politics. The problems involved in taxation agreements reach far beyond the ground covered in an analysis of legal rules. Yet the problems cannot be understood and no satisfactory solution can be worked out unless they proceed from an analysis of the legal norms established in the fundamental law.

It is only too apparent that in Canada one great difficulty is to reach agreement on the kind of federal-provincial relationships that the constitutional rules imply. On many technical points such as have been discussed here, final decisions of the Privy Council or the Supreme Court of Canada give us an answer, but on much more fundamental matters the court decisions are silent or confusing. It is precisely these deeper issues which elevate constitutional discussion in Canada to the plane of philosophical debate and which intrude themselves into every aspect of federal-provincial relations.

The point can be illustrated by asking some simple questions. What is the nature of the BNA Act? Is it a statute or a compact, or, as Père Arrhès holds, both a statute and a compact?[16] Or is it to be explained by the 'théorie de l'institution' as Edouard Laurent maintained?[17] If it is a compact, between whom was it made; between the four original provinces, between all the provinces and the Dominion, or simply, as the prevalent theory in Quebec seems to maintain, between races? If it is a compact between races, is it between the French race and all other races in Canada collectively, or between French and English, using English in the Quebec sense of meaning anyone from the British Isles?[18] Again, is the aim of the constitution the retention of what Lord Atkin calls 'the watertight compartments,'[19] or is it rather, as Lord Sankey once said,[20] 'to give the central government those high functions and almost sovereign powers by which uniformity of legislation might be secured on all questions which were of common concern to all the provinces as members of a constituent whole?'

It is unlikely that a single answer will ever be given to these questions by all

16 See *La Confédération: Pacte ou Loi*, éditions de L'Action Nationale, 1949, p. 72.
17 See *Quelle est la nature de l'acte de 1867?* Cahiers de l'Ecole des Sciences Sociales, Laval (n.d.).
18 The only race mentioned by name in the BNA Act is the Indian race, and Indians were made wards of Ottawa.
19 [1937] A.C. at p. 354.
20 [1932] A.C. at p. 70.

Canadians. Each will answer according to his basic philosophical approach and according to the ends he has in view. In a bicultural country, the backgrounds, educational systems and political aspirations are too varied to permit of single explanations of constitutional rules. To someone trained in Dicey's *Law of the Constitution*, the BNA Act is simply a statute to be obeyed by our courts because of the ancient doctrine of imperial sovereignty. Is it reasonable to expect so technical a view to be held by a graduate of a classical college in Quebec? Is he not right when he reminds us that the great central facts of Canadian life – the race relationships, the religious guarantees, the bilingualism – cannot be subsumed under narrow legal concepts? Is it surprising that he finds a continuing difficulty in expressing his French realities in the terms of English legalities? The Canadian constitution is not even written in one of the two official languages of this country – his own.

It is unfortunate for the economists who wish Ottawa to adopt a fiscal policy based on Keynesian principles, that taxation arrangements have now become involved in, and perhaps dominated by, Quebec's insistence on the recognition of her status and her rights under the Canadian constitution. It is also unfortunate for the unemployed in Quebec and elsewhere, since battles over status seldom aid in solving economic problems. As a member of the Quebec delegation said after the first sessions of the federal-provincial fiscal conference in April, 1955, 'When other provinces come to Ottawa they bring their problems and leave their rights behind. Quebec brings her rights and leaves her problems behind.' But few will doubt that Quebec is standing on very strong ground in stressing the non-economic factors in this debate. Quebec's view is based on the theory that the maintenance of Canadian federalism requires that each province, and particularly Quebec, should be able to finance its own functions of government out of its own resources; otherwise it ceases to have any autonomy worth the name. This is claimed as a right, not as a privilege or concession. Since taxation agreements as hitherto devised seem to imply an abandonment of this right, their rejection is an act of honour. They become mixed up with feelings of status and prestige, and cease to be merely practical devices for solving common problems. And since Quebec's income tax of 1954 brought these issues vividly to the Quebec public, the income tax itself became, in a sense, a symbol of cultural defence. This explains why there has been so much insistence over deductions for an income tax in Quebec, whereas a far wider group of Quebec taxpayers – including the lowest paid workers – pay a double and sometimes a triple sales tax without any sense that their culture is at stake. Yet why, one may ask, is an income tax more honourable than a sales tax? It affects far fewer people.

The currents of constitutional thinking in Quebec suggest that to-day the identification of the government of Quebec with the whole French-Canadian race is greater than ever before. This identification once assumed as a major premiss, a number of new concepts about Canadian federalism seem to follow. Canada is seen not just as one central government and ten provincial governments, Quebec being merely one of the ten: rather is it looked upon as composed of two races, equal in status, one of which speaks through the government of Quebec and the other through Ottawa. Hence Quebec on this view is one of two governments. The notion of Canada as a dyarchy, or a dual monarchy, is implicit in much of the contemporary discussion on federal-provincial relations.

Fiscal policy in Canada is thus enmeshed in minority rights. When financial arrangements achieve the importance and magnitude of current tax agreements this is scarcely surprising. For the inner conflict in all federal states between growing welfare responsibilities resting on the local governments, and new fiscal responsibilities for promoting overall economic welfare resting on the central government, is difficult enough to resolve even in a homogeneous society. It assumes added complexities in a bicultural society. With us taxation agreements must be understood as achieving two objectives simultaneously: Quebec's autonomy, as well as economic stability. Autonomy for English-speaking provinces is, of course, also a serious factor, but without minority complications. This is no criticism of past agreements; they may have been the best that could be devised. They were not so understood in Quebec, however, and too little attention was paid to the necessity of securing that widespread acceptance of the aims and objectives of the agreements, which is necessary if so significant a change in older constitutional relationships is to rest on some adequate degree of popular consent. In this issue two powerful ideas are contending for recognition – provincial self-government and federal responsibility for overall economic stability. Provincial resistance creates a countervailing power to balance federal control. Too much resistance could create economic chaos, too little might endanger federalism itself. Finding the acceptable mean is the art of Canadian fiscal policy.

# XXIII

# Areas of Conflict in the Field of Public Law and Policy

*This paper discusses some of the new concepts of Canadian federalism asserted by Quebec spokesmen and the challenge they pose to the traditional views held in English Canada.*

From the *McGill Law Journal*, 3, 1957, 29-50

The public law of Quebec, unlike the private law, derives its principles and general content from the public law of England. By the *Treaty of Paris* in 1763 the sovereignty over New France passed from the King of France to the King of England; and automatically the law relating to the Crown, the government and the political rights of citizens, became those of an English colony. The legislative, executive and judicial organs, which were established and developed after the cession, copied the patterns of the new mother country, as formerly they had those of the old: in this sense New France became New England. But the underlying social institutions, such as the Church, the seigneurial system and the family, with the French language, private law and traditions, did not change:[1] in this sense New France became Old France. Thus Quebec offers an early example of British institutions of government being first imposed upon and then accepted, by a non-British people, who in other respects guarded jealously their own laws and customs.

Through the successive constitutional changes in Canada after 1763, such as in 1792, 1841 and 1867, the public law of Quebec remained English in character, though new institutions of government were introduced. These new institutions, with few exceptions, were not peculiar to Quebec but followed the model set up also in other Canadian jurisdictions. Quebec was integrated into a developing imperial system. Though French Canadian nationalism steadily increased during the nineteenth century, the law of the constitution takes little note of it. The BNA

---

1 I leave aside the question as to whether the French private law was temporarily displaced by the Royal Proclamation of 1763.

Act of 1867 contains few special provisions for Quebec. Outside sections 71-80, establishing the Quebec legislature, most of which concern the Legislative Council, there are few references to the province by name. Some of the clauses applicable to Quebec were for the protection of the Protestant minority only, or were equally beneficial to Catholic and Protestant; an example of the former is the special vote required for changes in the representation from the Eastern Townships (sec. 80), predominantly English in 1867; of the latter the equal protection for Catholic and Protestant schools existing at the Union (sec. 93), and the protection for the two official languages in the federal and Quebec legislatures and courts (sec. 133). These rules, far from enlarging autonomy in the province, all impose restrictions on it in the interest of minority rights which are not exclusively French or Catholic.

The most noticeable singling out of Quebec, as a province, in the Constitution is to be found in the uniformity provisions of sections 94,[2] where Quebec is omitted, and in section 98 which provides that judges in Quebec courts must always be drawn from the Bar of Quebec. Section 94 does not permit the Legislature of Quebec to delegate to Ottawa jurisdiction over 'property and civil rights' by the easy process which other provinces may employ, and shows that the preservation of the French law was one of the purposes of the Union of 1867 as it had been of all previous constitutions since the Quebec Act of 1774. This is also the reason for the requirement that judicial appointments in Quebec must be made from among the members of the provincial Bar (sec. 98). Like the guaranteed use of the English and French languages, these provisions recognize the bicultural nature of Canada. They do not add to provincial autonomy, however, but rather restrict it. Nor do they prevent a transfer of jurisdiction, as for unemployment insurance and old age pensions, by the amendment of the constitution. Cultural differences in 1867 were not expressed in greater legislative autonomy for provinces; indeed, the dangers to unity which they entailed were one of the reasons for establishing a strong government at Ottawa with the residue of power in the hands of the central authorities.

In the basic distribution of legislative powers under sections 91-92 of the constitution, there is no mention of Quebec: the original legislatures are all given the same powers. Preservation of the two cultures was a principle on which the Canadian nation was built, but the constitution did not create in Quebec a special kind of 'state' to which was entrusted an exclusive guardianship over French culture. On the contrary, minority rights and provincial autonomy are kept quite distinct, and autonomy is frequently subordinated to the higher value of minority rights. This is shown by the fact that Ottawa is specifically given a power to legislate on education in certain circumstances, in Quebec as elsewhere, for the

2 This section, which has never been used, enabled provinces to abandon jurisdiction to the federal Parliament by consent.

protection of minorities (sec. 93–4), and by the federal veto power over provincial laws (sec. 90), which was intended to operate as a control over any legislature abusing its power. As Cartier himself said during the Confederation debates, 'I would recommend it (disallowance) myself in case of injustice.'[3]

The superstructure of the constitution, however, is one thing; the living forces within peoples are another. The States of the American Union, under its constitution, are treated with even more equality among themselves than are Canadian provinces, yet the deep-seated differences between North and South are still patent though not based on language and religion, and produced a doctrine of nullification and claims to secession which could not be resolved by judicial process. From 1867 Quebec became an autonomous community in the sense in which any state in a federation is autonomous, namely, it could exercise its legislative powers as it chose in any way that did not conflict with the law of the constitution. In particular, its jurisdiction over 'property and civil rights' which it shares with other provinces, gave it a wide field for self-expression, particularly as its content was greatly expanded through judicial interpretation. Over the course of the years its provincial legislation has changed certain parts of the public law in Quebec in ways that differ from the direction taken in other parts of Canada, though a basic similarity remains. More important even than the differences which such local legislation produces – and Quebec is not unique in this form of regionalism – are the attitudes and feelings in the province about 'provincial autonomy'; here the opinions expressed with increasing conviction in Quebec often stand in strong contrast to those prevalent elsewhere. While opinions are not law, they tend to produce interpretations of law and certainly produce conflict in the judicial as well as in the political sphere.

Some of these contrasting views will now be analysed. But while the emphasis is on differences of outlook, it must be remembered that not all French-Canadians think alike and still less do all other Canadians. Quebec is by no means the only defender of provincial autonomy, though under Premier Maurice Duplessis, as often in the past, this has been a leading characteristic of its policy. Hence crosscurrents blunt the edges of opinion which, if too sharpened, might make impossible that degree of ethnic co-operation without which Canadian federalism could not survive. The areas of conflict here outlined must be seen against a much wider background of day-to-day collaboration in almost every phase of Canadian activity.

STATUTE OR COMPACT?

A primary question, still unresolved by Canadian publicists, is this: What is the

---

3 Confederation Debates, pp. 407–8. See also F.R. Scott, 'Dominion Jurisdiction over Human Rights and Fundamental Freedoms,' 27 *Canadian Bar Review* at p. 530. (Essay XVIII above)

nature of the British North America Act of 1867? Is it simply a statute of the British Parliament, distributing powers afresh among Canadian governments through the exercise of an ancient imperial sovereignty? Or is it a solemn compact or treaty not only between provinces but between the French and English races in Canada? On the answer given this question many others will inevitably depend.

The view that the constitution is a statute – a view which commands wide though not universal support in English Canada – sees all the present provinces as deriving their governmental powers from a superior legislative grant which is equally binding upon federal Parliament and provincial legislatures. The authority of the Parliament at Westminster, which established the present system of government, is still used to change its fundamental provisions, and for the amendments this Parliament alone can make, no provincial consent is legally necessary, however politically wise it may be to secure it. The law of the constitution does not give any province, or any number of them, a veto on changes requested by the federal Parliament. Moreover, with this approach 'provincial autonomy' is no more a chief purpose of Confederation than federal autonomy, or decentralisation than centralisation; the BNA Act was an Act for the Union of provinces, not for disunion, and while a federal form of government was adopted, the provinces, in the words of the BNA Act, 'shall form and be one Dominion under the name of Canada' (sec. 3).

On this understanding of the BNA Act, the struggle of the French-Canadian minority for its due share of status and power in Canada and for the recognition of its fundamental rights must express itself through the Parliament of Canada, as well as through the Quebec and other provincial governments. Federal institutions, as well as provincial ones, are its proper outlet. Quebec is and doubtless will remain a 'homeland' to all French Canadians, except perhaps the Acadians, but this is an historic fact rather than a constitutional rule. All Canada is the homeland for all Canadians. Canada is thus two cultures but not two states; a federal system and not a dyarchy. The ten provinces are equal in status and French culture, while geographically centred in Quebec, radiates outward through various social and political channels but not through any special governmental institutions. The government of Quebec, though controlled by French Canadians, is neither French nor Catholic, being designed for all its inhabitants, 20% of whom are not of French origin. 'Dans notre pays il n'existe pas de religion de l'État,' says Mr Justice Taschereau.[4] Indeed, since all government in Canada is carried on in the name of the Crown, and the Queen must by law be in communion with the Church of England, Quebec has a Protestant as formal head of the government, whatever may be the religion of the Premier and Cabinet.

If the BNA Act is viewed as a compact or treaty rather than a statute – an

4 In *Chaput* v. *Romain*, [1955] S.C.R. 834 at p. 840.

opinion almost official in Quebec[5] – at once different aspects of the federal relationship are stressed. Ottawa becomes, in a very real sense, the 'creature' of the provinces,[6] who agreed in 1867 to set up a new form of government. The creators, being equal in rights, would seem to have an equal voice in proposing and approving changes in the constitution. On this argument every province has – or should have – a veto power over amendments. Though it is true that some provinces were established or admitted after Confederation, and cannot strictly be considered as parties to the compact, and though Quebec and Ontario were united in a single Province of Canada when the compact was formed, the basic fact of provincial pre-existence remains in so far as Quebec opinion is concerned. French Canada had its separate existence as New France until 1763, as Lower Canada from 1792–1841, and was recognised as a distinct entity by the tacit federalism that was practised under the Union government of the Province of Canada from 1841–1867. Its sense of identity survives and pervades every form of constitution. Lower Canada also had its own delegation, separate from that of Ontario and composed of both French and English members, at the Quebec and London Conferences preceding Confederation. These facts lend special strength to the compact theory in Quebec.

Some recent thinking in Quebec goes far beyond the compact theory and defines Confederation as a fundamental agreement, not merely between provinces, but between the two races, French and English. This notion, like the compact theory, opens up new lines of constitutional analysis but leads to quite different conclusions. Not unnaturally, among all the influences that shaped the constitution, the French-English relationship stands out most vividly in the Quebec mind. There seems no straining of history in calling the eventual agreement a treaty between races, even though the text of the BNA Act mentions no race at all except the Indian. On this approach there exists a dualism in the constitution reflecting a predominant fact of Canadian life, and the government of Quebec at once appears as a 'French' and 'Catholic' government, a champion of the race, set over against the English-Protestant government of Ottawa. Symbolisation of the racial and religious struggle takes place on the constitutional level, though the language of the law is neutral. The treaty-between-races theory explains the importance for Quebec of having its own flag, as a sign of nationhood, and its own anthem – *O Canada!* – whose French version hymns the traditions of Old France rather than the aspirations of the new federal state stretching from sea to sea.

If the races in Canada are equal, so the theory goes, then the governments representing the races should be equal. Therefore Quebec is the equal of Ottawa

5 It has been written in to the preamble of the Quebec statute 2–3 Eliz. 11, cap. 17.

6 This view has also English-Canadian support: see e.g. S.J. Watson, *The Powers of Canadian Parliaments* (1880) p. 51, D.A. O'Sullivan, *A Manual of Government in Canada* (1879) p. 21.

and not just one part of a larger whole. Such is the easy transition from the aspirations of the people to the supposed law of the constitution. This concentration on the provincial government as defender and sole representative of Quebec's rights, as distinct from merely regarding the province as a focus of culture, is something relatively new in Quebec though the ideas being defended are as old as the cession of 1763. The degree to which these ideas have penetrated into the realms of constitutional theory can be seen in the following typical statements. One is from a speech of the Honourable Antonio Barrette, Minister of Labour in Quebec, who said in May, 1955:[7]

There is now such a thing as a French-Canadian nation. Not only have we accomplished the miracle of survival, but we have reached the point where we have our own government, our own religion, our own language, our own culture, our own universities and our own literature.

The acts of heroism of Quebec's early settlers were beginning to pay off in a tangible manner.

We have reconquered our autonomy and we are now well on the way to re-take possession of our taxation rights which are at the very basis of our existence. Without our power to tax, our freedom of legislation would be a sheer illusion.

Another is from the recommendations of the Tremblay Commission on Constitutional Problems, the second of which states: '2. With regard to French-Canadian culture, the Province of Quebec assumes alone the responsibilities which the other provinces jointly assume with regard to Anglo-Canadian culture.'[8] A third is from an article by a member of the Bar of Quebec, M. Philippe Ferland, QC published in *Thémis*, the law journal of the University of Montréal.[9] Writing of the meeting of Prime Minister St-Laurent and Premier Duplessis in 'neutral' Montreal on October 5, 1954, to discuss a new taxation agreement, M. Ferland said:

'Nous sommes ramenés au point de départ, à l'origine de la Confédération. Deux parties sont en présence: l'Etat canadien-français et l'Etat canadien.

Pour la première fois depuis 1867, ces deux Etats se rencontrent seul à seul. Le dialogue doit s'engager entre les deux seules parties qui n'ont ni négocier ni signer: Québec et Ottawa. La discussion doit s'engager entre les véritables délégués qui se font face: l'Etat fédéral, représentant de l'union législative, l'Etat provincial du Québec, représentant le peuple qui veut refaire ses chances de survie, celui des Canadiens-français. Deux Etats, deux conceptions, deux peuples.

7 Quoted by J. Harvey Perry, 'What Price Provincial Autonomy,' *Can. Journal of Economics and Political Science*, Vol. 21 at p. 445.
8 Summary of the Report, 1956, p. 18.
9 No. 14 Dec. 1954, p. 105 at p. 109.

What would surprise the Canadian from Nova Scotia or Alberta who might read this last statement (assuming he understood French), is the notion that Ottawa speaks for all the other 'English' provinces as well as for itself, and that because the population of Quebec is predominantly French and Catholic, all provinces except Quebec disappear, leaving only two 'states' on the Canadian scene. Yet this has become a deeply felt reality in Quebec, where the idea that federalism in Canada exists solely to guarantee the survival of French culture, and that without it Canada would be a unitary state, finds ready acceptance. The regional loyalty of the Maritimes, for example, or the separatism inherent in geography, which imposed federalism on Canada quite regardless of Quebec feeling, are factors to which no attention is paid.

The 'dual state' theory is quite inconsistent with the compact theory, since the latter claims only that all provinces are equal sovereign entities whose rights cannot be changed without their consent, whereas the former denies the existence or importance of all provinces save Quebec. The attractiveness of the theory for Quebec lies in its attribution of equal status to the smaller of the two Canadian communities: it thus plays the same role as 'Dominion status' within the Commonwealth and 'sovereignty of states' within the international order. That it is revolutionary in its implications is obvious. It could not be worked out to its logical conclusions without totally destroying the present constitution of Canada. Already certain extremists in Quebec have no hesitation in dismissing all French-speaking federal Members of Parliament from Quebec (though duly elected) as *vendus*, as indeed by definition they must be for associating with 'the other side.' Even though *Le Devoir*, traditional defender of Quebec nationalism, may protest at the injustice to Quebec of having too few French Canadians in the federal civil service, any Quebecer who takes an Ottawa post is likely to suffer the accusation of having lost his essential French character.

Unless Quebec is to become an independent state outside Confederation, which virtually no one in Quebec seems to desire, the limitation of legislative and executive powers imposed by the present constitution on the Quebec government would seem to make it wholly inadequate as the *exclusive* defender of French culture, even if all French minorities in other provinces are disregarded. The elevation of this government as the sole champion of the race has therefore grave dangers for that race: it might have the unexpected effect of imprisoning the vital energies of the French-Canadian people. A 'state' such as a Canadian province, deprived by the constitution of control of money and banking, foreign and inter-provincial trade, transportation and tele-communications (including radio and television), the armed forces and the criminal law, whose taxing powers are limited and whose laws can be vetoed, is not in a position to control all the important areas in which a culture flourishes, still less to provide a secure economic base for that culture. Besides these legislative limitations, the constitution gives to the government at Ottawa the appointment of all the Senators from Quebec, all the Superior Court and Court of Appeal judges in Quebec, and the Lieutenant-Governor of Quebec, while the Parliament of Canada can declare any public work in Quebec to be for the 'general advantage of Canada' and thus gain control over it.

These provisions were not aimed at Quebec, but apply to all provinces equally; they are part of the traditional fabric of Canadian federalism. The Fathers of Confederation, witnessing the American civil war, drew therefrom the lesson that an exaggerated provincial autonomy could spell disaster, and took steps to avoid any such danger in the Canadian constitution. There is little in Canadian history to suggest that they were mistaken in this view. The Quebec nationalist is far from being alone in his dislike of federal authority. Before Confederation was a year old, Nova Scotia (not Quebec) was endeavouring to secede entirely; secessionist movements were developing on the prairies during the 1930's; the Social Credit Party's attempts to secure financial autonomy for Alberta under Premier Aberhart fully match the similar efforts of Mr Duplessis in Quebec. The Canadian nation, in demographic shape still a long ribbon of population broken at several points, has difficulty holding itself together against strong centrifugal forces at all times. This is the reason why Canadian federalism contains the unitary features, already referred to, which mark it off from other systems, more typically federal.

Behind the rather outspoken claims of supporters of the compact and racial theories of Confederation lies a natural desire for survival and expansion that is constantly seeking new symbols to express its aspirations. The French Canadian is at home in Quebec. So is the English Canadian in the province, though some other minorities are perhaps not so secure. The French Canadian wants to feel as much at home when he lives in Ontario; that is, he wants his own language, his own school, his church and parish, and his French Canadian way of life. To some extent he has achieved this in districts adjacent to Quebec. But his minorities farther from the homeland have not achieved it, and the English-speaking inhabitants of other provinces are surprised, if not startled, to discover that they are expected to adapt their local laws (e.g. as to separate schools) so as to make possible the steady development of a French-speaking cultural minority as an island colony in the midst of their already heterogeneous populations. Meeting this resistance, the French minorities look to Quebec for help, which in turn reacts with stronger claims. The fact that an exaggerated provincial autonomy may actually weaken the outside minorities by subjecting them still further to local majorities and depriving them of the protection of Ottawa does not deter the nationalists in Quebec. An 'autonomous' Quebec is a fortress in a dangerous land, without which the struggle for survival seems hopeless. Thus a strong Quebec government seems necessary to pry loose more freedom for its minorities outside as well as within, using at the same time provincial autonomy, influence at Ottawa, and pressures of every kind to achieve the single purpose. The conflicting interpretations of the constitution as between statute and compact, or as racial treaty, are phases of this wider engagement. For this reason legal argument is of little avail in changing opinions, and proofs that the BNA Act is or is not founded on a compact or treaty do not go to the real issue, which is one of power rather than of law.

## NEW FUNCTIONS OF GOVERNMENT

While debates about the nature of the Canadian constitution continue, new functions of government arise to alter the basic foundations of federal-provincial relations. These new functions create new conflicts of opinion. The provision of social services, and the maintenance of economic equilibrium, make demands upon Canadian governments which the original constitution was ill-equipped to fulfill. Economic equilibrium and high employment are inevitably federal responsibilities, for no province has sufficient control over taxation or finance to be capable of maintaining them. The Social Credit government's record in Alberta between 1935-1940 exposed this provincial weakness, both in fact and in law. Social legislation, about which Quebec is deeply concerned, is more easily conceived of in provincial terms in so far as administration goes, and even the financing of minor services can be borne by provinces, but the larger social insurances affecting unemployment, health and old age are too costly for most provincial budgets without federal participation. Already unemployment insurance and old age pensions have been attributed to Ottawa by constitutional amendment. Other provincial services are developing so fast that they too are demanding federal aid. University education is a case in point. National economic policies and social service demands tend toward centralization, no matter what interpretations the courts place upon the constitution or what arguments are brought forward for provincial autonomy. Hence Quebec's fears for the future of her distinctive way of life are increased, and the conflicts of opinion which are always present in the federal system are exacerbated.

The most powerful centripetal forces are created by the fundamental dynamic in Canadian society – industrialisation. This is the real enemy to provincial autonomy as conceived in racial or any other terms, and the most serious challenge which French Canada must face – more dangerous than the English majority in Canada, also carried along by the forces of change, or than 'Ottawa' or any other external symbolisation of the 'threat to Quebec.' Industrialisation and technical change are sweeping Quebec as never before in her history, for the rugged Laurentian country which for so long maintained the near-subsistence agriculture on which Old France could survive in North America, is now found to be rich with minerals and resources which an expanding economy requires for its voracious mills and factories. The remotest regions of the province are being brought under exploration and development. Great amounts of capital are needed that few

French Canadians can provide, and the large private corporations which, in a capitalist society, are the chief instruments used in development, relentlessly transform the ancient pattern of Quebec life, introduce new centres of authority, and tie the province to world markets. The movement from farm to factory is accentuated, despite Quebec's belief in 'colonisation' of marginal lands; immigrant labour can for the first time be absorbed in French communities; international trade unions reach out to protect workers who feel themselves to be unsympathetically treated even by their own government. The cultural curtain which history and institutional policy have placed around Quebec is brushed aside at every point.

It is ironic that the man who most invokes the political appeal of provincial autonomy, Premier Maurice Duplessis, is the one who has most encouraged the very process which is undermining his own philosophy. Being conservative in background and political outlook, he promotes private enterprise in its purest forms, so that while it is true, as *Le Devoir* said,[10] that 'the only government over which the people of Quebec exercise absolute control is the Quebec Government,' the Quebec population has very little control over the policies of the financiers and entrepreneurs who are shaping the future relationships of Quebec to Canada and to the outside world. Corporate undertakings of the modern type are themselves a form of government, and to use the words of an American constitutional authority, 'corporations, in the process of conducting their operations in a number of states, render control by any state extremely difficult, leaving the federal government the only potentially effective master.'[11] Even Ottawa seems powerless in face of the general trend. The forces threatening Quebec are international in scope, and battles over provincial status seem peculiarly beside the point.

It is not only economic forces, however, which play this formative role in the federal system. Canada's international obligations, and her essential part in the defence system of the western world, also change the basis of federalism. During World War II, Canada became virtually a unitary state. Emergency conditions necessitated a high degree of centralisation. That this did not permanently destroy the autonomy of provinces is evidenced by their present strength. But some after-effects of war show no signs of disappearing. One is the continuing need to spend large sums on defence, which necessitates a high level of federal taxation. Both in law and in policy defence demands have priority over provincial claims. Money for this programme must be obtained from taxation spread over the whole country, including Quebec. In addition, Canadian industry must be available as needed for defence supplies; this has necessitated federal legislation under which very stringent controls can be imposed by Ottawa upon sources of production. Each

10 Quoted and translated in Montreal *Gazette*, 31 March 1955.
11 Swisher, *The Growth of Constitutional Power in the United States*, p. 208.

individual industry in a province forms part of the national defence potential. No industry falls exclusively within the jurisdiction of the province in which it is situated, though 'property and civil rights' are provincial matters under the constitution. Given nothing worse than a cold war, the defence power leaves room for provincial freedom, but no concession can be made to provincial governments which threaten defence planning for the security of Canada and her western allies. The conflicts that occur in the field of public law in Canada, and the constant attempt to find new solutions to the financial problems facing provincial governments, are carried on under the overriding necessity of facing the realities of the international situation.

## FISCAL POLICY AND PROVINCIAL AUTONOMY

It may be admitted that provincial autonomy must have a sound financial base or it is an empty formula. In insisting on this point, Quebec voices a widespread belief. With federal taxes geared to the double requirement of equilibrium economics and defence spending, the field of taxation is so largely occupied by the federal government that provincial legislatures are hard pressed to find the additional funds needed for their expanding social services. Under the constitution they are denied the right to levy any but direct taxes. All provinces other than Quebec – and, for a time, Ontario – accepted Ottawa's solution to this problem up to 1957, in the form of five-year tax rental agreements by which, in return for their withdrawal from the income and corporation tax fields, they received additional grants from the federal treasury on formulae equally available to all. Quebec refused to enter these arrangements after 1945, though she was a party to the War-Time Tax Agreements, 1941–45. Mr Duplessis has consistently interpreted his refusal as a defence of the fundamental rights of Quebec, and Ottawa's taxation policies as an attack upon those rights. The following extracts from a speech he delivered at Rouyn, PQ, on August 21, 1955,[12] state his position clearly enough:

The Premier said the efforts of the Government were limited by the amount of taxes collected ... 'To do what is required to meet the growing needs of our province and our people, additional funds will be required ... '

'As far as I am concerned,' the Premier asserted, 'I don't know how many more years Providence will allow me to continue as the head of the Government. I know it would be simple for me to take the easy way out and sell the rights of Quebec for a few million dollars. It would be easy but it would not be honourable. I have said before and I say it again,' declared the Premier, 'that I will never betray the province of Quebec whether the price is a few pieces of silver or millions of dollars ... '

12 As reported in Montreal *Gazette*, 23 August, 1955.

'We must have additional funds to provide our schools with the educational facilities to which they are entitled; we must have financial independence to build our own hospitals and to provide the people of this province with the social services which they have come to expect from their government.'

Stated in these general terms, these propositions have evoked almost universal support in Quebec and a good deal outside. The problem is to know whether in fact the rejected taxation agreements, or others which may replace them, are the real danger to autonomy which they are painted to be. Sharp conflicts of opinion between Quebec and the rest of Canada have arisen on this point. Other provinces find it difficult to believe that a French-Canadian Prime Minister of Canada, or the Quebec members of the Senate and House of Commons, would have approved the tax arrangements had they contained a betrayal of Quebec's rights. The general view outside Quebec seems to be that some such form of financial co-operation between all Canadian governments is essential for the economic well-being of the whole country, and that any province attempting to 'go it alone' will not only injure its own people but others as well. The smaller and poorer provinces in particular want a federal policy which redistributes national income through federal support of social insurances and direct subsidies to provincial governments. The opposition of so powerful a province as Quebec could mean the collapse of national plans and a general free-for-all in which existing inequalities between regions and classes would be greatly accentuated.

From the Quebec point of view, however, the problem is not at bottom economic. Or rather, its economic aspects are not as important as its cultural implications. To be subsidised is to be in some degree dependent. The donor is psychologically and politically stronger than the recipient of the gift; hence if Quebec accepts money from Ottawa, the dual-state theory of Canadian government is difficult to maintain. In receiving subsidies the people of Quebec learn to look outside their borders for assistance; their local loyalty is weakened; they become less defensive of their special position. If it is pointed out that subsidies have always existed in the constitution, and that they were an integral part of the agreement of 1867, obviously not destructive of provincial autonomy, the reply is that the original provinces were weak and undeveloped, not obliged to assume the wide functions of their present government, and not faced with the challenge to autonomy which now threatens them. The very strength of the present centripetal forces justifies further measures for safeguarding local self-government. Even though some 'efficiency,' from the purely economic point of view, be lost, the value of autonomy, particularly for Quebec, far outweighs this cost.[13]

13 This danger is not felt exclusively in Quebec: see e.g. H.F. Argus, 'Two Restrictions on Provincial Autonomy,' *Can. Journal of Economics and Political Science*, Vol. 21, p. 445.

Even deeper motives can be sensed in Quebec's hesitancy to commit herself to certain forms of tax centralisation. Long range fears, as much as present dangers, compel caution. A particular scheme, such as the Tax Rental Agreements, on its surface may appear fair and reasonable. It avoids dual taxation, supports national fiscal policy, and effects a redistribution of wealth toward the poorer provinces. What can be said against it? The answer often given in Quebec is that it is the beginning of a road, the end of which no one can foresee. Today there may be nothing but benefit in the scheme, tomorrow the strength of Quebec may be undermined beyond repair. Such is the line of thought which has produced a refusal to co-operate in national fiscal plans even when this refusal has cost Quebec millions of dollars of revenue. And since fiscal needs constantly increase, the government of Quebec chooses to impose dual income taxation and to demand that the federal government withdraw from direct taxation fields which the province wishes to enter. Unless Ottawa moves out there is little room for Quebec to move in, since under the law a province has no priority in the exercise of the direct taxation to which it is restricted.[14] But if the federal government is obliged to withdraw from a given field of taxation at provincial request, then not only does national fiscal policy go by the board but a doctrine of nullification or veto by provinces over Parliament becomes part of Canadian constitutional practice, regardless of what the law may be. It was on this point that Mr St-Laurent stood firm when Mr Duplessis first imposed his provincial income tax in 1954, and on which the Quebec government eventually gave way by removing the claim to priority from the statute.[15]

In every federal state the division of taxing powers and public revenues presents grave difficulties. In the United States, Australia and Switzerland, as well as in Canada where they are part of the original law of the constitution, subsidies to the states and cantons have had to be instituted.[16] Yet these countries have remained federal in form, though the central authority has grown stronger. Quebec's claim for fiscal autonomy is by no means peculiar to herself; it is echoed by other Canadian provinces and in other federations. But in her case it takes on added strength and colour because it becomes part of the general defense of a minority culture.

EDUCATIONAL CONFLICTS

Some of the most acute conflicts in the field of public law have occurred over the educational provisions of the Canadian constitution. The story is a long one, reaching back to the vain attempts of the English not long after the cession to es-

14 See discussion in F.R. Scott, 'The Constitutional Background of Taxation Agreements,'
   2 *McGill Law Journal*, p. 1 (Essay XXII above).
15 See amendment in 1955 Quebec Statutes c. 15.
16 Wheare, *Federal Government*, 3rd. ed. pp. 115–6.

tablish the Royal Institution for the Advancement of Learning as a general educational system for the province. Against this unifying tendency Quebec stood firm, claiming the right to separate French parochial schools. In the course of the constitutional evolution since those days Canada has achieved a peculiar school system which varies from province to province and which ranges in theory from the complete separation of Protestant and Catholic schools, as in Quebec, to the notion of the single, undenominational state-supported public school, as in British Columbia. In between are several variations on these two themes, with varying types of separate schools in Ontario, Saskatchewan, Alberta and the Northwest Territories. Newfoundland has added a new note with five kinds of religious schools receiving state support: Roman Catholic, Anglican, United Church, Salvation Army and Pentecostal Associations. Needless to say, the Canadian constitution does not contain a fundamental rule barring 'an establishment of religion,' as in the opening clause of the First Amendment to the United States constitution.

The conflicts that arise in this area are numerous and stem from different motives. They are by no means exclusively disagreements between French-Catholics and English-Protestants. Sometimes English-speaking Catholics are ranged against French-speaking co-religionists, as in the lawsuit which tested the validity of Ontario's attempt to restrict the use of French as the language of instruction.[17] Sometimes two different churches are allied in their opposition to a school law, as in the attack upon the Manitoba School Act of 1890 when Anglicans and Catholics joined forces.[18] The Jewish communities in Quebec have difficulty in fitting themselves into a system divided into two Christian groups, and some Doukhobors refuse to send their children to any school, resulting (in British Columbia) in the forceful separation of children from parents. Ontario law still has provision for separate schools for 'coloured people,' though the last of such schools ceased to exist in 1891.[19] The heterogeneity of the Canadian population, which steadily increases as new immigrants arrive, produces many claims on provincial governments for educational privileges.

From the point of view of Quebec, however, there is one claim which has priority over all others, and that is the right of the French-Canadian minority in all other provinces to possess as favourable a system of separate schools as exists for both Catholics and Protestants in Quebec. Spokesmen for Quebec take justifiable pride in pointing out the favourable situation of the Protestant minority in the province, and claim that no other provincial government treats the minority so well. They contend that the principle of separate schools, written into Section 93 of the constitution, while not universally extended in the early days to all

17 *Ottawa Separate Schools* v. *Mackell*, [1917] A.C. 62.
18 *Winnipeg* v. *Barret*, *Winnipeg* v. *Logan:* [1892] A.C. 445.
19 Information supplied by the Ontario Dept. of Education.

Canada, should be admitted in every province as the French-speaking population grows. They have been bitterly disappointed in certain leading court decisions which have denied their claims, notably with regard to separate schools in New Brunswick and Manitoba, to the use of the French language in Ontario, and to the distribution of school funds in Ontario. They feel aggrieved that British Columbia does not accept their views. Gérard Filion, Editor of *Le Devoir*, lists the inequalities in the school system as one of the great causes of friction between the two races, and he adds somewhat optimistically:[20] 'On the day when every French-Canadian, wherever he may be in the country, enjoys the same advantages and the same privileges as his English-speaking compatriot, the last obstacle to the unity of the country will have disappeared.'

The opponents of this view employ much the same argument as can be heard in the United States against the claims of parochial schools to a share of tax revenues, though in Canada there is no constitutional barrier to such payments. The need to develop a common sense of citizenship, and to overcome the racial and religious hatreds that too often follow segregation, exists in Canada as well as in the United States. Groups that feel unable to use state schools on conscientious grounds are at liberty to set up and pay for private schools. A belief in the advisability of the complete separation of church and state is firmly held in many parts of Canada, though not written into the fundamental law. The conflict of ideas here is one of principle, not easy to resolve since there is no common point of departure. In the result, Canada remains partly committed to separate schools, and partly not.

The differences of view over schools reach out to other fields of education. Universities in Canada have traditionally been established or regulated by provincial legislation. Some have, like McGill, a Royal Charter antedating Confederation; others, like the University of Montreal, have both a civil and a pontifical charter. All are having difficulty in securing the necessary finances. In 1951 the federal government, which had long been making special grants for particular forms of university research, adopted a recommendation of the Massey Commission and embarked upon a scheme of subsidisation for all universities based on a formula equally applied in all the provinces. In Quebec, a special committee appointed by the Quebec government supervised the distribution of the funds. All Quebec universities at first accepted the plan, but after one year the Quebec government refused to participate further and declared that Ottawa's subsidies were an invasion of the province's exclusive jurisdiction over education. As no other province took this view, the result has been that all universities save those in Quebec have continued to receive federal funds. Meanwhile the Quebec government has insti-

20 In *Saturday Night*, Nov. 24, 1954.

tuted payments on a year to year basis to replace those lost by its own institutions. This additional drain on its resources is urged as a further argument for exclusive use of the direct tax fields allotted to it under the constitution.

The same dispute goes beyond school and university into the realm of culture generally. Is 'culture' a provincial matter? The very idea seems to denude the word of any meaningful content, yet many defenders of provincial autonomy claim that it is included by analogy in the term 'education,' over which provinces have the main jurisdiction. It would follow that Ottawa should not assist at all in the development of the arts and sciences, or in adult education. Yet radio and television broadcasting have been ascribed to federal jurisdiction by legal interpretation of the constitution, the federal responsibility for the whole Northwest Territories and for Canada's 160,000 Indians as well as its need for trained personnel in every branch of government, as patent facts. Legally there is no invasion of any legislative field in a province if the federal Crown, legal proprietor of public funds, offers a subsidy to any institution or group engaged in educational or cultural work, since the making of gifts is not the same as enacting laws.[21] Moreover, as the Massey Report said: 'If the Federal Government is to renounce its right to associate itself with other social groups, public and private, in the general education of Canadian citizens, it denies its intellectual and moral purpose, the complete conception of the common good is lost, and Canada, as such, becomes a materialistic society.' Despite these facts and this argument, opposition from Quebec is credited with the prevention of the establishment of the Canada Council, as recommended by the Massey Report, thus leaving Canada without any Arts Council or any National Commission for UNESCO.[22] Meanwhile Canadian artists and writers must rely on the generous assistance of American Foundations and such help as may come from provincial institutions (among which the Quebec government is most generous) supplemented by federal aid in the form of radio and television contracts or fellowships paid out of blocked European currencies. This *Kulturkampf* has its casualties in fewer creative artists and lost cultural opportunities.

LANGUAGE DISPUTES

The law of the Canadian constitution recognizes English and French as the two official languages of the country, within certain limits. They are on an equal footing as regards their use in the Parliament of Canada, in federal statutes, and in

21 Cf. note (14) above.
22 On November 12, 1956, Mr St-Laurent announced that his government intended to establish the Council.

federal courts. Since these statutes and courts may operate anywhere in the country, every province is in this sense bilingual. But in provincial legislatures, statutes and courts outside Quebec, English is the sole official language. This results from the wording of section 133 of the BNA Act, reading as follows:

133. Either the English or the French Language may be used by any Person in the Debates of the Houses of the Parliament of Canada and of the Houses of the Legislature of Quebec; and both these Languages shall be used in the respective Records and Journals of those Houses; and either of those Languages may be used by any Person or in any Pleading or Process in or issuing from any Court of Canada established under this Act, and in or from all or any of the Courts of Quebec.

The Acts of the Parliament of Canada and of the Legislature of Quebec shall be printed and published in both those Languages.

Thus the simple description of Canada as a 'bilingual country' is misleading, unless understood in the special Canadian sense.

The incompleteness in Canadian bilingualism is a source of irritation in Quebec, just as any extension of French annoys certain elements in English-speaking provinces. Attacks upon the whole notion of bilingualism have come from several parts of the country. Instead of seeing in these two languages, which happen today to be the two working languages of the United Nations, a source of cultural richness, bilingualism is frequently felt to be a handicap to be overcome. Thus in 1890 Manitoba repealed that section of its original constitution which had made French an official language for the province. In 1877 Ottawa introduced French into the Northwest Territories, but in 1891 permitted the Legislative Assembly of the Territories to decide the question itself, and in 1892 it abolished the use of French for debates – a further example of how local autonomy may be used to restrict minority rights.[23] Ontario's decision in 1913 to limit the use of French as a language of instruction in her schools raised a storm of protest, not alleviated by Court rulings that the law was constitutional. In 1937, Mr Duplessis put through an amendment to make the French text of the Civil Code and statutes of Quebec prevail over the English in case of conflict, but as this was clearly contrary to section 133 of the BNA Act he was induced to repeal the law, so that the two languages remain on an equal footing in Quebec.

French has thus lost some of the status it once held in the law of western Canada. On the other hand the federal control over broadcasting has brought French programmes into areas which, had radio been a provincial matter, would not have

23 French continues, however, as an official language in the Courts of the Territories.

permitted it. Strong pressure from Quebec, and a somewhat more rational attitude toward bilingualism, have resulted in the establishment by the Canadian Broadcasting Corporation of French-language stations on the prairies. A French network has been set up, bringing programmes to French minorities far from their homeland. Radio and television are important influences in the extension of the French language in Canada and of English in Quebec. Since, however, the French are concentrated in the Quebec region and represent less than 30% of the total Canadian population, a widespread familiarity with the second official language is hardly to be anticipated, however desirable it may be.

## CIVIL LIBERTIES

The Canadian constitution does not contain a Bill of Rights such as is found in the American and other written constitutions. Some constitutional guarantees, such as those for separate schools, the two languages, and annual sessions of Parliament, are in the text of the BNA Act, but freedom of religion, speech, press and assembly are not mentioned in the written law. As in England, they remain sacred by tradition but at the mercy of legislation. The only question for Canada is which legislature has jurisdiction – federal or provincial; the rights themselves are seemingly not beyond parliamentary modification.

Perhaps nowhere in the public law of Canada is the difference of outlook between French and English more marked than in respect to civil liberties. The order of values is not the same in the two peoples; the tradition and situation of Quebec make its people emphasize their own minority rights at all times, while in other provinces the stress is much more on individual rights. The 'village Hampden' that Wolfe was reputedly hearing about as he was rowed under the cliffs of Quebec in September 1759 was unknown to New France, where representative institutions, even on the municipal level, had never existed. The Declaration of the Rights of Man, France's great contribution to modern liberal thought, came after the cession, and was then so associated with anti-clericalism as to render it ever afterwards suspect by the Catholic Church in Canada. On the other hand, English public law had not worked out any theory of minority rights guaranteed by law.

The British conquest was the first revolutionary experience French Canada had ever had, and though the new sovereign soon introduced an elected legislative assembly, and replaced the *lettre de cachet* by Habeas Corpus, the cession created racial tensions not favourable to the growth of an indigenous sense of personal freedom. Individual liberties thenceforth had an English face, and the democracy thus begun was discovered by the French to possess unexpected limitations when it seemed likely to transfer power to their hands. Lower Canada's fight for responsible government, as Durham rightly perceived, was a struggle not of principles but of races, though democratic slogans were used. The prime purpose was to assert minority rights against the English, rather than, as in Upper Canada, to secure personal freedom from arbitrary power of any kind. Since those days the concept of the 'état de siège' has persisted in Quebec and in French minorities in other provinces, making them subordinate individual liberty to the common racial goal, and to ostracise those of their own group who deviate from the official line of action.

In the matter of religious toleration, similar differences of outlook appear. No Protestant was ever allowed into New France after 1627; Protestantism was the religion of the conquerors which the French were forced to tolerate. The British, intolerant of Catholicism at home, were obliged to give legal status to Catholics in Quebec by the sheer necessities of Canadian life as well as by the need for allies against the growing threat of revolt in America. Toleration in these circumstances did not carry much conviction. The strong Catholic tradition in Quebec has remained ultramontane rather than Gallican, and authoritarian rather than liberal. Quebec has seen in parliamentary institutions a valuable instrument for asserting cultural differences, while the English accepted toleration and minority rights in inverse proportion to their distance from Quebec.

These various strands have shaped and are still shaping the evolution of the laws relating to civil liberties. Examples can be found on both sides of a disregard for the types of fundamental rights proclaimed in the Universal Declaration of Human Rights of the United Nations. Only since World War II, for instance, have the federal election laws removed several forms of racial discrimination, and Ottawa's attempt to deport some 4,000 Canadian Japanese in 1945-46 will stand as a solemn reminder that racial prejudice can spring up anywhere in Canada. Quebec did not grant votes to women until 1941, and her Civil Code still subjects married women to serious incapacities. But while Ottawa and various provincial governments were removing discrimination from their laws, Quebec has been moving in the opposite direction. Recently, certain Quebec statutes have curtailed the traditional freedom of religion, of speech and of the press in a manner which has marked off its legislation sharply from that of other provinces, and has created conflicts both in public opinion and in the courts.

These statutes were all introduced by Premier Duplessis and backed by his Union Nationale Party. The most notorious of them, adopted in 1937, and popularly known as the *Padlock Act*, makes it an offence to propagate 'communism or bolshevism' by any means in a 'house' in the province, or to publish or distribute any literature propagating or even 'tending to propagate' these undefined doctrines. Any house may be padlocked, and the occupant evicted, by the Attorney-General 'on satisfactory proof' that the Act is being violated, without any notice or trial in a court of law; to remove the padlock the owner must institute an action in court and prove either that the house was not in fact being so used or that he was ignorant of it. Thus there is punishment without trial, and the burden of proof is cast upon persons presumably innocent. Since the federal government refused to disallow the Act, it remained in force and has been applied on numerous occasions to activities of suspected communist groups. Its constitutionality was upheld by Quebec courts, but a final appeal to the Supreme Court of Canada is pending. While Canadian opinion, both in Quebec and outside, is overwhelmingly opposed to the spread of communism, this type of legislation is in direct conflict with traditional freedom concepts and nothing similar to it has existed in Canadian law in peacetime. [Even the notorious Section 98 of the Criminal Code, repealed in 1936, required trial in open Court before a judge and jury.]

Other examples may be given of recent Quebec legislation restricting ancient civil liberties. A provincial statute enacted in 1947 enables municipalities to prohibit the distribution on their streets of any literature or pamphlets without the permission of a municipal chief of police. Thus a local policeman becomes a press censor. Many municipalities have adopted such by-laws, and even federal candidates at federal elections have found themselves obliged to submit their election literature to police approval.[24] The prohibition appears to be aimed at the activities. of Jehovah's Witnesses and communists; like all such laws, in striking at minorities, it deprives everyone of rights. In 1950 the Quebec legislature adopted the *Act Respecting Publications and Public Morals*, by which the Board of Cinema Censors may issue a censure order against magazines and certain other publications which are found to contain 'immoral illustrations,' whereupon all copies may be seized by the police with or without warrant. Another Quebec statute enabled municipalities to close commercial establishments on certain Catholic feast days, whether or not they were owned by Catholics. Montreal's attempt to apply the law was, however, held unconstitutional by the Supreme Court of Canada, overruling the Quebec Court of Appeal, and the statute itself was held to be criminal law, a subject outside provincial powers under the BNA Act.[25] Still other Quebec statutes have seriously restricted the rights of trade unions. One bars all strikes and lock-outs, and imposes compulsory arbitration, in all 'public services' in the province, including municipal and school corporations, public transportation systems and public utilities. No other province in Canada feels such drastic curbs to be necessary. Another Quebec law requires that the certificate of recognition of all trade unions must be refused or revoked if they tolerate so much as one organizer or officer adhering 'to a communist party or movement,'

24  See F.R. Scott, Correspondence, 31 *Can. Bar Review* (1953) p. 591; also *Dame Dionne* v. *The Municipal Court* [1956] S.C. 289.
25  See *Birks & Sons* v. *City of Montreal*, [1955] S.C.R. 799.

thus limiting the unions' freedom to choose its own leaders. And in 1954, the Freedom of Worship Act, dating from before Confederation, was amended so as to narrow considerably the toleration hitherto allowed.[26]

While these Quebec laws are in conflict with traditional freedoms in Canada, provisions not so dissimilar have been found in other parts of the country at various times. Certainly the Quebec community is not alone in reacting against communists, Jehovah's Witnesses and trade unions. British Columbia prevented a qualified student from practicing law because he was a communist;[27] the Labour Relations Board of Nova Scotia refused to certify a union whose secretary-treasurer was a communist;[28] Prince Edward Island in 1948 adopted a law amounting almost to total prohibition of trade unions;[29] Alberta has passed a statute limiting the right of Hutterites colonies to purchase land.[30] The Quebec laws, particularly the *Padlock Act*, are severe, but may well represent a temporary reaction to a new situation. There are some signs that within Quebec society itself, particularly among trade unionists, there is a growing awareness of the need for protecting individual rights against Quebec authorities. Industrial disputes place the French-Canadian worker in opposition to French-Canadian employers and provincial police. Racial categories break down before economic facts. Catholic teachers once went on strike in Montreal against the Catholic School Commission, and their union fought valiantly, though unsuccessfully, for its rights to collective bargaining.[31]

Surveying the recent battles over civil liberties which have for the first time been presented to the Quebec courts, it seems fair to say that the judges in Quebec are far more inclined than are the common law judges to uphold the authority of the state as against the individual, though generalisations here must be used with caution. In five recent leading cases, dealing with the definition of sedition,[32] with arbitrary decertification of a trade union,[33] with the control of pamphlet

---

26 Statutes of Quebec, 1953–54, cap. 15. The amendment forbids 'abusive or insulting attacks against the practice of a religious profession.'

27 E. Meredith, 'Communism and the BC Bar,' 1950 28 *Can. Bar Review* 893.

28 *Smith & Rhuland Ltd.* v. *The Queen* [1953] 2 S.C.R. 95; 1954 *Can. Bar Review*, pp. 85, 353.

29 E.A. Forsey, 'The PEI Trade Union Act,' 1948 *Can. Bar Review* 1159.

30 See *Communal Property Act*, 1947 Alberta Statutes Cap. 16.

31 The Union, having been illegally decertified by the Quebec Labour Relations Board, won back in the Supreme Court of Canada (overruling the Quebec Court of Appeal) its right to recognition as the bargaining unit, only to have the right taken away by retroactive legislation put through the Quebec Legislature. See *Alliance des Professeurs Catholiques* v. *Labour Relations Board* [1953] 2 S.C.R. 140: 2–3 Eliz. 11, Cap. 11 (Quebec).

32 The *Boucher* case: [1951] S.C.R. 265; 1951 *Can. Bar Review* p. 193.

33 The *Alliance* case: [1953] 2 S.C.R. 140; 1953 *Can. Bar Review* p. 821.

distribution by cities,[34] with liability of police officers for unlawfully disturbing a meeting of Jehovah's Witnesses,[35] and with compulsory observance of Catholic feast days,[36] the Supreme Court of Canada took a more liberal view of private rights than did the Quebec Court of Appeal, which was overruled every time. Two further cases, involving the validity of the *Padlock Act*[37] and the legality of the cancellation of a liquor licence held by Witnesses of Jehovah[38] seems to show the same support of authority by Quebec judges. It is only to be expected that Quebec Courts, like any others, will reflect in large part the prevailing attitudes of the community from which they are drawn, and that community is still highly authoritarian.

CONCLUSION

It is necessary to repeat again what was said earlier about the relationship between areas of conflict and areas of co-operation. Conflict in any acute sense between Quebec and the rest of Canada is the exception, not the rule, but it is often vivid and sometimes profound, and its existence throws light upon the root differences in the two cultures. Within the legal order, cultural conflicts present no different problem from class conflicts or international conflicts; they are one among the many types which it is the purpose of the law to resolve by peaceful means with the minimum of effort. If contained within the bounds of constitutionalism, they are a creative force moulding the law and adapting it to the satisfaction of larger numbers of people. Canadian public law, with its mixture of English and Canadian rules, has shown itself to be sufficiently humane in principle and adaptable in practice to suit the needs of most Canadians, as is evidenced by the small number of substantive changes made in the Constitution since 1867. That the French minorities however, still feel dissatisfied on certain issues has already been indicated, and conflicts of opinion about the nature of Canadian federalism are as acute today as they have ever been.

What immediately lies ahead of Canadians is the problem of completing the 'nationalisation' of the constitution. The BNA Act remains a British statute; its very name belongs to an age that is past. Fundamental changes in its provisions cannot be made wholly within Canada, for the quaint procedure known as the

---

34 The *Saumur* case: [1953] 2 S.C.R. 299.
35 The *Chaput* case: [1955] S.C.R. 834.
36 The *Birks* case: supra note (25).
37 The *Switzman* case: Padlock Act upheld by Quebec Court of Appeal, [1954] Q.B. 421. Appeal pending in Supreme Court.
38 The *Roncarelli* case: cancellation upheld by Quebec Court of Appeal, [1956] Q.B. 447. Appeal pending in Supreme Court.

'Joint Address' of the Senate and House of Commons to the United Kingdom Parliament for proposed amendments has survived Canada's achievement of nationhood. Until a new procedure is agreed upon for these amendments, capable of being carried out inside the country, legal sovereignty cannot be finally transferred from England to Canada. The Constitutional Conference of 1950 failed to achieve this solution because Quebec insisted on the right of veto on every amendment affecting 'property and civil rights,' though the other provinces were quite willing to entrench the minority rights clauses.[39] Hence the English-French complex is responsible for the continuing element of colonialism in Canada's relations with Great Britain. The fear of Ottawa is seemingly greater in Quebec than the fear of London, though since London by constitutional convention must always act at Ottawa's request, the retention of the sovereignty of Westminster does not remove the danger of overriding by the majority.[40] By tacit agreement the political parties now leave in abeyance a question fraught with such danger of race conflict. Perhaps the drafting of a Canadian Bill of Rights, placing fundamental freedoms as well as minority rights beyond the risk of diminution without the unanimous consent of all provinces, might provide a basis on which a reasonably flexible amending process for other parts of the constitution might be established, and the legislative independence of the country finally secured.

39 See the two volumes of *Proceedings of the Constitutional Conference of Federal and Provincial Governments*, Ottawa, 1950.
40 Despite the contrary argument in Gérin-Lajoie, *Constitutional Amendment in Canada*. Same author, 'Du pouvoir d'amendement constitutionnel,' 29 *Can. Bar Review*, 1136 at p. 1149.

# XXIV

# The Bill of Rights and Quebec Law

*The Canadian Bill of Rights was adopted in 1960. It belongs in the field of Public Law, and hence has its sources in the English Common Law which underlies the Public Law of all the provinces. In Quebec, however, the private law derives from the French Civil Law, and to enforce the Bill of Rights it may be necessary to institute a private action against someone who has violated a protected right. The application of the Bill of Rights may thus differ as between Quebec and the other provinces. Some of these problems are discussed here.*
From the *Canadian Bar Review*, 37, 1959, 135–46

Mr Diefenbaker's proposed Bill of Rights, as drafted, confines itself to matters within federal jurisdiction. Since in these fields the law of Quebec is the same as that of the other provinces, the Bill will presumably have the same effect, and the same lack of effect, in Quebec as elsewhere in Canada. Section 3, its operative clause, instructs the courts to construe and apply all federal statutes and orders so as not to 'abrogate, abridge or infringe' the named human rights and freedoms, and Quebec judges will face the same problems as their brethren outside the province in applying this rule of interpretation. What is the meaning of such phrases found in the Bill as 'due process of law,' 'discrimination,' 'other constitutional safeguards,' 'cruel, inhuman or degrading treatment or punishment,' 'principles of fundamental justice?' What is the effect of the Bill upon the interpretation of a future statute running to the contrary? Do the tenor and content of the Bill enlarge the concepts of public order and good morals to be applied in the interpretation of contracts? These are the kinds of questions that will arise, requiring answers in Quebec similar to those that will be found elsewhere.

As no new remedies are given to any individual by the Bill, the basic law protecting civil liberties in Quebec will remain unchanged. That law, like its counterpart in common-law jurisdictions, rests in large part upon the right to an action in damages against anyone, whether private citizen or public officer, who causes damage to another by his negligence or fault. Further important protections for individual freedoms are given by the prerogative writs – habeas corpus, mandamus, prohibition, certiorari, quo warranto. In the wider field of administrative law, Quebec courts insist upon their right to review administrative acts, and have adopted the same 'principles of natural justice' as operate in common-law jurisdictions as criteria for administrative behaviour.[1] This is to be expected, since the public law of Quebec is English in origin, and will vary from English or other Canadian precedents only where a local statute has altered it. The criminal law, on the definitions and procedure of which so much civil liberty depends, being in the Criminal Code of Canada, offers no contrasts in Quebec save in the vagaries of judicial interpretation and judicial severity in imposing sentences. Constitutional law, important to civil liberties in its restraints upon legislatures, is also the same for Quebec as for other provinces in so far as the interpretation of sections 91 to 93 of the British North America Act is concerned.

Thus the differences between the civil and common-law jurisdictions in Canada, in respect of the general law protecting human rights and fundamental freedoms, are not as great as might be imagined, since so much of this law is either uniform throughout Canada (criminal law, constitutional law on distribution of legislative powers) or else is public law of English origin (prerogative writs, administrative law). Only in the civil law proper, and in local statutes, do we find particular rules for Quebec, and here the general action in damages before the ordinary courts – Dicey's 'rule of law' in action – is permitted on principles not dissimilar from the tort action at common law.

These general propositions deserve closer analysis. The civil law of delict and quasi-delict, for example, not being the same as the common law of torts, provides a somewhat different protection for the victim of wrongdoing. The civil law has evolved a general principle of liability for wrongs, applicable to all situations that present themselves. It is a law of delict and not of delicts; new sets of facts may arise in society to which the rule has never been applied before, yet which it is adequate to cover.[2] Quebec judges do not legislate when so applying the all-embracing principle, they merely subsume new facts under the ancient rule. The common law of torts has not yet been reduced to a single general principle, and a

---

1 See LeDain, The Supervisory Jurisdiction in Quebec (1957), 35 *Can. Bar Rev.* 788.
2 See, for example, *Robbins* v. *Canadian Broadcasting Corporation*, [1958] S.C. 152, where damages were awarded against the Canadian Broadcasting Corporation for injury to plaintiff's practice and invasion of his privacy caused by an invitation to viewers of a television programme to 'cheer him up' by telephoning his home. Scott CJ said: 'There is no need to attempt any precise definition of this fault which defendant's servants committed' (at p. 157).

plaintiff must bring his action within a tort already known to the law, though 'extensions' of the old concepts may occur.[3] Moreover the civil law has developed the notion of 'abuse of rights' as a protection against the exercise of a right merely for the purpose of injuring another; and while Quebec courts have been hesitant to apply the principle it is available for use in civil-liberties cases in this province to a degree not open to the common-law judge.[4] Thus in theory at least the civil law of Quebec on delicts and quasi-delicts as set out in articles 1053–1056 of the Civil Code should give a wider protection for civil liberties than does the common law. As Mr Justice Taschereau said in *Chaput* v. *Romain;*[5]

Il [le dommage moral] comprend certainement le préjudice souffert dans la présente cause. Il s'entend en effet de tout atteinte aux droits extra-patrimoniaux, comme le droit à la liberté, à l'honneur, au nom, à la liberte de conscience ou de parole. Les tribunaux ne peuvent refuser de l'accorder, comme par exemple, si les *sentiments religieux ou patriotiques* ont été blessés.

According to this view, civil liberties such as freedom of conscience, freedom of speech, and freedom of the person are extra-patrimonial rights, any unjustified invasion of which renders the guilty party liable to a damage action. Hence article 1053 of the Civil Code which states: 'Every person capable of discerning right from wrong is responsible for the damage caused by his fault to another, whether by positive act, imprudence, neglect or want of skill,' underpins the basic human rights.

Some examples of the application of this rule may be given. The illegal deprivation of the right to vote is actionable in Quebec.[6] Cases abound in which police

3 See for instance, Goodhart, *English Law and The Moral Law* (1953), pp. 98–99: 'We do not even know whether there is a law of tort or a law of torts. The law has even been reluctant to hold that all intentional 'injuries' involve tortious liability. There are a considerable number of ways in which one person can intentionally injure another without subjecting himself to an action, but it would not be in the public interest to state them in detail'

4 See the discussions of the comparative legal situation in Baudouin, *Le droit civil de la province de Québec* (1953), p. 1283 *et seqq.* Also Nadeau, *Traité de droit civil du Québec* (1949), Chap. V. Mignault, *Premier Congrés de l'Association Henri Capitant* (1939), p. 643; *cf. Bradford* v. *Pickles,* [1895] A.C. 587 (H. of L.) (use of property case). Of course the notion of abuse of rights might be considered merely as an application of article 1053 and not an independent notion. Responsibility arises when a right is exercised in a faulty manner, whether or not the actor intended to injure the victim. Applying this rule in the field of administrative law, the test is: Would a prudent administrator have exercised his authority in this manner?

5 [1955] S.C.R. 834, at p. 841. [Italics in original text.]

6 Mignault, *Le droit civil canadien* (Vol. 5, 1901), p. 363 and cases there cited.

officers have been condemned to pay damages for false arrest, or for the use of excessive force in making an arrest.[7] Malicious prosecution also gives rise to an action under article 1053.[8] The same article covers all forms of defamation; such a case as *Morin* v. *Ryan*[9] is a good illustration of the civil law protecting an individual unjustly accused of being a communist – a healthy check on incipient McCarthysm. *Ortenberg* v. *Plamondon*[10] shows that defamation can be committed against a group of persons such as a small Jewish community in Quebec City. No case is reported in Quebec of damages awarded for a direct interference with freedom of speech, unless *le Club de la Garnison de Québec* v. *Lavergne*[11] be so considered; the court upheld the action of Lavergne against the club which had expelled him from membership because of a speech made in the legislature, but rested (somewhat dubiously) its decision on parliamentary privilege rather than on the civil law. Yet we have the authority of Taschereau J in the *Chaput* case,[12] for the proposition that any invasion of this right to free speech is a civil wrong.

Within the ambit of article 1053 comes also the general rule, and a very important one, that an act of a public officer exceeding his powers, or a faulty act within his powers, creates a liability to repair the consequent damage. As put by Mackinnon J in *Roncarelli* v. *Duplessis*,[13] 'If acting outside the statutory defined functions of his office defendant has committed a faulty and unauthorized act causing damage he should be held personally liable.' Abbott J in the same case[14] held respondent liable 'under Art. 1053 of the Civil Code for the damages sustained by the appellant, by reason of the acts done by respondent in excess of his legal authority,' and he expressly found that respondent was acting in what he conceived to be the best interests of the province. Fauteux J, dissenting on the ground that notice of action should have been given, said[15] 'Dans l'espèce, l'annulation du permis est exclusivement imputable à l'intimé et précisément pour cette raison, constitue dans les circonstances, un acte illicite donnant droit à l'appelant d'obtenir réparation pour les dommages lui en résultant.' This is but the state-

7 Nadeau, *op. cit., supra*, footnote 4, p. 208.
8 *Ibid.* See also *Dufour* v. *Tremblay*, [1954] S.C. 343.
9 [1957] Q.B. 296.
10 (1915), 24 K.B. 69.
11 (1918), 27 K.B. 37.
12 *Supra*, footnote 5. See Dalloz, *Nouveau repertoire* (Vol. 3), p. 831.
13 [1952] 1 D.L.R. 680, at p. 699 (S.C.). This, in my opinion, states the rule too narrowly, since it suggests that a mere exceeding of authority is not enough unless faulty, whereas the excess is the fault.
14 (1959), S. Ct. Can., not yet reported. In regard to authority for the rule, Abbott, J said: 'I do not find it necessary to cite from the wealth of authority supporting the principle that a public officer is responsible for acts done by him without legal justification. I content myself with quoting the well known passage from Dicey's *Law of the Constitution*, 9th ed., p. 193.'
15 *Ibid.*

ment in civil-law terms of the rule of public law given by Halsbury as follows:[16]

416. The so-called liberties of the subject are really implications drawn from the two principles that the subject may say or do what he pleases, provided he does not transgress the substantive law, or infringe the legal rights of others, whereas *public authorities (including the Crown) may do nothing but what they are authorized to do by some rule of common law or statute.*

In Quebec we must consider that this rule holding public officers to account before the ordinary courts for all their activities derives from English law, since it is part of public law. Yet the measure of the liability it imposes, the definition of fault, the defences available, and the finding of the causal connection between the act and the damage, will seemingly be based on the civil law. Thus common law and civil law blend in Quebec administrative law. The civil law excludes anything in the nature of punitive or exemplary damage, since the purpose of the delictual action is to compensate and not to punish. This at any rate is the way the problem is dealt with in the more recent Quebec cases against public officers. Doubt has been cast upon this interpretation, however, by Kellock J, in the *Chaput* case, at least in so far as concerns actions which fall within the scope of the Magistrates Privileges Act[17] of Quebec. The statute is designed to give certain procedural protections to public officers provided that (1) they were acting within their functions and (2) they were in good faith. The words of the statute expressly allow the court or jury to award such damages 'as they think proper.' Said the learned judge:[18]

In *Lachance* v. *Casault, ubi cit.* the Court of Appeal, after argument on the point, felt entitled to award punitive damages and did so. Whether that result was in harmony with the view that the defendant had ceased to bear the character of a public officer engaged in the performance of his duty need not be here considered. In a case to which the statute is applicable it may be that the right to recover 'such damages as they (the court or jury) think proper' (s. 2, R.S.Q., c. 18) is to be construed, like other provisions of the statute, in accordance with English law, and authorizes an award of common law damages. The statute is a special, while the Code is a general Act. Both have stood side by side since the enactment of the Code in 1866. It is, however, not necessary to decide that question on this occasion.

The point is therefore still open. It did not have to be decided in the *Roncarelli*

---

16 Halsbury, Laws of England (3rd ed. 1955) 1 vol. 7, par. 416. Italics mine.
17 R.S.Q., 1941, c. 18.
18 *Supra*, footnote 5, at p. 860.

case any more than in the *Chaput* case, since in neither were the defendants acting within their functions when causing damage, and hence neither was within the ambit of the Magistrates Privileges Act. It would be an odd result, however, if it were found that the public officer acting in bad faith outside his functions was liable to pay less damages, being restricted to civil-law compensation, than the officer who comes under the protecting statute where good faith and acting within the functions are required, and where defendant can be made to pay whatever damages are 'proper.' The protected official would then be worse off than the unprotected.

In view of the wide applicability of article 1053, how are we to explain the restrictive attitude of the Quebec courts in the recent important civil-liberties cases coming from that province? True, not all of these involved civil law principles: *Boucher* v. *The King*,[19] *Saumur* v. *City of Quebec*,[20] *Birks* v. *City of Montreal*[21] and *Switzman* v. *Elbling*[22] turned on points of constitutional and criminal law. In each of these cases, however, the Quebec Court of Appeal upheld the more authoritarian view of the law against the more liberal view, and in each it was overruled by the Supreme Court – in *Boucher* and *Saumur* by majorities of five to four, in *Birks* unanimously and in *Chaput* by eight to one. In the *Chaput*, *Roncarelli* and *Lamb*[23] cases the civil law of delict was invoked to support a claim for damages against public officers violating civil liberties; in each article 1053 of the Quebec Civil Code was in question; in each the plaintiff lost his action before the Quebec Court of Appeal and won it before the Supreme Court, unanimously or by substantial majorities (9–0, 6–3, 6–3). There seems little point in calling attention to the safeguards for civil liberties inherent in the Civil Code if in fact the Quebec courts refuse to apply them in concrete cases. The law at any given time is what the judges say it is, not what is written down in the books. The climate of Quebec, it must be admitted, has not recently been favourable to certain opinions, and with rare exceptions the judiciary has merely expressed the prevailing social outlook. If to these seven leading cases one adds the *Alliance*[24] case, where the Supreme Court held invalid the decertification of a trade union by the Quebec Labour Relations Board for lack of any notice to the union officers, which decertification the Court of Appeal had upheld, we have eight recent examples where the Supreme Court of Canada overruled the highest court in Quebec and gave a better support for human rights and fundamental freedoms. Sure-

---

19 [1951] S.C.R. 265.
20 [1953] 2 S.C.R. 299.
21 [1955] S.C.R. 799.
22 [1957] S.C.R. 285.
23 (1959), S. Ct. Can., not yet reported. See [1958] Q.B. 237.
24 *L'Alliance de Professeurs Catholiques de Montreal* v. *the Labour Relations Board of Quebec*, [1953] 2 S.C.R. 140.

ly the time has come for the tide to turn in Quebec. The civil law is waiting for a wider application than the Quebec judges seem willing to give it.

A special protection for religious freedom exists in Quebec, and also it seems in Ontario, through the existence in those provinces of the Freedom of Worship Act.[25] Enacted by the old province of Canada before Confederation, and hence covering the two central provinces, it has been continued in the Revised Statutes of Quebec till the present day, but was last consolidated in Ontario in 1897.[26] The present Quebec version of the Act declares that:

2. The free exercise and enjoyment of religious profession and worship, without discrimination or preference, provided the same be not made an excuse for acts of licentiousness, or a justification of practices inconsistent with the peace and safety of the Province, are by the constitution and laws of this Province allowed to all His Majesty's subjects living within the same.

After the Supreme Court decision in the *Saumur* case, and apparently to offset its possible effects, the Quebec legislature amended the Act[27] by adding a section which states that it does not constitute the free exercise or enjoyment of religious profession and worship to distribute, in public places or from door to door, books, magazines or tracts containing abusive or insulting attacks upon the religion of any portion of the population. The constitutional validity of this amendment is now before the Quebec courts.[28] In the light of the *Birks* decision, it would seem that laws affecting freedom of religion and religious observance fall within federal jurisdiction under the criminal law power. If this proves to be the constitutional law on the point, and it is submitted that it is, then the original Freedom of Worship Act of 1851 is now binding on both Quebec and Ontario, by virtue of section 129 of the British North America Act, and cannot be amended by either legislature in so far as the principle set out in section 2 is concerned. It is a 'Bill of Religious Rights' for two provinces, more precise than Mr Diefenbaker's Bill, and containing penalties for its breach.

Little need be said about the manner in which the prerogative writs and injunctions are applied in Quebec in civil liberties cases, since the law governing their use, with minor variations set out in the Quebec Code of Civil Procedure, is the same as that in other jurisdictions. The writs remain the essential weapons for the individual who is attempting to assert his rights and protect his freedoms

---

25 R.S.Q., 1941, c. 307.
26 R.S.Q., 1897, c. 306.
27 Stats. of Que., 1953–4, c. 15.
28 See *Procureur Général de la Province de Québec* v. *Saumur*, [1956] Q.B. 565, dealing with interlocutory questions that have arisen in the action.

against public authorities and public officers. The Quebec rules seem unnecessarily complicated in some instances, particularly with regard to the issuance of injunctions, and a procedural reform is overdue. Trade unions in Quebec find themselves handicapped by long and costly court battles which seem to belong to a primitive stage of industrial law, though it is not only in Quebec that this happens. There is evident need to reconsider the proper use of injunctions in labour cases. Habeas corpus operates in Quebec in both private and public law situations, and the other prerogative writs are ready for use in appropriate cases. There is, however, a growing use of privative clauses ousting the supervisory power of the superior courts public authorities, and article 87a of the Quebec Code of Civil Procedure contains the following sweeping provision:

87a. No proceeding by way of injunction, mandamus or other special or provisional measure shall lie against the Government of this Province or against any Minister thereof or any officer acting upon the instructions of any such Minister for anything done or omitted or proposed to be done or omitted in the exercise of the duties thereof including the exercise of any authority conferred or purporting to be conferred upon same by any Act of this Legislature.

This leaves open the action in damages against the ministers or officers of the Crown acting under their instructions, but severely reduces the area left subject to the special writs. Like all privative clauses, however, it will be strictly interpreted by the courts so as to restrict their supervisory power as little as possible.

How can we relate these principles of Quebec law to Mr Diefenbaker's Bill of Rights? There would seem to be very little direct relationship, since the Bill relates to federal matters only. The judges may perhaps be strengthened in their none too evident determination to uphold the liberties of the subject, if the Bill is enacted, but respect for the Supreme Court and the danger of being overruled there might seem more potent influences. As already pointed out, any Quebec judge who feels an injustice has been done to human freedoms can find ample reasons in Quebec law, administrative or civil, for giving protection to the individual, especially since the recent holding in *Roncarelli* v. *Duplessis*. Of course a specific rule of law cannot be set aside merely because it violates human rights and fundamental freedoms, unless it be *ultra vires* the legislature. Where the Civil Code discriminates between the rights of married and unmarried women, as in the right to contract or to sue (ester en justice), the judges must of course apply, and continue to apply, the written law. The Quebec legislature in 1953 set an evil example when it deprived a trade union by retroactive legislation of the effect of a judgment in its favour rendered by the Supreme Court.[29] No one would contend that such legislation was beyond the powers of the province, however much it may be thought to violate democratic principles and human rights. Nor will the passage of the Bill of Rights make any difference, for it does not attempt to abridge provincial sovereignty.

The possible effect of the Bill of Rights in the enlargement of human rights in Quebec may be illustrated by taking a specific case and asking ourselves whether the decision would be changed by the passage of the Bill. In *Christie* v. *The York Corporation*,[30] plaintiff was a negro who held a box ticket to the Montreal Forum for the hockey season. He was accustomed to enter the York Tavern, which is in the Forum building, for refreshments. On the night in question he went in as usual with two friends and asked the waiter for three glasses of beer. The waiter refused to serve him because he said he had orders not to serve coloured people. Christie called in the police, but the refusal was repeated. In an action for breach of contract and damages, the trial judge awarded $25.00, but the Court of Appeal and the Supreme Court of Canada reversed the judgment on the ground that freedom of commerce made every proprietor a *maître chez lui*, able to carry on his business in the manner that seems best to himself. The obligatory duty to serve travellers, imposed on hotels and restaurants, was held not to apply to this tavern though it operated on licence. The insult to Christie went unpunished.

What difference would a federal Bill of Rights make in such a situation? The case turned on the interpretation of Quebec civil law and Quebec statutes. But it is significant that not only the trial judge, but Galipeault J in the Court of Appeal and Davis J in the Supreme Court dissented. These dissents were based upon an analysis of the same law that the majority used to deny plaintiff's claim. Had the case gone the other way we would still have said that Quebec law was being applied. Thus the courts here, as in many situations, become the determining factor in the preservation of civil liberties, more important than new Bills and Declarations. They so often have liberty in their hands, to dispense or to withold. The most we could hope for in future *Christie* cases in Quebec if Mr Diefenbaker's Bill passes is that the judges themselves will feel urged to limit the effects of this judgment and to distinguish new situations on the facts. We can scarcely hope they will cease to follow it altogether. The decision must be overruled, by reinterpretation or by legislation, if a gross form of racial discrimination is to be checked.

Despite the apparent ineffectiveness of the proposed Bill in respect of much of the law of Quebec, there are some ways in which perhaps it will strengthen the

29 Stats. of Que., 1952–53, c. 11, setting aside the *Alliance* judgment, *supra*, footnote 24.
30 [1940] S.C.R. 139, and note by Laskin in (1940), 18 *Can. Bar Rev.* 314.

law protecting civil liberties and fundamental freedoms. We must start by remembering that federal law does not impose any personal liability upon federal officers in Quebec; it is imposed by provincial law. The damages occasioned by individual postmen or Canadian Broadcasting Corporation employees or officers of the Royal Canadian Mounted Police, in Quebec, will be judged by Quebec law. When the further question arises as to whether the federal Crown or agency or department which employs the wrongdoer can be sued, then federal law must be looked to. If liability is to be imposed on the federal instrumentality of government, the rule must be found in the Crown Liability Act or other relevant federal statute; and if it is found, and the Crown or agency is liable, provincial law measures that liability. But in so measuring it, provincial courts will look to any standards that may be laid down in the federal law. The Quebec rule that a public officer exceeding his powers commits a fault that renders him liable for subsequent damage, when applied to federal officers, must depend upon the actual powers set out in the federal law. The postman's powers are found in the Post Office Act, and so on; damage within the powers will be *damnun sine injuria.* Hence it follows that any restraint upon federal officers that may be found in the Bill of Rights, any limitation it may impose upon discretions they possess under existing statutes, will operate to impose stricter standards upon them and hence to increase the likelihood that they may act in an *ultra vires* fashion. Thus the ambit for the application of article 1053 of the Quebec Civil Code may be enlarged, and the law in Quebec (much of which is necessarily federal law) extended, by the passage of the Bill.

We can foresee a similar enlargement of the exercise of the power of judicial review over administrative actions. The supervisory power of the Quebec courts extends to federal as well as to provincial agencies in Quebec.[31] That power, as has been said, is employed to protect the principles of natural justice in the working of administrative tribunals. The well-known rules that a man should not be tried unheard or by his accuser, that he should be given notice of any charges against him and allowed a fair hearing, are part of Quebec law, deriving from the public law. To the presently accepted rules of natural justice the Bill of Rights appears to add some others. The right to 'retain and instruct counsel without delay' is spelled out in section 3 (b); denial of this would seemingly constitute grounds for quashing the decision of the 'tribunal, commission, board or other authority.' A bold judge might now assert that the right to retain counsel before federal agencies is an extra-patrimonial right within the meaning of the passage from Taschereau J's judgment in the *Chaput* case, giving rise to moral damages if refused. Once again we are in the hands of the judges.

31 *The Montreal Street Railway Co.* v. *The Board of Conciliation and Investigation et al.* (1913), 44 S.C. 350 (Ct. Rev.).

A further question may be asked. Will the Bill of Rights constitute a legislative definition of part of the content of 'public order and good morals' as that phrase is used in the Civil Code? The possibility should not be set aside on any simple notion that federal statutes cannot invade the field of property and civil rights. This of course is true, but does not dispose of the problem. It is the Civil Code itself which says in article 13 that 'No one can by private agreement, validly contravene the laws of public order and good morals.' But the Code does not define the terms. Various cases have applied the rule to establish the validity or invalidity of contracts, gifts and testamentary dispositions. In *Weingart* v. *Stober*[32] a stipulation in a marriage contract limiting access of the parties to the courts of justice was held illegal; in *Renaud* v. *Lamothe*[33] the Supreme Court of Canada, overruling a previous Quebec decision in *Kimpton* v. *La Compagnie du Chemin de Fer du Pacifique Canadien*,[34] held valid a legacy conditional on the legatees being Catholic. If non-discrimination between Canadian citizens is proclaimed by Parliament in the Bill of Rights as public policy, it would not seem to be straining the law were the courts in Quebec to admit this principle when interpreting article 13 and similar provisions of the Code. In other words, judicial discretion in Quebec is wide enough to embrace non-discrimination without departing from the Civil Code, since the Code refers the courts to a concept the content of which must be found outside its provisions. Moreover, if Girouard J was right in *Renaud* v. *Lamothe*,[35] and there can be two kinds of 'public order' in Quebec, depending on whether the question arises in a field of civil or of common law, then non-discrimination should be considered as belonging to an area of public law in which the federal Parliament, with its jurisdiction over citizenship, may validly proclaim a rule of public policy for all Canada.[36]

32 (1919), 57 S.C. 321; (1922), 60 S.C. 55 (Ct. Rev.).
33 (1902), 32 S.C.R. 357. See also (1953), 31 *Can. Bar Rev.* 227.
34 (1888), 16 R.L. 361 (Que. S.C.).
35 Baudouin shares this view: *op. cit., supra*, footnote 4, p. 876.
36 Note that in *Gauvin* v. *Rancourt*, [1953] R.L. 517 (Que. C.A.) which recognized the validity of a Michigan divorce, Marchand J (at p. 575) and Gagné J (at pp. 576–580) dissenting, maintained that the recognition of foreign divorces was against Quebec public order and good morals as expressed in article 185 C.C., while divorces rendered in other parts of Canada would have to be recognized in this province owing to federal jurisdiction over divorce.

# XXV

# Federal Jurisdiction over Labour Relations: A New Look

*When Lord Haldane, speaking for the Privy Council in* Toronto Electric Commissioners v. Snider, *(1925 A.C. 396), struck down the federal Industrial Disputes Investigation Act, he created a legal morass in labour matters from which the country has never recovered. Ten provinces find themselves shouldered with the responsibility of settling labour disputes, separately and individually, with large corporations which may do business in every province and negotiate with a single trade union. Result: Ottawa has no jurisdiction to interfere, and the provinces are virtually helpless. This paper notes some of these difficulties and suggests some remedies.*

An address delivered to the 11th Annual Meeting of the Industrial Relations Conference of McGill University, 1959; from *McGill Law Journal*, 6, 1960, 153–67

Just thirty-five years ago the case of *Toronto Electric Commissioners* v. *Snider* was before the Judicial Committee of the Privy Council. A dispute had arisen between the Toronto Electric Commission – a body operating the light, heat and power system of Toronto – and its employees, at whose request a federal Conciliation Board was set up. The Commission took a writ of injunction against the Board, contending that it had no authority to deal with the dispute because the Parliament of Canada had exceeded its jurisdiction in enacting the Industrial Disputes Investigation Act under which the Board was established. In the result, their Lordships held that this Act (hereafter called the IDI Act) was beyond the powers of the Federal Parliament.[1] The decision overruled previous decisions of the Court of Review of Quebec[2] and the Appellate Division of the Supreme

---

1 See [1925] A.C. 396.
2 *Montreal St. Rly.* v. *Board of Conciliation and Investigation*, (1913), 44 S.C. (Que.) 350. Text is also in 'Judicial Proceedings respecting Constitutional Validity of the Industrial Disputes Investigation Act,' Dept. of Labour, Ottawa, 1925, pp. 255 ff.

Court of Ontario;[3] in other words, the five Law Lords (or a mere majority of them – this cannot be known) disagreed with the opinion of the Parliament of Canada, presumably acting upon advice from the Department of Justice, and with two appellate courts in Canada's most industrialised provinces. The judgment, rendered by Lord Haldane, marked the extreme point in that jurist's career as a special interpreter of the Canadian Constitution, which is tantamount to saying it marked a low point in the judicial definition of federal authority. On two points of constitutional law enunciated in that judgment – one affecting the trade and commerce clause, the other the criminal law – Lord Haldane has already been overruled by the Privy Council itself,[4] and on another of his leading ideas – the 'emergency' doctrine – his views have been badly shaken.[5] But his decision still stands on the central matter at issue, which was the extent of federal authority over the subject of industrial disputes. In consequence, the present Industrial Relations and Disputes Investigation Act which replaces the old Act held *ultra vires* in the *Snider* case is so limited in application that it covers only about 10% of the Canadian labour force amenable to dispute settlement procedures. Ten provinces now have the major responsibility for legislation in a field which grows daily more important from the national point of view, and in which the centralisation of the decision-making power on both the management and labour sides has proceeded rapidly.

It is proposed in this paper to take a new and common-sense look at this situation in the light of the present realities of industrial and trade-union development. The question is not the fairness or utility of any provisions in the present laws dealing with industrial disputes, but rather the distribution of legislative powers in this field, and the effects of that distribution upon the processes of collective bargaining. It is the old problem of the relationship between constitutional law and social fact. It is always dangerous for a country to allow its constitutional law to disregard or get out of line with the facts. If the disparity grows too great, something must give, and usually it will be the constitution. If the constitution holds, as it may for a time, then social relations can be distorted and wise policies frustrated. Unless a federal system of government adapts itself to changing social conditions by amendment or new judicial interpretation, it creates confusion, slows progress and contributes to social tensions. The purpose of state intervention in labour relations is to relieve tensions.

3 *Toronto Electric Commissioners* v. *Snider*, 55 O.L.R. 454.
4 On Haldane's special views on trade and commerce, see what was said by Lord Atkin in *Proprietary Articles Trade Association* v. *A.G. for Canada*, [1931] A.C. 310 at p. 326; and on his view of criminal law as confined to acts which by their very nature belong to the domain of 'criminal jurisprudence,' see *ibid.* at p. 324.
5 By Lord Simon in *Canada Temperance Federation* case, [1946] A.C. 193.

To place the problem in perspective, it is necessary to glance back at the evolution of Canadian law concerning labour relations. The provinces were the first to deal with industrial disputes, Ontario's legislation of 1873 leading the way. Since this Act was restricted to disputes not involving wages (these were then thought to be outside the legitimate sphere of state action) it remained a dead letter and was later repealed. Other Ontario statutes followed, of which the Ontario Railway and Municipal Board Act of 1906 is perhaps the most important. Margaret Mackintosh[6] says that from 1907 to March, 1923, during which time the federal IDI Act was operative, there were 51 applications to the Ontario Department of Labour for the appointment of Boards of conciliation and investigation in connection with disputes between electric railways in Ontario and their employees. We have thus had experience in Canada of overlapping jurisdictions in labour disputes, the parties having the option of provincial or federal Boards. In Nova Scotia, British Columbia and Quebec there were statutes providing for conciliation and arbitration before the federal government assumed its wider jurisdiction in 1907, but they were either abortive, as in the case of British Columbia, or of minor importance.

Federal legislation affecting trade unions dates from the Trade Union Act of 1872, but we may say that federal concern with the law of industrial disputes begins with the appointment of the Royal Commission on the Relations of Labor and Capital in Canada in 1886. This Commission's report, submitted in 1889, after reviewing some startling evidence on working conditions in Canada, recommended the establishment of local boards of conciliation in all the large centres of trade, combined with a permanent central board. Under certain conditions an appeal would lie from the local to the central board whose decision would be final and binding. Thus as early as 1889 it was assumed that the federal government had a role to play, though the Commissioners cautiously observed that they could not 'venture to determine where, in legislation affecting labour and capital, the authority of the Dominion Parliament ends and that of the provincial legislatures begins.' No legislation followed this Report until the federal Conciliation Act of 1900 which applied to any industrial dispute, though it contained no compulsory features. The Railway Labour Disputes Act of 1903 also applied to *all* railways, not only to federal lines.

Then came the Industrial Disputes Investigation Act of 1907. This was called

6 'Government Intervention in Labour Disputes in Canada,' reprinted in Dept. of Labour, 'Judicial Proceedings ... ,' *supra* note 2, at p. 291. A thorough survey of Canadian legislation in labour disputes will be found in W.S. Martin, 'A Study of Legislation Designed to Foster Industrial Peace in the Common Law Jurisdictions of Canada,' unpublished doctoral thesis at Univ. of Toronto, 1954.

'An Act to aid in the Prevention and Settlement of Strikes and Lockouts in Mines and Industries connected with Public Utilities'; the distinction between industries affecting the public interest and convenience, and other industry, was crucial in the Act. It covered all mines in the country (it was passed after a strike among the coal miners of Alberta) and all agencies of transportation and communication, as well as public service utilities. This was a broad, but still limited, coverage; however, by section 63, it was possible for the parties to any dispute whatever, in any business or trade, to agree to refer the matter to a federal board, whereupon the provisions of the Act applied. Thus all industries in Canada in which there was an element of wide public interest were compulsorily covered, and all the rest voluntarily covered. Of the 619 applications for Boards received between March 1907 and March 1924, 120 were for disputes not falling clearly within the direct scope of the Act.[7] Canada had grown accustomed, till the *Snider* case intervened, to the use of what we would now call national labour boards. Even after the *Snider* decision, with the consent of the parties, federal boards were quite often appointed.

It was unfortunate that the *Snider* case arose out of a dispute between a municipal body and its employees, for even before the Privy Council decision doubts had arisen about federal jurisdiction in this particular area in view of the provinces' jurisdiction over municipalities. The IDI Act was often used in municipal street railway disputes, but in its later years the federal Minister of Labour adopted the practice of appointing federal boards only in the absence of a protest by the municipality on the ground of jurisdiction.[8] One wonders whether the IDI Act might not have been upheld had the dispute which gave rise to the litigation occurred in, say, the coal mining industry on which, at that time, so many industries in so many provinces depended, and which had given rise to the Act in the first place. Certainly the national aspect of labour relations would have been more apparent, though it may be doubted whether this would have been enough to change the current of Lord Haldane's interpretations.

Few contrasts are more striking in our constitutional law than that between the judicial reasoning about the IDI Act which prevailed in the Canadian courts and that adopted in the Privy Council. When the question came before the Quebec courts in 1912 Mr Justice Charbonneau issued a writ of Prohibition against a federal Board appointed to investigate a dispute between The Montreal Street Rly Co. and its employees, though he expressed the view that the claim of un-

---

7 *Ibid.*, at p. 281.
8 Report of Deputy Minister of Labour, 1919, quoted in Margaret Mackintosh, *op. cit.*, *supra* note 6, at pp. 300–1.

constitutionality was invalid.[9] Mr Justice Lafontaine delivered the Superior Court judgment upholding the Act. The following passage indicates his approach to the problem:[10]

Whereas, the Industrial Disputes Investigation Act, 1907, has for its apparent and ostensible aim the prevention of strikes, which are one of the manifestations, often troubling and irritating, and causing disorder from one end of the country to the other, of a social and economic condition existing throughout the Dominion, to wit: labour and capital; this condition, by its nature, effects and various and multiform manifestations, considerably surpasses the judicial nature and effects of relations between employers and employees resulting from the contract for the hire of labour; this economic and social condition extends beyond the limits of any locality and province and extends indeed throughout the whole country, and is consequently of a general character, and not of a purely local and private character in the province. (Translation)

There we see surely a common-sense, realistic attitude, based on an appreciation of the social facts which gave rise to the legislation being attacked. On this point Mr Justice Lafontaine was upheld by the Court of Review consisting of Justices Tellier, De Lorimier and Greenshields.

A similar realism pervades the judgments of Mowat J in the Supreme Court of Ontario, and of Ferguson JA in the Appellate Division of that Court. Mowat J said, for example:[11]

It appears to me that 'labour' legislation such as the Industrial Disputes Investigation Act is one of national concern. It is important that a close touch should be kept of the movements and variations of industrial strife and that this can best be done, as such strife existed in 1907 and until the present time by the Federal Government. A general strike in Winnipeg in 1919 was only brought to an end through the voluntary efforts of the non-industrial citizens to break it, and to prevent the misery and underfeeding of children which seemed likely to ensue. All important labour unions in Canada were sympathetically affected by it from ocean to ocean, and if it had spread, as at one time feared, ruinous conditions would have ensued to trade and stable industry. In such a case provincial lines are obliterated and the provinces, not having the means of free and instant com-

9 *Ibid.*, at p. 255.
10 (1913), 44 S.C. 350, at pp. 351–2.
11 *Supra*, note 3, at p. 467.

munication with each other, or for concert, could ill avert dominion-wide trouble. The simple local strikes, which alone could have been in contemplation of the Fathers in 1864 and 1867, have given place to those of brotherhoods composed in some instances of hundreds of thousands, and dominion-wide in their operations and probably beyond the resources of each province to deal with.

Ferguson JA, with whom Mulock CJ and Magee and Smith JJ concurred, approached the question in this way:[12]

Industrial disputes are not now regarded as matters concerning only a disputing employer and his employees. It is common knowledge that such disputes are matters of public interest and concern, and frequently of national and international importance. This is so, not because the disputes may result in many plants being shut down, or tens, hundreds and even thousands of employees drawing strike pay instead of wages, but because experience has taught that such disputes not infrequently develop into quarrels wherein or by reason whereof public wrongs are done and crimes are committed, and the safety of the public and the public peace are endangered and broken, and the national trade and commerce is disturbed and hindered by strikes and lockouts extending, not only throughout the Dominion, but frequently to the United States, where most of our trade unions have their headquarters. Being of opinion that the Act is not one to control or regulate contractual or civil rights, but one to authorize an inquiry into conditions or disputes, and that the prevention of crimes, the protection of public safety, peace and order and the protection of trade and commerce are of the 'pith and substance and paramount purposes' of the Industrial Disputes Investigation Act and of the enquiry authorized and directed thereby, I think the legislation may and should be supported on the powers conferred upon the Dominion Parliament by section 91, British North America Act, to make laws 'in relation to' 'the regulation of trade and commerce,' and to make laws 'in relation to' 'the criminal law' 'in its widest sense,' even though it does not enact a criminal law or a law defining how or in what manner trade and commerce shall be carried on.

How similar is this Canadian approach to that of Chief Justice Hughes when upholding the Wagner Act in 1937. He said:[13]

---

12 *Ibid.*, at p. 476.
13 *National Labor Relations Board* v. *Jones & Laughlin Steel Co.*, (1937), 301 U.S. 1, at pp. 38, 41–2.

We are asked to shut our eyes to the plainest facts of our national life and to deal with the question of direct and indirect effects in an intellectual vacuum ... When industries organize themselves on a national scale, making their relation to interstate commerce the dominant factor in their activities, how can it be maintained that their industrial labor relations constitute a forbidden field into which Congress may not enter when it is necessary to protect interstate commerce from the paralyzing consequences of industrial war? We have often said that interstate commerce itself is a practical conception. It is equally true that interferences with that commerce must be appraised by a judgment that does not ignore actual experience.

Two Ontario judges, Orde J and Hodgins JA, upheld the provincial point of view (both with expressed reluctance), chiefly on the ground that municipal institutions were involved and that property and civil rights were improperly trenched upon by the federal law. Thus out of 12 Canadian judges who considered the question, 10 were in favour and 2 against the validity of the Act.

In the Privy Council Lord Haldane found 'clear' and 'obvious' those propositions which the Canadian courts had rejected. 'It is clear that this enactment was one which was competent to the Legislature of a province under s. 92.'[14] 'It is obvious that these provisions dealt with civil rights, and it was not within the power of the Dominion Parliament to make this otherwise by imposing merely ancillary penalties.'[15] He kept his mind on the private law aspects of the matter being dealt with, and did not see the larger realities, the avoidance of public danger and the maintenance of industrial peace, which the Canadian courts had stressed as being the prime purposes of the legislation. He saw no evidence of any emergency 'putting the national life of Canada in unanticipated peril'[16] without which, in his view, the 'peace, order and good government clause' of the Constitution could not operate if property and civil rights were affected. As stated above, on this point as on his own peculiar limitations upon the exercise of federal jurisdiction over trade and commerce and criminal law, more recent Privy Council decisions have either dissented or have reinterpreted the law.[17] It is in this judgment[18] that there occurs Lord Haldane's famous passage about the evil of intemperance in Canada amounting to so great a menace to our national life in

14 *Supra*, note 1, at p. 404.
15 *Ibid.*, at p. 408.
16 *Ibid.*, at p. 415.
17 *Supra*, notes 4 and 5.
18 At p. 412.

1878 as to compel the Federal Parliament to intervene with the Canada Temperance Act to save the nation from disaster. Perhaps the simplest way of commenting upon this extraordinary judicial performance is to say that it was wrong, at least in its wider generalisations. With that wrong we are still wrestling.

What happened after the *Snider* judgment came out shows how strong was the feeling in Canada in favour of federal responsibility for industrial disputes. Mr Lapointe, then Minister of Justice, said he was petitioned by both employers and employees to revive the IDD Act.[19] The Parliament of Canada immediately revised the Act so that instead of applying to the former industries affected with a public interest, it now applied to a specific list of federal undertakings about which there could be little or no question of authority. The basic idea of the old IDI Act was public interest and convenience; it made no attempt to cover all employment even within federal jurisdiction. The basic idea of the revised Act of 1925 was that all federal industries and undertakings should be covered, regardless of the degree of public interest involved. The law had to be tailored to fit the rules of interpretation of the BNA Act rather than the size and shape of the problem being dealt with. But over and above the enumerated federal undertakings there was a provision that the Act would apply to 'any dispute which is within the exclusive legislative jurisdiction of any province and which by the legislation of the province is made subject to the provisions of this Act.'[20] The provinces were invited to legislate away the *Snider* judgment.

This invitation to co-operate was promptly accepted. By 1928 six provinces had responded; even Quebec and Ontario adopted the federal law in 1932. Only Prince Edward Island remained out. The divisive results of the *Snider* case seemed effectively to have been overcome, and once again the Canadian intention to have uniform legislation was clearly seen. Professor H.A. Logan[21] states that the powers granted to the Federal Parliament by this permissive legislation were regularly invoked to deal with disputes involving coal mines and street railways which, apart from the enabling legislation, would have been beyond the scope of the Act. He also says that there was considerable opposition, at least on the part of employers, to the provincial adoption of the federal Act.

The depression of the 1930s, among its many social consequences, produced a great development in trade unionism and hence in labour law. The Wagner Act in the United States became a kind of beacon light shining over the troubled industrial waters, and to its concepts of certification, collective bargaining and un-

---

19 *Hansard*, 1925, p. 3153.
20 R.S.C. 1927, c. 112, s. 3(d).
21 *State Intervention and Assistance in Collective Bargaining*, (1956), p. 6.

fair labour practices, Canadian opinion was gradually drawn. Federal legislation was still restricted by the *Snider* judgment, and the *ILO Conventions* case in 1937 still further narrowed the area of potential federal intervention. In consequence the provinces started to come back into the field, each in its own way. A new era of provincial labour legislation began, and we are in the midst of it now. World War II restored federal authority for the duration, giving us in PC 1003 the first taste of uniformity on Wagner Act principles, but the coming of peace deprived Ottawa of its emergency powers and restored the *status quo*. By 1947 the wartime federal labour relations had ended.

Two important Conferences of Labour Ministers met during the war period, one in November 1943 when the Dominion was seeking agreement on its proposed wartime legislation – later PC 1003 – and the other in October 1946 in preparation for the transition to peacetime relationships between the governments in labour matters. Even at the 1943 Conference certain provinces, such as Quebec and British Columbia, were anxious to limit federal authority to war industries, and wished to keep the administration of the law in their own hands.[22] At the 1946 Conference[23] some lip-service was paid to the desire for uniformity, and apparently some of the smaller provinces were in favour of federal jurisdiction. But the larger provinces were opposed, and the federal government itself made no proposal for any amendment to the BNA Act or any form of National Labour Code which Labour was ardently demanding. The only concession was provided in Sections 62–63 of the new federal law of 1948, by which a joint administration of federal and provincial laws could be arranged wherever they were substantially similar. This is a far cry from the enabling legislation made possible in the revised IDI Act of 1925.

One cannot escape the conclusion that the small concern for uniformity and the preference for provincial jurisdiction reflected the prevailing employers' viewpoint. The Canadian Manufacturers' Association brief to the House of Commons Committee on Industrial Relations on Bill 338, later to become the present federal Act (which I shall call the IRDI Act) contained no recommendation for a wider federal coverage, whereas this was the main burden of the briefs from the two labour Congresses.[24] Professor Logan criticises the federal government for its failure to rise to its responsibilities on this occasion; he wonders whether a stronger and more resourceful Minister of Labour might not have gone further toward securing an enlarged jurisdiction. But we know that the Liberal government at

22 *Ibid.*, at p. 21.
23 *Ibid.*, at pp. 38–43.
24 *Ibid.*, at pp. 43–5.

this time was entering upon its blissful period of easeful death, carrying out Mackenzie King's policy of 'orderly decontrol,' and it is perhaps not surprising that it gave no strong leadership for a national labour policy. Political pressure from the left by this time had greatly eased.

This historical story may be resumed in a few words. Industrial disputes in industries affected with a public interest were appropriated by the Federal Parliament in 1907, with widespread approval from all sections of Canada, whether French or English speaking; when the startling news was received from abroad that the IDI Act was unconstitutional, the country reacted to offset the decision by a revised federal Act followed by provincial enabling legislation in every province except PEI; the rise of trade unionism in the 1930's accentuated the conflict between capital and labour and compelled new legislation which (apart from the war period) came mostly from the provinces with labour almost alone in calling for uniformity. Class consciousness had apparently increased, and the question of jurisdiction became involved in the power struggle which is surely as evident today as at any time in our history. The extremely large degree of provincial jurisdiction over industrial disputes even in industries almost wholly engaged in interprovincial and international trade, and organised by a single national or international union, leaves us, therefore, exposed to the sudden swings of opinion which occur more frequently and more violently on the provincial than on the federal level – witness the anti-labour legislation of Prince Edward Island in 1947,[25] in British Columbia and Newfoundland in 1959 – so that anything that might be called a national labour policy seems farther off than ever before. The gap between law and fact, the 'décalage,' increases instead of decreasing. It is submitted that this is not a healthy situation from any rational point of view.

It may be postulated that Canadians are desirous of seeing sound democratic principles emerging in our federalism. But it must be obvious that in federal states – and this applies to bi-cultural countries as much as to homogeneous ones – the alternative to federal authority is not always or necessarily provincial autonomy; it may well turn out to be anarchy. If the subject-matter of legislation is too vast for a province to control (for instance, an attempt at provincial control of commodity prices set by a national or international market) then an interpretation of the constitution which leaves it to the provinces simply means that no government control of any kind is possible. Private interest, whether of capital or labour, or even of both in collusion, dominates the society, and the public interest tends to get lost in the power struggle. We see this in the international sphere, where the nation state plays the role of the province in a federation, and

25 See E.A. Forsey, The Prince Edward Trade Union Act, 1948, in (1948), 26 *Can. Bar Rev.* 1159.

where excessive national autonomy wrecks so many needed forms of international regulation. As a single human race, we have not grown up to the oneness of our living, and, in a smaller context, as a Canadian nation we have not grown up to the enlarged scale of relationships now existing between capital and labour. Sooner or later we shall have to bring our law into line with the realities that confront us, and if we believe that good laws can reduce tensions, the sooner we prepare for a change the more likely we are to avoid further conflicts.

Two practical illustrations may be given of the difficulties and dangers that can arise through the inadequacy of our present law dealing with industrial disputes. The first is the story of the strike in the packing industry in 1947. In that instance, there was a single union, the United Packinghouse Workers of America, acting as the bargaining agent for all important plants in eight out of the then nine Canadian provinces. There were three dominant firms negotiating the new contract – Canada Packers, Burns, and Swift Canadian, the last being a wholly owned American subsidiary. One union, three firms, all negotiating in Toronto, where national bargaining had begun in 1944. A federal Controller had been appointed in 1945, and federal conciliation had kept the peace till 1947. But in May of that year federal emergency powers ended and with them federal jurisdiction ceased. Theoretically, before a nation-wide strike could be called separate provincial negotiations should have been started in each province where there was a plant affected, with separate conciliation boards consisting of different people all investigating the same problem and making separate reports to separate Departments of Labour. What a legal absurdity! So absurd was it that little attention was paid to the law; on the passing of the strike-deadline work stopped in all plants. It is a personal opinion, after some investigation of this situation, that had federal authority existed there would have been no strike, since the employers would have realised that the union could easily legalise the strike action which was thought to be impossible in face of the provincial barriers.

This strike gave a revealing example of the anarchy that results from big issues being left to small jurisdictions. Because Ottawa could not act, the provinces thought they would try to combine forces and bring about a settlement. At Premier Drew's suggestion representatives of seven provincial governments met in Toronto on Sept. 26th, 1947, to work out a common plan. There were six Ministers of Labour, one Deputy Minister, one 'observer' (PEI) and one message of sympathy (BC).[26] Rumour has it that one Minister said the strike was illegal in each province and should be smashed, to which Saskatchewan replied that it was not illegal in Saskatchewan. Nothing came of the meeting except a good lesson in

26 See report in Labour Gazette, 1947, p. 1791; also Montreal Gazette for Sept. 26th and 29th, 1947, p. 1.

federalism; even the appointment of a common conciliator could not be agreed upon. The delegates went sorrowfully home nursing their provincial autonomies. The strike was settled without benefit of law, but it might not have occurred, and it will be less likely to occur in the future in this or other big industries, if jurisdiction keeps pace with or is brought into line with the facts.

Another example illustrates the cumbersome procedures and dubious expediences which are promoted by the present division of jurisdiction. The Provincial Transport Company runs buses in Quebec and in the city of Kingston, Ontario; it also owns the Colonial Coach Lines which operate from Quebec into Ontario and thus have extra-provincial connections. At one time the PTC buses crossed the provincial boundary at Hull and the US boundary at certain points, thus bringing the Company within the ambit of the federal IRDI Act for all its operations except the Kingston buses. Employees on all three branches are organised by the Canadian Brotherhood of Railway, Transport and General Workers. A short while ago the Company stopped its PTC Quebec buses from crossing the boundary at any point, thus taking these services out from under the Canada Labour Relations Board and bringing them under the Quebec Public Service Employees Act which prohibits strikes and provides for compulsory arbitration. So here is a single Company dealing with a single Union with respect to a single operation of bus driving in central Canada, which now (a) comes under Quebec law for the Quebec operations, (b) under Ontario law for the Kingston operations, and (c) under federal law for its Colonial Coach Lines operations. This state of affairs cannot promote industrial peace or efficient service. Nor does the present law seem to benefit the Company, since the Quebec drivers, though deprived of the right to strike, have to be paid the same rates as Colonial Coach Lines which operate out of the same terminus in Montreal and who have the right to strike. The original IDI Act would have covered all the operations, and the revised Act of 1925 would also have applied because Quebec and Ontario had both passed enabling legislation. Constitutionally we have moved backwards.

Our present labour relations Acts are based on the principles of certification, compulsory collective bargaining, compulsory conciliation procedures, and then, as a last resort but always in the background, the strike or lockout. The freedom to strike is still essential to the whole concept. This freedom is curtailed if the law surrounds it with such complicated procedures that it cannot effectively be exercised within the law, which is precisely the situation which the existing division of powers produces in industries which are national in scope. Hence labour is faced in certain industries with the choice of disregarding the law or foregoing its undoubted rights and bargaining under less favourable conditions than the law allows in other industries. This is unfair and inconsistent; the result of judicial accident and not of deliberate national policy. Strong unions faced with a choice either of accepting poor agreements or striking regardless of the confused law will from time to time choose the latter course; if their leaders do not, wild-cat strikes are likely to break out. Hence the present state of the law tends to lawlessness.

Does all this mean that there must be a complete abandonment by the provinces of their jurisdiction over disputes? Remember we are not discussing labour legislation in general, but only those aspects of it which relate to collective bargaining and conciliation procedures. The answer to this question would surely be in the negative. It would not be wise, and politically it would be next to impossible, to provide an exclusive federal jurisdiction. The point is rather that the public interest and the protection of the country against disputes too large for provincial intervention demand an enlargement of federal authority. Some division of jurisdiction will remain, but should be more closely related to economic realities. Nation-wide collective bargaining has already begun and is likely to increase. It should not be compelled by the law, but it should not be inhibited by the law as it is at present. If we enlarged the area of efficient collective bargaining by enlarging the coverage of the IRDI Act, management and unions would be free to work out their own levels of agreement, but under a uniform law.

## THE ENLARGEMENT OF FEDERAL JURISDICTION – SOME ALTERNATIVE PROCEDURES

What could we do about the present situation, assuming there was or there might develop a desire to achieve greater uniformity of law? It seems to be taken for granted in Canada that we are incapable of amending our constitution. Yet as recently as 1951 we did so, with the consent of all the provinces, by making old age pensions a concurrent power. At any rate, any discussion of jurisdiction over labour relations that does not contemplate the possibility of constitutional amendment is incomplete. There is a choice in types of amendment: the federal power may be placed in the list of exclusive federal matters in section 91 of the BNA Act, as was done with unemployment insurance, or may be added to the concurrent powers along with agriculture and immigration. An exclusive power is one which the Parliament of Canada alone may exercise; federal law covers the country to the extent chosen by Parliament, and any part of the field not occupied by federal law remains empty and cannot be occupied by provincial law. This rule operates today with respect to labour relations in federal undertakings. A concurrent power, such as our constitution now contains for immigration and agriculture, is one which both Parliament and the provinces may exercise, with the federal law prevailing over provincial law in case of conflict. Provinces can only legislate outside the area selected by Parliament.

Sound argument can be made for each of these alternatives. The pros and cons of exclusive and concurrent powers are carefully analysed by Professor Cox in a paper read to the National Academy of Arbitrators in Washington in 1954,[27] and while he was dealing with the American situation similar considerations apply in Canada for preferring an exclusive jurisdiction in the central government. But he would not exclude the States from legislating with respect to industries not brought under the authority of Congress; he would merely make sure that State governments did not pile additional laws upon those industries that are taken over nationally. Thus federal authority would be exclusive, but would not cover all industries. This seems to be a sensible approach; it is in fact the existing situation in Canada, our difficulty being that federal authority is too restricted whereas he inclines to the view that in the United States it is already too extensive. Translating this idea into Canadian constitutional terms, it would mean adding some such words as these to section 91: 'Labour Relations in such industries and services as are declared by the Parliament of Canada to be of national interest and importance.'

Such a concept is not altogether foreign to our fundamental law. The Parliament of Canada can already declare 'works' to be for the general advantage of Canada or of two or more of the provinces, whereupon they come under federal jurisdiction. Their labour relations today are under the IRDI Act. There would be no constitutional barrier, for instance, to a declaration by Parliament that all the packing houses in Canada, presently existing or to be built, are for the general advantage; whereupon a national law would underpin the nation-wide bargaining that in fact takes place. In theory this could be extended to the plants of all large-scale industry in Canada, as it had to all grain elevators, for instance, for the purpose of enforcing the federal wheat-marketing policy. The trouble with this solution is that by the declaration Parliament takes over much more than the labour relations of the industry, and this it may well not wish to do.

Short of amending the constitution, there are still other roads open. Section 94 of the BNA Act permits the legislatures of the common law provinces to assign to Parliament any matter belonging to the field of property and civil rights, where labour relations belong. Hence these provinces could help to build up a nation-wide law, much as they did after 1925 by their enabling legislation. Some of the smaller provinces have shown a willingness to abandon the field, or part of it, to the Dominion, but not so the larger provinces, and Quebec lacks the constitutional power to make a delegation under Section 94. It should be pointed out, however, that Quebec law on labour relations is not so different in kind from that of other provinces as to suggest that any enlargement of federal jurisdiction would threaten to obliterate cultural institutions that are part of her heritage; there was

27 Reprinted in *The Profession of Labor Arbitration*, ed. by Jean T. McKelvey, 1957, p. 76.

no substantial law on this subject in Quebec till 1944, and then it was modelled on the Wagner Act. The Professional Syndicates Act, under which the Catholic unions are incorporated, would be unaffected. The Catholic syndicates were founded and developed under the aegis of federal legislation, first in the original IDI Act and then under the 1925 Act which Quebec adopted.

What about judicial interpretation? Might not the Supreme Court of Canada take a broader view of federal jurisdiction than that suggested in the *Snider* case? That case is still law, but strictly speaking all it decided was that the IDI Act could not apply to municipal institutions. The wider language used by Lord Haldane was beside the point at issue. The Supreme Court upheld the present IRDI Act in 1955 on a reference,[28] and an Ontario Judge, in the *Pronto Uranium Mines* case,[29] has upheld its application to workers in uranium mines and concentrating plants. In the IRDI Act reference Judge Rand, as usual seeing clearly the social realities of contemporary society, said 'Labour agreements, embodying new conceptions of contractual arrangements are now generally of nation-wide application, and as we know, strike action may become immediately effective throughout the systems.'[30] While he was speaking of railways, the argument holds for many other industries. But we cannot expect a new interpretation until there is either (i) new federal legislation, (ii) a constitutional reference framed to elicit opinions about federal authority over labour relations in inter-provincial industries, or (iii) a daring lawsuit challenging the jurisdiction of some provincial board in a dispute arising in some major industry. We should remember also that the revised IDI Act of 1925 was made applicable to federally incorporated companies and to disputes declared to be subject to the Act by reason of a national emergency, provisions not repeated in the present federal law, and the validity of which has not been tested. The possibility of some judicial rethinking in the future should not be excluded, particularly with respect to the trade and commerce and the peace, order and good government clauses of the Constitution – the *Murphy* case in 1959, upholding the Canada Grain Act,[31] and the *Pronto Mines* case,[32] gave some new leads – but the obstacles to be overcome are considerable.

There is one last provision for uniformity that needs to be mentioned. This is the method of federal-provincial arrangements for federal administration of provincial labour legislation when it is substantially uniform with that of the Dominion. The IRDI Act, as already indicated, provides for such arrangements in sections 62–3. It is interesting to note that seven provinces have adopted somewhat

28 [1955] S.C.R. 529.
29 [1956] 5 D.L.R. (2nd) 342.
30 *Supra*, note 28.
31 [1958] S.C.R. 626.
32 *Supra*, note 29.

similar provisions in their labour laws, though the wording, as usual, varies considerably, and the two biggest provinces, Quebec and Ontario, with PEI, have remained aloof.[33] Alberta and British Columbia confine their possible arrangement with Ottawa to the meat-packing and coal-mining industries. Saskatchewan makes provision for the application to the province of the whole IRDI Act, which shows a willingness to go back to pre-*Snider* days. Most provinces confine their offer to federal administration of provincial law. This is different from, and, it is submitted, not so useful as, the enabling legislation invited in 1925 by which provinces made the entire federal Act applicable to themselves. Here the provincial law remains within provincial jurisdiction; only administration is simplified. If there was a general will for uniformity, no doubt the provinces could improve somewhat the present situation by modelling their legislation exactly on the federal Act and then entering into an arrangement under section 62, but if there were this degree of desire for uniformity then we might look for new enabling legislation or even for an amendment to the BNA Act covering major industries. At any rate, no such arrangements as the IRDI Act and the provincial statutes contemplate have yet been made.

This review of the law poses a question. Why was the desire for uniform labour relations legislation stronger in Canada in the first third of this century than it is today? Are we more disunited? Certainly the disputes to be regulated are larger and more threatening than ever before. When introducing the IDI Act in 1907 in 1907 the Hon. Rodolphe Lemieux, Minister of Labour, said, 'as the country grows, as the area covered by these strikes increases, the danger becomes greater and greater every day.'[34] History has borne out the accuracy of this prediction. Once already in the past the ill effects of the *Snider* judgment were overcome, and they could be again if the desire existed, without having to amend the BNA Act. Labour's position is clear. At its 1958 Convention the Canadian Labour Congress adopted the following resolution.[35]

BE IT RESOLVED that the Congress urge the Government to declare inter-provincial industries, of nation-wide scope and importance, works for the general advantage of Canada, and so bring them under the exclusive jurisdiction of Parliament, and within the purview of the Industrial Relations and Disputes Investigation Act.

---

33 The statutes in question are to be found in the following Revised Statutes: Newfoundland, 1952, c. 258 s. 63; Nova Scotia, 1954, c. 295 s. 70; New Brunswick, 1952, c. 124 ss. 57–8; Manitoba, 1954, c. 132 ss. 60–1; Saskatchewan, 1953, c. 259 s. 30; Alberta, 1955, c. 167 s. 108; British Columbia, 1948, c. 155 s. 79.
34 *Hansard*, 1906–7, p. 3013.
35 *Proceedings*, p. 11.

But no voice of equal weight has been raised on the employer's side. Can the answer to the question be that some employers like divided jurisdiction and confusing laws? If so they stand in the way of much needed progress. It is preferable to believe that political inertia and the well-known Canadian capacity for accepting what seems to be but is not inevitable are deeper reasons. Let us hope we do not have to have the rude shock of further national strikes to shake us out of this inertia.

# XXVI

# Expanding Concepts of Human Rights

*An address delivered to the mid-winter meeting of the Ontario Branch of the Canadian-Bar Association, February 1960.*
From the *Canadian Bar Journal*, 3, 1960, 199-208

I find it interesting to observe how in the field of constitutional law - and I think the same is true of other branches of the law - certain parts of the total structure seem to become floodlighted and to stand out from the rest at particular periods of time. The law surrounds and clothes the body politic and economic, and as that body stirs restlessly so does the surface of the law disclose where the tensions and the pressures are being most felt. Thus we can explain the great expansion of administrative and labour law in the past half century, as industrialisation and its inevitable consequence, state regulation of economic activity, developed side by side. Most of the great cases in Canadian constitutional law, of course, have turned on questions of jurisdiction under sections 91 and 92 of the BNA Act, and these we have always with us; here it is interesting to note the swing of the pendulum as between federal authority and provincial autonomy. But if we take a short look backward over the past dozen years, and survey leading decisions of the Supreme Court of Canada as well as the substance of much federal and provincial legislation, we cannot but be struck by the emergence in our law of a remarkable combination of cases and legislative purposes which we can properly classify under the heading of human rights. These new cases and laws raise fundamental issues - issues which we have always known about in theory but which we have seldom had to incorporate into our own legal order. The determination of these cases and the enactment of these laws have in turn raised questions as to the adequacy of the protection afforded to civil liberties in the basic law of our present constitution; hence for the first time in our history, we are offered the draft of a national Bill of Rights which it is now proposed should be adopted by Parliament. Constitutionally speaking, the 1950s was predominantly the decade of human rights.

My topic is 'Expanding Concepts of Human Rights,' and I propose to divide all I have to say into three parts. But before I embark upon this Caesarian operation let me describe briefly the progress of our Canadian law in this field in the period I am talking about. Two cases of major importance have denied provincial jurisdiction in matters vitally affecting freedom of religion and freedom of speech. The first was the *Birks* case, in 1955, which held it unconstitutional for a municipality acting under provincial statutory permission to compel the closing of all stores on Catholic feast days. This is tantamount to saying that any compulsory laws on religious observance belong, if anywhere, in the federal jurisdiction over criminal law. So religious toleration is made more secure, at least as against provincial interference. The second case was the *Padlock Act* case, which I think can be said to have held that the proscription of political ideas also belongs, if anywhere (and here we have an express doubt on the part of Mr Justice Abbott as to whether it does exist in Canada) in the area of criminal law. So peaceful co-existence becomes more possible.

These two cases involve questions of jurisdiction as well as principles of civil liberties. The *Boucher* case, decided in 1951, did not touch upon legislative jurisdiction, but it did interpret the Canadian law of sedition very liberally – and here I use the term 'liberal' in its most conservative sense. So we now are free to utter quite dangerous thought without fear of criminal prosecution. This is a comforting reflection in an age when every other influence in our society seems to be tending to conformity.

Besides these three notable triumphs for civil liberties, we have had three other cases which are good examples of Dicey's Rule of Law in its simplest form. You remember the proud boast of Dicey when he said: 'With us every official, from a Prime Minister down to a constable or a collector of taxes [below which, apparently, his imagination could not sink], is under the same responsibility for every act done without legal justification as any other citizen.' The *Roncarelli* case involved the liability of a Prime Minister, and the *Chaput* and *Lamb* cases involved the liability of constables, and all the officials sued were held liable for acts done without legal justification. Only the tax collector was missing to make Dicey's picture complete. So the great principle of the supremacy of the law was re-affirmed, and in situations, be it noted, involving liability under the Civil Code of Quebec. These cases do not affect any distribution of power as between Parliament and legislatures, and the legislature of Quebec or any other province could if it wished alter the law so laid down, but we have in them a demonstration of what independent judges and good legal principles can do to defend basic freedoms from arbitrary interference by state officials.

In the legislative history of this period, we have witnessed the emergence of new statutes aimed to strengthen certain human rights. On the negative side, our electoral laws have been cleared of almost all racial discrimination, (the granting of the vote to Indians, provincially as well as federally, will complete this operation) and on the positive side we have the Fair Employment Practices Acts, the Fair Accommodation Practices Acts, and the statutes requiring equal pay for equal work as between men and women. The first two of these, aimed to prevent discrimination in employment and in the securing of accommodation in public establishments, have not been long enough in operation for us to be able to measure their success; they do not, of course, cover all the situations in which discrimination exists; and they have not yet been accepted in all provinces of Canada. Similarly, the laws requiring equal pay for equal work are not found everywhere yet, and economic discrimination against women undoubtedly continues. This is surely a reminder that we cannot feel complacent about our progress, and that the passing of a law may be only the beginning of the fight to eradicate the evil.

What interests me most about Ontario's approach to this new type of legislation is the method of enforcement through the Anti-Discrimination Commission. I am convinced that what we need today as well as new legislation, are new procedures or more expeditious procedures for making rights effective. *Ubi remedium, ibi jus*, has always been the practical approach of English law, and in this area of human rights the maxim is particularly applicable because the people who need protection most are usually people who simply have not the means to stand up to the officials or employers or whoever it is that violates their rights. Five of the victims whose cases reached the Supreme Court of Canada in the last decade, and who have contributed so greatly to the clarification of our law, were Jehovah's Witnesses – namely *Boucher, Saumur, Chaput, Roncarelli* and *Lamb*. Suppose they had had no organisation behind them: would we have rectified the wrongs? Is the action in damages, with its delays and heavy costs, sufficient protection for the violation of fundamental rights? English lawyers developed Habeas Corpus as a remedy for unlawful imprisonment, and by that one procedure achieved perhaps as much as the Bill of Rights itself to safeguard personal liberty. Maybe we can also devise new methods. The Anti-Discrimination Commission of Ontario enquires into charges of discrimination as one would investigate an industrial dispute prior to efforts at conciliation. Good administration can here take over part of the function of litigation, and with advantages to both the complainant and the defendant. I am not suggesting the action in damages be eliminated; it is basic. I am pointing out that the excellence of the law is not always matched in its procedures.

This brief survey of recent developments, which is a record of steady progress in civil liberties, would be unbalanced if I made no mention of a contrary trend which has showed itself only recently. I refer to the statutory limitation of traditional trade union rights, as evidenced by amendments to the Newfoundland and British Columbia Trade Union Acts, and by proposals for the so-called 'right to work laws' which emanate from respectable but I think very misguided quarters. Of all the forces threatening civil liberties today, I should put the trade unions last, since the exceptional cases of individual union misgovernment are vastly outweighed by the constant pressure of the labour movement for human rights in all their forms. I know of no single body in the whole of Canada doing as much continuous and consistent work for civil liberties as the National Committee on Human Rights of the Canadian Labour Congress. It is not flattering to us to compare their monthly publication, called *Canadian Labour Reports*, with its live discussion of real issues all across the country, with the annual reports of the Civil Liberties Section of The Canadian Bar Association. Let those who doubt my statement, make their own comparison. No doubt we have not yet reached finality in our labour laws any more than we have in other branches of the law, but attacks upon the fundamental right of association, as in Newfoundland, or upon the status of the trade union, as in British Columbia, are in my opinion turning the clock backward and not leading us into more human relationships.

All that I have said so far is by way of reflection and reminder of where we stand today. Now I wish to come to my tripartite division of the subject, and to leave with you three ideas about civil liberties and human rights that seem to me to be meaningful. These are broad generalisations, and as such liable to oversimplification, but I think they can be supported by our past history and present experience.

In the early struggles for liberty, it was nearly always the state or some part of it that was the enemy. Kings, tyrants, dictators – these are state officials. The police are the state in action. Government had to be kept under the law, or liberty did not exist. Hence the very strong tradition grew up – a tradition particularly strong among members of the Bar and Bench – that it was liberty against government that mattered. Hence the efforts to curb governmental power, by Bills of Rights, concepts of natural law, doctrines of the separation of powers and theories of checks and balances. This approach fitted perfectly the individualist philosophy which believed that the least government was the best government, and that the more private initiative there was the better and richer society would be. This is the easiest kind of liberty to understand, the one that has sunk deepest into our consciousness, and the one most frequently stated to be the be all and end all of civil liberties.

This concept, however, has had in recent times to be supplemented by another idea, which I may call liberty through government. Certain human rights, of great value to a great number of people, can only be realised through governmental action. This should not surprise us, for government action means the making and enforcing of laws, and we are all accustomed to say that without law there is no liberty. We are not so traditionally accustomed, however, to say that without an unemployment insurance law, or without an old age pensions law, or laws providing for free universal education, there is no liberty. Particularly among members of the legal profession are these newer forms of human rights apt to be either forgotten or neglected, because these social insurances require administration through government commissions and enforcement in administrative tribunals rather than consultation with lawyers and actions in the regular courts. Lawyers tend to pay attention mostly to judicial review over administrative agencies; law school courses in administrative law usually concentrate on this aspect of the matter. Yet this, though of great importance, is not the central issue. The object of these laws is to free men and women from known and certain risks which exist in our industrialised society, and which if not insured against can destroy so much liberty among so many individuals as to make Bills of Rights to them a hollow mockery. The hungry man must be fed, the sick must be attended to, the old must be provided for, the young must have a chance to enter to the fullest degree into our cultural heritage through education. To deprive people of these essentials to the good life, or to allow the still unresolved problems of our economic system to deprive them of them without taking steps to alleviate the deprivations, is to take away human rights.

Now it is obvious that liberty against government and liberty through government pose separate problems. Liberty against government can be secured by restrictions upon state action. Specifically we can order legislatures, by constitutional means, not to enact certain types of law. This is what I think we would do in our Bill of Rights, and frankly I am not interested or impressed by any other kind of Bill of Rights. If, as has now been announced, we are to seek authority from the United Kingdom Parliament to amend all portions of the BNA Act by appropriate Canadian action, if we are going to go back to the mother of our parliaments one last time, if we are going to keep what I have called 'our rendezvous with the BNA Act,' then I say let us do two things at once, and replace the present Bill C-60 which Mr Diefenbaker has offered us with some further entrenched clauses in the constitution. These clauses, and the new amending clause, can be contained in the final UK statute, and we shall not only have nationalised our constitution but have firmly endowed it with those principles of freedom which it was always intended to safeguard. Let us make more explicit that which was implicit but imperfectly protected in the phrase 'a constitution similar in principle to that of the United Kingdom.'

What, then, of those other human rights which must be sought not against but through government? The constitution can tell the legislatures not to do something: can it not instruct them also to do something? Such instruction, unlike the prohibition, produces no result until the legislatures act, and they must be free to choose the form of action. Hence many people – certainly I think most lawyers – feel that ideas of freedom from want, from disease, from unemployment, from penurious old age, have no place in a Bill of Rights. They certainly have not had in the past, but they certainly do have in many constitutions of the present day, at least as directives of national policy. I shall be happy if we can include a true Bill of Rights of the traditional sort in our nationalised constitution, but I say frankly that I would be happier if we also included some words or phrases, if not in the text of the constitution then in its preamble, expressing the now universally accepted notions of social security and human welfare. Do not forget that the word 'welfare' was included in the definition of federal powers in both the Quebec Resolutions and the London Resolutions. The great phrase of Section 91 was chosen by Canadians to be 'peace, welfare and good government,' not 'peace, order and good government.' That, too, was the phrase used in The Constitutional Act of 1791. The emphasis should be, not on a police state, but on a welfare state. The preamble of the American constitution has its 'general welfare' clause, and this has been operative in several important cases involving federal spending for the national welfare. Our present preamble already states purposes and objectives for Canada which are certainly not legal rules; what does 'promote the interests of the British Empire' mean in law? If we were to state other purposes consonant with our present practices and our agreed goals of securing the largest possible freedom and security for all citizens regardless of race or religion, we should, I submit, have a more lively, more contemporary, and a more human constitution. It would be a citizen's constitution and not just a lawyer's constitution.

Freedom from arbitrary state action, freedom from the risks inherent in an industrialised society through social security involving state action – these are properly the domain of law and therefore properly the concern of the legal profession in all their aspects. There is a right to unemployment insurance: a moral right before a statute is passed, a legal right after it is passed. There is the same right to old age pensions, to education, and so on. These are truly rights, not just airy nothings or visionary dreams outside the legal and constitutional order. Our concept of human rights includes them and new ones will be added as our democracy clarifies its aims and increases its capacity to fulfil those aims by expanded production. Human rights are not static, but dynamic; were it not so, what objective do we set before ourselves as a nation? To multiply worldly goods and not enlarge human rights is to head toward disaster. To put all the emphasis on production and not to ask the question 'Production for what use and purpose' is to see only half the need. Besides, if I help to produce a first-rate legal mind, am I not a producer as much as the corporation that produces a new automobile, or the inventor that invents the better mouse-trap? We as a profession are surely meant to be producers of the highest kind of social good – liberty under law, and freedom from unlawful interference with rights.

I come now to the third aspect of my subject, and one which is more difficult to talk about. It is, also, less legal, more sociological, and some may think for that reason less appropriate for discussion here. But I do not apologize for introducing it, because I am more and more impressed by the fact that if we look around our society we find that the greatest restrictions upon human rights come, not from government action, or from government inaction in the face of social needs, but rather from our own behaviour toward one another. Private decisions affect human rights just as easily as public laws, and much more frequently. The employer who refuses to employ a coloured person, the trade union which refuses to admit one, or which expels a member without due process, the proprietor who refuses to lease premises to certain races, the corporation which denies to its employees the right to take part in politics, the editor who kills the important news story which he does not personally like, or colours it out of all recognition – these are all interferences with freedom. How do we protect ourselves against ourselves? How do we liberalise our attitudes and practices in those infinitely numerous daily activities where rights and freedoms are at stake? This is indeed a fruitful area for investigation.

May I take two examples of what I mean, and I offer them as examples merely and without any desire to raise controversy. We have rightly been concerned about the recent outbreaks of antisemitism in Canada and throughout the world, evidenced by the painting of swastikas on the walls of synagogues. Though it cannot represent among us anything as serious as a wave of persecution, it does remind us that race-hatred is always with us and that prejudice dies hard. Yet we all know that in various parts of Canada there are invisible swastikas on the doors of many clubs, on the lists of directors and governors of reputable institutions, on certain properties and in fraternities and other places where they should have disappeared. There are forms of discrimination here which are not amenable perhaps to legal prohibition, but I like to think that leadership in opposing this kind of behaviour is coming and will come from the ranks of the legal profession, a profession fitted by its tradition to stand for equal treatment for all, and by its daily practice to meet with and to set an example to Canadians in all walks of life and in every kind of activity.

My other example concerns the dissemination of news on matters of public interest in Canada. There began last autumn in Montreal one of the biggest combines cases to come before the courts of that province for a very long time. Seven-

teen pulp and paper companies are on trial, and issues of significance to the country as a whole as well as to the province are being aired. Yet the *Montreal Star*
has not reported the trial since the first day, (Oct. 13th) – one small item appeared
on Oct. 13th, the day the trial opened; no defendants were named – and the
*Montreal Gazette*, after one report, (Oct. 14th) closed its columns and printed
not a word. Since the Canadian Press relies on local reports for Montreal news,
nothing more went over its wires; nor did the United Press carry it. Thus as far as
I can find out, the rest of Canada also heard virtually nothing of it. The silence
of the press also silenced the CBC, which relies for such news on the same sources
as the newspapers. These same two papers both failed to report a major decision
of the Liberal Party in Quebec at the time of its autumn convention, namely to
re-nationalize the distribution of natural gas if re-elected – a decision that rated
an eight column headline in *Le Devoir*. I find it hard to believe that these omis-
sions were accidental.[1] I cite these examples because I have long quoted with
pleasure the words of Mr Justice Cannon in the Alberta Press case, where he said:

Freedom of discussion is essential to enlighten public opinion in a democratic
state; it cannot be curtailed without affecting the right of the people to be informed through sources independent of the government concerning matters of
public interest. There must be an untramelled publication of the news and political opinions of the political parties contending for ascendancy.

We welcomed then the decision of the Supreme Court in declaring unconstitutional the Alberta Accurate News and Information Act; that was government interference with freedom of the press. What if there is private interference? It can
be more dangerous because it is much harder to control and more subtle in its
operation. As newspapers fall into chains, and the same owners acquire radio and
TV outlets, we move into dangerous territory indeed. Whether you think anything should be done about this kind of situation, whether you feel we should establish a Press Council to allow for self-regulation and disciplining of the industry
or not, you will I hope agree with me that any thinking about civil liberties that
does not go beyond the text of the law and probe into the actual behaviour of
people and institutions is shallow thinking. No Bill of Rights can save us here.
   What I have said is perhaps only another way of saying that the measure of
liberty in a society is a reflection of the total society, and not just of its laws and
their administration. A good play or novel may do more to free men's mind from

---

1 Subsequently the *Star* claimed that the evidence in the trial was not appropriate for
  reporting since it mostly consisted of documents filed without discussion: the *Gazette*
  claimed that in long and technical cases its practice is to report only the summing up
  and the judges' decision.

prejudice than new legislation. The expansion of the arts in Canada is a freeing of the imagination and the achieving of a sense of community not only within Canada but between Canada and the world. It is also helping greatly to break down the walls of incomprehension that still separate our two cultures. The work of Canada Council is an influence making for human freedom. All of which should concern us as lawyers, for the lawyer should not only be a legally learned man, he should also be a broadly cultivated man. And this I like to think is the direction in which we are moving.

# XXVII

# Canadian Federalism:
# The Legal Perspective

*A paper read as one of the Centennial Lectures on Canadian Federalism, 6 March, 1967, sponsored by the Department of Political Science, University of Alberta.* From the *Alberta Law Journal*, 5, 1967, 263–73

Within the writer's short lifetime the Canadian constitution has had to withstand two particular crises: that of the 1930s, caused by the general economic collapse, and that of the 1960s, caused principally – but by no means exclusively – by the revolutionary changes taking place in Quebec.[1] In the first of these crises, it was the economic system which had failed. Unemployment and stagnation brought ruin to the industrial east, while drought and low prices devastated the agricultural west. Yet the constitution remained unshaken in all its essentials, and when the *Sirois Report* was issued its main recommendations were intended to strengthen the central government, the provinces having been shown to be helpless in face of such a calamity. Today we seem to be in the reverse situation: the constitution is under fierce attack, provincial autonomy and separate policy-making have brought the central government to its lowest ebb since Confederation, and what seems to be holding us together is the strength of the economic system and our dependence on its continued expansion for a rising standard of living. We may see a comparable situation in Belgium, where two warring linguistic groups are held by the economic advantages of union not only in the same country, but in a unitary state.

---

1 Severe as were the conscription crises in the two World Wars, they were of short duration and did not directly affect the constitution; the Francoeur revolution on the secession of Quebec in 1918 was debated but withdrawn. See Elizabeth H. Armstrong, *The Crisis of Quebec*, 1914–18, at 209 ff.

## THE IMPORTANCE OF THE CONSTITUTION

In this situation the law of the constitution may seem to be an irrelevancy. The whole emphasis is on constitutional change rather than upon the application of existing rules. Professor Alfred Dubuc of the University of Montreal has recently written of the BNA Act: 'Today this document no longer serves as the principal guide to the elaboration of central economic policies. The new realities of the 20th century simply cannot be guided by its light ... The federal-provincial and inter-provincial conferences at the political level now fulfil the function formerly carried out at the juridical level by the Constitution and the courts.'[2] More explicitly, Professor D.V. Smiley has explained that ' "Canadians and Canadiens" do not agree on the community to which they give their primary allegiance – Canada or French Canada – and this difference in allegiances makes impossible any agreement on the appropriate distribution of powers and privileges between federal and provincial governments.'[3] Similarly Professor Cheffins has recently said: 'It appears as if the [Supreme] Court is being by-passed as an important arena for the making of vital constitutional decisions.'[4]

The social scientists of every type are in the saddle, and if the cold voice of the constitutional lawyer is heard at all, it carries little weight. The firm statement that 'This is the law' is apt to be met by the rather irreverent comment 'So what!'

Now I would be the last to pretend that the law which is, is the law which should be. The pace of change has accelerated in every sphere of human activity, and the law cannot be exempt. As a great American jurist has said: 'Existing rules and principles can give us our present location, our bearings, our latitude and longitude. The inn that shelters for the night is not the journey's end. The law, like the traveller, must be ready for the morrow. It must have a principle of growth.'[5]

You will note that this statement contains two main ideas: first, that the law must change, but secondly – and equally importantly in my opinion – that the law which is about to change gives us a present location, a latitude and longitude, and thus our bearings. In other words, it tells us the point from which we must start. Our situation is therefore quite different from that of a man lost in the forest who does not even have the choice of direction since he knows no direction. The existence of a functioning constitutional law prevents us wandering

2 *Nationalism in Canada*, Peter Russell ed., at 126, 129.
3 'Two Themes of Canadian Federalism,' 31 C.J.E.P.S., at 88.
4 'The Supreme Court of Canada: A Quiet Court in an Unquiet Country' (1966), *Osgoode Hall, L.J.*, at 259.
5 Benjamin N. Cardozo, *The Growth of the Law*.

around in circles. We are not in the sad position of the motorist who, having lost his way, asked a farmer whom he met on a by-road how to reach the next town; the man scratched his head, suggested going down the road and turning right, or better, going up the road and turning left, and then ended up by saying: 'If I was going to the next town, I wouldn't start from here.' If we start to change our constitution, we do so from the basis of the law that exists. It may be desirable now and then to remind ourselves of some of its important characteristics.

The reason why it is possible to treat the Constitution today as though it was a kind of remote nuisance is precisely because it has one great virtue: flexibility. It permits a very wide freedom of choice in respect of governmental policy and intergovernmental relationships. Constitutional law in some respects is different from other kinds of law. The ordinary laws tell us what to do and what not to do; constitutional law does not make these laws, but tells us who has the right to make them. The Constitution rarely says what must be done, in respect of government policy. Hence the comments of Professors Dubuc and Cheffins just quoted seem to me to be somewhat beside the point; policy-making is not the prime concern of the courts. The Constitution confers jurisdiction and authority upon various bodies, leaving them free to exercise their powers in any way they see fit. The legislature endowed with jurisdiction is not even obliged to exercise it; it may prefer not to legislate. And if the area happens to be one of concurrent jurisdiction, like immigration or agriculture, or some overlapping parts of sections 91 and 92, then the withdrawal of federal legislation leaves the field wide open to the provinces. The so-called handing over of part of the income tax field to the provinces, for example, did not involve a change of sovereignty, but merely a change in the direction of the tax, and all governments have as much legal right to raise or lower their taxes after as they had before the agreement.

PUBLIC AND PRIVATE GOVERNMENTS

Should, however, all the public authorities refrain from legislating, then the private authorities – which include you and me, of course, but over much of our lives today means principally the large private corporations – make their own policies and govern us in the way that best suits themselves. We do not escape government, but we do have a choice between public and private government. The electors who choose and can call to account our public governments are you and I and other adult citizens; the electors who choose and theoretically are in control of private governments are those entitled to vote at shareholders' meetings (theoretically, because in practice the managers control), and while you and I have only one vote at elections a single shareholder (which may be another corporation) may have ten thousand. What I may call the constitutional law of the private corporation is in many respects today quite as important to Canadians as what we call constitutional law proper. There are very large private governments in Canada that have no Canadian electorate whatever since all the shares are owned by the parent company in the United States. J.K. Galbraith in the Reith Lectures, recently given over the BBC in England, points out that we now live under an increasingly planned economy, in which the large corporation has become a planning unit. He writes:

We have difficulty in thinking of the private firm as a planning instrument because we associate planning with the state. But the modern industrial enterprise operates on a scale that is far more nearly comparable with that of government than old-fashioned market-oriented activity. In 1965 three American industrial corporations, General Motors, Standard Oil of New Jersey, and Ford Motor Company, together had more gross income than all of the farms in the United States. The income alone of General Motors of $20.7 billion about equalled that of the 3,000,000 smallest farmers in the country – around 90 per cent of all farmers. The gross revenues of each of the three corporations just mentioned far exceed those of any single state. The revenues of General Motors in 1963 were fifty times those of the state of Nevada, eight times those of the state of New York, and slightly less than one-fifth those of the Federal Government.

Such is the corporation as a planning authority. It rivals in size the state itself. It has authority extending over and uniting the capital and organized talent that modern technology requires. Its authority extends on its supply of capital. And its power is safely removed and protected from the extraneous or conflicting authority either of the state or its own owners or creditors.[6]

I have called the large corporations private governments because I think it is essential we include their powers, their jurisdiction and their policies in our thinking about the constitution and government of Canada in general. It is obvious that some of these corporations have a definite foreign policy, or, what is more striking, are told from the parent company outside Canada what policy they should follow. Thus our public international policy may be frustrated by our private international policy. For example, some of these corporations have involved us directly in the Vietnam war on the side of the United States, though our public government professes to be a member of a neutral Control Commission. The two roles are contradictory, and if Canada chooses to allow the sale of arms and munitions to the United States to be used in the country we are supposed to be supervising, then I think we must ask ourselves how long we can hope

6 Quoted in *The Listener*, Vol. LXXVI, 1966, at 756–7.

to maintain a neutral reputation. If we want to play a Scandinavian role, we must pay a price for it. I think it is time that political scientists, constitutional lawyers and others who pay so much attention to federal-provincial relations, should turn their analytical powers to the field of corporation law and practice. A *de facto* constitution will be seen alongside the *de jure* constitution. Most scholarship today is directed to the issue of federal versus provincial government; an equally important issue is that between public and private government. In that context it might be found that new common interests exist for all public governments, federal and provincial, in Quebec as elsewhere, and that they are all confronted with a challenge to their power that they can only collectively withstand.

## CONSTITUTIONAL PURPOSES

Every written constitution – and the Canadian constitution is partly written and partly unwritten – serves two general purposes. It first of all constitutes a framework of law under which the government of the country is carried on. It distributes authority, authorizes various activities, and above all proclaims certain social and political values. Parliamentary democracy would be one such value. Though the working out of the Constitution may be very different from the written law, so that merely reading the words in the text may convey a very false impression of how government is carried on, nevertheless these values are explicitly or implicitly contained in the law and in that sense constitute profoundly important guidelines for future policy. The written words may be only the dry bones, but they shape the manner in which the flesh and blood may grow.

Constitution-making is a political art, widely practised in recent times with the development of so many new independent states. I call it an art, because a constitution is a kind of artifact; it is designed by man and may have infinite variety of form and content. Ultimately, we know, it is no stronger than the will to accept and to work it. If that will vanishes, so does the constitution. This ultimate reliance on something other than the law is however not peculiar to constitutions. All human societies and institutions depend upon a more fundamental sense of social solidarity. A constitution may itself develop that sense of solidarity if it enables a given society reasonably to evolve according to its inner directives.

But beyond this general function of constitutions there is in each particular state a special purpose which the constitution seeks to attain. The Canadian Constitution was drawn up a century ago to suit the needs of the country then being created. The Fathers of Confederation were not theorists in constitution-making; they were practical politicians with a long experience of previous constitutional battles and proposals, and a strong sense of Canadian history. The chief impulse toward Confederation and the principal ideas about it came from the Upper and

Lower Canadians, not from the Maritime provinces and of course not from the Western provinces which were then not in the Union. The most vivid memories and experiences in the lives of the most prominent Fathers, particularly Cartier and Macdonald, came from the immediate past experience of the old province of Canada established in 1841 after the two rebellions. It was in central Canada that the economic power lay, and that was where the confrontation between English and French, Protestant and Catholic, was most real. What was true then has continued to be mainly true of the entire subsequent development of Canada, though in recent years the economic and political power at least of Western Canada has made itself more evident. The present cultural and linguistic crisis is but a continuation of that noted so vividly by Lord Durham.

What then were the prime purposes accepted and written into our constitutional law one hundred years ago? These may be briefly listed. The first purpose was Union. The BNA Act is an act for the Union of provinces into a new state. It was not an act for disunion, though it is crucially important to remember that in so far as Lower Canada was concerned it was an act which for the first time freed Quebec from the domination, first of an English oligarchy and then of an English majority, in respect of all those matters – and we realize today how large they were – which were assigned exclusively to provincial legislatures. For Quebec, Confederation was a partial application of the separatist principle. It is precisely the harmonizing of the two conflicting concepts of union, and independence, which makes federalism so peculiarly adaptable to so many contemporary communities blessed with cultural diversity. A 'new nationality' was envisaged in 1867, of a political character, which some of the Fathers rashly thought would be 'redeemed from provincialism.'

It was also assumed in 1867 that an economic unity would match the political unity. The old provincial tariffs disappeared, and free trade across provincial boundaries was written into section 121. Here the American example was followed; the Fathers sought to provide a system of government which would enable an economic development across the whole of the northern half of the continent to take place as successfully as it had in the southern half. The BNA Act, particularly explicit on the distribution of economic powers, was evidently designed to enable businessmen and entrepreneurs to go ahead with their plans for development under the aegis of the central government. This government was deliberately made strong, both that it might bring into the new state those undeveloped portions and unallied colonies that were still outside the system in 1867, and also that it might undertake basic developments of its own, too large for any province, in the form of railways, canals, telegraphs, etc. essential for the rapid expansion of private business. Ottawa was the big new centre to which the most able and imaginative politicians were attracted. It could hardly have been foreseen that the very success of the federal government in completing the Union from coast to coast and providing these basic economic services would itself transform the nature of the federal structure by casting upon the supposedly insignificant provinces obligations and opportunities so vast as to magnify enormously – with much unexpected help from the Privy Council – their political and economic powers.

The Union, though intended to be strong at the centre, was nevertheless to be federal. Provincial autonomy was guaranteed, subject to the federal power of disallowance and paramountcy, though I do not believe the concept of autonomy was intended to dominate the future interpretation of the Constitution in the manner subsequently laid down by the courts. But provincial autonomy obviously meant something very special to the province of Quebec. It provided a constitutional basis for cultural diversity. There were important provisions in the Constitution designed to safeguard minority rights, understood then as including protection for the use of the French and English languages and for existing Protestant and Catholic separate schools. These protections benefited the English minority in Quebec, but, as it turned out, did next to nothing for the French minorities outside Quebec. The constitutional guarantees nevertheless resulted in an extension of the official use of the French language far beyond anything that had previously existed in British North America, for the laws of the Parliament of Canada, which of course operate across the entire country, were to be in the two languages. Thus when British Columbia entered the Union in 1871, and Prince Edward Island in 1873, all the federal laws in those provinces were as authoritatively written in French as they were in English. Moreover, when the federal Parliament created the three Prairie provinces it did so in statutes written in the two languages. Thus the constitutions of Alberta, Saskatchewan, and Manitoba are still written in French as well as in English, and in this sense French is an official language even here. The Manitoba decision to abolish the use of French in its provincial statutes in 1890 did not abolish the French text of the Manitoba Act. If Ottawa were to decide to publish its statutes in parallel columns on each page in both languages, as Quebec does for her statutes, the whole of Canada would suddenly awaken to the presence of the French language in its official laws. Able lawyers would then begin to enquire whether their clients might not be better protected by the French rather than the English version.

A further evident purpose in the original Canadian Constitution was the preservation of the monarchical principle and the parliamentary form of government. But the monarchic principle in Canada was from the start and is today quite different in its social implication from its position in Great Britain. Not only do we have no resident sovereign, but in the law we talk more about the Crown than we do about the Queen. We do not speak about the Queen's corporations, we call them Crown corporations. We speak of the Crown in right of Alberta and the Crown in right of Quebec. The term 'Crown' is simply a variant on the term 'state.' There is no theory of the state in English public law, nor is there in Canadian public law, because the concept of the Crown suffices as a substitute. The BNA Act itself uses non-monarchical language in many sections, as when it says 'Canada shall be liable for the debts and liabilities of each province existing at the Union'; 'Nova Scotia shall be liable to Canada ... '; 'The assets enumerated in the Fourth Schedule to this act belonging at the Union to the province of Canada shall be the property of Ontario and Quebec conjointly.' As Maitland once pointed out,[7] this is the language of statesmanship and of common life; to introduce the strict legal concept of the Queen as owner of the various assets and liabilities would be as stilted as it is accurate.

This monarchical principle, moreover, was to express itself in the traditional constitutional form of parliamentary government, with all that that implies about free elections, fundamental freedoms of the individual, and indeed the constitutional basis of a free society. Here it is essential that we distinguish between the constitutional provision of a parliamentary system and the way parliaments actually conduct their business. To say that Parliament should be reformed so that it can more efficiently conduct the increasing amount of business that comes before it, is one thing, and there is a growing body of opinion to this effect. To say that the parliamentary system itself should be scrapped and replaced by the American presidential system, as some far out individuals have done,[8] is quite another thing. We must be careful not to throw the baby out with the bathwater. Mr Gérin-Lajoie has suggested that Cabinet Ministers should not sit in the Legislature because it wastes too much of their time; this change would play havoc with cabinet government as we have known it, but a province has the power to change its constitution in this way if it so chooses. A province has not the legal power, however, to turn itself into a republic, for this would interfere with the office of Lieutenant-Governor, something not permitted in the present constitution. Such a decision involves the whole of Canada.

AMENDMENT OF THE BNA ACT

Surveying the present situation in Canada, and comparing it with what existed at the end of the great depression of the 1930s, it is obvious that very great changes in governmental practice have occurred with remarkably little change in the formal law of the Constitution. How many amendments have been made in that period requiring the participation of the United Kingdom Parliament? There was

7 In his essay *The Crown as Corporation.*
8 *E.g.* François Aquin, M.P.P., quoted in *Le Devoir*, Feb. 27, 1967.

the 1940 amendment adding unemployment insurance to federal powers; there was the 1943 amendment postponing readjustment; there was the amendment making new provisions for representation in the House of Commons, enacted in 1946 but since 1949 within federal control; there was the union with Newfoundland in 1949; there was the important addition of the federal power to revise the Constitution in purely federal matters, also in 1949; there was the addition of a federal jurisdiction over old age pensions in 1951, amended in 1964; and there was the limitation of the age of judges to seventy-five years, added in 1961. It is therefore true to say that the only changes in legislative jurisdiction as between Ottawa and the provinces have been the unemployment insurance and the old age pension provisions, both of which increased federal authority. The provinces have so far had no additional jurisdiction granted them by fundamental change in the Constitution. All their increased authority has come from within the Constitution itself. Even Quebec's accord with France for the exchange of teachers has been authorized by an overall agreement between Ottawa and France made under the federal power to conduct international relations. And it is clear that we have by no means exhausted all the permutations and combinations possible under the existing constitutional law.

The foregoing remarks may convey the impression that the writer does not believe we need to make any change in the fundamental law laid down in the BNA Acts. If so, let that impression at once be corrected. The writer has said repeatedly that 'we have a rendezvous with the BNA Act,' and believes it still to be true. Everyone will agree, for instance, that sooner or later we must repatriate the Constitution, so as to avoid the necessity of appealing to an exterior Parliament to make our own law. This task itself is one of fundamental difficulty, as the slow formulation, acceptance, and then rejection of the Fulton-Favreau formula made clear. A method for amending a federal constitution cannot be formulated without the entire theory of the nature of that constitution being also explicitly or impliedly stated. The present Constitution in strict law is easy to define; it is based on statutes (the BNA Acts and others) emanating from a Parliament that had and still has legal authority over Canada in certain respects, and which can therefore amend its own laws – our Constitution – at any time it so desires without even, some inveterate Diceyans would still hold, the necessity of prior Canadian agreement. It may be said that such a statement, to use the words of Lord Sankey, 'is theory and has no relation to realities.'[9] The reality is that Canada controls the legislative powers of the United Kingdom Parliament for Canadian purposes. We press the button, and the House of Lords and House of Commons

9 In the *British Coal Corporation* case, [1935] A.C. 500, 520.

at Westminster spring into action. So much is this true that when Mr Lesage was contemplating abolishing the Legislative Council in Quebec, and could not obtain its consent, he was apparently prepared to invoke this overriding jurisdiction to procure the direct abolition of a part of the Quebec legislature without the necessity of a Quebec statute. But if we are to rid ourselves of the United Kingdom as a constituent assembly for Canada, then we must have a clear alternative which expresses our notion of the proper relationship between the central government and the provinces, a task complicated by the factor of giving place to the will of the people. Observers cannot but note that it was as much the influence of Quebec as of any province that insisted in the consideration of the Fulton-Favreau formula on a drastic right of provincial veto over future amendments; yet at the last moment it was Quebec which wrecked the very formula it had so very actively supported. In future we may bless Mr Lesage's change of mind. He saved the country from committing what would have been, in my opinion, a fatal, suicidal error. The Fulton-Favreau formula is fortunately forgotten.

TWO CULTURES AND A COMMON POLITICAL NATIONALITY

So all would agree we must face up to the problem of fundamental constitutional amendment. But that, of course, is only part of the story. Once we come face to face with the Constitution, we open up many other profoundly important questions that are now being debated. Foremost among these will be the question of the relationship between the two cultures, the two official languages, and as some would say, the two nations, of which this country is composed. As a continuing member of a Royal Commission specifically charged with enquiring into some of these matters, and which has not yet issued its final report, I am debarred from saying what I think should take place. But, like any judge, I can take judicial notice of certain facts and certain movements of opinion. The thirty-five per cent of the population of New Brunswick whose mother tongue is French do not have the guaranteed rights that are given by the Constitution to the now thirteen per cent in Quebec whose mother tongue is English, though we must remember that the thirteen per cent are three times as numerous as the thirty-five per cent. In absolute numbers (and it is wise to think of absolute numbers as well as percentages of total population) there are twice as many people of French mother tongue in Ontario as there are in New Brunswick. In a modern industrial society mobility of personnel is an essential need, and we take steps, such as making pensions portable, to promote it. How far should the two official languages be portable? This issue must be faced. Then, too, it is true to say that nearly all provinces have some form of special status under the law of the present Constitution, even if it is only a negative status such as the inability of the Prairie provinces to tax the property of the CPR. The special status for Quebec under the present Constitution is particularly noticeable; should it be increased? Or should it be rendered less special by the elimination of the English minority rights in Quebec? If all human rights are taken away, all citizens can be said to be equal in status. All are slaves.

A combination of forces – military, political, and economic – made it possible to find a common ground for the original Constitution one hundred years ago. We seem to be at the stage that Canadians had reached just before the BNA Act was adopted. To a lesser degree, the war in Vietnam (Senator McCarthy's legacy to America) is playing the part of the American Civil War, by sharpening our sense of separateness from the United States. All sorts of forces are making for change, some of them centripetal, such as the pressure of technology, computerized industry, telecommunications and the other attributes of the post-industrial revolution; some of them, of which Quebec nationalism is easily the most important, are centrifugal. Nationalism has proven strong enough to render obsolete the notion that communism was monolithic and would produce similar results in all countries. In short, nationalism knocks the basis out of what appears to be the foundation of much American foreign policy. We must not think that we can be exempt from its creative force in our own country. Nehru once said that there is a good form of nationalism, and a bad form of nationalism; the good form is that inherent desire in man to live in a society that enables him to express himself to the fullest; the bad form is the rigid application of racist doctrines that can lead to disaster. Both the good and the bad forms of nationalism are usually to be found simultaneously in any nationalist movement, and the question is, which one will prevail? The answer to that depends on many factors, but among them the receptivity of the movement by its environment plays a major role. A frustrated nationalism turns to primitive weapons, just as a frustrated individual may seek release in a primitive nationalism. On the other hand, a strong sense of national identity can be a protection against the crushing conformity toward which technology is constantly driving us.

In the midst of our present controversies, certain points of law stand out clearly. Neither the federal government nor any provincial governments have by law a racial or religious character. Ottawa is not the 'national government of English Canada,' nor is Quebec the 'national government of French Canada.'[10] Both types of government are representative of all the racial elements that come under their jurisdictions. French Canada is bigger than and cannot be wholly represented by Quebec. English Canadians are part and parcel of every provincial government.

10 See *Quebec Year Book*, 1963, at 23.

Both Ottawa and Quebec have a unique position under the Constitution, in that each is officially bilingual in its parliamentary debates, its statutes, and in the administration of justice through its courts. Nevertheless, both these governments should serve with equal consideration all the Canadians that come within their territories.

In regard to subjects which are predominantly provincial in character, such as education and health, the autonomy of the province permits it to make agreements of a political character with other jurisdictions. To take away this power to make agreements would be to limit provincial autonomy. Thus an agreement between a province and the federal government in regard to education is quite lawful. It is not an invasion of a provincial sphere by the federal government even if federal money is spent. Quebec, under the aegis of an exchange of notes between Ottawa and France, has made an agreement with the French government regarding the exchange of teachers; no one has suggested that France is interfering in a matter of Quebec's educational autonomy. It would surely be odd to learn that France had more constitutional right than Ottawa to help in the development of provincial education.

Both the federal and provincial governments make use of the spending power to promote their objectives. It is my opinion that neither government is debarred from spending money, duly appropriated by its legislature, even in regard to matters over which there is no legislative jurisdiction. The province can always refuse an offer. No province can legislate extra-territorially, yet every province can make a contract of loan in New York or buy property in England or France. This is spending money outside the jurisdiction. The same is true for Ottawa, though its jurisdiction is not limited territorially but only in regard to subject matter. I am not here discussing the wisdom, but only the legality, of spending public money.

It is my view also that any government in Canada is entitled to spend money on any kind of research which it feels would be helpful to it. There is no 'class of subjects' called research which is ascribed by the BNA Act to any particular jurisdiction. Moreover, in undertaking research, no law is passed which affects any rights of the citizen. The Royal Commission on Constitutional Questions in Quebec, known as the *Tremblay Commission*, was within its powers in conducting research into every aspect of the Canadian Constitution and of the position of other provinces, though it never left Quebec and did not invite any other governments to present their views. Similarly, Ottawa is quite free to investigate the situation regarding education, the promotion of the arts, the development of scientific research, or any other matter which it feels would assist it in its responsibilities for the peace, order and good government of Canada. The federal government, of course, has one further ground to justify its educational and research activities, since it is also a provincial government. We are apt to forget that Canada's eleventh province is the Northwest Territories, and that the federal government is its legislature. The centennial design very properly symbolises this fact. Every subject matter within the jurisdiction of the other provinces is also within the jurisdiction of the Parliament of Canada with respect to the Northwest Territories. The federal government also has a conditional right to legislate on education in any province under section 93 of the BNA Act, as well as a clear duty to care for the education of its armed forces. It is important that we do not allow the legislative division of powers to spill over into the area of executive action not involving the making of laws but merely the acquiring of information. To do so would be to restrict unduly and improperly the freedom of both the federal and provincial governments. Research today is a prime function of government.

Every problem met by an individual or a country in the course of their lives is both a challenge and an opportunity. Our problems in Canada today are large enough to offer us great opportunities for a clearer definition of the nature and purpose of Canadian federalism. The building of stable multi-cultural societies is a task being faced by a majority of the worlds' governments, and as the nation-state grows more and more obsolete will increasingly demand our attention. Canadians of this generation are challenged to bring a large outlook and a generous humanism to the solution of our constitutional difficulties. But in searching for solutions let us not forget that the Constitution is the supreme law of the land, and that it cannot be fundamentally amended without a common consent that in recent times has had to come from every province as well as from the federal government. The winning of that consent is a prerequisite to orderly change.

# XXVIII

# Language Rights and Language Policy in Canada

*The sixth annual Manitoba Law School Foundation Lecture, 1970, in which I look back on the work of the Royal Commission on Bilingualism and Bicultural-ism, of which I had been a member.*
From the *Manitoba Law Journal*, 4, 1971, 243-57

Before I enter upon the main burden of my topic, I would like to take this oppor-tunity of saying how happy I am to be addressing this audience in Winnipeg dur-ing your centennial year. I have followed your centennial celebrations by means of television and the press, and it has given me occasion to reflect upon the quite unique position Manitoba holds in Canadian history. I envy the excitement of Kelsey and La Vérendrye as they debouched upon the vast central plain of North America. A new chapter in the development of Canada started here; a whole new society grew out from here. As in Eastern Canada, the French were the first white men to invade these Indian lands, and showed their remarkable adaptability to Indian ways, but the English authority and settlers soon came south from Hud-son's Bay to create in Manitoba the basic dualism of Canadian society. At its cre-ation in 1870, the province had a population in which English and French were nearly equally matched. So it is not surprising that protections for language and separate schools were written into the provincial Constitution - the first written constitution in Canada to be enacted by a Canadian legislature. Being a federal statute it was of course enacted in French as well as English, and both texts are authoritative; even today. Then came the immigration from all parts of Europe and the United States, bringing those *Strangers Within Our Gates* - now among our foremost citizens - of which J.S. Woodsworth wrote so sympathetically. Out of the resulting linguistic confusion grew a demand for one public school system using one language. As Professor Morton has put it in his history of the province, you passed from duality to plurality and, by inevitable paradox, to uniformity.

Now uniformity itself (never a very attractive idea!) is giving way before the rising concept of an equal partnership all across Canada between the two founding peoples, which welcomes the contribution of other cultural groups.

During my long teaching of constitutional law, I, of course, had to study the important constitutional cases to which your political movements in Manitoba gave rise from time to time. The names of Barrett and Brophy were familiar to my law students as well as yours, as the consequences of those cases are familiar to all Canadian historians. I have sometimes speculated on the degree to which our history might have been different had we succeeded in abolishing appeals to the Privy Council in 1875 when the Supreme Court of Canada was created, instead of in 1949, for then the unanimous judgment of our highest Court protecting the denominational schools in Manitoba would be the law today, and much of the racial bitterness deriving from that series of events might have been avoided. The three Protestant judges on the Supreme Court were in agreement with the two Catholic justices in their defence of the separate school rights. But it is the facts of history and not the 'ifs' of history with which we must deal, and we Canadians will always, I am sure, find new reasons for disagreeing with one another.

Now we have reached a time in Canada when we are at least as much concerned about the language used in the school as we are about the religious aspect of the school. This represents a very profound change in our outlook, and it has important consequences. Oecumenism has reduced religious tensions but language disputes are ready to hand for those who need to feel angry. Throughout our early history, the principal treaties and statutes touching upon biculturalism referred only to religion; this was true of the treaty of Utrecht 1713, the treaty of Paris 1763, and the Quebec Act of 1784. In these, the free exercise of the Roman Catholic religion is promised, but language is not mentioned, though the Quebec Act, in restoring French civil law, must have contemplated the use of the French language. The Union Act of 1840 required all statutes to be in English only, though translation was authorized; this provision was repealed in 1848, but language use was left to the discretion of the legislature. Not until the BNA Act of 1867, and the Manitoba Act of 1870, do we find specific guarantees for dual language use in Canada, and then only in reference to the enactment of statutes, debates in the legislature, and pleadings before the courts. No specific mention of language was included in the sections dealing with schools in the first BNA Act [though if a choice of language was established for any denominational schools 'by law' at the Union it could not be 'prejudicially' affected by provincial legislation today.]

Apart from historical and constitutional interests, I have other and more personal associations with Manitoba and in Winnipeg which I should like to acknowledge here. As a young man in Quebec city I think I was hardly aware of the existence of Winnipeg until my father, then Canon F.G. Scott recently returned as Senior Chaplain to the First Canadian Division in World War I, decided during your 1919 general strike that 'his boys were in trouble,' as he put it, and that he should come here to see if in any way he could help. He was not motivated by a desire to bring victory either to the Citizens Committee or to the One Big Union, but rather to resume the friendships he had had with officers and men in your regiments with whom he had seen active service. Nevertheless, the authorities apparently decided that his goodwill was more helpful to the strikers than to the forces of law and order, for he was told to leave late one night and had to return to Quebec. He was not the first Scott in your history to attain some notoriety.

Later when I returned from Oxford in the 1920s, Winnipeg again began to loom in my life. I came under the influence of several great Canadians who have emerged from this city, notably John W. Dafoe, E.J. Tarr and others who were so prominent in the founding of the Canadian Institute of International Affairs, and in defining a new form of Canadian nationalism which led inevitably to our independent status in world politics. It was then too, that I first met and began to appreciate the stature of J.S. Woodsworth, who perhaps more than any other Canadian helped me to clarify my ideas about the kind of democratic Canada we should seek to build and the kind of political instrument that would most contribute to the attainment of our ideals. These are still living memories which I deeply cherish.

I realize that in choosing as my topic for this lecture 'Language Rights and Language Policy in Canada,' I am opening up a subject on which there are many strong feelings. This at least, means that, to use a current term, the subject is 'relevant.' Of course the whole question of constitutional revision is also relevant, but we have made already far more positive decisions with respect to changes in the use of the two official languages than we have in regard to the future distribution of legislative jurisdiction between Ottawa and the provinces. I feel on much more solid ground in talking about the language question than about the constitutional question, because I can discuss actualities rather than possibilities. Moreover the language issue gives me an opportunity to say something about the work of the B. and B. Commission, now at last drawing to an uneventful close. To borrow from T.S. Eliot, it began with a bang, and is ending with a whimper. But I think you will agree that because of its work, Canada will never be quite the same again.

Canadians often question the utility of Royal Commissions, and our Commission and its cost stimulated more criticism. Let me just give you a few of the facts. We were given a mandate which, on examination required us to do an amount of work that I think could legitimately have been assigned to seven or eight separate Royal Commissions. How do you operate the armed forces in a bilingual country? Canada is a member of NATO where English and French are the two working languages, as they are at the United Nations. A whole Royal Commission could have been devoting its time to this military problem. How do you change the imbalance in the use of the two official languages in the Federal Civil Service and Crown Corporations? This is another vastly difficult subject, of crucial importance. What is the situation regarding the teaching of English and French in the various provincial school systems? This rated an entire volume of our studies. Did it not rate a separate Commission? How do the modern media of communication, such as the newspapers, film, radio and television affect the development of bilingualism and biculturalism? Here again we have a question of major importance. What is the role of the 'Other Ethnic Groups' in Canadian society, many of whom are conscious of their language and culture and wish to preserve them? Some 24% of the Canadian population falls in this category. And of particular importance in Quebec, but of growing importance elsewhere, is the question of the proper relationship between private business enterprises and the cultural environment in which they are placed. Even where there is no language problem, we can be and are, deeply concerned about the foreign ownership of essential Canadian resources; this foreign ownership looks more dangerous in Quebec where to the ownership is added a dominant use of English at the top levels of industrial government. A career use of French becomes less and less possible as the young Quebecer rises in business and finance.

One Royal Commission, our Royal Commission, was handed this whole package of problems. You must forgive us if we took much time and spent – was it much money? Whenever we had a twinge of conscience, and even Royal Commissioners do have a conscience, we remembered the aircraft carrier Bonaventure. It will be discovered that the greater part of our expenditure went on research. This was an essential activity because we were inquiring for the first time into a maze of problems on which there were no reliable statistics. One of the beneficial side effects of our work will be that a very large number of experts, both inside and outside the universities, and both French and English speaking, were brought to put their minds to these vital questions. These men and women, now better informed, are part of our whole educational structure.

So much by way of an introduction. To prove that I was not unaware of the unpopularity, particularly in the early days of our work, of much that we were doing, I wrote this little verse about it:

How doth the busy B. and B.
Enlarge each whining hour,
By hearing griefs from sea to sea
And turning sweet to sour.

Apparently, many Canadians believed that we should have let sleeping dogs lie. 'We had no problem here till you came' was a frequent observation we met on our travels; we usually found that the problem was very deep and had not been faced realistically. It is true that some enquiries can stir up trouble that perhaps in the course of time would die away, but the kind of problem facing Canada when we were appointed, and the problem that still faces it, and which we must learn to live with and adapt to, is not of that sort. History and demography have committed us to a course from which there is no turning back. Even so extreme a solution as the independence of Quebec would not in fact dispose of the problem. An independent Quebec would start with over a million English speaking people, a very large minority for a new country of six million. There would also be a million francophones in the other provinces, mostly in Ontario and New Brunswick. Their claims to recognition could not be ignored by English Canada without violating established rights. I know there are some nationalists in Quebec who would like to have a unilingual French State, as there are many anglophones (I trust this new word we coined is winning general acceptance) who would like to see an all English Canada, but these are extremes of opinion which we must tolerate but cannot realistically endorse.

Let me now give some of the facts which our studies brought to light and which are basic to any thinking about language rights and policy for Canada. We are dealing not just with a Canadian problem, but with a world-wide problem in its Canadian application. Linguists tell us there are 2,500 identifiable languages in the world, and there are only 130 countries to put them in. Some people, indeed many people, are going to have a language problem. Language being an essential part of a culture, and the love of one's culture being natural to men who live in a cultural group, language use is seen by most people as an essential part of their individuality and personal freedom. Our terms of reference made it clear that we were to assume some degree of bilingualism in Canada, and were to recommend ways in which the Canadian Confederation could develop on the basis of an equal partnership between the two founding peoples, but we also had to take into account the contribution made by the other ethnic groups. We have only two official languages in Canada, French and English, and to have recommended three or more official languages would have been beyond our mandate – besides an exercise in futility.

Given the world-wide dimensions of our problem, the experience of other bilingual states became extremely relevant. We made an intensive study of four countries with comparable situations, namely Belgium, Switzerland, Finland and South Africa. We might, of course, have visited all these countries, following the examples of many other Royal Commissions that feel a need to look at situations in other parts of the world before making a report, but we chose instead to have experts write about them and tell us what they found. Here at least we were not extravagant.

What are some of the significant things we learned from these studies? First, I would say, we learned that every country that has a language problem, attempts to solve it in its own way. There are no universal rules, except perhaps the rule that language rights must be respected if you wish to have domestic peace. We also learned that there are two kinds of bilingualism which must be distinguished. These may be called territorial bilingualism and personal bilingualism. Territorial bilingualism means that the country with two languages divides itself into regions within each of which only one language is officially used. Language is tied to the land, as it were. For example in Belgium, with some minor exceptions, everything north of a line across the country is Flemish, and everything south of it is French; there is a mixed area around Brussels where the two are officially recognized. Personal bilingualism means that each individual may use his own language wherever he happens to be in his country for all official acts. Most countries use some combination of the two forms of bilingualism: Territorial bilingualism is thus attached to a defined territory while personal bilingualism travels with the person. In our recommendations we drew upon both these principles for our proposed solutions.

We found it necessary to make another distinction. A bilingual person, of course, is one who can speak any two languages, but for our purposes, because of our terms of reference, we confined the term to those who can speak English and French. I won't trouble you with the distinctions that must be made in the degrees of bilingualism; these are hard to measure but very important. If you can speak and understand another language when it is spoken to you, you have a very simple but useful bilingualism; if you can also read it and write it you have complete bilingualism. Often it is quite sufficient for a person to be able to talk the language and to understand it when it is spoken.

Institutional bilingualism is another kind of concept. Here the institution – let us say Federal Post Office or the Canadian National Railways – is bilingual if it can provide services to the public in both languages, even though the great majority of its employees may speak only one language. To satisfy the reasonable requirements of personal bilingualism, so that a French speaking person getting off at a railway station in Vancouver can have his needs met, it is only necessary that in the station there be a wicket or a place where he can get the information he needs in his own language. A very few bilingual people are sufficient to staff such a service, and then we can say the institution is bilingual.

We noted another fact about these countries, which is certainly true of Canada. In a bilingual country you will find large blocks of people who only speak one language. In Quebec, according to the 1961 census, 61% of the population could not speak English. Other figures suggest 75% are unilingual. Right now Quebec is predominantly unilingual. So is English Canada where even fewer are bilingual. This situation is not going to change very fast: the widespread notion that our Commission expects everyone to learn two languages, however desirable this may be, is wrong. Official bilingualism in a province does not force the minority to become bilingual, as the example of Quebec amply proves. If everybody spoke both languages equally well, there would really be little need in trying to make any special rules.

South Africa is a country where the majority of the white population is already bilingual, and in consequence they are able to adopt such rules as having a department of Government speak English for one month and Afrikaans the next month – something we could not do. They publish their statutes in the two languages, but only one of them is authoritative and the bills are assented to alternately in English and Afrikaans. They thus avoid the problem of interpretation when there is a difference between the two versions. We have to struggle with that problem in Canada, because our two versions are equally authoritative, and this is now true of the judgments of the Supreme Court of Canada which appear in parallel columns in the two languages. I am sure lawyers in English Canada have been somewhat startled to discover that from now on, the statutes of Canada and the Supreme Court judgments are printed in both languages in the same volume. Formerly the statutes were all bound in an English volume and separately in a French volume, so it was easy for the practising lawyer in Victoria, BC, perhaps violently opposed to bilingualism, to forget that Canada was already a bilingual country in certain essential respects, even in British Columbia. Now he sees on his desk the language that has produced the great masterpieces of French literature.

Finland was a country that we found particularly interesting and from which we borrowed one of our basic ideas, namely the 'bilingual districts' – special areas within which a defined language régime would be established for federal, provincial and local governments. Finland used to be part of Sweden and was for long governed by Swedes; now it is independent and the Swedes make up about 7% only of the population. Yet their language rights are generously protected. The commune is the unit of local government, and it is recognized as officially bilingual if it includes in its territory a linguistic minority of at least 10% or 5,000 persons. And Finns may use either language in their dealings with governmental authorities anywhere. Finland thus uses a combination of the territorial principle, the bilingual communes, and the personality principle, the right of the individual, even outside the commune, to choose the language of communication with governments.

Belgium is another, and not very happy, bilingual country. But here the territorial principle is rigidly applied, except for the area around Brussels and some small exceptions on the border. Everything north of the dividing line, as I have said, is Flemish, everything south is French. With one million anglophones in Quebec, and one million francophones outside, this kind of solution would be wholly unsuitable to Canada. There is no place where the dividing line can be fairly drawn: certainly not at the boundary of Quebec. Switzerland showed us another example of a combination of the territorial and personality principles: the cantons are mostly unilingual for schools and local administrative services, while federal services are given in the individual's language no matter where he lives. South Africa, in its use of Afrikaans and English, showed further variations: no overall territorial principle is applied because bilingualism is widespread and the two communities are interspersed. Members of the official language groups are fully integrated with the public service and can work in their own language, while each child has a right to education in his mother tongue wherever the numbers warrant it.

It is interesting to note that of the four countries we specially studied only one – Switzerland – is a federal state. South Africa's 'provinces' do not possess coordinate powers as do the Canadian provinces. Biculturalism and bilingualism can be well safeguarded in a country that has a single central government. Decentralisation in the form of federalism may be helpful, but does not appear to be essential.

These are some of the ways in which four countries with language problems similar to Canada's have attempted to apply the principle of equal partnership. From each there was some lesson to be learned. But each found its own solutions and there was no uniform pattern of law or custom. So too it would have to be in Canada: our special Canadian conditions would require special Canadian arrangements. What those conditions were, how Canadians lived and worked and felt in an environment already bilingual and bicultural to a considerable degree, was what we sought to discover through our massive research programme. Volume I of our Report lists 146 studies prepared for our use, and there were innumerable other documents made available to us, of which the 1961 census was of first importance. It was on the basis of this mountain of evidence that we sought to make our recommendations achieve 'the greatest equality with the least impracticality.' There are 14 such recommendations dealing with the official languages, 46 relating to education, 57 regarding the work world, both for the federal administration and the private sector, 16 for the other ethnic groups, and 17 for the federal capital district – 150 in all for the volumes already published.

Royal Commissions create a stir when they are appointed and when they report, but all too often the effect is short-lived. It is hardly to be expected that all of our proposals will be widely known, but the basic ideas and the philosophy behind them should be kept before the public if there is to be a meaningful change in our national habits. Many important steps – more perhaps than is generally realized – have already been taken to give effect to some of our recommendations, at least in the making of new laws, like the official languages acts of the federal and New Brunswick governments, and the amended school acts in Ontario, New Brunswick and, most recently, Manitoba. For the first time in Canadian history the four contiguous provinces between Nova Scotia and Saskatchewan, where the minority questions are most acute, are applying the principle of the complete dual school system in the official language chosen by the parents.

However, to change the feelings and outlook of people is a more difficult matter than to change their laws. We cannot legislate love, but at least we can by legislation lessen the causes of hate. Since our objective was an effective equal partnership between French-speaking and English-speaking Canadians, our very first recommendation was that this equality should be recognized by proclaiming French and English as the official languages in the Federal Parliament, courts and administration, and also in the provinces of New Brunswick, where the French constitutes 35% of the population, and Ontario, where though only 7% they make a global mass of about 600,000 people. We also laid down the principle that any other province where the official language minority reaches 10% should make the same declaration. We made no similar recommendation for Manitoba partly because the law of 1890 purporting to make the province unilingual has never been tested in the courts and might turn out to be unconstitutional, and partly because the francophones there do not reach the 10% we adopted as a general rule for all provinces nor constitute a sufficiently large global mass (there were 61,000 in 1961) to meet this other criterion.

Certain corollaries inescapably flow from this general principle. Federal services should be made available in either of the official languages in all parts of the country. This is the personality principle, and since the enactment of The Federal Official Languages Act in 1969 and the appointment of the Official Languages Commissioner in Ottawa – a sort of language Ombudsman – is on its way to being realized. This by itself, though much, is only part of the problem. It does not touch the inside working of the federal services. Here we took as the ideal that no Canadian should be handicapped in his career as a servant of the federal government or its Crown Corporations by reason of his having English or French as his mother tongue. Our proposed solution was the creation of work units, appropriately placed at all levels of administration, where French could be as normal a language of work as English is at the present moment. The difficulties in the application of this principle should not blind us to its practicability and great utility; only thus will we be able to make full use of French talent and capacity in the federal civil service.

Making the federal government services bilingual is not enough: the provinces and municipalities, the Commission felt, should play their part. Where the official language minorities actually live in sizeable groups, there should be found in Canada as in Finland, a complete range of provincial and municipal as well as federal services in the two languages. This is where the territorial principle applies. All provinces should respect this obligation, and not only the officially bilingual ones. The services would include of course public education given in the official language chosen by the parents. Hence the Commission proposal for the creation of bilingual districts – selected areas in which at least 10% of the population uses the second official language.

To locate these bilingual districts the Commission could use only the federal census districts, of which there were 273 in the 1961 census. It was found that all but two provinces – British Columbia and Newfoundland – had such districts meeting the 10% test. This makes the French minorities outside Quebec quite unlike all other language minorities, which are not so dispersed across the country, and on this ground alone, quite apart from the obvious historical differences, could not expect to be placed on the same constitutional footing as the French. Our recommendation was that bilingual districts be established throughout Canada, their exact limits to be defined by negotiation between the federal and provincial government concerned. Such negotiations have already begun. In Quebec the need is less pressing as the English minority has its own schools, and receive bilingual services already from the provincial government and in municipalities where it is most concentrated. Yet Quebec too should accept the rule.

One area requiring particular attention was the city of Ottawa and the whole federal capital district. The hitherto purely English character of Canada's capital is an anomaly that must be ended if the concept of equal partnership is to be given real as well as symbolic meaning. Most countries composed of more than one cultural community have had difficulty determining the location and character of the capital, and here again we found a variety of solutions. South Africa divides its capital functionally; the legislature meets in Cape Town, the administrative capital is Pretoria, and Blomfontein is the seat of the Appellate Division of the Supreme Court. Bern is mostly unilingual German despite Switzerland's multilingual constitution. In the old United Province of Canada before Confederation the Capital perambulated between Kingston, Montreal, Toronto and Quebec. Ottawa was then chosen as the most acceptable compromise. There it obviously must remain, though the 'Federal District' extends far beyond the single city of Ottawa into Quebec, and some federal administrative offices are now situated in Hull. Our Commission set out in Book V the detailed recommendations designed to make the whole area reflect the new concept of a bilingual and bicultural federal state.

Another important federal agency examined by the Commission was the armed forces. These employ roughly one-quarter of all federal government personnel, and should obviously be subject to the same general principles of language use with suitable adaptation, which were applied to other branches of the public service. The Royal 22nd Regiment – the Vandoos – have already shown the possibility and efficiency of this kind of 'work unit,' and there has been a steady development of bilingual practice within the services in recent years. The story is told in Volume III as part of the description of the federal administration.

The armed forces are a significant area of the total work world to which the Commission's recommendations are directed. By far the most important part of this world, however, from the point of view of the numbers employed, is the private sector – the world of private business. This was dealt with in the third part of Volume III.

It is not too difficult, though difficult enough, to develop new procedures and practices within governments which give effect to the officially bilingual character of the country. It is more difficult to work out and give effect to such procedures and practices within the field of private business, because here there are literally thousands of employers each enjoying the freedom of private enterprise. If language is a human right, then private individuals should presumably be able to associate together for business purposes and carry on that business in the language of their choice. This is of course a right being exercised in all parts of Canada, given the heterogenous composition of this population. There are, for example, Chinese newspapers being published, where one may assume that the editors and other employees speak Chinese to one another in their daily work. A Ukrainian in Winnipeg told the Commission he might spend a week practising his profession, meeting clients and friends, and scarcely speak a word of English. There is no reason why such forms of work using any language should not be allowed to grow and to flourish in their own way and at their own pace.

If we are to encourage the contribution of the 'other ethnic groups,' such forms of private enterprise should be welcomed as well as merely permitted. In business enterprises, there will almost inevitably be a distinction made between the language of internal management and that used in external communication with the public. An Italian restaurant in Montreal will use English or French with the great majority of its customers, whereas the chefs and waitresses may only speak Italian to one another. But it would be undemocratic to prohibit by law an Italian restaurant from speaking only Italian to its customers, and no Canadian should feel insulted if he is not dealt with in either French or English in a private undertaking. The customer's choice will soon determine the size and extent of such a business.

Complications arise when the business run in one language begins to engage large numbers of employees who use English or French, and carries on business in a large way with governments and other enterprises. A bilingual country ought not to impose any impediment upon successful advancement in a chosen career because the mother-tongue of the employee is one or other of the official languages. This means that in Quebec large business enterprises, which at present are mostly owned and managed by anglophones, ought to permit the French speaking employee to rise in the business to the top posts without being handicapped by the fact that his normal tongue is French. At the present moment he is so handicapped, unless he is exceptionally bilingual, whenever English is the working language. This is particularly true in the upper echelons of business. The English-speaking Quebecer is similarly handicapped if he chooses a career in the public administration of Quebec and cannot speak fluent French.

It was to meet this problem, which is also found in government enterprises, that the Commission proposed the creation of language units within the private corporate structure similar to those recommended for government enterprises. What this means is that the daily activities of these work situations ought to be so arranged that some of the work can be carried on in the second language, though of course it is essential that there be bilingual individuals at these top levels who can communicate with other work units. A man may thus spend almost his whole day working in the language he knows best and in which he is most efficient. For the private sector of Quebec the Commission recommended as the objective that French must become 'the principal language of work at all levels,' and specified certain steps to be taken to reach this objective, including a change over from English to French as the main language of work units in the middle and upper brackets of major work institutions.

I was obliged to differ with my colleagues on the Commission on this wording, not because I was opposed to the idea that French must become the principal language of work in Quebec, for I believe that to be the case, but because in the formulation of its recommendation the Commission did not, it seemed to me, sufficiently distinguish between the types of business to which this principle would apply. Business activities today are carried on in so many different kinds of institutions, with so many varieties of internal and external relationships, that it is impossible to impose a uniform rule on everyone.

The Commission recognized this fact insofar as it sought to distinguish between 'major work institutions' and 'smaller or specialized firms,' and in recommending that 'the main language of work in activities related to operations outside the province remain the choice of the enterprise.' But its stipulation that French should be the principal language of work 'at all levels' in all the major work institutions in the Province seemed to me quite unrealistic in the light of corporate enterprise today, which may be nation-wide or world-wide. A company may have a head office and only one plant in Quebec, with ten elsewhere; obviously at the topmost levels in the head office English will have to be the principal language used.

It would still be true to say of some enterprise, however, that French was their 'principal language of work' if, as in the case of the pulp and paper industry, the majority of the work force was French Canadian and were speaking French daily on the job. The amount of French spoken per day in such an industry is far greater than the amount of English used. The statement often heard, that no French-Canadian can get a job in Quebec unless he speaks English, is much more incorrect than correct; 61% of the Quebec population cannot speak English at all, yet presumably are not all unemployed, and the prevalence of English is confined to the far less numerous though more influential posts in the middle and upper management brackets. It is here, at the top of the industrial pyramid, that the language problem presses. It is here that the inequality exists and where some solution must be found.

Many people believe that 'private business,' because it is private, should control its 'in-door management' in any way which the owners determine. I have suggested that this idea is valid for smaller businesses and that, not only in bilingual districts, the choice of the business language should be the free choice of the owners. But it is unrealistic to apply this principle to the so-called private businesses that are in fact large industrial undertakings employing thousands of people and offering important careers to the young men and women coming out of the schools and universities. These businesses affect the public interest so widely that they can no longer be called private. They are a form of government exercising powers delegated to them in their corporate charters by the state, and the principles of language use which we would apply to a government must apply to them.

As a method of approaching the whole problem of the language of work in Quebec, the Commission made a very practical recommendation. It is quoted here in full:

We recommend that the government of Quebec establish a task force to consist of representatives of government, industry, the universities, and the major labour unions with the following general terms of reference: a) to launch discussions with the major companies in the province concerning the current state of bilingualism in their organizations and the means of developing institutional bilingualism more fully; b) to design an overall plan for establishing French as the principal language of work in Quebec and to set a timetable for this process; c) to initiate discussions with the federal government and with the governments of New Brunswick and Ontario, to discover areas of potential co-operation in implementing the plan; and d) to make recommendations to the provincial government for the achievement of the goal and for the establishment of permanent machinery of co-ordination. (1310)

Unfortunately, this approach has not yet been accepted. Instead there is another commission called the Gendron Commission studying the same questions on which the B & B Commission reported. Its composition is unfortunate. Neither the English business community nor the Quebec trade unions are represented, and the only anglophone, though a distinguished professor, was not a native Canadian, and had lived only two years in Quebec when appointed. Whatever the recommendations of the Gendron Commission may be, and no doubt its research will throw more light on the problem, there will inevitably arise questions as to the authority with which it speaks.

Canadians must approach the language question with two special qualities: realism and goodwill. Realism means accepting facts. French-Canada is a fact, and English-Canada is a fact. The English minority in Quebec now numbers one million, the French minorities outside Quebec also number about one million. If Canadian federalism is to survive, it must accept bilingualism sensibly applied, in Quebec as well as in Canada as a whole. It is *one* of the essential conditions of our survival. It is not the only one, for economic benefits must come to all Canadians from our association. We must believe we are worthwhile as a nation. But it must be a bilingual nation.

We must also have goodwill. We must see the plus as well as the minus, the great advantages as well as the difficulties. To accept bilingualism means a greater respect for human rights, a greater domestic tranquility, and, above all, the development within our country of the richness and creative ability that have made England and France two of the great centers of western civilization. That it will give Canada a national identity unique in the Americas goes without saying.

Quebec is painfully making up its mind as to what should be its political relations with its neighbours. So is English Canada, though its more secure position and difference of temperament make it more content to accept minor adjustments in the status quo. Will an independent Quebec provide a safe haven within which an uncontaminated French culture may flourish, or will this not be a fortress state driven in upon itself, cut off from its growing minorities outside, and doomed to the tensions and antagonism which such a situation tends to create? Will English Canada move toward some form of special status for Quebec which will still leave a viable federalism? This is the position as the B & B Commission ends its labours. We did not attempt the task of proposing basic constitutional reforms because it was doubtful if we were appointed for that purpose, we had not embarked upon the necessary background research, and we would have been entering an area in which other more specialised official committees were already at work. But my experience convinced me that an equal partnership between the two cultural communities in Canada was a workable concept, and one which would help Canada make a distinctive contribution to world history and world peace. Whether Canadians will accept the idea and bring it steadily into being is their decision. I for one have faith that they will accept the great challenge rather than fall back into obsolete forms of the nation state.

# XXIX

# Our Changing Constitution

*The Presidential Address to Section II of the Royal Society, 1961.*
From *Transactions of the Royal Society of Canada*, 55, Series III, June 1961,
83–95

In a presidential address before this Section of the Royal Society, whose members are drawn from so many different fields of knowledge, one is tempted to choose a subject that can be treated in a manner less technical than would be expected by a more specialized audience. This paper is about our changing constitution, but from a point of view broad enough, I hope, to cut across many of the boundaries that divide us. I have selected for discussion certain aspects of our constitutional development that are particularly relevant to problems we face today, the most important of which is the 'repatriation' of the constitution itself. Part of my paper – indeed much of it – will be historical, a reminder of things past, even a *recherche de la constitution perdue*; part will be autobiographical; and part of it will be rash enough to include foretellings, and perhaps forebodings, of the future. As I shall frequently refer back to a date of which we shall shortly be celebrating the centenary, namely 1867, the first all-Canadian year, I feel that a short title to my talk might simply be 'Life with Fathers.'

I had the good fortune, as a young student in the McGill Law Faculty, to be introduced to constitutional law by the late H.A. Smith, until recently Professor of International Law at London University. He was not only a stimulating teacher but a jurist with a strong sense of history, who looked through the legal terminology of the constitution, and of its judicial interpretations, to the body politic it was designed to create. It was he who taught me to see the problems which the Act of 1867 was intended to remedy, to look at the conditions in the British North American colonies in the 1860s, and to seek the intentions of the Fathers of Confederation not only in the words of the statutes but also in all the material available to historians, including the Confederation debates and other *travaux préparatoires*. He was well aware that English and Canadian courts exclude references to most of this material, and he has strongly urged[1] that this rule of exclusion should be changed to the more sensible practice, well established in continental jurisdictions, of permitting the judges to admit all historical evidence and to use their own discretion in respect of it.

Professor Smith was among the first commentators in Canada to point out that the trend in Privy Council interpretations of the BNA Act – he was writing just after the disastrous judgment of 1925 in the *Snider* case had reduced federal jurisdiction to its lowest point – had been towards a type of constitution quite different from that which the Fathers of Confederation had clearly intended. To use his own words: 'Whether the principle of federal government devised by our forefathers or that more recently established by the Privy Council is the better for Canada is a question of policy beyond the scope of this article. I hope that I have written enough to show that they are not the same.'[2]

The Fathers had stressed the importance of the federal government's being given ample authority for the great task of nation-building[3] that was entrusted to it. Unlike the American Congress, the Parliament of Canada possessed the residue of powers not otherwise distributed, as well as its specified powers. The Privy Council, in certain leading cases, had paid so much attention to the preservation of provincial autonomy, as though this was the chief or only aim of the Fathers, and had so expanded provincial jurisdiction over property and civil rights, as virtually to transfer the federal residuary power to provincial hands, at least in peacetime. Apart from the residuary clause, Privy Council judgments drastically curtailed federal jurisdiction over trade and commerce, fisheries and agriculture. Such a *volte face* could only have occurred in a court which substituted its own idea of the intentions of the Fathers from that which was on the record it barred itself from examining.

Professor Smith's thesis took some time to win acceptance in legal and academic circles. The historical record, it is true, was not wholly clear, either before or after 1925. A change of heart seemed to occur when the Privy Council in the years 1930–32 attributed to federal competence two matters of national and in-

---

1 'Interpretation in English and Continental Law,' *J. Comp. Leg.*, Third Series, vol. IX (1927), p. 153. See also 'The Residue of Power in Canada,' 1926 *Can. Bar Rev.*, 432 at p. 433.

2 'The Residue of Power in Canada,' 1926 *Can. Bar Rev.*, 432 at p. 439.

3 Cartier, Brown, Galt, and other Fathers of Confederation used the word 'nation' to represent all Canada. See references in F.R. Scott, 'Political Nationalism and Confederation,' *C.J.E.P.S.*, VIII, 3 (1942), pp. 387–90 [reprinted in this volume].

deed international importance, namely aeronautics and broadcasting,[4] but this was a short-lived respite. After the judicial massacre of Mr Bennett's 'New Deal,' legislation in 1937,[5] weakening if not destroying federal competence over unemployment insurance, interprovincial marketing, and the implementing of Canadian treaties, there were few commentators left in Canada who had not put themselves on record as sharing Professor Smith's point of view.[6] Instead of being 'a living tree capable of growth and expansion,' as the constitution was described in 1930, it was now likened to a ship of state sailing on larger ventures but still retaining the 'watertight compartments' which were an essential part of her original structure. So, as Professor McWhinney points out,[7] the 'marine metaphor' of Lord Atkin offsets the 'arboreal metaphor' of Lord Sankey. The *Sirois Report* in 1940, perhaps not wanting to wound provincial susceptibilities, came to the remarkable conclusion that the historical interpretation and references to the intentions of the Fathers of Confederation proved nothing, and that anyway the enquiry was not worth pursuing.[8] The enquiry, in my opinion, was very well worth pursuing and is still more worth pursuing as we come to face the problem of nationalizing the constitution. In turning our back on history we may forget values and experiences which are still valid.

I think perhaps in this debate, now almost forgotten but having a relevance I shall attempt to show in a moment, there were some important considerations overlooked. A constitution establishes a structure and framework for a country based on certain values. If, like ours, it is largely a written constitution for a federal state, it is a law for making laws, looking to the future exercise of the powers distributed for the attainment of the desired ends. The value of the historical approach is not that it necessarily settles the points of contention that the courts must wrestle with, or that it renders more precise the meaning of words and expressions whose ambiguities are only brought to light by experience, though it sometimes may help even here. The value is rather in the broad objectives it discloses, the political concepts shown to have gone into the making of the constitution, which point in the general direction that the courts would be expected to follow.

The great constitutional values that the Fathers of Confederation considered

4  Both judgments are reported in 1932 A.C., pp. 54 and 304 ff.

5  See the Appeal Cases for that year; also comments in 1937 *Can. Bar Rev.*, pp. 393–507.

6  I have compiled a list of these authorities in 'Centralisation and Decentralisation in Canadian Federalism,' 1951 *Can. Bar Rev.*, p. 1095 at p. 1108 n. 44 [reprinted in this volume].

7  *Judicial Review in the English-Speaking World* (2nd ed.; Toronto, 1960), p. 74.

8  *Report of the Royal Commission on Dominion-Provincial Relations* (Ottawa, 1940), vol. I, pp. 32–6.

important cannot easily be disputed. Those men valued provincial autonomy, of course, or there would not have been a federal state. But they equally clearly valued a federalism that leaned towards strength at the centre when the choice had to be made, or they would not have placed the residue of powers in federal hands, unified the court structure, and provided for federal appointment of Lieutenant-Governors and disallowance of provincial laws. They held the duality of cultures to be a value; they wanted protection for certain school and language rights. The two cultures, moreover, were to enjoy equal status in the Province of Quebec, despite the numerical superiority of the French-speaking element there. They clearly intended Canada to possess a system of parliamentary democracy, for the whole Act, as well as the Preamble, contemplates the free working of parliamentary institutions with all that that implies in the way of fundamental liberties. And that the new federal government was to be the chief builder of the national economy, having the main responsibility for our future material well being, is abundantly evident from all that was said at the time as well as in the provisions of the Act relating to economic matters. In the words of Dr Macintosh, speaking of the Fathers of Confederation: 'They had conceived a great and daring project: the development of inter-provincial trade, the acquisition of the West from the Hudson's Bay Company, the construction of a transcontinental railway and the administration of a scheme of immigration and land settlement.'[9] It is in the light of these values and objectives that the main criticism of the constitutional commentators was directed at the results of so much of the judicial interpretation.

Among French-speaking lawyers and jurists the study of constitutional law has, quite naturally perhaps, been accorded less time and received less attention than the broad field of the civil law, Quebec's proud and exclusive possession. The aspects of the constitution which most occupied French Canada until comparatively recently were those dealing with language and school rights, and with Canada's status in the Empire and Commonwealth. Under the powerful and colourful leadership of Premier Duplessis, however, and emerging from the extreme centralization of World War II, ardent defenders of Quebec's autonomy discovered their provincial government as a potent symbol (with a flag) and protector of their rights and revendications. The full value of certain Privy Council trends in interpretation came to be appreciated, though the developing opinion did not stop there. When Quebec's Royal Commission of Enquiry on Constitutional Problems in 1956 did make the kind of political, social, and economic analysis of the constitution to which English-speaking Canadians had been more habitu-

9 In *Federalism: An Australian Jubilee Study*, ed. Geoffrey Sawer (Melbourne, 1952), pp. 87–8.

ated, it produced, in both French and English, the five weighty volumes of its *Report* that we call the *Tremblay Report*.[10] Though little known, I suspect, outside Quebec, and perhaps confined to certain circles inside, this *Report* is in my opinion as important reading for serious students of our constitution as any other work we possess – at least if you believe, as I do, that thoughts in people's heads are potent forces making for constitutional change.

Like the *Sirois Report*, to which it is in effect a point by point reply, the *Tremblay Report* crystallizes a certain attitude of certain people at a certain time, and also like the *Sirois Report*, its recommendations are not all going to be accepted. It puts forward a view of Canadian federalism based (if I may be forgiven an over-simplification) upon the treaty-between-races concept, the notion that the constitution is primarily designed to preserve and promote the duality of cultures. Note that this concept is not the same as the concept of provincial autonomy, since the notion of cultural partnership does not favour any province except Quebec. From the treaty concept, however, conclusions are drawn which would require a relinquishment of federal control and jurisdiction far greater than any to be hinted at even in Privy Council judgments and such as would have astounded the Fathers of Confederation. The duality of cultures was, as I have said, one of the values, and a great value, accepted at Confederation, but then it was not believed to be incompatible with the other values also affirmed at the time, one of which was that our federalism should be strong at the centre rather than weak. The *Tremblay Report* is one possible view, if not of what Canadian federalism is (though in some degree this claim is made), but of what it ought to be; it touches on matters which are so much a part of our national life as never to be far from our political choices; and it adds a number of challenging ideas to that total stream of thought and discussion in Canada, whose variety of claims and whose contradictions make our constitutional history and law so interesting.

I know it sounds a little old-fashioned still to be talking about the Fathers of Confederation and the kind of country they foresaw. The choices they made are not necessarily the best for today. But it seems to me both interesting and relevant to know why they made them, so that if we decide to reject or alter their scale of values, we do so deliberately and consciously. We seem to be facing constitutional issues comparable, in some ways, to theirs. We are certainly having to think out our relationship with the United States afresh. Canada in the 1860s received the opposite treatment from that which is now accorded us: instead of seducing us by the embrace of great corporations, which has brought so many of us to bed with affluence, the Americans then cast our forefathers out into the

10 *Report of the Royal Commission of Inquiry on Constitutional Problems* (Quebec: Queen's Printer, 1956), and Annexes.

economic wilderness by cancelling the Reciprocity Treaty, just as England had earlier rejected them by repealing the corn laws. So there we were in the 1860s, English- and French-speaking Canadians, Maritimers and distant western colonials, having to meet the challenge of continental isolation with boldness and imagination, or else to remain in a petty provincialism exposed to all the dangers of stagnation and ultimate absorption.

I am still impressed, every time I reflect upon it, with the largeness of outlook of the men who believed, though they had only the simplest and slowest means of communication with remote parts of a vast country, that they could make of the bigger northern half of the continent something like what the Americans had made of the southern half so far as economic development was concerned. At that time the prime mover in the whole business had to be the new government at Ottawa; provinces were necessary for the preservation of local customs and institutions, and had their guaranteed rights, but they could not be the chief builders of the new federal state. Many of the leading Fathers of Confederation, particularly in central Canada, moved out of the provincial sphere into the new national sphere because the opportunities there were larger and the outlook more exciting. Even Joseph Howe ended rather ingloriously in Ottawa, and though he supported the idea at first, confederation knew no more formidable opponent. All this took place without anyone's imagining that it jeopardized the separate schools in Quebec and Ontario, the language rights, or the Quebec Civil Code, all of which were established and accepted at the time the BNA Act became law. Federal and provincial governments were not thought of as competing units, almost sworn enemies, but as complementary institutions all engaged in their allotted tasks for the benefit of the whole people of Canada. Within the wide boundaries of legitimate provincial autonomy there was thought to be ample room for cultural freedom.

It would take too long to trace here the fading of this early Canadian dream towards the end of the nineteenth century. The prolonged economic depression that began in 1873 seemed to prove the failure of the national economic policies,[11] and increasing tension between races was caused by conflicts over schools and language. What a difference it would have made in Canada if the Privy Council had not overruled the unanimous decision of the Supreme Court setting aside the Manitoba School Laws of 1890.[12] We would have avoided the intense bitterness of the racial feeling that preceded the 1896 election. French Canada felt that on the first great test of her rights the BNA Act had failed her. It was of course London, not Ottawa that failed her. These various influences resulted in a great in-

11 *Report of the Royal Commission on Dominion-Provincial Relations*, vol. I, p. 50.
12 *Winnipeg* v. *Barrett*, 1892 A.C. 445.

crease in provincial autonomy at the close of the century. The interprovincial conference of 1887 was the first expression of provincial revolt against federal dom-
inance. It is remarkable how many of the specific requests for constitutional
change then made have since been accorded the provinces, chiefly by judicial interpretation.[13] The great western boom in the decade before World War I brought
a revival of federal prestige, seeming to justify the expenditures in railway building, immigration, and land settlement, and the war years 1914- 18 added to federal importance by the requirements of national policy and by bringing Canada
out into the international arena. But these years also widened the racial gap by
reason of the school language issue in Ontario and the conscription issue of 1917,
and the centralized emergency powers were swiftly dissipated by constitutional
interpretation after the war.

Canada was a very divided country during the 1920s, and men of my generation will remember how much the theme of national unity was the object of our
discussion and thought in that decade. Though we may not have seen it clearly
at the time, new economic factors were increasing the centrifugal forces in Canada and enlarging provincial authority, for the economic expansion was now, not
in railways and land settlement, primarily a federal responsibility, but in developing provincial resources by private capital with the consent of provincial governments. Pulp and paper, lumber, base metals, hydro-electric power, opened new
fields for investment, most of it private, much of it American. The era of great
corporate expansion had begun. In the law courts, the federal government saw its
first important effort at economic regulation, its 1919 Board of Commerce Act
and its Combines and Fair Prices Act, struck down,[14] and then lost its jurisdiction over labour relations except for a small number of federal undertakings.[15]
The way was cleared for an almost unlimited exploitation of Canadian resources
by US capital with the assurance of a minimum of governmental control – far
less, certainly, than the same capital would have had to face in the United States
itself, where the Inter-State Commerce Commission, the Federal Trade Commission, and the anti-trust laws were in effect.

When the great depression of the 1930s converted even the Conservatives into
New Dealers, the federal government made another effort at economic leadership,
only to meet a second defeat in the law courts. The Natural Products Marketing
Act, the Employment and Social Insurance Act, and the three statutes providing
minimum wages, maximum hours, and a weekly day of rest were all held uncon-

---

13 I have listed these in *Evolving Canadian Federalism*, ed. A.R.M. Lower, F.R. Scott, *et al.*
(Durham: Duke University Press, 1958), pp. 69–70.
14 *In re* Board of Commerce Act, 1922 1 A.C. 191.
15 *Toronto Electric Commissioners* v. *Snider*, 1925 A.C. 396.

stitutional.[16] 'The economic needs of the nation' have had little relevance to our constitutional law, though they have every relevance to our daily lives, our level of employment, and our standard of living.

So far this account may be leaving the impression that the economic situation ought to be much worse in Canada than in fact it is. How have we enjoyed the post World War II prosperity, such as it was? There are two constitutional answers to this; I do not attempt to give economic ones. One is that we did do something about the constitution: we amended it twice so as to give the federal government the power to enact unemployment insurance and old age pension laws. This established Ottawa firmly in the field of social security and added to its freedom in fiscal policy. In the light of present conditions we can see more clearly that while these forms of welfare legislation provide cushions to ease the shock of economic decline, they do not prevent that decline. Some more positive forms of economic leadership and control are going to be necessary unless we want to fold our hands and watch the current hardships, the regional declines, and the growing injustices with total indifference. Something else besides amendment to the BNA Act took place, however, without formal constitutional change but with even greater constitutional significance. This was the growing use of monetary policy, taxation, and planned government spending, as factors in maintaining economic equilibrium. From the time of its economic proposals in 1945, the federal government became committed to a policy of high and stable levels of income and employment. Keynes became a kind of post-natal Father of Confederation.

The emergence of fiscal and monetary policy as economic regulators has become so important a factor today as almost to make us forget the question of legislative jurisdiction. It seems to have by-passed Sections 91 and 92 of the BNA Act. The lawyers are moving out and the economists are moving in. Since Ottawa has the most money, and exclusive control of banking and currency, this fiscal approach restores federal influence in the total governmental picture though no new judgments are forthcoming from the courts to enlarge federal jurisdiction. Ottawa learns to induce where it cannot command, and federal policy is made by bargains with provincial governments. The economic system of course goes on its own way quite apart from this spending power, though greatly affected by it.

Perhaps before handing over entirely to the economists at this point I may be allowed to keep my foot in the constitutional door for a moment longer. The federal spending power has not gone altogether unchallenged. Indeed, the *Tremblay Report* challenges it directly as being a violation of the federal principle, especially when the spending is for welfare and educational projects. If the authors

16 These decisions are all reported in 1937 A.C., pp. 326–418.

of the Tremblay Report had their way, Ottawa would move out of unemployment insurance, old age pensions, family allowances, university and research grants, health insurance, and any other forms of direct subsidy for national welfare or cultural expression. This would indeed be a vast change in our constitutional behaviour. Professor Corry has remarked that it is strange that no one has challenged the spending power in the courts, though he admits it is not likely to be denied at this stage.[17] Actually the Family Allowance Act was challenged on one occasion and was upheld by one judge in the Exchequer Court.[18] The refusal of Quebec universities to take federal grants was a challenge to the spending power, though of a somewhat uncertain kind since these universities first accepted them and then, under what I am convinced was external pressure and not a genuine academic decision, changed their minds.[19]

I wish to put myself on record again as of the opinion that the prerogative right of the Crown to make gifts of any money it possesses is unimpaired in Canada, whether it be the federal Crown or the provincial Crown – assuming, of course, that the legislature votes the appropriation. The reason (stated without argument) is that both aspects of the Crown may dispose gratuitously of their own moneys as they see fit.[20] The first of the federal enumerated powers in the Act of 1867 is the exclusive jurisdiction over the 'Public Debt and Property,' and money in the Consolidated Revenue Fund is public property. So I believe the federal Crown may decide to invest money in a new industry, like Polymer Corporation, or to subsidize an old one like the coal industry in Nova Scotia, or to buy all butter offered to it at $x$ cents a pound, or to build a War Memorial in France, or a dam in India, or to purchase Old Masters for the National Gallery. It is difficult to see how this country could be governed if this power were to be

17 In *Evolving Canadian Federalism*, p. 119.
18 *Angers* v. *Minister of National Revenue*, 1957 Ex. C.R. 83.
19 See *Survey of Higher Education 1952–54* (Dominion Bureau of Statistics, 1957), pp. 9–12, for a brief history of Federal Government University Grants. Premier Lesage, when saying that Quebec universities were free to receive Canada Council grants for buildings, explained that they had failed to obtain them in the past only because of a 'caprice' of the former National Union government. See *Montreal Star*, June 1, 1961. The N.C.C.U., of which Quebec universities are members, asked the Massey Commission for *per capita* grants for all students registered in professional faculties, and at its meeting in 1951 passed a unanimous Resolution approving the recommendations of the Massey Report. See *Proceedings of the National Council of Canadian Universities 1951*, p. 73.
20 Mr Barrette when Premier of Quebec shared this view. When asked why he made gifts to educational institutions outside Quebec, he replied, 'La province peut faire un don aussi bien qu'un individu' (See *Le Devoir*, April 9, 1960). It is interesting to note that the first Legislature in Quebec in 1868 appropriated $4,000 for 'Aid to Distressed Seamen in Nova Scotia.' A nice example of the spending power. (See 31 Vict. (Que.) Cap. I, p. 10.)

denied; though this is not the same as saying that every government expenditure is a good one or a wise one. By the same spending power a province may open an office in London or New York, contribute to a *Maison Canadienne* in Paris (though it can only make laws 'within the province' according to the wording of the BNA Act), may send students abroad on scholarships, may make gifts of food or money to victims of famine in foreign lands, or may even, as is the case in Quebec, give provincial taxpayers' money to a few selected universities in other provinces.

And while I am in this vein, may I add a word about the concept of welfare in our constitution. There are so many vested interests fighting any extension of public welfare expenditure in Canada, and so much advertising and propaganda against it, that we are in danger of being brainwashed into believing that welfare is an evil word. There can be argument about the quantity and forms of welfare, but it cannot be denied that to serve the public welfare is a proper function of all governments in a democratic state. Not just the provincial, not just the federal, but federal, provincial, and local governments have this duty. Every state worthy of being called free, as well as some that are not, is a form of welfare state today. The Fathers of Confederation were very familiar with the word welfare: both in the Quebec Resolutions and in the London Resolutions the residuary power of the federal parliament was expressed as a power to make laws for the peace, *welfare*, and good government of the provinces. 'Peace, welfare and good government' are the operative words conferring all jurisdiction to the Legislature in the Act of Union, 1840. No doubt the word had a less inclusive meaning then than now, as had many other words in the constitution, but today's concepts are a logical extension of earlier ones. The Consolidated Statutes of the Province of Canada, 1859, contained laws on Public Health, Innoculation and Vaccination, Emigrants and Quarantine, Charitable and Provident Associations, Private Lunatic Asylums; all these applied to both Upper and Lower Canada, and were over and above the local laws on welfare matters in the two sections of the Province.

Some unknown draftsman changed 'welfare' into 'order' in the BNA Act, so the Section now reads 'Peace, Order, and Good Government,' but the word was not taken out of the Preamble of the constitution, which still reminds us that 'such a Union,' that is, a federal Union under the Crown, 'would conduce to the welfare of the provinces.' Welfare was to be the result of union: how then is the government of the Union not concerned with it? Of course it must be a concern with welfare that is of a different order from that exclusively reserved to provinces, but the federal entry into the field, unless there is a transfer of jurisdiction, leaves provincial jurisdiction intact. The problem of cost is another matter, a practical matter involving concepts of equity, balance, and fair treatment, and particularly bringing to light the important function of Parliament in minimizing the discrepancies in our regional incomes. But this belongs to the politics of federalism more than to the law. That it requires a more co-operative kind of federalism than we have had in the past, and more instruments of co-operation, there can be no doubt. Federal-provincial conferences seem here to stay, and they are likely to play a part in our evolution to which there is no real parallel in United States constitutional behaviour. Let us remember, however, that rightly considered every parliament of Canada is also, in a sense, a federal-provincial conference, since its members represent all sections of the country. The provinces of Canada have two governmental voices, not just one, and Ottawa speaks for Quebec, Ontario, and the rest on all matters within federal competence.

Let us come back to this question of jurisdiction. Some things cannot be done by federal-provincial conferences. They can only be done by federal legislation that is national in scope. There is no escape from this, however much it smacks of centralization. It is just another way of saying that freedom of action for the central government is just as important in a federal state as freedom of action for the component parts. Indeed, in a world moving towards integration, in many respects it is more important. Either certain things are done by an authority with larger jurisdiction than that conferred on provinces, or they are not done at all. The command of the law must bear some relationship to the size of the problems sought to be regulated. We have met this difficulty on the municipal level, where metropolitan government becomes impossible if left to a multitude of separate local municipalities. We have met it on the international level, where state sovereignty continues to hamper efforts at regional and world government. We still find it, and I suppose always shall find it, on the national level.

The point will become clearer if I give some examples of existing deficiencies in the federal power. Canada's capacity to enter into treaty relationships with other states is wholly inadequate to the needs of today. The damaging effect of the ILO Conventions case,[21] which in effect overruled the more liberal interpretation of the Privy Council in the Radio case,[22] have not been overcome. Every time Canada abstains from participating in multilateral conventions aimed at achieving good international standards, because of lack of jurisdiction to implement them, she withholds her influence for peace and co-operation. In internal matters, there is a lack of federal jurisdiction in the fields of marketing legislation, and control of the sale of corporation securities. Provincial jurisdiction over industrial disputes is quite incapable of regulating the situations which can arise when nation-wide employers are dealing with nation-wide unions.[23] Many important aspects of trade and commerce, affecting all provinces, have been held to fall

21 1937 A.C. 326.
22 1932 A.C. 304.
23 See F.R. Scott, 'Federal Jurisdiction over Labour Relations – A New Look,' *McGill Law Journal* (1960), p. 153. [reprinted in this volume].

into the provincial jurisdiction over property and civil rights. If we should attempt to exert a wider control over the national economy in peacetime the jurisdictional gaps would become very evident.[24] And there is no ultimate power in Canada to amend the constitution itself.

These realities we must keep before us. Adaptation of the present constitution might come, in part, from judicial interpretation, but this is a lengthy and unsure process. We are confronted again with the need for constitutional amendment. Even if no specific amendments are now being sought, an amendment to give ourselves a complete amending procedure must be secured, or Canada remains in an equivocal position. This is what 'repatriation' means in legal terms.

This brings me to my final point. We are now in the process of holding federal-provincial conferences of Attorneys-General, to seek this all-embracing amending formula and the 'repatriation' of the constitution. We have to transfer to Canadian legislatures the last vestiges of sovereignty over Canada still remaining in the United Kingdom. When this is done, some body or bodies in Canada will alone make all constitutional changes. But how? This is where we have always failed in the past. Just eleven years ago I read my first paper to this Section of the Society on the topic: 'The Redistribution of Imperial Sovereignty.' Since then that redistribution has accelerated, and the Mother of Parliaments has been 'signing off' its authority over new state after new state. Canada has been left out of this process because we could not agree on the terms on which we would take our freedom. We are like Mr Melpomenous Jones in Leacock's story, who never could make up his mind to say good-bye; finally after visiting some friends for dinner and being kept on as a house-guest for weeks, he acquired a fatal fever and departed this life murmuring 'I think I must go now.'

What is happening at the Attorneys-General Conference is mostly confidential and cannot be discussed here. This is itself a fact of some importance. It is our country and our future that is being planned and we – the citizens – should have our chance to be heard at the appropriate time before our governments have taken up fixed positions. Not being able to enlarge upon the suggestions now being considered, I shall content myself with bringing this paper to a conclusion by summarizing my ideas in the form of a series of propositions.

1 The Canadian constitution has not yet recovered from the damaging effects of judicial interpretation in the past. The argument for flexibility in the amending procedure is therefore particularly strong provided it can be achieved without endangering the cultural partnership which is fundamental to our federalism. If we freeze the present distribution of powers the federal government could be gravely hampered in dealing with future problems.

---

24 Some of these are discussed in F.R. Scott, 'Social Planning and Federalism' in *Social Purpose for Canada*, ed. Michael Oliver (University of Toronto Press, 1961).

2 Canada is facing constitutional choices comparable in their importance and their future implications to those which were made a hundred years ago by the Fathers of Confederation. They established a federal system: we must now define its nature.

3 The 'repatriation' of the constitution involves replacing the theory of the legal sovereignty of the United Kingdom Parliament, on which the BNA Act now rests, with a new theory. The amending clause will imply that theory.

4 The crux of the problem lies in the degree of provincial consent necessary to effect a transfer of legislative jurisdiction as between Parliament and Legislatures. The compact theory of Confederation, now seemingly uppermost in the present discussions, would require the unanimous consent of provinces for any such change. Such rigidity would I think be fatal to Canadian federalism. The treaty-between-races theory is somewhat more flexible, since it would require the consent of Quebec but not necessarily of all the other provinces. A theory that balanced the need for cultural guarantees with the need for constitutional adaptation to the rapidly changing conditions of the modern world would entrench minority rights without entrenching all other provincial powers in their present form – least of all the whole of 'property and civil rights' as those words are presently defined by the courts.

5 Before 1867 it took at least a decade of conferences and discussions before a constitutional solution was found acceptable to a majority of Upper and Lower Canadians and Maritimers. While a decade has passed since the last Federal-Provincial Constitutional Conference of 1950, the interval has been marked, not by intensive discussion, but by the absence of discussion.

6 The nation today is not prepared for the choices it seems to be on the point of making. Any final decisions should be delayed until much wider groups of people have been brought into the picture and invited to participate in the formulation of an amending procedure appropriate to our traditions, our experience, and our present needs.

7 While the present position of Canada vis-à-vis the United Kingdom is equivocal and obviously temporary, the dangers of delay in terminating it are far less than the dangers of too hasty an acceptance of 'repatriation' at any price.

8 The continuation of the reserve constituent powers of the United Kingdom Parliament in the amending of the Canadian constitution is no more a limitation on Canadian sovereignty than is the continuation of the position of the Crown in respect of Canada. In both instances the political control of the exercise of the United Kingdom legal powers is in the hands of Canadians. The Crown acts only on the advice of its Canadian ministers, and the United Kingdom Parliament acts only on the advice of the Canadian Parliament.

9 Future conferences on repatriation should include representatives of opposition

parties as well as representatives of parties in power. The constitution is for all Canadians and not just for present governments.

Canada is built on a series of paradoxes. East-west versus north-south pulls, central power versus provincial autonomy, economic integration versus cultural dualism – one could extend the list of opposites which must be harmonized and accommodated if we are to remain as a single nation-state in a changing world. Other solutions could be found to the one which the Fathers of Confederation, backed by a majority of the peoples of Canada of both races at the time, chose and thought to be viable. Nationalism is a force as powerful today as ever in the history of mankind, and nationalism in Canada is again a paradox, perhaps the greatest paradox, because it is not a single but a dual nationalism, French-speaking Canada feeling itself to be a nation fully as strongly as the other provinces feel themselves to be a nation. If these understandable and valid forms of nationalism seek their outlet primarily in cultural partnership, on terms of equality, then the political federalism we now possess will not be broken, though it may well have to make further accommodations to internal pressures. If the requirements of cultural dualism are pushed to political extremes, as evidenced in the renewed strength of the separatist movement in Quebec, then of course we shall have failed to maintain the original concept of Confederation and the Union will end in disunion. I am one of those who believe that the original constitution of Canada, changing as it must in face of new demands and new challenges, is still basically adapted to the sum total of our various hopes and aspirations.

# Selected Bibliography of Other Writings on Canadian Government and Politics

BOOKS AND PAMPHLETS

*Social Reconstruction and the BNA Act.* Toronto, Nelson, 1934
*Canada Today; a Study of Her National Interests and National Policy. Prepared for the British Commonwealth Relations Conference, 1938.* Toronto, Oxford University Press, 1938. 2nd rev. ed., 1939
*Canada and the United States.* Boston, World Peace Foundation, 1941
*Make This Your Canada; a Review of C.C.F. History and Policy*, by David Lewis and Frank Scott. Toronto, Central Canada Publishing, 1943
*Un Canada nouveau; vue d'ensemble de l'historique et de la politique du mouvement C.F.F.*, par David Lewis et Frank Scott. Montréal, Bernard Valiquette, 1944 [Translation of *Make This Your Canada*].
*Cooperation for What? United States and British Commonwealth.* New York, American Council, Institute of Pacific Relations, 1944
*The Canadian Constitution and Human Rights.* Toronto, Canadian Broadcasting Corporation, 1959 [Four radio talks as heard on CBC University of the Air].
*Civil Liberties and Canadian Federalism.* Toronto, University of Toronto Press, 1959
*Le Déclaration universelle des droits de l'homme; aspects historique et juridique.* Montréal, Association canadienne d'éducation de langue française, première plenière, 21. Congrès, Montréal, 20 août 1968 (Document 2608)
*Quebec States Her Case.* Edited by Frank Scott and Michael Oliver. Toronto, Macmillan, 1964

CHAPTERS AND SECTIONS OF BOOKS

'Evidence before the Special Committee on British North America Act, House of Commons of Canada.' In Canada, Parliament, House of Commons, Special

Committee on British North America Act, *Minutes of Proceedings and Evidence, no. 4, Tuesday, March 26, 1935*, pp. 80-92

'Freedom in the Modern World.' In *Our Heritage of Freedom*; A Series of Broadcasts Sponsored by the Canadian Broadcasting Corporation. Toronto, Nelson, 1937, pp. 43-8

'Canada and Hemispheric Solidarity.' In W.H.C. Laves, ed., *Inter-American Solidarity*. Chicago, University of Chicago Press, 1941, pp. 139-73

'The Constitution and the Post-War World.' Chap. 3 of Alexander Brady and F.R. Scott, eds, *Canada After the War; Studies in Political, Social and Economic Policies for Post-War Canada*. Toronto, Macmillan, 1944, pp. 60-87

'French-Canada and Canadian Federalism.' In *Evolving Canadian Federalism*, by A.R.M. Lower, F.R. Scott, and others. Durham, NC, Duke University Press, 1958, pp. 54-91

'Social Planning and Canadian Federalism.' In Michael Oliver, ed., *A Social Purpose for Canada*. Toronto, University of Toronto Press, 1961, pp. 394-407

'Address/Allocution Delivered at the Joint Dinner of the Association of Canadian Law Teachers and the Canadian Political Science Association at Charlottetown, PEI, on Thursday Evening, June 11, 1964.' In P.A. Crépeau, and C.B. Macpherson, eds, *The Future of Canadian Federalism*. Toronto, University of Toronto Press, 1965, pp. 181-8

'Evidence before the Standing Senate Committee on Legal and Constitutional Affairs concerning Bill S-21, To Amend the Criminal Code (Hate Propaganda).' In Canada, Parliament, Senate, Standing Committee on Legal and Constitutional Affairs, *Proceedings, no. 9, Tuesday, April 29, 1969*, pp. 201-13

PERIODICAL ARTICLES

'The Privy Council and Minority Rights.' *Queen's Quarterly*, 37, 1930, 668-78

'The Permanent Bases of Canadian Foreign Policy.' *Foreign Affairs*, 10, 1932, 617-31

'The CCF and the Constitution.' *Saskatchewan C.C.F. Research Bulletin*, no. 6, January 1934, 11-14

'The Efficiency of Socialism.' *Queen's Quarterly*, 42, 1935, 215-25

'Penal Reform; a Series of Four Articles.' *Saturday Night*, 51, nos 34-7, 27 June, 4 July, 11 July, 18 July, 1936

'The Royal Commission on Dominion-Provincial Relations.' *University of Toronto Quarterly*, 1938, 141-51

'Embryo Fascism in Quebec.' [by 'S']. *Foreign Affairs*, 16, 1938, 454-66

'A Policy of Neutrality for Canada.' *Foreign Affairs*, 17, 1939, 402-16

'Canadian Nationalism and the War.' *Canadian Forum*, 21, 1942, 360-2

'What Did "No" Mean?' *Canadian Forum*, 22, 1942, 71–3. Published also as pamphlet under title, *The Plebiscite Vote in Quebec*

'Socialism in the Commonwealth.' *International Journal*, 1, 1945-6, 22-30

'Abolition of Appeals to the Privy Council.' *Canadian Bar Review*, 25, 1947, 566-72. Part of a symposium.

'Administrative Law: 1923-1947.' *Canadian Bar Review*, 26, 1948, 268-85

'Social Medicine. English Text of a Speech Delivered to the Medical Students of the University of Montreal on January 19, 1949.' *CAMSI Journal*, 8, 1949, 9-16. Also published in French under title, 'La médecine sociale' in *Revue médicale Université de Montréal*, 1, 1949, 57-72

'Brief Presented to the Senate Committee on Human Rights and Fundamental Freedoms.' *Revue du barreau*, 10, 1950, 325-35

'A Survey of Canadian Federalism.' *International Social Science Bulletin*, 4, 1952, 71-88

'Technical Assistance and Economic Aid through the United Nations.' *Royal Society of Canada Transactions*, 47, ser. 3, sec. 2, June 1953, 17-31

'The World's Civil Service.' *International Conciliation*, Carnegie Endowment for International Peace, no. 496, 1954, 257-320

'American Pressures and Canadian Individuality: III.' *Centennial Review*, 1, 1957, 372-8

'The War Measures Act in Retrospect.' *CAUT/ACPU*, 2, no. 4, May 1971, 1-2

# Index of Cases

# Index of Topics